Applied Psychology

Variety and Opportunity

Robert Gifford

University of Victoria
Vancouver, Canada

Allyn and Bacon

Boston ◆ London ◆ Toronto ◆ Sydney ◆ Tokyo ◆ Singapore

Managing Editor: Susan Badger
Series Editorial Assistant: Dana Lamothe
Production Administrator: Annette Joseph
Production Coordinator: Susan Freese
Editorial-Production Service: Tage Publishing Service, Inc.
Manufacturing Buyer: Louise Richardson
Cover Administrator: Linda K. Dickinson
Cover Designer: Susan Slovinsky

Chapter-opening photographs courtesy of: Chapter 1, Loren Acker; Chapter 3, Gerald Koe; Chapter 4, Richard P. Halgin; Chapter 6, Cynthia Belar; Chapter 8, Donald Baumann and Charles Holahan. All other chapter-opening photographs courtesy of Robert Gifford.

Library of Congress Cataloging-in-Publication Data

Applied psychology : variety and opportunity / [edited by] Robert Gifford.
     p.   cm.
    Includes bibliographical references and index.
    ISBN 0-205-12664-2
    1. Psychology, Applied.   2. Psychology, Applied—Vocational guidance. I. Gifford, Robert.
    [DNLM; 1. Psychology, Applied.   2. Psychology, Clinical. BF 636 A651]
BF636.A64   1991
158—dc20
DNLM/DLC   90-14544
for Library of Congress   CIP

Printed in the United States of America

10 9 8 7 6 5 4 3 2 1   96 95 94 93 92 91

Brief Contents

1 Welcome to the Neighborhood ♦ *Robert Gifford* 1

2 The Clinical Child Psychologist ♦ *Michael Joschko* 21

3 The School Psychologist ♦ *Gerald Koe* 49

4 The Clinical Psychologist ♦ *Richard P. Halgin* 77

5 The Clinical Neuropsychologist ♦ *Louis Costa* 101

6 The Health Psychologist ♦ *Cynthia D. Belar* 123

7 The Sport Psychologist ♦ *John Durkin* 147

8 The Community Psychologist ♦ *Donald J. Baumann and Charles J. Holahan* 173

9 The Consumer Psychologist ♦ *Robert Sommer and Howard G. Schutz* 195

10 The Applied Behavior Analyst ♦ *Loren Edward Acker* 217

11 The Lawyer-Psychologist ♦ *Paul Hofer* 245

12 The Organizational Psychologist ♦ *Larry M. Coutts* 273

13 The Ergonomist ♦ *Ruth M. Heron* 301

14 The Environmental Psychologist ♦ *Robert Gifford* 327

15 The Geropsychologist ♦ *Kathy Montgomery* 355

Contents

Preface   xiii

1 Welcome to the Neighborhood ♦ *Robert Gifford*   1

What Is Applied Psychology?   2
The Background of Applied Psychology   2
The Scope of Applied Psychology   3
    A Neighborhood of Application, Optimism, and Method   4
    The Methods, in Brief   4
    The Purposes: Local Solutions, Global Understanding   7
    Who, What, How Many?   8
Becoming an Applied Psychologist   10
    Education   10
    Applied Psychology and Money   13
    Accreditation   14
    Employment   17
Suggested Readings and References   18
Memberships   18

2 The Clinical Child Psychologist ♦ *Michael Joschko*   21

What Is Clinical Child Psychology?   25
    The Background of Clinical Child Psychology   27
    The Scope of Clinical Child Psychology   30
Case Studies   33
Becoming a Clinical Child Psychologist   43
    Education   43
    Employment   45
Suggested Readings and References   46

3   The School Psychologist ♦ *Gerald Koe*   49

What Is School Psychology?   51
    Current Practice   52
The Background of School Psychology   54
    Philosophical Foundations   54
    Historical Foundations   55
The Scope of School Psychology   56
    Referrals   57
    Data Collection   57
    Hypothesis Testing   58
    Report   60
    Access to the Results   60
    Program Planning   61
    Progress Evaluation   61
Case Studies   61
Becoming a School Psychologist   70
    Employment   72
Endnotes   73
Suggested Readings and References   73

4   The Clinical Psychologist ♦ *Richard P. Halgin*   77

What Is Clinical Psychology?   79
The Background of Clinical Psychology   80
The Scope of Clinical Psychology   82
    Psychotherapist   82
    Expert in Psychological Assessment   84
    Consultant   87
    Research   88
    Other Roles   89
    Advantages and Disadvantages of Clinical Psychology   89
Case Studies   91
Becoming a Clinical Psychologist   95
Suggested Readings   98

5 The Clinical Neuropsychologist ♦ *Louis Costa*   101

What Is Clinical Neuropsychology?   105
The Background of Neuropsychology   105
The Scope of Clinical Neuropsychology   107
   Clinical Neuropsychological Practice: An Overview   *108*
   The Strategy of Assessment   *109*
Case Studies   110
Becoming a Clinical Neuropsychologist   116
   Training   *116*
Guidelines for Doctoral Training Programs in
Clinical Neuropsychology   117
   Getting Started   *120*
Suggested Readings and References   120

6 The Health Psychologist ♦ *Cynthia D. Belar*   123

What Is Health Psychology?   125
The Background of Health Psychology   126
   Basic Concepts in Health Psychology   *127*
The Scope of Health Psychology   130
Case Studies   132
Becoming a Health Psychologist   141
Endnotes   143
Suggested Readings and References   143

7 The Sport Psychologist ♦ *John Durkin*   147

What Is Sport Psychology?   150
Background of Sport Psychology   151
The Scope of Sport Psychology   154
   Breadth of Field   *154*
   Research Approaches   *155*
   Relaxation, Concentration, and Visualization   *158*
   Ethics and the Sport Psychologist   *161*

Case Studies   162
Becoming a Sport Psychologist   167
    Training   167
    Accreditation   168
    Employment Prospects   168
Suggested Readings and References   169

8 The Community Psychologist ♦ *Donald J. Baumann &*
   Charles J. Holahan   173

What Is Community Psychology?   175
The Background of Community Psychology   176
The Scope of Community Psychology   176
    Two Ways Community Psychologists Solve Problems   177
Case Studies   178
Becoming a Community Psychologist   191
    Education   191
    Employment   191
Suggested Readings and References   192

9 The Consumer Psychologist ♦ *Robert Sommer &*
   Howard G. Schutz   195

What Is Consumer Psychology?   196
The Background of Consumer Psychology   197
The Scope of Consumer Psychology   197
    Support for Research   199
    Organizations and Journals   200
    Market Segmentation   201
    Methods of Consumer Research   202
Case Studies   207
Becoming a Consumer Psychologist   212
Suggested Readings and References   214

10   The Applied Behavior Analyst ♦ *Loren Edward Acker*   217

What Is Applied Behavior Analysis?   218
The Background of Applied Behavior Analysis   221
Scope of Applied Behavior Analysis   223
   Not Just Flashing   223
   Better Living through Experimentation   225
   Don't Let Data Scare You   226
Case Studies   227
Becoming an Applied Behavior Analyst   237
   Education   237
   Employment   241
Suggested Readings and References   242

11   The Lawyer-Psychologist ♦ *Paul Hofer*   245

What Is Law and Psychology?   248
The Scope of Law and Psychology   248
   The Psycholegal Perspective   250
   Legislation-Oriented Research   255
   Litigation-Oriented Research   257
   Settlement-Oriented Research   260
   Testimony-Oriented Research   261
Case Studies   263
Becoming a Lawyer-Psychologist   268
Suggested Readings and References   270

12   The Organizational Psychologist ♦ *Larry M. Coutts*   273

What Is Organizational Psychology?   275
Organizational Psychology as a Science and Profession   276
The Background of Organizational Psychology   277
The Scope of Organizational Psychology   278

Measurement of Jobs   278
Personnel Selection   279
Performance Appraisal   280
Personnel Training   280
Motivation   281
Job Satisfaction   282
Group Dynamics   283
Leadership   284
Communication   285
Decision Making   286
Organizational Design   287
Case Studies   287
Becoming an Organizational Psychologist   297
Suggested Readings and References   299

13   The Ergonomist ♦ *Ruth M. Heron*   301

What Is Ergonomics?   303
The Background of Ergonomics   305
The Scope of Ergonomics   307
The Ergonomics Model and Its Implications   307
Ergonomics in Laboratory and Applied Settings   313
Case Studies   314
Becoming an Ergonomist   322
Education   322
Employment   324
Suggested Readings and References   325

14   The Environmental Psychologist ♦ *Robert Gifford*   327

What Is Environmental Psychology?   328
The Background of Environmental Psychology   329
A Capsule History   329

The Scope of Environmental Psychology   331
Case Studies   334
Becoming an Environmental Psychologist   350
    Education   350
    Employment   351
Suggested Readings and References   351

15 The Geropsychologist ♦ *Kathy Montgomery*   355

What Is Geropsychology?   356
The Background of Geropsychology   357
The Scope of Geropsychology   358
    Work Settings   358
    Research Concerns   360
Case Studies   362
    Concluding Comment   368
Becoming a Geropsychologist   369
    Interests and Education   369
    Research Support   370
    Employment   371
Suggested Readings and References   372

Index   373

Preface

Applied Psychology: Variety and Opportunity introduces 14 varieties of professional applied psychology. The major topics, issues, and approaches of each applied specialty are described, but the chapters are also about each applied psychologist as a professional person: They introduce, through actual case studies, the work of experts in the field. The inclusion of 14 specialties is a deliberate attempt to increase awareness of the many ways to apply psychology beyond the popular stereotype of one-on-one psychotherapy.

This book addresses many readers. The authors have done their best to avoid technical language or, if they could not avoid using a term, to explain the concept in plain English. Thus, the book is suitable for readers who have not yet had an introductory psychology course. In a very practice-oriented setting, it could even serve as a replacement for the standard introductory psychology textbook. In settings where both application and basic psychological processes are valued, it could serve as a companion to the standard introductory text. The book could serve as a text in a course on applied psychology.

Those who will work with applied psychologists—such as nurses, teachers, administrators, police, and others—will benefit from learning what applied psychologists do. Mature readers who are considering a career change may find this survey illuminating as a source of information on applied psychology. For similar reasons, the book will also be of interest to advanced undergraduates and new graduate students in psychology who are interested in exploring various avenues for improving the world. This view of real life as a professional applied psychologist should help young psychologists decide which field is best for them.

The book is carefully organized: Topics occur in the same order in every chapter. Each chapter opens with a *brief example* of the kind of work done in that specialty, followed by a *definition* of the specialty, information on the *background* of the specialty, and a brief look at its origins, principal heroes, persistent issues, and famous studies.

Next, the *scope* of the specialty is described: a summary of the topics, issues, and problems usually handled by that specialty. Then, several true *case studies* (usually three) are presented to illustrate the day-to-day work done in the specialty. Finally, requirements for *becoming* that kind of applied psychologist are addressed, including observations on education and employment. Each chapter closes with some *suggested readings* for further information on that specialty.

Apart from being experts in their fields, the authors of these chapters are clearly individuals. Their views of their fields are generally widely shared by their peers. But most have offered some personal views, too. These personal views do not agree with those of other authors in every respect, in particular those views expressed on graduate school. However, these diverse views are accurate: Graduate schools and student experiences in graduate schools *do* vary considerably. As the editor of this text, I have treated this diversity as a rich resource rather than a shortcoming. The collective variety of viewpoints expressed by the authors is probably more accurate than any one viewpoint, which would suffer from the limitations of an individual author's experience.

I hope these personal views enliven the book for you and move it from being a dry list of requirements and topic headings to a human celebration of diversity. These authors all love their specialties and want you to know both the "official line" and their own, often strongly held, perspectives.

Acknowledgments

This book is the product of many hands. I am grateful to John-Paul Lenney for suggesting it; to the authors and their assistants for producing the chapters; to Susan Badger, Dana Lamothe, and those others at Allyn and Bacon who shepherded the manuscript through production; to Neva Beckie, Dee O'Connor, Melanie Geist, and Kim Syer for valuable editorial assistance; to Bill Barke for another memorable lunch; and certainly not least, to the University of Victoria, a very supportive employer.

I also wish to acknowledge those individuals who reviewed this book at various stages: David Dinning, Acadia University (Wolfville, Nova Scotia); Bruce Dunn, University of Calgary (Alberta); Janice Hartgrove-Freile, North Harris County College (Houston,

Texas); and Erwin Janek, Henderson State University (Arkadelphia, Arkansas).

Special thanks go to Sarah for carrying a very precious weight while this book was produced; to Jonas for asking questions; to Anna for being steady; to my mother, Dorothy, for selfless support; to Robert Sommer for continuing inspiration.

R. G.

ROBERT GIFFORD

Robert Gifford is Professor in the Department of Psychology at the University of Victoria, in British Columbia. He received his BA from the University of California at Davis and his MA and Ph.D. from Simon Fraser University. His interest in applied psychology began in the 1960s when, with Robert Sommer, he investigated whether advice in how-to-study books was useful. The books often say you should study in a hard, high-backed chair at a well-lit desk. But Gifford and Sommer found that students who followed this advice had no better grades than students who studied in soft chairs, in bed, or even on the floor (Gifford & Sommer, 1968). So find any comfortable place to read this book! ♦

1

Welcome to the Neighborhood

Today's applied psychologists are solving problems brought to them by anxious parents, office workers with chronic back pain, governments who want to select better managers, figure skaters who can't concentrate, frustrated teachers, eager students, depressed construction workers, professionals with brain injuries, agencies concerned about the homeless, flashers, marketers of oranges, lawyers seeking an edge, the disabled who have trouble getting around, boards of directors who want to create more habitable buildings, and persons who are confused or fear they are losing their minds.

These are a mere sample of more than 40 actual cases you will read in this book, and these cases, in turn, are a mere sample of the thousands of cases that applied psychologists around the world are working on at any given time. Incidentally, the word *case* is not always accurate. It implies a one-on-one therapeutic situation, when many applied psychologists do not work that way. *Problem requiring a solution* is often a more accurate phrase, but it lacks the advantage of brevity enjoyed by the word *case*.

What Is Applied Psychology?

Many definitions of the field have been offered. The following one tries to be all-encompassing yet reasonably straightforward. *Applied psychology* is the part of psychology that, while retaining the goal of advancing knowledge through a scientific approach to human behavior, is dedicated to research and practice that can ameliorate the immediate and developing problems of individuals and organizations.

The Background of Applied Psychology

Later in this book, an author observes that people have been applying psychology from the first time a parent patted a child on the head after a good hunting trip or whacked the hand that tried to steal food. In fact, those parents probably discovered applied psychology before—or in the process of—having that child!

In modern times, applied psychology developed near the end of the last century. The first manifestation of applied psychology as we know it was probably the opening, in 1896, of Lightner Witmer's psychological clinic at the University of Pennsylvania. Because his main clients were students who were having difficulties, this represents the beginning of both clinical and school psychology.

The next area to develop was probably what we now call consumer psychology, in the form of work by Walter Dill Scott on advertising. His book, *The Theory of Advertising*, was published in 1903. This was followed by the area of law and psychology, when the famous psychologist Hugo Munsterberg published his book, *On the Witness Stand*, in 1908.

About the same time, industrial psychology (later industrial-organizational psychology) was established when Frederick Winslow Taylor developed an approach to work efficiency known as *scientific management*. His book, *The Principles of Scientific Management*, appeared in 1911.

Next, psychologists realized that an entire new discipline was developing. Munsterberg followed his book on law and psychology with a broader one, called *Psychology: General and Applied*, in 1915. Then, in 1917, one of the outstanding early psychologists, G. Stanley Hall, established the *Journal of Applied Psychology*, which is still one of the premier publications in the discipline. The number of applied psychologists increased from a handful in the first decade of the century to hundreds in the 1940s to thousands today.

Each area of applied psychology has its own history, landmark studies, and key figures. In the chapters ahead, I will let the specialists tell you more about the backgrounds of their own fields.

The Scope of Applied Psychology

Which problems are brought to applied psychologists, and who brings them? The opening lines of this chapter suggests that a very broad range of the community becomes involved with the applied psychologist at some point. The best known applied psychologists probably are the clinical psychologist and the organizational psychologist, to whom are brought the problems of suffering individuals and those of puzzled or unproductive organizations. However, I must confess that one purpose of this book is to introduce the many other applied psychologists who work in your community. This is the basis for the *variety* in the subtitle of this book.

A Neighborhood of Application, Optimism, and Method

I think of applied psychology as a neighborhood—hence the title of this chapter—even though the authors work all over North America. Instead of sharing a single physical community, applied psychologists share a certain orientation to problem solving. This shared orientation is the applied psychologist's "neighborhood." Just as in any neighborhood, these neighbors do have differences: They solve different problems, their methods and techniques vary, their training and work settings differ. Nevertheless, I believe the similarities are more important than these differences.

Which similarities lead me to use the word neighborhood in describing the field? I have already mentioned the most important one, the preference for using or discovering knowledge that can assist someone in everyday life. A second, but related belief is that the world—at least the little corner of it where the applied psychologist is working—*can* be helped, changed, or improved. This may sound obvious, especially if you share this view, but my experience is that pessimists who believe the world is negative and essentially unchangeable are not at all uncommon.

The Methods, in Brief

Applied psychologists agree in broad terms that certain ways of acquiring useful knowledge are best, even though not every requirement of those methods can be met in every study. A loose term for these ways is *the scientific method*, but applied psychologists employ numerous versions of the scientific method, methods that are usually adapted to investigations in the difficult terrain outside laboratories. Each chapter will describe the typical methods of that particular specialty, but you should be aware of the general nature of these methods.

The tools of the applied psychologist's trade include, in general: structured and semistructured interviews, standardized psychological tests, questionnaires and surveys, trained observation, case studies of individuals and organizations and, sometimes, true experiments, descriptive and inferential statistics. Many entire books have been written about each tool; what follows are very brief, informal introductions.

Interview

The *interview* is a prepared series of carefully worded questions, usually asked of one person at a time. In the semistructured interview, room is allowed for unanticipated topics to arise and be discussed; in the structured interview the agenda is adhered to closely, often because of the possibility that straying from the prepared set of questions may bias the interview outcome.

Standardized Psychological Tests

To measure a large number of psychological aspects of people, standardized psychological tests are used, the most common of which are intelligence and personality tests. Items on properly developed psychological tests have survived many steps of a test development process intended to ensure their *reliability* (i.e., their consistency from item to item within the test and from one testing occasion to another) and their *validity* (i.e., the extent to which they measure what they are intended to measure).

Questionnaires and Surveys

Although questionnaires and surveys are sometimes standardized and used in more than one study, most often they are constructed specifically for a particular problem. Nevertheless, they must also be carefully constructed. They are traditionally given to many people in a paper-and-pencil format, although both standardized tests and questionnaires are now sometimes administered on a computer. Questionnaires have been devised to study virtually every topic investigated by applied psychologists.

Trained Observation

To study actual behavior (as opposed to what people *say* they do on questionnaires and in interviews) requires trained observation. Even well-intentioned individuals sometimes act differently than they *think* (and say) they do. The observations may be of ongoing ("live") behavior, behavior that has been recorded on tape or film, behavioral records (e.g., last year's grades, performance figures, or analyses of the content of written material), or traces of behavior (e.g., worn spots on a bank teller machine, graffiti, or paths worn across a grassy area on campus). Coding systems for the observations must be developed with the same care devoted to the other methods. Observers are trained to follow the coding system precisely.

Case Studies

Case studies of individuals or organizations employ combinations of the above methods to learn something (or, sometimes, everything) important or relevant about a person or organization. The focus in the case study is more on understanding the subject of the case study than on discovering new scientific principles. An unusual case, however, may be described in the professional journals to help other psychologists who may encounter similar cases.

True Experiments

Applied psychologists sometimes perform true experiments. The primary characteristics of a true experiment are that (a) subjects are randomly assigned to conditions (e.g., bright light versus dim light), and (b) the experimenter controls the conditions being investigated so that other influences (e.g., how well the boss treats the employees who are working in different lighting conditions) will not affect the outcome (e.g., employee productivity). True experiments are very hard to do in everyday settings because organizations often cannot permit the experimenter so much control. However, some true experiments are done: One strategy is to perform the experiment on one unit of a large organization, so that disruption to most normal activities of the organization are minimized.

When numerous individuals are studied, two kinds of statistics are used to draw conclusions. *Descriptive statistics* are the kind often used in polls and sports: How many of this or that action has occurred? What is the average number of behaviors? What is the range of behaviors across individuals? We say, for example, that a baseball player has 150 hits in a season, that his batting average is .285, that the most hits in that season by any player was 215, and so on. Common descriptive statistics are *measures of central tendency* (e.g., mean or average, mode, median) and *measures of dispersion* (or how widely scattered the scores are; two common measures are the range and the standard deviation). *Inferential statistics* go beyond descriptive statistics; they indicate the extent to which two variables are related or one variable causes another. To continue the baseball analogy, inferential statistics could be used to discover whether batting averages are better in day games than in night games or whether experience (e.g., number of seasons played) is associated with higher batting averages. Such relationships usually are not perfect (e.g., not every player's batting average increases every season), but many are true to a degree. Inferential statistics show how strong the connection between variables is.

Some inferential statistics reveal the degree to which scores rise and fall together (e.g., correlation and multiple regression), and others show whether scores are significantly different from one another (e.g., t-tests, analyses of variance). Inferential statistics are subjected to *tests of significance*, which show whether the association between scores (or the difference between scores) is likely to be true for the entire group or population of interest (e.g., all baseball players) even though only some of them were studied (e.g., a sample of 200 major league players). In any comparison of scores, *some* association (or difference) is likely; the tests of significance indicate how likely it is that these are true of the whole group of interest.

But why do all this? What's the purpose?

The Purposes: Local Solutions, Global Understanding

Most psychologists hope that their work will be useful and eventually increase our understanding of human beings. In their daily work, however, some psychologists focus on careful laboratory work and trust that someone else will eventually use the knowledge they have gained to help people. The applied psychologist is the one who, despite appreciating the value of laboratory research, just can't wait to use knowledge to improve the world.

The applied psychologist does this despite being acutely aware that very often what is already known about how to solve the problem is scant or imperfect. The request for help with an immediate problem is so touching, so interesting, or so rewarding that the applied psychologist decides assistance really must be rendered. This decision is almost always a leap into the dark, done only when he or she believes one of two things: (1) that the existing store of knowledge is good enough that more good than harm will come from applying it or, more often, (2) that the stock of methods and techniques he or she has acquired through years of training and experience will yield useful information *as* the problem is investigated. Every applied psychologist can describe problems that have been solved through such efforts. There are over 40 accounts of such problems, or cases, in this book.

Every applied psychologist can also point to a multitude of problems that *could* be solved, if only more time, assistance, and funds were available. That is what the *opportunity* in the book's subtitle refers to. The growth of applied psychology over the last century has been phenomenal, and there is room for more eager, talented young psychologists. The authors of this book assume that you are at least mildly interested in these opportunities and therefore will often address you rather directly, as in "you will find that. . . ."

As I mentioned earlier, the applied psychologist also cares about understanding human behavior more generally; solving the immediate problem is not the only concern. It may seem that applied and theoretical psychology are incompatible, but they are not. One of the most important figures in applied psychology, Kurt Lewin, said over 40 years ago that "there is nothing so practical as a good theory." It doesn't happen every day, but professional practice can contribute to theory; conversely, good professional practice is guided by knowledge of relevant theories. The applied psychologist dreams that the solution to *this* problem will help others to solve similar problems, that the research done locally will reveal glimpses of a global set of principles by which human behavior in everyday life can be understood.

Who, What, How Many?

It is impossible to say just how many psychologists are active today. Some belong to no organization; many belong to one or more of many specialist organizations. A conservative estimate of how many psychologists of each kind is provided by membership in national associations. Even these numbers are underestimates because, in addition to the reasons just listed, (a) membership in the national associations is voluntary, and (b) the national organizations are undergoing important reorganizations and may split into separate groups.

The American Psychological Association (APA), founded in 1892 and incorporated in 1925, had 68,321 members in May 1989, a total that includes both applied and other kinds of psychologists. Membership in its 45 divisions is also voluntary, and about 41% of APA's members belong to no division. Each of those who choose to join the divisions, however, belong to an average of two divisions.

The British Psychological Society (BPS) was founded in 1901 and incorporated in 1941. It had over 13,100 members at the end of 1987. The BPS has 13 sections that members may join if they wish.

The Canadian Psychological Association (CPA) was founded in 1939 and incorporated in 1950. It has 26 sections devoted to particular areas of psychology and 3,740 members as of March 1988. Tables 1-1 and 1-2 give you an idea of the amount of

TABLE 1-1   Divisions of the APA of Special Interest to Applied Psychologists

Division	Division Membership (May 1989)	Proportion of APA Total (percent)	Change Since 1980 (percent)
Clinical Psychology	5,831	7.8	+29
Counseling Psychology	2,717	3.6	+5
Psychotherapy	4,567	6.1	+11
Psychoanalysis	2,583	3.5	+179
Clinical Neuropsychology	2,606	3.5	+502
Consulting Psychology	909	1.2	+35
Psychologists in Independent Practice	5,293	7.1	*
Industrial and Organizational Psychology	2,566	3.4	+31
Psychologists in Public Service	895	1.2	−31
Evaluation, Measurement and Statistics	1,236	1.7	+13
Applied Experimental and Engineering Psychologists	517	.7	+3
Consumer Psychology	448	.6	+41
Community Psychology	1,069	1.4	−29
Population and Environmental Psychology	382	.5	−21
Rehabilitation Psychology	928	1.2	+6
Mental Retardation and Developmental Disabilities	791	1.1	−16
Teaching of Psychology	1,895	2.5	−18
School Psychology	2,252	3.0	−9
Psychology of Women	2,334	3.1	+24
Child, Youth, and Family Services	1,397	1.9	+78
Family Psychology	1,752	2.4	*
Health Psychology	2,742	3.7	+195
Exercise and Sport Psychology	522	.7	*
Psychology-Law Society	1,237	1.7	*
Society for the Psychological Study of Social Issues (SPSSI)	2,785	3.7	+14
Lesbian and Gay Issues	587	.8	*
Ethnic Minority Issues	452	.6	*
Experimental Analysis of Behavior	1,095	1.5	−30
Media Psychology	370	.5	*
All APA Division Memberships**	74,355		+32

Source: *APA Monitor, 20,* October 1989, p. 4.

  *Division was not established in 1980.

**Including those for divisions not listed here.

interest in the different areas of applied psychology that are represented by those divisions and sections of the United States and Canadian national associations of special interest to applied psychologists.

TABLE 1-2   Sections of the CPA of Special Interest to Applied Psychologists

Section	Section Membership (1988)	Proportion of CPA Total (percent)
Clinical Psychology	*	*
Counseling Psychology	87	2.3
Clinical Neuropsychology	202	5.4
Criminal Justice Systems	93	2.5
Community Psychology	82	2.2
Environmental Psychology	26	.7
Industrial and Organizational Psychology	159	4.2
Program Evaluation	40	1.1
Psychological Gerontology	66	1.8
Health Psychology	237	6.3
Sport and Physical Fitness Psychology	74	2.0
Educational Psychology	132	3.5
Teaching of Psychology	107	2.9
Students in Psychology	140	3.7
Social Responsibility Psychology	82	2.2
Women and Psychology	276	7.4
Total CPA Memberships**	3,740	

Source: *CPA Annual Reports*, 1988.

*New in late 1989; no membership figures available yet.

**Including members not in sections listed above.

Becoming an Applied Psychologist

Education

The Degrees

To independently practice applied psychology today, a doctoral degree (Ph.D. or Psy.D.) is required in nearly every jurisdiction and specialty. With less than a doctoral degree, you may still be able to help people in various ways, but your work will be supervised by a qualified applied psychologist. A doctoral degree is earned after a master's degree, which comes after a bachelor's degree. The bad news is that the doctoral degree is rarely attained in less than eight years of college or university work. Many individuals take 11 or 12 years to achieve this goal because they work inside or outside school while they learn. If someone told me these facts when I first entered college, I might have been too discouraged to continue.

The good news is that although it takes a long time and much effort, life does not stop while you are on the path. You can still do most of the things that you thought you would do along the way. Assuming you are able and interested in doing the work, the time will pass much more quickly than you might think.

If you are unable or unwilling to pursue a doctoral degree, you can still obtain a job that will benefit from your psychological knowledge although you will not be able to call yourself a psychologist. With some psychology but not a bachelor's degree, you may be able to work in human service fields such as social welfare, corrections, agencies serving the elderly and the disabled, group homes, crisis intervention units, community mental health centers, drug and alcohol rehabilitation centers, early childhood education sites, and the like. In such positions, you would be supervised by someone with more advanced training, but at least you would be on the front lines, helping people.

If you obtain a bachelor's degree, positions requiring more psychological training will be open, but the title psychologist will still not be available. Typical positions for employees with a bachelor's degree in psychology include psychiatric assistant, parole officer, employment interviewer, marketing, administration, personnel, teaching, and geriatric work.

Students who earn a master's degree (but not a Ph.D.) will begin to see *parts* of the word *psychology* in their title: two positions often open are psychometrist (one concerned with psychological testing; the psychometrician with a master's degree usually is restricted to administering tests rather than developing them) and psychological assistant (one who assists or works under the supervision of a doctoral-level applied psychologist).

The Undergraduate Courses

If you think that you might want to be an applied psychologist, you are in one recommended course right now! What else should you take? The direction for a student aiming for a Ph.D. is described here, but at the undergraduate level the same advice applies for those who will not be going that far.

Normally, of course, you should fulfill your school's basic requirements for a bachelor's degree in psychology. Usually you have some choice of courses beyond that. Because every school is different, ask your professor or advisor which courses in your school are best for applied psychology in general and for the specialty that appeals most to you. In most cases, this is fairly obvious: Take courses with the same themes as the specialty you prefer—clinical, organizational, and health psychology, for example. Take developmental psychology if you are interested in the child clinical specialty, physiological psychology if you prefer clinical neuropsychology, aging for geropsychology. Social psychology is a useful basis for several specialties.

Other courses in psychology and other disciplines help broaden your horizons. Outside psychology, courses in English composition (good writing skill is very important in graduate school and beyond), sociology (to understand the problems the applied psychologist will deal with from a societal perspective), biology (to gain a fuller understanding of basic physiological processes), and philosophy (to sharpen your thinking) will be useful.

The Changes
It is very likely that you will change your interests between now and the end of your education. If you are unsure of your career direction now, that is OK; don't worry. In fact, I would worry more if, in the first two or three years of college, you felt absolutely certain which specialty you wanted. You may well take a course from a very admirable professor and see new value in that area. (This is what happened to me and to many others.) You may find that the material in a certain course matches your own interests very well, despite the instruction provided by a less-than-scintillating professor. The point is this: Make your own decisions, but take it easy about selecting a specialty until later. Many students even change their interests during graduate school.

Graduate School
Graduate school is different from undergraduate school. Again, this varies from place to place, but, generally speaking, you will spend much less time in class and your class size will shrink drastically. Some students make the dreadful mistake of thinking that this means graduate school is easy. Untrue! This is merely another step toward self-motivated work. Remember the difference between elementary school and high school? Between high school and college? Each time, there was less structure and less time spent in class. But did it become easier?

In graduate school, much (or even most) of the learning is self-directed; it occurs on your own or with a few fellow "sufferers." You will probably have one professor as your advisor and two or three others who serve on your committee. These are generally benevolent "demons" who guide you through a new process of growth that involves (a) learning more about the important people, organizations, theories, and pieces of research done in your field; (b) how to write (even) better; and (c) how to conduct your own research and evaluate research done by others.

You will write more papers and take fewer multiple-choice exams. However, you should actually enjoy writing most of the papers, because everything you do will be in an area of interest to you. (If it *isn't* interesting with a challenging twist, you should switch areas or get out.) You will take a comprehensive examination that supposedly covers everything in your specialty and is meant to demonstrate that you really deserve to call yourself a doctor of philosophy. In addition, you will undertake at least two big research projects (under the watchful and supportive direction of your advisors), one for the master's degree and one for the doctoral degree. How big? The Ph.D. dissertation usually takes at least a year and many students need two or more years to plan, execute, analyze, write, and defend it in an oral examination.

Applied Psychology and Money

You probably won't become rich as an applied psychologist, but you don't have to be rich to become one.

Let's start with the second part of that sentence. If you are a very good to excellent student (roughly A− or better, especially in your last two undergraduate years), you have a very reasonable expectation of receiving financial assistance in your graduate program. You may receive scholarships or fellowships that free you from working while in school. If your grades are in the B to B+ range, you may be accepted into a graduate program (not one of the top programs) and you may be able to work as a teaching or research assistant to pay your way; this will slow your progress a little. Both forms of assistance depend on the student (the best are offered more) and the school (the best are hardest to win assistance from). However, it is important to remember that this *is* accomplished by thousands of graduate students every year!

Now to the first part of that sentence. The assistance you receive is generally enough to keep you at a subsistence level, no more. You will temporarily envy friends who did not even complete college but are earning "big bucks" in a field that does not require a

Ph.D. Then, when you finally get that first real job, at age 30 or so, you will still be earning less than many friends.

But gradually, studies show, your salary will increase until you finally earn more than most of your friends who did not stay in school until the bitter end. Your total lifetime earnings will, despite your slow start, exceed that of those in many occupations. As for that friend of yours who makes a million in the trucking business, ask yourself (preferably after you have read the rest of this book!) whether you would rather make less money but be engaged in applied psychology. If the answer is no, there is still time to drop out and get into the trucking business!

Accreditation

Accreditation is the process by which an official organization grants professional recognition. Both programs (that is, courses of graduate study in universities and other institutions) and individuals (you) can be accredited. In applied psychology, accreditation is not always required for employment as an applied psychologist, but it is increasingly important in some specialties, for certain jobs, and in some places. Because accreditation requirements are still actively evolving, the information provided here should be regarded only as a guideline, to be checked as you get closer to becoming a professional psychologist.

Accreditation of Programs

For some specialties, attending an accredited graduate program is important or essential. (There is no official accreditation at the undergraduate level; you should simply attend the best university or college that you can.) These programs are all at the doctoral level. Most lead to the Doctor of Philosophy (Ph.D.) degree, but some lead to the Doctor of Psychology (Psy.D.), a newer type of degree that puts more emphasis on the practitioner role and less on the researcher role.

In the United States, the APA grants accreditation to programs that meet carefully monitored standards. Accreditation may be full (meets all requirements), provisional (not all requirements have been met, but they are expected to be met soon), or probationary (accredited but currently unsatisfactory).

In 1988, 147 programs were accredited by the APA in clinical psychology in the United States, plus 8 in Canada. Another 51 were accredited by the APA in counseling psychology, all in the United States. In school psychology, 38 programs were APA accredited, all in the United States. Most of the clinical programs are based in departments or schools of psychology, and many of the counseling and school psychology programs are based in departments or schools of education or educational psychology.

APA-accredited programs are found in nearly every U.S. state and Canadian province, but if you wish to know whether a particular institution's program is accredited, a full list is published every December in the *American Psychologist*, which can be found in your library. You can also write for more information to the American Psychological Association (see "Memberships" at the end of the chapter).

In Canada, the CPA accredits clinical programs. As of 1988, 12 universities and hospitals had received full or provisional accreditation. For more information, write to CPA (see "Memberships" at the end of the chapter).

Many other schools have degree-granting programs but are not accredited. Generally speaking, the accredited programs have more applicants and are more difficult to enter, because many view them as offering excellent programs and better opportunities for future advancement. However, some nonaccredited schools offer good programs and, as noted earlier, some positions do not require training in an accredited program. Nevertheless, if you wish to become a professional in an area of applied psychology that has an accreditation process, your goal should be to enter an accredited program. By the time you are ready for graduate school, further accreditation programs in applied psychology may be in place. Clinical neuropsychology, for example, is one specialty that is actively developing an accreditation process.

Accreditation of Individuals

For some varieties of applied psychology and for some jobs, earning a Ph.D. degree (even from an accredited program!) is not enough to obtain the right to practice. Individuals may be accredited, just as programs are. There are two basic forms of individual accreditation, licensing (also called certification) and boarding. This topic is a little complicated because of variations across the specialties, across the states and provinces, because accreditation practices are still developing (very actively in some specialties), and because of the two basic forms of accreditation. Let's start with licensing (or certification).

Licensing or certification. In all 50 states and 9 Canadian provinces, licensing or certification is required to work as an independent, unsupervised psychologist, particularly in the mental health specialties and sometimes in organizational psychology. The licensing board examines your training and gives you an exam; many jurisdictions also require two years of supervised work.

An internship, which may occur either during graduate training (a predoctoral internship) or after (a postdoctoral internship), is a frequent requirement in clinical and counseling psychology, but internships are also offered in other areas of applied psychology. The intern typically works full time for one academic year under the supervision of an experienced psychologist in a hospital or other setting that deals with actual clients. Because real work is done, many internships are salaried positions, but because the intern is still actively learning about the profession, the salaries are usually at the bare survival level.

Just as attendance in an accredited program is not always necessary for employment, being accredited as an individual is not always necessary. For example, a job within an organization that primarily deals with its own employees may not require that you are licensed. Also, licensing is often not required (and sometimes not even available) for applied psychologists who work in fields other than clinical, counseling, organizational, or school psychology.

Boarding. The fully qualified applied psychologist who seeks further recognition of his or her skills and experience should seek board accreditation. Boarding is usually done by national organizations, rather than states or provinces, and is usually not required for practice or employment. In the United States, several licensing boards exist. One of the most prominent is the American Board of Professional Psychology (ABPP), which certifies psychologists in the following specialties (the number in parentheses is how many of each specialty were certified as of 1988): clinical* (1,943), clinical neuropsychology (153), counseling* (272), forensic (82), industrial and organizational* (169), and school* (294). (Specialties marked with an asterisk are those ABPP certifications that are also officially recognized by the APA.)

In the United Kingdom, the BPS was granted a Royal Charter in 1987 to maintain a Register of Chartered Psychologists. The Register was set up during 1988 and implemented in 1989. The BPS maintains five divisions in which members can be chartered: clinical, occupational, criminological, legal, and educational (here there are two divisions—one for Scotland and one for members who practice elsewhere).

Employment

As noted earlier, most employment as an applied psychologist requires the doctoral degree, and independent practice requires licensing or certification. Those fields for which a psychology bachelor's degree is useful but other training is required (such as nursing, corrections, teaching, social work, and administration) have their own programs and requirements.

Assuming for the moment that you are interested in becoming an applied psychologist, what are the employment prospects? Of course, they vary by specialty, and each chapter in this book concludes with the author's view of employment prospects in his or her specialty. But what about the field as a whole?

The National Science Foundation (NSF) produced a special report in 1988 on employment in psychology. The report says that in the decade prior to 1988, psychology was the third-fastest-growing scientific field in the United States (after computer and mathematical specialties). The NSF estimates that between 1986 and 2000, the growth in psychology employment will be between 27% and 39%. (In comparison, its estimate for all occupations is an increase of 13% to 23%.) The largest increase within psychology is expected to occur in health-related services (between 55% and 68% growth by the year 2000). Psychology has always been a leader in the employment of women, the report says, and by 1986 women held 45% of all psychology positions.

The chapters to follow represent many of the classic areas of applied psychology. However, recent Ph.D.s in applied psychology are finding employment in many hybrids of these classic areas and in many new kinds of positions that value psychological training. A recent article describing the positions held by recent Ph.D.s from one graduate school lists some of these positions: manager of a Rideshare department, computer database analyst, research analyst for a mental health clinic, supervisor of an alcoholism unit, and others (Oskamp, 1988). However, many other positions described in the article directly follow from the classic specialties to be described in the next 14 chapters.

Welcome to the neighborhood!

SUGGESTED READINGS AND REFERENCES

The APA publishes several books and booklets that provide further information. Your school's psychology department or counseling center may have copies available.

Careers in Psychology. This brief (28-page) 1986 pamphlet describes the fields of and careers in psychology. Single copies are free to students.

Graduate Study in Psychology and Associated Fields. A comprehensive guide (652 pages) to graduate programs in the United States and Canada; the current version is 1988 with a 1989 addendum. You can learn which schools offer which specialties, admission requirements, housing facilities, financial assistance, tuition, and so on.

Is Psychology the Major for You? This 137-page 1987 volume is oriented toward students who wish to make a career in psychology: which careers are available, how to find a job, how to utilize career counseling, how to survive as a new employee.

Preparing for Graduate Study in Psychology: NOT for Seniors Only! A 1980 96-page sourcebook, this book outlines steps needed for graduate school, with an emphasis on students who do not have the credentials yet! Acquiring recommendations, writing resumes, practicing interviews, and so on are discussed.

The CPA also publishes material for prospective graduate students. Check your department advisor or write to the CPA (address follows).

Gifford, R., & Sommer, R. (1968). The desk or the bed? Personnel and Guidance Journal, *46*, 876–878.

Graduate Guide: Description of Graduate Psychology Programs in Canadian Universities (8th ed., 1989–1990).

National Science Foundation. (1988). *Profiles—Psychology: Human Resources and Funding* (NSF 88-325) (Washington, DC).

Oskamp, S. (1988). Nontraditional employment opportunities for applied psychologists. *American Psychologist, 43*, 484–485.

MEMBERSHIPS

You can join a national organization as a student affiliate. The APA's annual fee for students is $25, for which you get (a) discounts on books published by APA, (b) lower prices on APA journal subscriptions, and (c) the APA *Monitor* (the organization's monthly newspaper) and the *American Psychologist* (its official journal) at no extra cost. The APA's address is 1200 Seventeenth Street, N.W., Washington, DC 20036.

The CPA's student membership is only $10, for which you receive equivalent news and journals. The CPA's address is Vincent Road, Old Chelsea, Quebec J0X 2N0.

Another organization of interest is the International Association of Applied Psychology (IAAP). This worldwide group, formed in 1920, holds congresses every four years (the 1990 congress was in Kyoto, Japan). The

♦ Becoming an Applied Psychologist

IAAP has ten divisions: organizational psychology; psychological assessment; psychology and national development; environmental psychology; educational, instruction, and school psychology; clinical and community psychology; applied gerontology; health psychology; economic psychology; and psychology and law. For more information, contact Harry C. Triandis, 603 East Daniel Street, Champaign, IL 61820.

MICHAEL JOSCHKO

Michael Joschko received his Ph.D. in Clinical Psychology from the University of Windsor in 1981. He has extensive clinical experience working in child development, children's mental health, children's rehabilitation, and children's psychiatric settings. He is currently the Director of Psychology at the Arbutus Society for Children, which includes the G. R. Pearkes Centre for Children, the Queen Alexandra Hospital for Children, and the Jack Ledger Child and Adolescent Psychiatric Unit. He is also a Visiting Assistant Professor in the Department of Psychology at the University of Victoria. ♦

2

The
Clinical Child
Psychologist

The overall purpose of a clinical child psychologist's involvement with a child or family is to provide specific information or psychological interventions to improve that child's day-to-day functioning so that her or his psychological needs can be realized and any hinderances to his or her psychosocial development can be minimized. The work of most clinical child psychologists involves the assessment and/or treatment of so-called special children who are experiencing social, cognitive, psychological, or physical limitations to some aspect of their development.

Here is an example. Nine-year-old Daniel was referred to me by his teacher because he was very "anxious"; she believed he was having a "stress reaction" to his ongoing difficulties in mathematics. She requested that I provide some treatment to reduce Daniel's level of stress through one of the groups I was running. She also requested that I conduct a psychometric assessment of Daniel with a view to providing some suggestions regarding the remediation of his difficulties in mathematics.

Presented with such a problem, where does the clinical child psychologist start? The first step was to understand exactly what the problem was. This required a careful assessment of Daniel's problem and the various factors that might be contributing to it. In doing this, my responsibility to Daniel was to resist the temptation to jump to simple conclusions based on limited evidence; therefore, I did not enroll Daniel in my next preadolescent stress management group or automatically schedule him for assessment in the clinic's learning disability program. As is so often the case, the initial problem described in the referral letter masked a different and more complex set of problems than had originally been suspected by Daniel's teacher.

When I called Daniel's parents to gather more information and to set up a first appointment, his mother told me that she did not think that I could be of any help because she was sure her son had been "possessed by the devil." She described Daniel as willfully aggravating her and her husband by spitting at the dinner table and in the kitchen sink, swearing "almost constantly" including while reading from the Bible in front of his father's congregation, yelling incoherent phrases, and making strange and obscene facial gestures and hand movements. After some discussion, Daniel's mother agreed to bring him to see me, and she provided me with some additional information prior to my first appointment with Daniel by rating him on a series of standardized behavioral checklists and personality questionnaires that are designed to give a reliable description of a child's day-to-day behavior. She also agreed to have his teacher complete some similar questionnaires.

The results of these questionnaires gave me some important insights into Daniel's difficulties prior to my actual appointment with him. These insights, however, were puzzling in that they were somewhat inconsistent with the concerns expressed by the teacher or by Daniel's mother. On the basis of these well-standardized behavioral checklists and personality questionnaires, it seemed that Daniel was neither particularly "anxious," as had been suggested in the teacher's referral letter, or a "conduct problem," as had been suggested by his mother. He was rated on these questionnaires by both his teacher and mother as more active and impulsive than other boys his age; both raters also indicated the presence of some strange mannerisms and they endorsed a number of test items that suggested that Daniel might be experiencing some depression and a tendency toward rigid and inflexible behavior. The patterns commonly seen in anxious or conduct-disordered children were clearly not in evidence when I reviewed Daniel's test profiles. (Anxious children are characterized by very high levels of fearfulness and worry, while children with conduct disorders are characterized by repetitive and persistent disturbances of social conduct or behavior. The questionnaires and behavior rating scales I had administered indicated that Daniel had neither of these characteristics.)

When Daniel came to see me in my office he was extremely well behaved. With the exception of some fidgety behavior and some mild facial tics, there was nothing obviously unusual about Daniel. After some discussion, I asked Daniel to make some drawings and to tell some stories in response to the pictures I showed him. These projective tests, which used vague, ambiguous, and unstructured tasks to elicit Daniel's characteristic modes of perceiving his world, indicated that he was experiencing considerable sadness in relation to his behavior at home, that he felt his parents did not really love him, and that he had very poor self-esteem. There were no indications that Daniel's behavior was generally a problem or that he had a conduct disorder. As I reflected these insights back to Daniel, he opened up, and with little prompting from me, he described in some detail his frequently uncontrollable urges to spit, curse, stick out his tongue, or move his hands. He told me he could suppress these urges for periods of time while at school or in my office, but that they built up like a "pressure cooker" and often just had to come out at home. He cried when he told me that "he couldn't help it," even when his parents yelled at him to stop.

I then asked Daniel's mother to join us. I asked her about the evolution of Daniel's mannerisms and difficult behavior. She described a long history of strange tics and vocal utterances that would wax and wane over time. She reported that her family doctor had said Daniel would grow out of these "transient" tics and behavior problems. I then told Daniel and his mother that it was likely that Daniel's symptoms were due to a non–life-threatening neurological disorder, Gilles de la Tourette Syndrome, and that his symptoms were most likely quite involuntary and not his fault. As I reviewed Daniel's test results and my discussion with him, Daniel's mother began to cry. I asked her to allow Daniel to see her cry, and I encouraged both of them to tell the other some of the reasons for their sadness. Daniel's mother then told Daniel that she felt extremely guilty that she had so often punished him so severely for things he could not help. The punishments she reported included slapping his hand or face, locking him in his room for long periods of time, washing his mouth out with soap, and allowing her husband to have Daniel undergo two exorcisms in their church.

On the basis of my preliminary diagnosis of Daniel's symptoms and the problems in mathematics reported by his teacher, I decided to have Daniel undergo extensive psychological testing (in this case, neuropsychological testing; see Chapter 5) in order to rule out any significant cognitive deficits or learning disabilities that are sometimes associated with Gilles de la Tourette Syndrome. Because some of the strange symptoms described by Daniel and his mother are sometimes associated with certain brain diseases, I arranged for the clinic's consulting pediatrician to see Daniel in order to rule out any obvious medical cause for these symptoms and to confirm the diagnosis of Tourette Syndrome.

The assessment indicated that Daniel did not have any learning disability and that he was quite bright. His problems in mathematics were due to difficulties in controlling his hand tics, which made it difficult for him to properly align the numbers on his work sheets. I also suggested in my report to his parents and teacher that his depressive feelings, poor self-esteem, and the effort required to control his symptoms at school were affecting adversely his ability to concentrate on his school work. The diagnosis of Tourette Syndrome was confirmed. The consulting pediatrician then prescribed a regimen of medication that helped to control his involuntary swearing and motor tics.

Over the next two years, I provided Daniel with a number of sessions of individual supportive psychotherapy. I used the mediums of play, art, and hypnosis to help him regain his self-esteem and cope with the problems associated with Tourette Syndrome. I also arranged family meetings to provide support and information and to help Daniel's parents and sisters adapt to Daniel's disorder and repair some of the maladaptive interactional patterns the family had developed in their honest attempts to cope with Daniel's problems on their own. Finally, when Daniel no longer seemed to tolerate his medication and his symptoms became more noticeable at school, I met frequently with Daniel's teachers and, at times, his classmates to help them understand and respond constructively to Daniel's symptoms.

Although the problems experienced by Daniel were unique in terms of the actual specifics of the behaviors and circumstances involved, the careful diagnosis and treatment of these problems highlights the major tasks of the clinical child psychologist. The approach taken to understand and deal with Daniel's problems involved standardized psychological assessment procedures, an understanding of the personality and developmental factors involved, an understanding of family interrelationships, and the application of developmentally appropriate psychological treatment approaches. The strategies chosen by the clinical child psychologist in solving the problems faced by children and youth reflect the interacting contributions of the psychometric and psychodynamic traditions of the science of psychology. The psychometric tradition has focused on the development and application of mental and personality tests to describe and understand behavior, while the psychodynamic tradition has focused on the unconscious causes and motivational aspects of behavior.

What Is Clinical Child Psychology?

In practical terms, clinical child psychology is the branch of applied psychology that helps solve problems such as Daniel's. Other problems representative of those solved by clinical child psychologists include, but are not limited to, children with

1. sensory handicaps such as blindness or deafness;
2. motor impairments such as cerebral palsy or amputations;
3. generalized or specific intellectual impairments such as mental retardation, developmental delay, speech and language disorders, or learning disabilities;

4. behavioral and emotional problems such as conduct disorder, childhood depression, or childhood psychosis;

5. chronic or acute medical conditions such as cystic fibrosis, diabetes, childhood cancer, or encopresis;

6. neurological disorders such as autism, epilepsy, attention deficit disorder, or acquired brain injuries; and

7. social problems such as sexual abuse, drug abuse, family violence, or parental separation.

Even gifted children with high IQs sometimes require the services of a clinical child psychologist in order to maximize their learning potential and psychosocial adjustment. Almost every common problem of childhood has received some attention from clinical child psychologists.

Clinical child psychology may be formally defined as the application of the knowledge and skills derived from the areas of developmental and general clinical psychology to the assessment and treatment of the wide range of psychological problems faced by children. The developmental perspective and the dual clinical functions of assessment and treatment are very important in the definition, because these terms indicate that clinical child psychologists do not simply apply unchanged the psychological principles and knowledge derived from work with adults to the assessment and treatment of children. Clinical child psychologists realize fully that the theories, assessment tools, and treatment approaches developed by other psychologists for work with adults are not always directly applicable to children.

The eminent Swiss developmental psychologist, Jean Piaget (1970), documented the differing modes of thought and the distinctive stages of mental development that children pass through as they develop and demonstrated that children clearly perceive the world differently from adults. As a result of knowledge derived from early investigators of children's psychological development, such as Piaget, and awareness of other developmental phenomena, child clinical psychologists provide six-year-old children with psychological treatments and test materials that are qualitatively as well as quantitatively different from those used with adults or even 12-year-old children. For example, play therapy as a treatment modality was developed for use with children and is quite different than psychological treatment procedures used with adults. Likewise, psychological assessment procedures designed for use with young children take into account the need to use less verbal and less abstract test materials, as well as developmentally appropriate testing strategies. A number of well-validated psychological tests for the assessment of children actually involve the parents or teachers completing the test rather than directly testing the child.

In addition to assessment and treatment functions, clinical child psychologists also conduct clinical research or teach in university or college settings.

The Background of Clinical Child Psychology

Clinical child psychology emerged in 1896 when Lightner Witmer opened a psychological clinic at the University of Pennsylvania for the study of children with school and learning problems. Witmer's earlier training in James McKeen Cattell's testing laboratory, with its emphasis on the measurement of mental abilities, provided him with some of the necessary assessment tools and procedures for his clinical examinations of children. Interestingly, general clinical psychology also derived from Witmer's Pennsylvania clinic and for many years clinical psychology and clinical child psychology were synonymous. Most clinical employment settings for psychologists during these early years were focused on service delivery to children. This focus changed gradually during the first and second world wars as increasing numbers of clinical psychologists were required to help in the assignment of military personnel to suitable occupations.

In 1908, H. H. Goddard, the director of the psychology laboratory at the Vineland Training School, introduced the Binet-Simon intelligence scale in North America (Binet & Simon, 1916). Other child-centered clinics followed Witmer's clinic with the 1909 openings of a clinic for children with intellectual problems at the University of Minnesota and the Juvenile Psychopathic Institute in Chicago, which serviced emotionally and behaviorally disturbed children. In 1910, Goddard made available a slightly revised version of the 1908 Binet-Simon scales, which he had standardized on a large group of American children. A clinic for children with educational problems opened at the University of Pittsburgh in 1912, and the same year, W. Stern (Stern, 1914) introduced the concept of mental quotient, or IQ. In 1916, Lewis M. Terman published the Stanford Revision and Extension of the Binet-Simon Intelligence Scale. These psychometric developments marked the beginnings of the testing movement in North America and provided important tools for clinical child psychologists in their evaluations of children.

As the child-guidance movement flourished in the United

States during the 1920s and 1930s, clinical child psychologists were employed in a wide variety of settings to assess the intellectual and educational functioning of children. In this same time span, and the years that followed, many other important advances in the assessment of children's intelligence, social skills, and special cognitive abilities occurred. The availability of new psychometric instruments and methods increased the sophistication of the clinical child psychologist's evaluation and the range of referral questions that could be answered. These advances included the development and availability of a number of now very familiar psychometric tools: the Stanford Achievement Test in 1923, Goodenough's Draw-a-Man Test in 1926, the Merrill-Palmer Scale of Mental Tests in 1931, the Vineland Social Maturity Scale in 1936, the Bender Visual Motor Gestalt Test in 1938, the Cattell Infant Intelligence Scale in 1940, and the Wechsler Intelligence Scale for Children in 1949 (see Anastasi, 1976, or Sattler, 1988, for references and descriptions of these tests). These early psychometric developments were followed by revisions of older tests and the development of tests such as the Illinois Test of Psycholinguistic Ability in 1961, the Bayley Scales of Infant Development in 1969, the McCarthy Scales of Children's Abilities in 1972, the Wechsler Intelligence Scale for Children-Revised in 1974, the Kaufman Assessment Battery for Children in 1983, the Stanford-Binet Intelligence Scale: Fourth Edition in 1986, and the Vineland Adaptive Behavior Scales in 1986 (Anastasi, 1976; Sattler, 1988). Knowledge regarding the administration and interpretation of these ability tests, many of which are still the major tools of the trade of clinical child psychologists, represents only part of the special training and skills held by the clinical child psychologist.

Early in the history of the field, clinical child psychologists were also involved in the diagnosis and treatment of behavioral and emotional problems of childhood. As the emphasis in the child-guidance clinics turned more to conceptualizations of the problems presenting in the clinics based on the writings of Sigmund Freud and his psychoanalytic theory of personality, the clinical child psychologist—as a member of the child-guidance team—increasingly was asked to assess personality factors such as psychological conflicts and defenses. These conflicts and defenses, derived from Freud's theory of personality, were thought to reflect the stresses resulting from instinctual sexual energy in conflict with the conscience or the environment and the patterns of unconscious behavior that the person used as defenses against feelings of guilt, anxiety, and shame. The need for new clinical tools to address these referral questions lead to adaptations of adult tests, and the new tests for children were made. Projective techniques and personality tests such as the Make-a-Picture-Story Method, the Thematic Apperception Test, the Rorschach Inkblot Technique, the Incomplete Sentences Technique, the Children's Apperception Test, Blacky Pictures, and various projective drawing tests (e.g., the House-Tree-Person Test, Draw-a-Person, and Kinetic Family Drawings) began to find their way into the test libraries of clinical child psychologists (see Palmer, 1970). These early developments and experience obtained in the use of projective techniques with children eventually led to more carefully designed tests suitable for children and the gathering of child and adolescent norms on tests originally designed for adults.

Initially, the treatment approaches taken by clinical child psychologists, consistent with the psychodynamic emphasis of the child-guidance clinics, were psychodynamic in orientation. Nonetheless, Watson and Raynor's (1920) famous fear-conditioning study of Albert and Mary Clover Jones' (1924) behavioral treatment of young Peter's fears were not entirely lost on clinical child psychology. In little Albert's case, Watson and Raynor demonstrated that strong emotional reactions to a white rat could be learned by associating a fear arousing stimulus such as a loud noise with the initially unfeared white rat. In Peter's case, Jones demonstrated that Peter's fear of a white rabbit, which seemed to generalize to other white, fluffy objects such as cotton or fur, could be systematically treated by presenting the white rabbit to Peter under relaxed and pleasant circumstances. But it was not until the 1960s that behavior assessment and treatment approaches (which are based on empirically validated principles of learning and behavior change and many experiments and studies such as those involving little Albert and Peter) were commonplace in the work performed by clinical child psychologists. Many clinical child psychologists now devote most of their clinical time to behavioral assessment and treatment of the problems faced by children. Others, however, remain primarily psychodynamic in orientation while still others are quite eclectic, using both dynamic and behavioral approaches in their assessment and treatment of the problems presented to them. In spite of the theoretical differences on which they base their understanding of childhood problems, modern clinical child psychologists are always sensitive to the importance of developmental phenomena in their study and treatment of children.

By the late 1950s, the methods and training of most clinical child psychologists and clinical (adult) psychologists had become quite generic. Psychologists entered these two fields from a variety of different backgrounds; at times it seemed that only the focus on children in the work setting differentiated the two. By the mid-1960s, a number of publications, professional organizations, and university programs, however, made it clear to would be clinical child psychologists and employers alike that clinical work with children required specialized training and skills that could not be easily obtained on the job.

The Scope of Clinical Child Psychology

As you can easily imagine, the range of problems clinical child psychologists are asked to solve is quite broad. It is impossible to review here in detail all of the childhood problems that confront the clinical child psychologist, but some representative examples in the way of brief case synopses will be described in this section. First, however, it will be informative to consider the professional activities, types of clients, and employment settings clinical child psychologists are involved with in their work.

Activities
The major professional activities involved in the practice of clinical child psychology are assessment, treatment, consultation, teaching, and research. The amount of time any one clinical child psychologist spends in any of these areas depends on his or her own interests and the nature of the employment setting.

The range of assessment tools used by clinical child psychologists is quite broad. These assessment tools include structured tests of intelligence such as the Wechsler Intelligence Scale for Children-Revised (WISC-R), projective measures of personality characteristics such as the Thematic Apperception Test (TAT), and personality and behavioral checklists such as the Personality Inventory for Children or the Child Behavior Checklist (see Goldman, Stein, and Guerry, 1983), which use the ratings of parents or teachers to describe personality or behavioral characteristics of children. The assessment strategies used by clinical child psychologists involve direct observation of the child in structured or unstructured situations and the collection and collation of information from other observers, such as parents and teachers, who know the child well in a variety of social settings. The structured observation usually involves the use of a test or behavioral observation form (which is generally a list of specific behaviors that can be checked or rated on a defined scale).

At this juncture, it seems appropriate to point out that the psychological test is really nothing more than a structured observation with specific rules for classifying and scoring the behavior samples obtained during the assessment. Unstructured observations might involve watching how the child behaves in the classroom or on the playground. Clinical interviews and the use of standardized questionnaires with parents or other professionals, and the review of the reports or records of other professionals, generally provide important clinical data for the clinical child psychologist's assessment that cannot be easily obtained through direct observation.

The major approaches to the psychological treatment of children include psychotherapeutic interventions with individual children (individual therapy), groups of children (group therapy), or the child's entire family (family therapy). Each of these general approaches to psychological intervention, depending on the needs of the child and the theoretical orientation of the psychologist, can take many different forms and can involve a number of specific intervention techniques. The psychological treatment might make use of the child's play with common toys or art materials to express feelings and emotions and thereby to help resolve inner conflicts and tensions. Other approaches might be based primarily on verbal discussions of the problems faced by the child and a verbal exploration of the child's emotional reactions to these problems. Other approaches might utilize structured information sharing regarding the causes of psychological difficulties and attempts at altering maladaptive thought patterns through a series of structured exercises. Still other approaches might focus on training parents or teachers to respond to the child in specific ways as a means of encouraging and rewarding the occurrence of desirable behavior. Other approaches might involve the simultaneous treatment of several children in a group through combined play or art activities, group discussion and peer modeling, or structured information sharing and education.

As I have indicated above, the theoretical orientation of the clinical child psychologist to some degree influences the assessment and treatment approach used in helping children and their families. These theoretical orientations can be grouped into the four major models of child development listed on the next page.

1. *Developmental-maturational models* (e.g., Gesell & Ilg, 1943) focus on normal patterns of development and view child development and behavior as very closely determined by neurological maturation.
2. *Psychodynamic models* (e.g., Freud, 1946; Erikson, 1963) assume that child behavior is determined by unconscious mechanisms of motivation.
3. *Cognitive models* (e.g., Piaget, 1970) assume that child behavior can be best understood by understanding how the child acquires and uses knowledge.
4. *Learning-based or behavioral models* (Sears, Maccoby, & Levin, 1957; Bandura, 1974) place great emphasis on the events that take place in the environment as determinants of child behavior.

Clients

Children through the entire continuum of development are seen by clinical child psychologists. Infants, toddlers, preschoolers, early school-aged children, and adolescents, as well as their teenage or adult parents, can be part of the caseload of the clinical child psychologist. Many clinical child psychologists limit their practice to children within a certain age range, although some provide services to children of all ages. Most often clinical child psychologists provide their assessment results, treatment recommendations, and training to the parents of the children they have seen. However, at times the situation is such that either child-specific or more general consultations are provided directly to teachers, family physicians, pediatricians, psychiatrists, occupational therapists, speech pathologists, child protection workers, lawyers, school boards, police departments, hospital administrators, social service agencies, or other professionals-in-training.

Settings

Clinical child psychologists work in many different health care settings (including hospitals, specialized clinics, rehabilitation complexes, institutions for mentally or physically handicapped children, family practice consortiums), mental health clinics, developmental disability clinics, community or residential schools, university or college psychology departments, government agencies including the courts, and in private practice settings. Frequently, the clinical child psychologist works part time in a number of these settings.

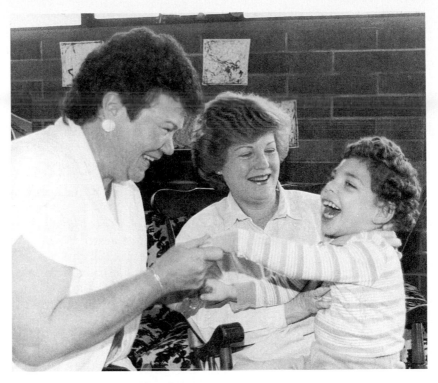

Working with disabled children can be rewarding. (Courtesy of Queen Alexandra Hospital for Children.)

When you consider the various combinations of professional activities rendered, clients served, and employment settings, you can see that the potential number of different childhood problems confronted by clinical child psychologists is very large indeed. Some representative clinical problems follow.

CASE STUDIES

Before describing specific examples, it is important to note that information about all the cases in this book have been disguised so that patients involved cannot be identified. It is important to protect the confidentiality of the patient or client.

CASE ONE: ALICE
The receptionist at the Children's Mental Health Center placed a note in front of me while I was on the phone. The note said, "Please

come to the conference room ASAP. Mrs. Smith (new client; no file available) is very upset! She needs to talk to someone about her daughter." As I finished my phone call, I wondered how upset Mrs. Smith might be and what she would tell me about her daughter. Although my graduate education and internship experiences had included crisis intervention training, I usually felt some slight apprehension when entering a clinical situation completely cold. I knew nothing about Mrs. Smith, her daughter, or the problems they were having. As a consequence, I would have to carefully use my clinical interviewing skills so that I could gather enough information to decide what to recommend as the next step in the process of providing service for her daughter, while at the same time providing some emotional support for Mrs. Smith. Because there was no file available, I stopped in at the receptionist's desk, hoping to gather a little background information. Sometimes even seemingly unimportant background details can be used to build rapport or to emphasize a point in a clinical interview. I wanted to know the child's name and something about her behavior before I talked to Mrs. Smith—very basic information that the receptionist could provide.

As I entered the waiting area, the receptionist was busy supervising a very active, blond preschooler who was trying to empty the contents of a desk drawer onto the floor. This little whirlwind of activity was able to stop long enough to tell me her name was Alice and that she didn't like her teacher. As I retrieved my clipboard from her, I asked the receptionist to take the girl to the play area out back until her mother and I could come for her. I assumed that the commotion caused by Alice, which could easily be heard in the conference room, would only contribute to Mrs. Smith's upset and would make it more difficult for me to gather the information I needed in order to be of help to Mrs. Smith and Alice. Learning Alice's name and the preliminary understanding of her problems afforded by this short observation of her behavior turned out to be quite helpful during my interview with Mrs. Smith.

Based on these clinical observations, my clinical experiences to date, and the time of the year, I began to formulate the likely problem Mrs. Smith would present. I hypothesized that the overactivity and difficulty sustaining attention that Alice displayed in the reception area were representative of her day-to-day behavior and that this already was creating problems at school after only three days into the year. I also hypothesized that Mrs. Smith had been "living for" the half days Alice would be in kindergarten and that this was now threatened by some feedback from the school indicating that Alice was too difficult to manage.

My hypotheses for the most part turned out to be correct. As indicated in the earlier discussion of Daniel's case, it is important not to jump to simple conclusions based on limited evidence. In order to be effective, however, a clinical child psychologist must formulate hypotheses that can be tested and then rejected or accepted on the basis of available evidence. These hypotheses guide the clinical interview and can help determine the interventions to make. I prefer to generate my hypotheses on the basis of careful clinical interviews, a review of background materials, and standardized descriptions of children's behavior as obtained through behavior checklists and personality inventories. Sometimes, however, these tools are not available.

When I entered the conference room, I was struck by the visual contrast between what I had witnessed in the reception area and the way in which Mrs. Smith presented. Mrs. Smith was a very tall, dark-haired woman who sat hunched over the edge of the conference table. With the exception of some tear stains on her face, she showed little sign of emotion, activity level, or normal interpersonal demeanor; she looked positively drained of emotion and energy. As I introduced myself, I was careful to sit as close as possible to her across the corner of the table. I wanted to communicate to her nonverbally that I was concerned for her and not at all put off by her emotional distress. Although she did not acknowledge verbally my introduction, she did look directly into my eyes; this suggested that her depression was not currently so great as to interfere significantly with interview process we were about to begin. In response to my next statement that she must find it really challenging to channel Alice's energy in productive ways, Mrs. Smith's features brightened momentarily and then returned to the same sad expression I had first noticed. I then told her that Alice was being well supervised and I suggested that she take some time to tell me about Alice and the difficulties that brought her to the Center. I also "gave her permission" to let her feelings out whenever she felt like during the interview by suggesting that I could see her pain and that there was no need to hide it when she was talking with me. Mrs. Smith responded by saying, "My name is Janice and I love Alice but . . ."; she then began to cry. Through many tears and with some support from me, Mrs. Smith told me Alice's story.

Alice, who was five years old, was described by her mother as "hyperactive." According to Mrs. Smith, this assessment of Alice was shared by Alice's preschool teachers, her father, friends, and members of Mrs. Smith's extended family. Mrs. Smith reported that Alice had been difficult since birth, that she slept poorly, that she still wet the bed, and, in comparison to other children her age, that she seemed to lack some understanding of simple language concepts. Mrs. Smith described Alice as frequently argumentative and unpleasant at home. Alice had been expelled from three different preschools because of her uncontrollable energy, disruption of other children's activities, and disregard for the requests and instructions of her teachers. She had wandered away from her home or preschool on numerous occasions and she apparently had no hesitancy in approaching strangers on the street. Mrs. Smith said she believed Alice had "minimal brain damage"; she reported that she had taken Alice to a number of pediatricians and neurologists who diagnosed her as having Attention Deficit Disorder. The stimulant medication prescribed for Alice by the last pediatrician had not improved her behavior.

Although Alice's behavior was reported as challenging for most adults, according to Mrs. Smith her husband had marginally better success controlling Alice. With some prompting from me, Mrs. Smith shared that Mr. Smith's approach was quite harsh and that Mr. Smith did not hesitate to point out Mrs. Smith's apparent inadequacy at dealing with their daughter. Mrs. Smith also shared that she was pregnant again and that she had just heard from Alice's school principal that the school might have to send her home unless her behavior could be improved. She was terrified that she would never get a break from Alice and that her next child would be equally difficult to manage.

Throughout this long interview, I consistently validated Mrs. Smith's feelings and acknowledged the struggles she was having with Alice. Wherever possible, I helped Mrs. Smith understand that her confused feelings and at times extreme frustration with Alice were understandable given the situation, similar to the experiences of other parents with children like Alice, and not indicative of poor parenting skills or a lack of love or caring for Alice.

In response to my request that Mrs. Smith try to formulate what she hoped the Children's Center would provide, she replied, "What is really wrong with Alice? What should we do to handle her behavior and help her fit in at school? Can you tell me if Alice is emotionally disturbed?" On the basis of this interview, I recommended the following steps and interventions:

1. I asked Mrs. Smith to sign the appropriate release forms so that I could obtain reports from the various medical professionals and preschool teachers who had seen Alice.
2. I arranged for Mr. and Mrs. Smith to return to the Center for a further interview and to complete a standardized developmental history and a number of behavior checklists.
3. I asked Mrs. Smith to do all she could to arrange for a babysitter, even if it meant paying double, to take Alice out of the house for a few hours on the weekend so that she could spend some uninterrupted time with her husband to express to him the frustrations and fears she had expressed to me.

I then escorted Mrs. Smith to the outside play area where she spent some time with Alice before going home.

The verbal and written reports I was able to obtain over the next two weeks confirmed the picture that had emerged during my interview with Mrs. Smith. Alice certainly seemed to be a child with a severe *Attention-Deficit Hyperactivity Disorder* (ADHD); this is a disorder characterized by inappropriate degrees of inattention, impulsiveness, and hyperactivity. The medical professionals had excluded any known medical or acute neurological causes for Alice's behavior. Food or other allergies were excluded as possible causes. The neurological evaluation elicited some nonlocalized "signs" (possible indications of mild brain dysfunction). Her "hyperactive" behavior was evident in most situations: at three preschools, in medical offices, in kindergarten, and at home.

The results of my next interview with Mr. and Mrs. Smith and the standardized checklists they completed excluded a major environmental contribution to Alice's behavior; there was no indication that the Smiths' home life or parenting strategies were in any way inadequate or chaotic. Because a generalized impairment in intellectual development could produce many of the features of ADHD and specific intellectual deficits are common in children with ADHD, I recommended a psychological evaluation to rule out the possibilities of mental retardation or learning disability. The results of this evaluation indicated that Alice was of average intelligence, that she did have some receptive language weaknesses, and that she had a very low self-esteem. Through the process of this evaluation, I provided additional verbal and written information about ADHD to Mr. and Mrs. Smith. I stressed that there was no known cure for the disorder and that it was something they and Alice would have to learn to cope with. They accepted my recommendation that they attend our evening behavior management course in order to fine tune some of the strategies for managing Alice's behavior we had already discussed. I also told them that they might need to seek professional intervention at various points through Alice's development, but that this intervention would most likely take the form of reviewing Alice's progress, providing some emotional support and reassurance, and updating some of the suggested coping strategies for home or school.

Alice's parents attended both our fall and spring behavior management courses, and the school responded positively to the consultations I offered them. Alice was placed in a special class for children of normal intelligence with behavior problems. Although Alice remained a challenge for her teachers and occasional problems had to be worked through, she gradually improved to the point that Mr. and Mrs. Smith reported both they and the school were happy with Alice's progress. My follow-up contacts with Alice indicated that she was using the strategies for focusing her attention and activities that were being taught at school and that her self-esteem had improved.

This case is important because it highlights some of the complexity of clinical practice. As so often happens, a clinical information gathering interview turned out to be a complex clinical interaction involving education (information giving), brief psychotherapy, and assessment. These conceptually different aspects of my work as a clinical child psychologist are so often entwined in actual clinical practice that it no longer makes sense to me to try to keep them separate except for teaching purposes. The art of clinical child psychology involves the ability to move back and forth between these activities in such a way so as not to cause discomfort for the client or confusion for the psychologist. ♦

CASE TWO: VICTORIA

As the Director of Psychology of a small psychology department in a children's rehabilitation center and developmental disabilities clinic, I provide practicum experiences for psychology graduate students from the local university. These practicum students who work under my close supervision generally have little academic training or clinical experience with preschoolers so I always save interesting school-age cases for them. When I received Victoria's referral in the mail from a local child psychiatrist, I immediately put it aside for one of my advanced practicum students.

According to the referral letter Victoria, age 13, had begun to hear voices and to be obsessed by sexual thoughts and a fear of germs. She apparently washed her hands for hours at a time, and she refused to touch any door knobs. Her grades had dropped dramatically over the last school year, and she was being shunned by her peers at school and in the community. She had been placed on psychotropic medication (a drug that affects mental activity) in an attempt to decrease the intensity of her symptoms and was receiving psychotherapy from the referring child psychiatrist who indicated concern with her lack of response to treatment. The referral question formulated in the letter to me was: Does Victoria have sufficient intelligence and language skills to benefit from psychotherapy? Does she have a thought disorder?

The actual psychological assessment necessary to answer these questions was relatively straightforward in terms of the strategies and clinical tools to use. However, I felt that this case would provide a good chance for one of my students to obtain some valuable clinical experience. Obsessive compulsive neurosis usually begins at adolescence or early adulthood and is relatively rare. It is characterized by recurrent obsessions or compulsions severe enough to interfere with usual social activities or relationships. Most graduate students would not see such a case during their training. In preparation for this assessment, I contacted Victoria's father, Mr. Field, to obtain further background information and an authorization to obtain a copy of Victoria's school records. During this telephone interview, I learned that Victoria had recently attacked her mother with a bread knife and that both Victoria and her mother were actively avoiding each other; they were even taking their meals in separate rooms. Mr. Field indicated that he would bring Victoria to the clinic for her appointments and that he did not expect his wife to be at all involved until Victoria was cured.

The school records confirmed the dramatic decline in Victoria's grades over the last year, but they also indicated a persistent pattern of lower than average academic performance in language arts areas. There was no record of Victoria ever having been assessed by a school psychologist. On the basis of this information, I hypothesized that Victoria probably had low-average to average intelligence and that she might have a mild language-related learning disability. I hypothesized that the thought disorder suspected by the psychiatrist might be an indication of some language-processing problems. The results of the standardized behavior checklists and personality inventories completed by Victoria's father and homeroom teacher indicated an internalized pattern of psychological adjustment that suggested that much of Victoria's day-to-day behavior was characterized by very high levels of anxiety and worry.

On the morning of Victoria's evaluation, I reviewed the case with the female graduate student I had chosen to do the assessment. Given the obvious difficulties between Victoria and her mother and the fact that both I and the psychiatrist were male, I hoped that a female examiner would elicit information Victoria might wish to suppress in the presence of a male. We discussed the sequence of test administration and the possible ways of handling any resistance Victoria might present us with during the evaluation. We decided to begin with the structured intelligence test because we reasoned that, given Victoria's level of anxiety, the less structured projective testing with its emphasis on the expression of thoughts, feelings, and unconscious motivations would be too threatening for her even after an initial interview and attempt to build rapport. We hoped that Victoria would find the intelligence test interesting and challenging and that this in turn would help to reduce her level of anxiety enough to handle the projective tests we would administer later in the morning.

When I introduced myself and the graduate student to Victoria, I immediately sensed that this young girl was extremely apprehensive and that she might choose not to cooperate with the assessment. I then decided to explain to her in more detail than is usually my practice the procedures we would follow that morning. I wanted to give Victoria every opportunity to ask any questions she might have and to obtain any reassurance she might need. While Mr. Field completed the various consent forms with the graduate student, Victoria and I moved into the viewing room I would be using to observe the assessment. After some initial surprise that she could see and hear her father behind the one-way glass, Victoria became quite interested in the physical setup and the activities she would be involved in that morning. After being assured that she would not be taped and that her father would not observe her test performance, she consented to my remaining behind the observation window while the examiner conducted the assessment. The assessment then progressed in a routine way; the only behaviors I noted as unusual as I observed the testing session were Victoria's frequent requests for clarification whenever the examiner used longer than average phrases in her instructions or questions and her rather stiff posture.

The results of the intelligence test indicated that Victoria was functioning in the high-average range of intelligence and that her language-related abilities were less well developed than her nonverbal abilities. This pattern of test results was consistent with, but not diagnostic of, a mild language-related learning disability. The results of the projective testing (including the Rorschach), a thematic apperception test, a family drawing, and a sentence completion test highlighted the obsessive quality of Victoria's thoughts. Throughout these test protocols, repetitive thoughts of being contaminated or unpure, and self-doubt were expressed through recurring themes of disease transmitted by germs or fears that doors or windows had not been closed. There was no evidence in her test responses of any thought disorder; she did not express any bizarre delusions or loosening of associations (difficulties sticking to a topic and drifting off on a train of associations stimulated by a word or idea). Victoria did not describe any auditory hallucinations; that is, she did not acknowledge hearing things or people that were not present. The only really strange responses were attributable to a misunderstanding of the questions posed to her. There was also no evidence of any sexual preoccupation in Victoria's test responses. I wondered, however, if the themes of locked doors and windows might relate to some concerns of a sexual nature.

As the assessment neared completion, I called the examiner out of the room for a brief conference. I suggested that she test the strength of Victoria's obsessions and that she ask Victoria directly about any sexual concerns. This resulted in Victoria acknowledging that she knew her fear of germs was unfounded in reality and that she did have nightmares in which men tried to enter her room to rape her. She also indicated that she had heard voices in the past but that they were no longer there.

The results of this assessment were discussed with Victoria and her father and a formal report was sent to the psychiatrist. I stated in the report that the data from the psychological assessment suggested that Victoria could benefit from psychotherapy but that the language level and concepts used in the therapy would have to be carefully monitored to ensure that Victoria actually understood them. I also recommended that Victoria undergo more comprehensive neuropsychological or educational assessment in order to determine whether her language weaknesses actually reflected a learning disability.

Although this case is unique in terms of the problems exhibited by Victoria, it is representative of the "assessment only" aspect of the work of the clinical child psychologist. Frequently, clinical child psychologists are asked by other professionals to use their expertise and clinical tools to confirm hypotheses or to further the understanding of the child. On other occasions, as in the case that follows, children are referred only for treatment. ♦

CASE THREE: RICHARD

Richard, age 17, was referred to me at the local children's mental health clinic by his pediatrician with a request that a behavioral program be designed to increase Richard's compliance with his prescribed treatment. The form of medical treatment and the nature of Richard's problems were not indicated on the short referral note. As is my usual practice, I contacted Richard's parents, Mr. and Mrs. Johnston, to verify their interest in pursuing the referral and to gather additional background information.

During the initial phone contact with Mrs. Johnston, she told me that Richard had diabetes and that he refused to follow his prescribed diet. Mrs. Johnston indicated that she and her husband were very concerned and constantly reminded Richard to watch his diet when he was out with his friends. She reported that on two occasions Richard had run away from home; both times Richard ended up in a hypoglycemic coma and had to be rushed to hospital. During the intake interview at the clinic, Richard's parents asked the social worker, "Does our son have a death wish? Is he trying to commit suicide by drinking coke and eating candy bars all the time? Doesn't he know we nag him only because we really love him and don't want him to die?"

On the basis of Richard's age and the nature of his problem, I decided that a behavioral program would be unlikely to meet with success unless Richard himself was motivated to change his behavior. I had reviewed Richard's school records and a three-year-old report from a medical psychologist that indicated that Richard was of above-average intelligence. I reasoned that unless the comas had produced some cognitive deterioration, Richard had the cognitive abilities necessary to understand the consequences of his behavior. I also reasoned that he was old enough to make most of his own choices and to actively and very effectively resist any attempts to get him to change. Consequently, I chose to meet with Richard alone to discuss his parents' and physician's concerns. My goal was to learn more about Richard and the possible explanations for his behavior and to see if I could encourage Richard to begin to take a more realistic approach to the management of his diabetes.

During my initial interview with Richard, he was quite open in expressing his anger at his parents for constantly interfering in his

life. He indicated that he was well aware of the possible consequences of his dietary habits but that he did not want to be different
from his friends. He also acknowledged that the last coma had
scared him and that some of his friends now seemed to be avoiding
him. He cried as he told me he was afraid he might die the next time,
but that he didn't know what to do. I recommended that Richard
come to see me again to talk about some ways in which he might
learn to take more charge over his feelings, and we made an appointment to meet again the next week. I had chosen to see Richard in
brief psychotherapy right away rather than to conduct a cognitive
assessment first because Richard reported that he was doing well at
school (which was confirmed by school records) and because he did
not complain of any cognitive deficits since his last coma. Because
Richard was quite open in discussing the issues I raised with him
and because he was seemingly aware of his emotional issues, a personality assessment did not seem to be necessary.

Over the next few weeks, I had four sessions with Richard and
one joint session with Richard and his parents. During the course
of these sessions, Richard was able to make a decision to be more
responsible regarding his diet, and he was able to negotiate with his
parents some increased independence in return for his more responsible behavior. Richard's self-esteem seemed to improve, and by our
last session he no longer referred to himself as "different" or as a
"sicko." During the session with his parents, Mr. Johnston was able
to share his deep concern for Richard and his fear that Richard
would die. The behaviors Richard had assumed meant his father
thought he was incompetent were reframed as messages of caring
and concern. A follow-up call six months later indicated that there
were still problems; Richard was coming home late, and he was
arguing for less control over his access to the family car. Richard's
diabetes, however, was well under control and no longer played a
major role in the family dynamics.

Richard's case is only one example of the increasing referrals
to clinical child psychologists for psychotherapy or other forms of
psychological intervention. ♦

Becoming a Clinical Child Psychologist

Education

The wide diversity in the theoretical orientations of clinical child
psychologists and the work settings employing them points to the

reality that there is no one prescribed educational course for someone wishing to enter the field. In most jurisdictions, the doctoral degree is a basic requirement necessary to be licensed or certified as a psychologist. Therefore, if you wish to become a clinical child psychologist, you will certainly require the undergraduate psychology courses necessary to gain admission to graduate school. Because there are many more applications for admission to any clinical psychology program than there are places available, you will need excellent undergraduate grades and high scores on entrance exams such as the Graduate Record Exam. You will also need to meet any other specific requirements of the program you wish to enter. At the undergraduate level, you should consider taking courses in developmental psychology, child psychopathology, and as many clinically focused courses as possible while still obtaining a broad background in general psychology.

Depending on the graduate school to which you gain admission, the course sequence you will take may be more or less prescribed by the program you have entered. Graduate schools offering formal training programs in clinical child psychology have relatively straightforward guidelines for the courses you should take. Within the constraints of these guidelines, you will be able to adjust your program of study to meet your specific interests, say, in the area of infancy or preschool children. Other graduate schools where clinical programs are more adult focused or where the program is developmental instead of clinical in orientation will challenge you with the opportunity to be creative in designing a program of studies that will provide you with advanced preparation in both the clinical and developmental areas of psychology. In such graduate programs, the integration of these two very important areas will be less structured and more dependent on your own abilities than is the case in more formally structured clinical child psychology programs. Increasingly, employers are demanding that clinical child psychologists must be trained in American Psychological Association (APA)-approved programs; this will provide obstacles to clinical child psychologists from less-structured programs.

Graduate school will mean significantly more individual study and less in-class time than during undergraduate studies. Clinical child psychologists must know something about adults if they are to be effective in their clinical work with children. Therefore, you will need to take a number of courses in common with general clinical psychology students, such as psychological assessment, theories of personality and psychopathology, and methods of psychotherapy and psychological intervention. You will study developmental psychology from infancy through to adolescence, and you will learn about childhood exceptionalities such as mental retardation, emotional disturbance, learning disabilities, and behavior problems. You will learn how to interview and observe children. You will learn that childhood problems occur in the context of relationships with significant adults; you will come to understand the various influences of school and family on the psychological problems faced by children. Depending on your graduate program, you may learn some psychological interventions that are effective in modifying the adverse influences schools or families can have on children.

Your graduate training, in addition to its developmental and clinical focus, will involve studying research design, advanced statistics, and other areas of psychology such as learning theory, physiological psychology, neuropsychology, and social psychology. You may be required to become involved in ongoing clinical research projects, and eventually you will have to conduct one or two pieces of original research (the M.A. thesis and Ph.D. dissertation) under the direction of your graduate supervisor and a supervisory committee.

Because of your clinical focus, many courses will have a practicum component in real-life settings. In these carefully supervised clinical settings, you will gradually be introduced to more and more responsibility for the assessment and treatment of children with psychological problems. These practicum experiences will prepare you for later pre- and/or postdoctoral internships, which will involve full-time work and training in clinical settings for extended periods of time; these closely supervised clinical placements may be a series of summer-long internships or a year-long internship near the end of your course of studies. In some circumstances, you may take your internship after you graduate. Internship experiences in hospitals, special schools, or child-related clinics will help you acquire practical clinical skills, a realistic understanding of the problems faced by children and their families, and a professional attitude; none of these can be learned solely in the classroom.

Employment

Clinical child psychologists work in a wide variety of settings. The most frequent settings include pediatric clinics or hospitals, child development or mental health clinics, schools, government agencies, or private practice settings.

The needs of children remain a high priority in our society, and the contributions made by clinical child psychologists to the care of special children are now widely recognized by professionals and parents alike. Because the training involved in becoming a clinical child psychologist is so specialized and so few child clinical psychologists are graduated each year, there has been no shortage of positions for new clinical child psychologists. Advertisements attempting to recruit clinical child psychologists appear regularly in professional publications and major newspapers. In the foreseeable future, there is little reason to suspect that a newly graduated clinical child psychologist should have any difficulty obtaining a position.

SUGGESTED READINGS AND REFERENCES

The Walker and Roberts (1983) book provides a scholarly in-depth overview of clinical child psychology. Other books on the list, which are written as first-person accounts or in the format of a novel, will provide you with extended case studies of some of the types of special children assessed and treated by clinical child psychologists.

ANASTASI, A. (1976). *Psychological testing* (4th ed.). New York: Macmillan.

AXLINE, V. M. (1964). *Dibs in search of self.* New York: Ballantine Books.

BANDURA, A. (1974). Behavior theory and the models of man. *American Psychologist, 29,* 859–869.

BETTELHEIM, B. (1950). *Love is not enough.* New York: Free Press.

BINET, A., & SIMON, T. (1916). *The development of intelligence in children* (E. S. Kit, Trans.) Baltimore: Williams & Wilkins (original work published 1908).

BROWN, H. (1976). *Yesterday's child.* New York: New American Library.

CRAIG, E. (1972). *P.S. you're not listening.* New York: New American Library.

ERIKSON, E. H. (1963). *Childhood and society* (2nd ed.). New York: Norton.

FREUD, A. (1946). *The psychoanalytic treatment of children.* London: Imago.

GESELL, A. & ILG, F. L. (1943). *Infant and child in the culture of today.* New York: Hoeber.

GOLDMAN, J., STEIN, C. L., & GUERRY, S. (1983). *Psychological methods of child assessment.* New York: Brunner/Mazel.

GREENBERG, J. (1964). *I never promised you a rose garden.* New York: Holt, Rinehart, & Winston.

GREENFELD, J. (1973). *A child called Noah: A family journal.* New York: Warner Books.

HAYDEN, T. L. (1980). *One child.* New York: Putnam.

Jones, M. C. (1924). A laboratory study of fear: The case of Peter. *Journal of Genetic Psychology, 31*, 308–315.

Palmer, J. O. (1970). *The psychological assessment of children.* New York: Wiley.

Piaget, J. (1970). Piaget's theory. In P. H. Mussen (Ed.), *Carmichael's manual of child psychology* (3rd ed.). New York: Wiley.

Sattler, J. (1988). *Assessment of children's intelligence and special abilities* (3rd ed.). San Diego: J. M. Sattler.

Sears, R. R., Maccoby, E. E., & Levin, H. (1957). *Patterns of child rearing.* New York: Harper & Row.

Stern, W. (1914). *The psychological methods of testing intelligence.* Baltimore: Warwick & York.

Terman, L. M. (1916). *The measurement of intelligence.* Boston: Houghton-Mifflin.

Watson, J. B., & Raynor, R. (1920). Conditioned emotional reactions. *Journal Experimental Psychology, 3*, 1–14.

Walker, C. E., & Roberts, M. C. (Eds.). (1983). *Handbook of clinical child psychology.* New York: Wiley.

GERALD KOE

Gerald Koe received his B.Ed. in counseling and mathematics at the University of British Columbia (UBC) in 1970. He later received his M.A. (1974) and his Ed.D. (1981) in school psychology from UBC. He taught grades four through seven, was an elementary school principal, and has practiced as a school psychologist since 1974. Dr. Koe has supervised the practical field experience of masters and doctoral-level students from UBC and Simon Fraser University (SFU). He has taught undergraduate and graduate courses in school psychology at the University of British Columbia. Dr. Koe is founding editor of the Canadian Journal of School Psychology *and chairs the British Columbia Psychological Association School Psychology Special Interest Group. Dr. Koe is currently researching the use of hypnosis in educational settings to improve student self-concept and performance. He is presently employed as District Psychologist for School District #75 (Mission, B.C.) and maintains a private practice dealing with medical referrals in the area of hypnosis.* ♦

3

The School Psychologist

School psychology is one of the oldest applied specialties in psychology. It originated in the practice of Lightner Witmer and the establishment of his clinic at the University of Pennsylvania in 1896. It gained official recognition in 1945 when the American Psychological Association (APA) created Division 16, the purpose of which is the application of psychological knowledge in the schools. In practice, this involves psychoeducational assessments and a wide range of psychological services.

The traditional role for school psychologists was one of identifying children for special classes. This activity was extremely important to the development of the profession as school officials sought to ensure proper placement of mentally retarded and learning-disabled students. School psychologists were hired to administer the standardized tests needed to distinguish developmentally delayed and neurologically impaired children from those who were not achieving adequately for other reasons.

A typical example of this traditional "gate-keeping" role is provided by the following example. A 10-year-old fourth-grade Sto Lo Indian girl was referred to me because of failure to make adequate academic progress. Wendy's developmental history revealed a premature birth and delay in major developmental milestones. The school records indicated that Wendy had been retained in first grade and was encountering academic difficulty in fourth grade. The referral was made to determine whether or not Wendy met criteria for Educable Mentally Handicapped (EMH) special class placement.

I screened Wendy's vision and hearing, administered an individual intelligence test, an achievement test, and a measure of adaptive social skills. These test results, combined with the developmental, school, and family histories, suggested that Wendy did meet the criteria for EMH placement. On the basis of this information, I could have recommended that Wendy be placed in a special class.

However, I did not feel comfortable with these results. Wendy did not seem to be a slow child. She seemed curious and enthusiastic during testing. Her teacher reported that she socialized and played well with other children. When she understood a concept, she responded quickly and did not seem to have difficulty processing information. Because Wendy belonged to a minority group, I recognized that my test results were limited by cultural bias. Appropriate norms were not available for Sto Lo children. In addition, a timed test had been used to measure the intelligence of a child whose culture did not place a priority on time.

I had reservations about placing Wendy in an EMH class and

wanted to find out more about her. I subsequently visited her home. Her parents indicated they were not concerned that Wendy learn to read or write English, that she obtain employment, or that she succeed in the white society. They were concerned that she view herself with pride, that she appreciate her heritage, and that she help preserve the native culture and language by learning to be a native speaker, for which she seemed to have a talent.

Wendy's test failure was partially related to her cultural background. She was not mentally handicapped. She simply was not being exposed to English, or white, culture, and her parents were not encouraging her to succeed in school.

I faced a dilemma, common for school psychologists who perform the traditional gate-keeper role. Wendy was not succeeding in the regular program and needed extra help. The academic assistance that Wendy needed could best be provided in an EMH setting. However, because Wendy was not mentally handicapped, I felt uncomfortable with such a placement. I therefore recommended against special class placement. Special class placement would stigmatize Wendy and emphasize academic development. This would be contrary to the heritage goals of Wendy's parents.

Wendy was subsequently kept in fourth grade, but placed on a modified program in language arts. This program incorporated Sto Lo stories and culture. Wendy's parents were invited to talk to the class about the tribe's history and traditions. Wendy was encouraged to take pride in her heritage. A priority was placed on social, emotional, and physical development. When Wendy recognized that her parents approved of and supported her academic program, she also began to make adequate academic progress.

This solution was dependent on the availability of materials and the cooperation of Wendy's teacher and parents. It necessitated a willingness on my part to look beyond the test results and focus on the individual and her needs. In less favorable circumstances, Wendy may have been inappropriately placed in an EMH class. At its best, the practice of school psychology is an art. It involves an ability to interpret the scientific data collected and a willingness to adapt educational programs to suit the needs of students.

What Is School Psychology?

School psychology is the branch of applied psychology that deals with problems or behaviors that interfere with the academic

A typical classroom from which the school psychologist might draw clients. (Courtesy of the editor, Robert Gifford.)

progress or social acceptance of children in the school system. In this context, the school psychologist encounters a wide range of clinical cases.

Current Practice

School psychologists assess cognitive functioning and identify giftedness, mental retardation, developmental delays, instructional difficulties, and learning disabilities. They recommend educational programs and consult regarding placements. They assess behavioral and emotional problems, support parents and teachers, and provide direct treatment. They deal with the full spectrum of social problems including family violence, peer interactions, substance abuse, sexual abuse, neglect, and the influence of these problems on school functioning. They act as a screening and referral resource for a wide range of medical, social, and emotional disorders that interfere with academic functioning.

In addition to working with individuals, school psychologists perform a variety of other functions including mediation, child advocacy, community consultation, program development, and program evaluation. In general, school psychologists study behavior, protect and promote mental health, and apply the principles of psychology to improve school adjustment and learning. An excellent definition of the wide range of school psychological services is provided in the service specialty guideline published by the APA.[1] Of course, specific services depend on the competencies of the school psychologist and the needs of the particular school system being served.

School psychologists report that they spend about 50% of their time in psychoeducational assessments, 25% in interventions, 20% in consultation, and 1% or less in research and evaluation (Fagan, 1989). They are contracted by schools for nine to ten months and earn over $25,000 (Fagan, 1989). Of course, these numbers will change in the future.

Future Roles

As school psychology moves into the twenty-first century, one can only speculate about impending changes. However, one could expect national-level certification, ethics, and standards of practice. Public demand will cause school systems to justify program development and to adopt scientific approaches to program evaluation. Social pressures will necessitate the implementation of programs such as grief counseling, suicide prevention, and drug counseling. School psychologists could expect to play a leading role in implementing and developing programs within the school setting.

Specialization will undoubtedly develop within school psychology. Service boundaries will likely be extended to encompass preschool and university students. Child-care legislation changes are precipitating the development of assessment skills and preventative programs at the preschool level. Educational initiatives are focusing attention on functional and vocational assessments.

Some school psychologists already specialize in program evaluation, neuropsychological diagnosis, behavior modification, and consultation. In addition to hiring general practitioners, school districts will contract services from these and other specialists.

There will also be major changes in diagnostic practice as school psychologists become aware of the inadequacies in current practices. Diagnosis will necessitate the development of symptom clusters allied more closely with medicine and neurology. These changes will precipitate multidisciplinary treatment approaches.

As the need for school psychology is recognized, school psychologists will be found helping all children, not only those experiencing problems. School psychologists will be asked to consult on course development and instructional strategies. Future school psychologists will have opportunities for many intriguing and challenging roles.

However, while specialization and technological changes will likely have a major impact on school psychology, the profession will continue to practice the fundamental role of data collection and problem solving. This role is based on a well-defined philosophical and practical tradition and provides the primary focus for school psychology.

The Background of School Psychology

Philosophical Foundations

The philosophical foundations of school psychology were established almost 300 years ago. John Locke (1695) in *Some Thoughts Concerning Education* wrote:

> He therefore that is about Childlren, should well study their Natures and Aptitudes, and see, by often Trials, what Turn they easily take, and what becomes them; observe what their native Stock is, how it may be improv'd and what it is fit for. He should consider, what they want; whether they be capable of having it wrought into them by Industry and incorporated there by Practice; and whether it be worthwhile to endeavour it. For in many Cases, all that we can do, or should aim at, is to make the best of what Nature has given, to prevent the Vices and Faults to which such a Constitution is most inclin'd and give it all the Advantages it is capable of. Every one's natural Genious should be carry'd as far as it could; but to attempt the putting another upon him will be but Labour in vain; and what is so plaister'd or will at best sit but untowardly, and have always hanging to it the Ungracefulness of Constraint and Affectation.

Although Locke's philosophical statement overemphasized the hereditary nature of behavior, it established a philosophical foundation for the evolution of school psychology. This philosophical foundation is still evident in the current practice of measuring intelligence and identifying cognitive strengths and weaknesses.

Since the APA Boulder (Colorado) Conference in the late 1940s, most applied psychologists view themselves as data-based problem solvers (Edwards, 1987); that is, they collect the pertinent data and facilitate the problem-solving process. In school psychology, this problem-solving process has traditionally been linked to the development of services in special education.

Historical Foundations

As mentioned earlier, the historical foundations of school psychology can be traced back to the first psychological clinic under the direction of Lightner Witmer at the University of Pennsylvania in 1896 (French, 1986). This clinic was founded to conduct psychometric evaluations of so-called "mentally and morally retarded" children, as well as those with physical defects and developmental delays.

Following on Witmer's work, the Chicago Bureau of Child Study, established in 1899, was the first clinical psychological service incorporated in a school system. Recognition of the need for psychological services in the schools spread quickly. New York developed similar services in 1900.

Changes in North American immigration policy and the passing of child labor laws in the early 1900s greatly influenced the number of children who remained in school. Education became compulsory. The retention of children in the school system complicated the instructional process and established a need for the application of clinical psychological services to children who resisted the ordinary methods of the classroom.

However, it was not until 1910 that Stern coined the title *school psychologist* in noting the emergent need for qualified persons to administer psychological tests in the school system. By 1913, there were about 115 individuals in North America administering psychological tests to school-aged children (Fagan, 1989). Two years later, Arnold Gesell was appointed as the first school psychologist by the state of Connecticut.

Acceptance of psychological services in the schools created a need for training programs. The first undergraduate and graduate training programs in school psychology were offered at New York University in 1929 (Fagan, 1985; 1986). The universities of Columbia, Pennsylvania State, Ohio State, Michigan, and Illinois provided leadership during the next two decades (Fagan, 1985). In 1923, Hutt published an article using *school psychologist* in the title. In 1930, Gertrude Hildreth of Columbia University wrote the first official textbook in school psychology. New York became the first state to certify school psychological practitioners in 1935.

The Great Depression and World War II slowed the development of school psychology. However, interest and growth resumed at the end of the war. In 1945, the APA established Division 16, acknowledging school psychology as a specialty. Prior to the Thayer Conference in 1954, there were 18 training programs in school psychology and approximately 1,000 school psychologists in the United States (Fagan, 1985, 1989). This conference examined the functions, qualifications, and training of school psychologists and established the early standards for professional development.

Following the Thayer Conference, school psychology grew rapidly. Today, over 210 institutions in the United States alone offer school psychology programs to about 6,300 students (Brown & Minke, 1986). The 24,000 practitioners in North America represent about half the school psychologists in the world.

The National Association of School Psychologists (NASP) was formed in 1969 and the Canadian Association of School Psychologists (CASP) was formed in 1985. There are now approximately 12,000 members of the NASP and 250 members of the CASP. Division 16 of the APA has about 2,000 members.

Twenty-four thousand practitioners may seem like a large number of school psychologists. However, when one realizes that between 10% and 20% of the 45 million students in North America will be referred to a school psychologist, the demand for services becomes very apparent. In many school districts, parents wait six months or more for assessments.

The Scope of School Psychology

As noted previously, the role of the school psychologist is complex and varied. However, data collection and problem solving are central to this role. The nature of data collection and problem solving depends on the problem characteristics and the needs of the individual requiring service. This problem-solving process is perhaps best illustrated in psychoeducational assessments.

School psychologists spend about half their time conducting psychoeducational assessments. A school psychologist usually assesses about 166 cases per year in servicing a school population of about 2,300 students (Fagan, 1989). Assessments are generally initiated by a written request for service or referral.

Referrals

Most referrals come from parents or teachers. However, referrals may also come from administrators, colleagues, medical personnel, and even students. In many districts, referrals are processed through a school-based team (SBT), which usually includes the school psychologist, learning assistance teacher, principal, and teacher. The SBT ensures that school personnel have exhausted their resources before making a formal request for psychological services.

In my district, all referrals are processed through the SBT. I participate in the SBT meetings. When the SBT approves a referral, the teacher completes the referral form, discusses the referral with the parent, and obtains a parental signature approving the referral. The teacher then forwards a copy of the referral form, student's file, permanent record card, learning assistance report, and SBT report along with any other pertinent data to me. This referral will usually specify the problem and detail the nature of the requested service.

Data Collection

School psychologists obtain data from behavioral observations; school records; previous psychological, psychiatric, and medical reports; developmental, social, and medical histories; and tests.

Observing the child in the classroom setting often provides insight into aspects of the child's problem, which could not be obtained from any other source. It enables a wider perspective than offered in the isolation of the testing situation.

On receiving a referral, I will usually make an appointment to talk with the teacher and to observe the child in class. I will also make an appointment to interview the parents. Home visits are scheduled when appropriate. Talking with the parents and teacher helps to clarify the referral concern. Also, many minor problems can be dealt with in this manner.

When testing is necessary, I prefer to test the child in my office. This enables me to ensure similar conditions for all students. I have flexibility in test selection, and it saves travel time. I test in the schools when parents are unable to transport the child. Many school psychologists prefer to test in the schools. They feel that this approach affords better teacher contact, fewer missed appointments, and a familiar setting for the anxious child.

Before testing the child, I usually review previous report cards, the permanent record card, test results, and examples of the child's school work. Parents are generally interviewed about the birth, developmental, genetic, medical, educational, and family history. I also like to go over a typical 24-hour schedule in the child's life, as this affords many clues to medical and emotional problems. Once sufficient information has been obtained, I begin to develop hypotheses regarding possible diagnoses.

Hypothesis Testing

Once I have developed some ideas about the child's presenting problems, methods of substantiating or confirming these hypotheses can be selected. The process is similar to a detective attempting to solve a case. I look for clues and methods of testing my hypotheses.

It is the responsibility of the school psychologist to select the most appropriate tests and to ensure standardization of testing conditions so that extraneous factors do not influence results. I generally discuss the tests that I plan to administer with the parent before the testing session starts.

School psychologists may administer a wide variety of tests, depending on their training and preferences. The tests will include developmental tests, school readiness measures, and perceptual tests. They may administer intelligence, language, and achievement tests. They may also use rating scales and diagnostic tests, aptitude and personality measures, and even neuropsychological tests. Most school psychologists rely on a few preferred tests that have excellent reliability, validity, and normative data supported by a wide variety of supplementary tests that are not as well standardized.

In the testing session, it is my responsibility to ensure that the child achieves the best possible performance while maintaining standardization procedures. It is also my responsibility to observe how the child performs on the tests in order to judge the validity of results.

The testing session usually lasts about two hours. However, in some cases, additional sessions may be booked. A second session is often advisable to confirm a finding when its reliability is questionable. Generally, a second session is also required when the referral is for special class placement or when something unexpected emerges in the initial testing session.

I usually start the testing session by describing the tests to the child. I also explore his or her feelings about the assessment, which usually helps to build rapport and reduce the child's anxiety. Once the child is comfortable in the testing situation, I test the child's vision and hearing. If potential problems are evident, I will ask for further assessment.

Not all school psychologists screen vision and hearing. Equipment may not be available, or screening may conflict with the role of other professionals. As such, many school psychologists must rely on their ability to infer problems from the child's response to other tests. They may also rely on reports from vision and hearing professionals long after the testing session.

It is important to know the status of vision and hearing on the day of testing, particularly when an intelligence test is administered. Hearing can change within a few hours. Many children have vision defects which, without this testing, would not be corrected during the crucial years when their eyes are still developing. Vision and hearing difficulties can seriously influence results. I am often

School settings become increasingly important in a young child's life. (Courtesy of the editor, Robert Gifford.)

surprised: At least 10% of the children I see have visual defects or hearing problems that might be undetected without formal assessment procedures.

After screening vision and hearing, I proceed with the administration of other tests. In order to maintain rapport, I talk with the child during appropriate breaks in the testing session. At the end of the testing session, I provide the child with appropriate feedback about his or her overall performance. Elementary age children are encouraged to select a reward, usually a small toy, school-related tool (pencil, eraser, etc.), or sticker. It is important that the child feels comfortable throughout the testing session and leaves with a positive feeling about the experience.

Report

I write a psychoeducational report when I have sufficient data to describe and validate the child's problem. There are three components to this validation process: (1) providing information regarding possible cause, (2) inferential and direct testing of the deficit, and (3) showing how the problem influences school performance. The report is essentially a description, rather than a diagnosis.

The format of psychoeducational reports depends on the psychologist and the intended use. Usually, the report will state the referral concern and describe observation and test data. I usually include pertinent developmental, medical, and school history. Conclusions may be drawn, based on the data, and recommendations will be stated. The report generally is sent to the child's teacher or school and to other professionals as necessary.

Access to the Results

Essentially, it is the parent who decides what information can be disseminated. In the United States, the *Family Educational Rights and Privacy Act* (Public Law 93-380) grants parents of children under 18 years old the right of access to educational records kept by schools relating to their children. Parents have the right to challenge the accuracy and appropriateness of these records, to limit public access to these records, and to receive a list of individuals and/or agencies that have been given access to the records. They have the right to be notified if and when the records are turned over to a court of law.

Canadian psychologists are bound by codes of ethics generally modeled on the codes of ethics of the APA and NASP. These codes require informed consent for dissemination of information. As such, psychoeducational assessment findings must be discussed with parents prior to release. I usually schedule an appointment with the child's parents to discuss the test results and then the parents sign a release form that indicates they are aware of the contents of the report and designates to whom it is to be sent.

Program Planning

The manner in which recommendations are generated and implemented depends on the school psychologist and the needs of the school system being served. I prefer a collaborative, multidisciplinary approach. As such, I limit recommendations on the psychological report to placement recommendations and professional referrals. I prefer to schedule a case conference to develop the educational treatment strategy with the parents, teacher, learning assistance teacher, principal, and other interested professionals in attendance. All individuals are expected to contribute their observations and experience. Recommendations are developed collaboratively. Minutes are kept that include observations, recommendations, follow-up findings, and evaluative procedures. These minutes form the basis of the Individual Educational Program (IEP) for the child.

Progress Evaluation

Once recommendations have been made and treatment initiated, school psychologists usually establish some means of evaluating the child's progress. This may be done informally by talking with the teacher or more formally by retesting or case conferences. Although the recommendations may be comprehensive, they may not solve the problem. The following case illustrates a situation where problems continued despite appropriate diagnosis and intervention.

CASE STUDIES

CASE ONE: CHRIS
Chris was a nine-year-old boy who was referred because of hyperactive, out-of-seat, and off-task behaviors. He talked with other

students and disrupted lessons with his wandering about the classroom.

The teacher had spoken to Chris many times about his inappropriate behavior. Reprimands, isolation, and detentions failed to alleviate the problem. The school counselor had placed Chris on a program that rewarded in-seat, on-task behavior. Still, as time progressed, Chris became more disruptive and aggressive in the classroom. After a particularly serious incident, the teacher requested that Chris be removed from the classroom and suspended from school.

Before she suspended Chris, the principal insisted that the parents be consulted. The parents indicated that Chris was generally well behaved at home and had not evidenced such severe behavior problems in previous grades. The counselor expressed concern that Chris had not responded to behavior modification procedures or counseling. The principal stressed that Chris's behavior would not be tolerated and indicated that any further disruption could result in suspension and possible expulsion from school.

In view of Chris's failure to respond to counseling, the principal suggested that Chris be referred to me for an evaluation. Perhaps there was some explanation for Chris's out-of-seat, off-task behavior and willful disobedience in the classroom. The parents were somewhat hesitant, at first, in accepting this suggestion. They were confused about the difference between a psychiatrist and psychologist and were concerned about the stigma of seeing a psychologist.

I explained to them that psychiatrists are physicians who treat mental disorders, whereas school psychologists study behavior, protect and promote mental health, and apply the principles of psychology to improve behavior and learning. With this explanation and the opportunity of meeting me, the parents became more amenable to a referral.

The referral form was completed, signed, and forwarded to me along with a photocopy of Chris's permanent record card and school file. I immediately contacted the parents to interview them and made an appointment to observe Chris in class, talk to the counselor, and interview the teacher.

Generally, the first step in an assessment is to clarify the reason for referral. What did the teacher mean by hyperactive and off-task behavior? Why and how often was Chris out-of-seat? In addition, there is often a need to identify ownership of the problem.

Whose problem was it? Was this a case of inadequate parenting, classroom management problems, or something else?

An interview with the teacher is often necessary to help clarify these concerns. In this case, Chris was reported to waste time talking with other students or wandering about the classroom. He was said to constantly interfere with other children and apparently would refuse to remain in his seat. His behavior ranged from extreme agitation to daydreaming.

Chris persistently stole candies from other children's lunches and provocatively ate the candies during class. He fought with other children and had been caught defacing school property. He was socially isolated because of his behavior.

The teacher reported that Chris was unable to keep his mind on his work. He often sat doodling or daydreaming. He refused to start tasks or would seem to forget what he was doing in the middle of a task. He was easily frustrated and would often rip up worksheets.

Chris was observed in his classroom on two occasions, for about an hour each time. He was a very large boy, for his age, who spent most of his time looking around the class and engaging in off-task activities. The classroom environment was highly distracting, with busy decorations and both doors open to a main hallway. When someone passed one of the doors, Chris would turn his head and then look in that direction long after the person had passed. He was aggressive toward a girl sitting directly in front of him. He cut his finger hitting her with his ruler. On several occasions, Chris manifested an exaggerated blink and facial grimace, then banged his head with his hand or objects. Unusual flushing of his face was observed in conjunction with the blinking and facial grimaces.

The other children in the classroom seemed well behaved and task oriented. The teacher used verbal direction and proximity control techniques in an effort to keep Chris on-task. The teacher did not make optimal use of visual aids, but classroom discipline seemed adequate.

Chris's permanent school record indicated average academic functioning (grades of C to C+). Report card comments suggested that he tended to be bossy during activities. He was described as very possessive of his desk and the area around it. There were a few comments about Chris's restless, distractible, and impulsive behavior. He was reported to be easily discouraged. These comments seemed to confirm the parents' observations and suggested that his disruptive and acting-out behaviors were relatively mild prior to fourth grade.

Chris's father did not attend the parental interview. All the information was obtained from the mother. She said there had been no significant prenatal or perinatal problems. Chris's major developmental milestones (walking, talking, toilet training, etc.) were achieved within normal limits. There was no significant history of medical or educational concerns.

During the parental interview, Chris's mother disclosed that her husband was an alcoholic and tended to be verbally and physically abusive toward Chris. She attempted to protect Chris from his father. Chris spent much of his time out of the home.

The home situation seemed to contribute to behavior problems. However, that situation had existed for some time. As such, it did not seem to explain the rapid onset of severe behavior problems in the classroom.

The information available on Chris suggested three major areas of concern:

1. Social isolation, aggressive behavior towards peers, theft from peers, fights, and destructive behaviors.
2. Distractibility, impulsivity, and hyperactivity.
3. Large size, staring episodes, facial flushes, and automatisms (staring, facial flush, grimaces/blinks, hits something repeatedly).

I told Chris's mother that he seemed to have both social and attention problems. The investigation of his social problems would involve an attempt to find out what was bothering him by talking with him, analyzing his drawings, and rating his behavior. The investigation of his attention problems would involve administration of standardized tests to permit comparison of his performance with that of groups of children who experienced similar problems. Because of the complexity of this case, the testing would take approximately five hours. Two appointments were scheduled.

On the first day of testing, vision and hearing were assessed before administering the Wechsler Intelligence Scale for Children–Revised (WISC-R). The WISC-R is frequently used by school psychologists for many purposes; it is a prognostic instrument designed to predict school success. In this case, the test was also used as a structured interview in which to observe Chris. A self-concept scale and tests of depression and anxiety were also administered.

On the second day of testing, Chris was interviewed. He was relatively noncommunicative. He did not want to talk about school, family, or feelings. Drawings were used to gain further insight into the dynamics of his difficulties. In addition, Chris was administered a neurological test and a test of language functioning. His teacher was asked to complete a rating scale that would compare him to children previously diagnosed as having an attention problem.

During both testing sessions, Chris appeared to use distractible, impulsive, and inappropriate behavior in an aggressive manner. He indicated that he did not like working in school and did not like tests. Noise making, pounding the desk, and kicking the walls increased during tests that were of an oral or academic nature and decreased during drawing or physical activities. Chris had to be frequently directed to sit throughout both testing sessions. He seemed capable of controlling his distractible behavior for short periods of time and had no difficulty controlling his attention for 20 minutes when he was interested in a task.

The drawings seemed to confirm that Chris used aggressive and distractible behavior as a means of hitting out at his environment. His drawings suggested he felt overpowered, confused, and helpless. There were indications of hostility toward his environment, fear of punishment, and strong dependency on his mother. He did not appear to feel accepted by his father. The teacher's rating of Chris indicated conduct problems.

Performance on the neurological screening test placed Chris in the "suspicious" range, indicating possible neurological dysfunction. He tended to overshoot objects in reaching for them, was unable to perform rapid alternating movements, and had difficulty balancing himself.

Then, during the second testing session, Chris had a seizure. The episode started with staring and a general flushing of the face and lasted for approximately 30 seconds. The flushing was followed by rapid eye blinking, chewing movements of the jaw, and symmetric arm jerking. At the end of the incident, Chris yawned but otherwise displayed no observable emotion. Similar behavior (flushing, facial grimaces, and automatisms) had been evident in the classroom observations.

Tests of Chris's cognitive abilities did not reveal any specific dysfunction. His vision and hearing were within normal limits. His IQ was normal. His anxiety, depression, and self-concept scores were all within normal limits.

The test findings were discussed with Chris's mother. The dysfunctional family situation was a concern. Chris seemed to serve as a scapegoat, removing the focus from an alcoholic parent. He also seemed to be modeling his father's aggressive behaviors.

During this interview, Chris's mother agreed to encourage her husband to try Alcoholics Anonymous, encourage Chris to try Alateen, and to join Alanon herself. She agreed to insist on family counseling should her husband fail to go to Alcoholics Anonymous. She also agreed to permit me to contact her family physician regarding Chris's symptoms.

Chris's mother read the report and signed a release that authorized the report to be sent to the family physician and teacher. In order to coordinate services, I called a case conference involving Chris's parents, teacher, principal, learning assistance teacher, school counselor, speech/language pathologist, and public health nurse.

Chris was seen by the family physician before the case conference. He was diagnosed as having psychomotor epilepsy and was placed on medication. His mother had followed through with the referral to Alanon. Chris was enrolled in Alateen. His father refused to join Alcoholics Anonymous but did agree to family counseling.

At the case conference, I explained that the psychomotor epilepsy appeared to cause Chris to be easily distracted in the classroom. It interfered with his ability to attend and with his short-term auditory memory. It also seemed to inhibit his ability to process language.

Chris's seizure symptoms were discussed and help was requested to monitor symptoms and report observations to the family physician. The public health nurse agreed to attach a medical alert to Chris's permanent record card.

The teacher realized that her emphasis on oral instruction might be very difficult for Chris. She agreed to provide more visual input in the classroom. She also agreed to close the door to her classroom, to limit distraction. The speech pathologist suggested an evaluation of Chris's language ability and agreed to provide recommendations for the teacher and parent.

Chris's distractibility, off-task, and resistant behavior was perceived very differently by school personnel in view of his epilepsy. The medication seemed to make Chris more willing to start tasks, and he did not seem to forget what he was doing part way through tasks. The teacher stopped reprimanding Chris, and Chris reduced his acting-out behavior in the classroom.

I placed Chris in a social skills group that I conducted in the school. Previously, he was physically unable to respond to the behavior modification program for in-seat, on-task behavior. This inability to achieve rewards may have been an additional frustrator for Chris. His continued distractibility, behavior problems, and social isolation had interfered with his ability to benefit from personal counseling regarding his behavior. The counselor initiated counseling to help Chris deal with his anger. The learning assistance teacher agreed to support verbal instruction in the classroom with visual aids and to debrief Chris after class to ensure he understood and retained material.

A follow-up case conference was scheduled two months after the initial intervention with Chris. This case conference revealed that Chris was still very distractible in the classroom. He was reported to respond negatively to oral tasks or any tasks he felt were too difficult. Academic problems continued to frustrate Chris and produce aggressive behaviors.

At this follow-up case conference, it was decided to refer Chris for placement in a specific learning-disabilities class where he was provided with a highly structured visual program. He responded very well in this environment. Within a year, Chris was reintegrated into his regular class and his behavior problems did not reemerge.

In this case, the school psychologist served in a variety of roles including "gate-keeper," assessor, consultant, and intervention team member. These roles represent a blend of the traditional and current roles that school psychologists engage in. Many referrals are not so complex. The following case study depicts the treatment of a boy with a similar presenting problem but illustrates a different role of the school psychologist. ♦

CASE TWO: JOHN
John was a nine-year-old boy who was referred because of distractible and irritable behavior at home and at school. His mother indicated that he was not paying attention in class and that his behavior was explosive at home, with frequent emotional storms. John was described as a very sensitive boy, and treatment for stress was requested.

It became apparent, during the initial interview, that John's anxiety or depressive symptoms were not typical. His academic progress was average, and there was no indication of social or emotional problems. There was no history of birth, medical, or developmental problems other than developmental nocturnal enuresis (bed-wetting). John was simply an extremely distractible and irritable child.

Because the therapeutic direction for dealing with John's distractibility and irritability was not clear, I initially chose to concentrate on the nocturnal enuresis. Nocturnal enuresis occurs in about 5% of children at age nine and is generally treated whenever it persists beyond age six. I initially thought that concentrating on the enuresis would help alleviate parental anxiety and provide time to further investigate John's distractibility and irritability.

The enuresis was discussed with John in the initial interview. He said that he was extremely embarrassed by his bed-wetting. John's parents were not aware of John's feelings about his enuresis. They had consulted with their family physician and realized the problem was developmental. They were simply waiting for him to outgrow it. However, they had failed to convey this information to John.

Because John had indicated that he was extremely embarrassed by his enuresis, I asked him what he was trying to do to stop his bed-wetting. He said that he tried to stay awake each night so that he wouldn't wet the bed. This strategy worked some nights but not other nights.

I discussed the developmental nature of the enuresis with John and began a program of bladder stretching and urinary awareness training. John's sleep improved when he stopped trying to remain awake at night. His distractibility and irritability disappeared almost immediately, and his nocturnal enuresis was controlled within a month. Therapy was terminated before treatment for stress could be initiated.

In this case, John's irritability and distractibility were associated with lack of sleep and frustration at his inability to prevent nocturnal enuresis. A simple developmental delay in his urinary system had been crucially affecting his emotional adjustment and academic functioning.

In the practice of school psychology, there are many opportunities for simple interventions that can profoundly influence the behavior of young children. This case illustrates the changing role of school psychologists from traditional psychoeducational assessment and treatment recommendations toward social interventions and direct treatment. ♦

CASE THREE: A SCREENING PROGRAM

A further example of the changing role of school psychologists is apparent in the development of screening programs. I recently developed, piloted, and implemented a multidisciplinary screening program in my school district. First-grade teachers were provided with a quick screening device containing the five items most highly correlated with failure in that grade. This test was used to help teachers identify children who might be at risk for failure early in the school year. Parents of children identified as at risk were offered

RICHARD P. HALGIN

Richard P. Halgin is a clinical psychologist in the Department of Psychology at the University of Massachusetts at Amherst, where he serves as Associate Director of the Psychological Services Center and Coordinator of the Postdoctoral Respecialization Program in Clinical Psychology. He teaches undergraduate courses in abnormal and clinical psychology and graduate courses in psychological assessment and psychotherapy. Dr. Halgin's scholarly work has focused on psychotherapy integration, attitudes about obtaining professional psychological help, issues in clinical training and supervision, and the provision of clinical services to underserved populations. In addition, he is currently co-authoring an abnormal psychology textbook. He is an associate editor of the Journal of Integrative and Eclectic Psychotherapy *and a consulting editor of the journal* Teaching of Psychology. *Dr. Halgin provides psychotherapy and consulting services through the Psychological Services Center and maintains a limited private practice. He holds a Diplomate in Clinical Psychology from the American Board of Professional Psychology.* ♦

4

The Clinical Psychologist

The case of Marie provides an excellent example of one of the most common activities of a clinical psychologist—conducting psychotherapy. At the time that Marie sought professional help from me, she was 28 years old and residing in her parents' home. She contacted me at the beginning of April a few years ago, stating that her problem with procrastination was having serious consequences in her life. She stated that she wished to engage in psychotherapy in order to resolve this problematic personal style. However, she had a critical short-term goal as well. Marie had an outstanding incomplete in her final college course, which had been unresolved for the past six years. In order to receive her bachelor's degree, she had only to write a ten-page paper. Marie had spent the past six years putting off completion of this single task.

In my initial meeting with Marie, I developed a limited understanding of the roots of this problem and was able to see how Marie's problems had much to do with her personality and developmental history. I saw from the outset that Marie was a person who was very dependent on others. The completion of her college degree was an anxiety-provoking symbol for Marie; it would mean that she would be responsible for taking care of herself. She could no longer be the "college kid" who depended on her parents for financial support or who could use the university as a protective environment.

I formulated a dual-faceted therapeutic plan for my work with Marie: (1) develop a behavioral program to help her finish her final incomplete, and (2) conduct some exploratory psychotherapy in an attempt to help Marie understand the roots of her problem and to translate these insights into changed behaviors.

I saw Marie on a weekly basis for six months. During the first five sessions, our work focused on the immediate task of completing her ten-page paper. We collaboratively developed daily and weekly work schedules that included built-in rewards for the achievement of goals. With relative facility, Marie completed her work prior to the grading period for that semester, submitted the paper to her professor, and formally completed her undergraduate degree.

In the subsequent sessions, our work focused on the evolution of Marie's problematic personal style. It became evident to Marie that her problem with procrastination was really a symptom of a more deeply rooted problem of dependency. We explored Marie's developmental history and came to understand how her overprotective parents had encouraged this dependency in their only child and continued to do so even in her adult years. As Marie came

to understand these issues, she was able to make some choices that were oriented toward autonomy rather than dependency. For example, she got her own apartment and took sole responsibility for her own financial support. At a point when it seemed that Marie was comfortably on her way to resolving her own problems, we agreed to terminate the therapy.

What Is Clinical Psychology?

When my undergraduate advisor suggested that I consider the field of clinical psychology for graduate training, I conjured up an image of what I believed a clinical psychologist would look like. In my mind, a clinical psychologist would be a person who wears a white coat, works in a clinic, and administers IQ tests and personality tests. It seemed rather uninteresting to me, but that was because my impression was incorrect. I investigated this profession further by reading extensively about it and by interviewing a clinical psychologist. I quickly discovered that clinical psychologists engage in a range of rather diverse activities, most of which are quite challenging and exciting.

In this chapter, I will discuss some of the various activities of clinical psychologists and provide some brief examples from my own professional work. Although the role of psychotherapist, as exemplified in the case example above, is the most common professional role of clinical psychologists, there are many other professional activities, examples of which will be given later. I will also discuss some advantages and disadvantages of being a clinical psychologist, and I will suggest how a person would go about becoming a clinical psychologist.

Clinical psychology includes many different activities, and no simple definition is entirely adequate. One textbook defines it as follows: "*Clinical psychology* is concerned with improving human function. . . . As a clinical field it is dedicated to improving the lot of individuals in distress . . . while striving through research to increase the knowledge and sharpen the techniques needed for improved intervention in the future" (Korchin, 1976, p. 3). As we shall see, clinical psychologists assist others through psychotherapy, psychological assessment, consulting, research, teaching, and administration.

The Background of Clinical Psychology

In order to understand how clinical psychology has developed into such a diversified professional field, some grasp of its history is helpful. Psychology historians cite the turn of the century as the birth years of clinical psychology. During this period, two very important areas of theory and application were emerging—psychological testing and psychotherapy.

The history of psychological testing dates back to pioneering work done by people such as James McKeen Cattell who coined the term *mental tests* and Alfred Binet who developed the first IQ test. The term *clinical psychology* was first used by Lightner Witmer when he established a clinic to study and treat children with learning and school problems. Witmer emphasized an important criterion for this new field that has been maintained to the present day—that interventions with clients be based on scientific methods and research.

Around the same time that science was being integrated with practice in the field of psychological testing, there was an emergence of interest in psychopathology and psychotherapy. The innovative and controversial work of Freud as well as the contributions of two important American psychologists, G. Stanley Hall and William James, introduced fresh approaches to understanding human development.

The academic setting nurtured these creative theoretical explorations, so it was natural that these ideas would be put into practice on university campuses. By 1914, many university campuses had established psychological clinics, and psychologists expanded their efforts to new settings, including mental hospitals and facilities for developmentally disabled and physically handicapped people. In those early years of the twentieth century, psychologists were respected for their expertise in research and their psychological testing abilities.

World War I was a particularly important event in the evolution of this new field. A group of psychologists accepted the U.S. army's challenge to develop intelligence tests that could be administered to large groups for the purpose of efficient and economical assessment of intellectual abilities. Group intelligence testing was soon followed by group testing of soldiers for emotional problems.

During the 1920s and 1930s, the limited role of the clinical psychologist as an expert in psychological testing was reinforced.

However, a major shift in professional activity took place during World War II and shortly thereafter. When directors of the Veterans Administration (VA) were faced with large numbers of emotionally disturbed soldiers, they turned to psychology for assistance in treating these impaired individuals. Because of the severe shortage of needed mental health clinicians, the VA provided considerable financial support for training in the mental health disciplines. Other government agencies, such as the National Institute of Mental Health (NIMH), also recognized the importance of this new field and added to the financial support of training.

The VA defined the work of the clinical psychologist to include diagnosis, psychotherapy, and research. This dramatic expansion of the role of clinical psychology permanently changed the nature of the field. Clinical psychologists were no longer limited to the activities of testing and research but were accorded responsibilities that covered a wide range of clinical activities. This evolution of professional role was also accompanied by an increase in prestige and educational requirements. The VA upgraded the educational requirements for clinical psychologists by requiring a doctorate.

Around this time, the American Psychological Association (APA) recognized the importance of establishing curriculum requirements for this field, and called a training conference in Colorado. The 1949 Boulder Conference provided a definition of *clinical psychologist* that would hold relatively constant for more than two decades; the clinical psychologist was to be a scientist-professional. Doctoral-level psychologists would be trained in both science and practice. In other words, graduate training that was limited to developing clinical expertise was regarded as insufficient; clinical psychologists must be trained in and committed to scientific investigation of the phenomena associated with their work.

By the mid-1970s, an alternative to Boulder model scientist-professional training had surfaced. At a 1973 conference in Vail, Colorado, a new training model for clinical psychology—professional-scientist—emerged. These professionals would continue to be trained in research methods, but there would be increased emphasis on the acquisition of clinical skills. Although the Vail Conference did not intend to delete the role of research from the training and professional activities of clinical psychologists, many people in the field construed that to be the case. By the 1980s, there was a surprising proliferation of professional programs and schools offering an alternative to the traditional university-based Boulder model programs.

The Scope of Clinical Psychology

The most exciting aspect of being a clinical psychologist is the fact that my particular activities are so diverse and the contexts within which I work are so different. Later, I will use my own professional activities as case examples of the endeavors of clinical psychologists. It is important to realize, however, that not every clinical psychologist engages in each of these activities. Some clinical psychologists limit their work to one or more specific areas. My own preference is diversification of activity in order to avoid boredom or burnout. My primary professional role is that of a university professor, a position that allows, and even encourages, participation in varied activities that can inform my endeavors as a teacher and researcher.

Psychotherapist

I start with the role of psychotherapist because I have found that this facet is particularly interesting to students who aspire to the field of clinical psychology. Most people who wish to become clinical psychologists have a desire to help others, and they see psychotherapy as an interesting and challenging means of doing so. Although many of you may have never been psychotherapy clients, you have probably been in analogous situations that can give you some understanding of what psychotherapy involves. For example, before choosing a college, you probably consulted with a counselor. Perhaps you discussed conflicts—such as a wish to move away from home but anxiety about doing so. Perhaps you were faced with the dilemma of whether to attend the college your parents preferred or the one where your friends were going. Such experiences of being helped by a professional can give you a bit of insight into what it might feel like to be a psychotherapy client. You can probably also understand how such factors as the personal style of the counselor, your feelings of comfort with the counselor, and the counselor's expertise would have significant bearing on the resolution of your concerns. These same factors hold true for psychotherapy.

Psychotherapy is a process in which a helping professional works with a client who wishes to resolve some emotional problem, change some troublesome behavior, or develop increased self-understanding. The client may be an individual adult, adolescent,

or child or may be a couple, family, or group. In many instances, people are able to achieve these goals without professional help. However, at times the distress becomes so great, the behavior so troubling, or the problem so confusing that assistance from a professional can be very beneficial.

Psychological problems cover a wide continuum, ranging from minor adjustment difficulties (such as homesickness) to severe forms of psychological disturbance (such as suicidal depression). Consequently, the methods of intervention differ from case to case.

Furthermore, psychotherapists adhere to a variety of psychotherapeutic models, each with its own theory and techniques. The psychotherapeutic models that have the greatest number of followers are: psychodynamic, behavioral, humanistic-existential, and neuroscientific. Each of these models is quite different, and adherents of each model have different ways of understanding client problems and very different approaches to therapy.

Psychodynamic psychotherapists derive their techniques from Freudian theory. Simply stated, psychodynamic psychotherapists view early life experiences as the primary determinants of current problems. They believe that many of these conflicts reside in a person's unconscious and that the resolution of current difficulties must be achieved through exploration of the unconscious. Central to the psychodynamic model is the notion that personality develops through a series of stages that are intricately connected with sexuality. Although Freud placed such a heavy emphasis on the role of sexuality, some of his later followers moved away from such an extreme view. In recent years, psychodynamic psychotherapists have focused more on the role of early life relationships in the development of personality. A troubled relationship between a parent and a child in the early years of life may cause long-term deficits in the person's ability to relate intimately with others as an adult.

Behaviorists are not concerned with the unconscious. Rather, they believe that current troubled behavior results from maladaptive learning; the resolution of difficulties lies in the learning of more effective behaviors. For many years, behaviorists were criticized for their exclusive attention to observable behaviors. A recent behavioral trend has expanded the focus to include concern with cognitive processes. For example, cognitive-behavioral therapists who treat depressed people would look for ways to alleviate the depression by helping such clients develop less depressing ways of thinking. For example, a depressed woman may be plagued by

thoughts such as "I'm no good." The therapist would work with the client in an attempt to replace such negative thoughts with more positive ones.

Humanistic-existential psychologists view human problems from a very different perspective. Reacting to what they believe are the dehumanizing aspects of the psychodynamic and behavioral approaches, they focus on the more positive aspects of human existence. Because humanistic-existential psychotherapists believe that abnormal behavior results from the blocking of personal development, their therapies involve the fostering of self-awareness, personal growth, and responsibility for one's decisions. These psychotherapists believe that it is important for the clinician to be warm and accepting of the client. Rather than focusing on conflicts and inadequacies that clients may feel, the clinician looks for ways to help clients reach their fullest potential in life.

Adherents of the *neuroscientific theories* focus their attention on the role of biology. In trying to understand and treat disturbed people, they are likely to rely on somatic interventions. For example, they would explain many forms of depression as resulting from disturbances in the neurochemical functioning of the brain. Their treatment would probably include some somatic intervention that would alter the brain's functioning. There are a wide range of somatic interventions including medication, dietary changes, and exposure to certain forms of light that have been shown to ameliorate depression.

These models are but four from a total of dozens of clinical models. Most psychotherapists choose from more than one model in their work. Surveys in recent years have shown that clinical psychologists have moved away from adherence to narrow approaches and have increasingly defined themselves as eclectic or integrative. In other words, they have studied various clinical models, and they select the components of each model that best meet the individualized treatment needs of each of their clients.

Expert in Psychological Assessment

As we discussed in the brief history of clinical psychology, psychological assessment has been an area of specialization since the establishment of the profession of clinical psychology. Unlike psychotherapy, which can be conducted by several other kinds of mental health professionals such as psychiatrists, social workers, and nurses, psychological testing can only be administered by psychologists.

In order to understand this facet of a clinical psychologist's work, it is helpful to briefly discuss the nature of psychological testing. Tests are used to measure human variables such as knowledge, intelligence, or personality. Every one of you has taken tests in your life. Some tests measure a specific ability—such as a state driving test, which determines whether you have acquired sufficient knowledge to safely drive a car. Others are concerned with aptitudes—such as the Scholastic Aptitude Test (SAT), which was used to predict your likelihood of succeeding in college. Clinical psychologists are concerned with the measurement of variables in the psychological sphere such as intellectual functioning and personality.

In the realm of intellectual testing, the tasks range from the assessment of IQ to complex neuropsychological assessments used to determine whether a person has deficits in brain function. In the realm of personality testing, the tasks range from a focused appraisal of a single factor (e.g., sociability) to complex assessment of a client's personality.

In determining which psychological tests, if any, to use for assessments, clinical psychologists first consider the referral question. Many referral questions can be answered by simple inquiries of the client. For example, suicidal predisposition can be assessed by asking the client directly about suicidal thoughts and attempts. Other referral questions necessitate the administration of a standardized procedure that helps the clinician to better understand how much this client is like normal people. For example, a clinical psychologist may be asked to assess whether a seemingly bright 19-year-old young man who acts and speaks in rather unusual ways is merely eccentric or whether he is showing the early signs of severe mental illness. In this instance, the clinical psychologist might choose to conduct an interview and administer a battery of psychological tests, including tests of intelligence and personality.

Intelligence tests account for a good deal of the assessments that clinical psychologists conduct. There are many kinds of intelligence tests, but the Wechsler scales are the most frequently used individual tests of intelligence. These tests are named after the late David Wechsler, the American psychologist who developed and refined these scales. There are three Wechsler tests, each of which is appropriate for a different age group: the Wechsler Adult Intelligence Scale-Revised (WAIS-R), the Wechsler Intelligence Scale for Children-Revised (WISC-R), and the Wechsler Preschool and Primary Scale of Intelligence (WPPSI). The Wechsler scales yield several useful forms of information. In addition to an overall estimate of IQ, they provide separate measures of verbal and performance intelli-

gence. A clinical psychologist can also use subscales of these tests to pinpoint particular cognitive strengths and weaknesses.

The many personality tests fall into two categories: self-report personality inventories and projective techniques. The most widely used self-report personality inventory is the Minnesota Multiphasic Personality Inventory (MMPI), which consists of 566 statements about personality to which the subject responds true or false. Just as intelligence tests provide information about various facets of intelligence, self-report measures provide information about different aspects of a client's personality. The MMPI has been devised so as to inform the psychologist about whether the client's responses are valid. Therefore, the psychologist is able to determine whether the subject is intentionally lying or exaggerating problems. In addition to the validity scales, there are ten clinical scales covering such personality variables as depression, hypochondriasis, and paranoia.

Projective techniques are quite different from self-report measures. The most commonly used projective techniques are the Rorschach and the Thematic Apperception Test (TAT). On the Rorschach, the subject tells the clinical psychologist what he or she sees in each of ten inkblots. Based on a careful analysis of a client's Rorschach responses, the clinical psychologist can discern a great deal about the client's personality. For example, a subject whose responses are characterized by an inordinate attention to minor details may be a person with prominent obsessive traits, who is unable to "see the forest for the trees." For the TAT, the subject looks at a series of drawings of people engaged in various activities and is asked to tell a story about what is happening in each picture. A subject who repeatedly tells stories filled with conflict and anger is very likely telling the clinician something about inner concerns. The assumption underlying the projective tests is that the subject will project onto a neutral stimulus relevant issues, concerns, and conflicts, some of which are unconscious.

Taking the case of the 19-year-old man, the clinical psychologist would conduct an integrated assessment that specifically addresses this individual's cognitive style vis à vis his personality. The psychologist would compare the psychological test data of this young man with responses from individuals who are psychotic and responses from other individuals who are very bright and eccentric in order to make a diagnostic determination.

In addition to intelligence and personality testing, many psychologists conduct assessments of brain functioning. Neuropsychological assessment techniques are used to assess brain damage or dysfunction. The Halstead-Reitan Neuropsychological

Battery is comprised of a number of tasks that assess the functioning of specific areas of the brain. Neuropsychological assessment is used in a variety of situations. For example, a clinical psychologist may use these techniques in an attempt to assess the extent of brain damage in a person who has sustained a head injury. Or at the other end of the severity spectrum, the clinician may use these techniques to assess particular learning disabilities in a person who is struggling with reading problems.

Consultant

Clinical psychologists are trained to be experts in human relations. As we have already discussed, the most common context for practicing this specialty is psychotherapy, where clinical psychologists help clients resolve problems. Many clinical psychologists are asked to apply their human relations expertise in contexts other than psychotherapy. When a clinical psychologist acts in the role of consultant, there is still a client, but the client in this case is usually an organization.

Just as there are many forms of psychotherapy, there are many forms of consulting. In part, the consulting role depends on specialty areas of the clinical psychologist and also on the consulting need of the organization that is requesting guidance. For example, a clinical psychologist may limit consulting work to human service agencies, possibly assisting their efforts to develop more effective treatment programs for clients. Another clinical psychologist may specialize in consulting to businesses or municipal groups, possibly assisting a company or a police department in the development of a stress reduction program.

Thus, the consultant works as an advisor. Clinical psychologists are recruited for such work because they have been trained in three relevant areas: assessment, intervention, and research. *Assessment* training is beneficial because it equips the clinical psychologist with the knowledge needed for defining the problem. For example, when a police captain tells the consultant that she has discipline problems with a few troublesome officers, the consultant will undertake an assessment in order to ascertain the degree to which several variables are causing the problem: (a) personalities of the officers involved, (b) personality and supervisory style of the captain, (c) situational factors such as work schedule, work assignments, relationships with co-workers, and so on. The clinical psychologist's *intervention* skills then come into

play.In this example, the clinician realizes that the problem is systematic in nature; in other words, the difficulty is rooted in and maintained by several people and factors. To solve the problem, it will be necessary to treat the system, perhaps using techniques similar to those that would be employed in family therapy. The clinical psychologist's *research* skills will enable the consultant to evaluate the intervention in order to ascertain that components of the intervention are responsible for improvement or worsening of the situation. For example, the consultant might have suggested a reassignment of the troublesome officers. Is the subsequent improvement attributable to the fact that each has a new co-worker, or a new immediate supervisor, or a new set of responsibilities, or might it even be attributable to the fact that the officers are appreciative that they are being given some positive attention, rather than punishment?

Research

Research plays a prominent role in the work of several different psychology specialties. Interestingly, relatively few clinical psychologists devote an extensive amount of their time to research; in fact, studies have shown that most clinical psychologists do not actively engage in formal research following receipt of the doctorate. This fact has been used by proponents of the professional schools who believe that it is wiser to devote doctoral training time to clinical endeavors rather than research endeavors.

The counterargument is made by proponents of Boulder model training that the acquisition of research skills benefits clinical psychologists even if they do not maintain active research involvement. It is argued that research training gives the clinical psychologist analytical skills. My own experience is that research training and research involvement positively affect my clinical work, particularly when my research efforts are directly related to my clinical efforts.

Research conducted by clinical psychologists is quite diverse, usually focusing on some facet of clinical diagnosis or treatment. For example, a psychopathologist may study the relationship between experiences of child abuse and subsequent emotional adjustment as an adult. Or, a psychotherapy researcher may study the differential effectiveness of various treatment programs for a particular emotional problem. It is assumed that the development of expertise in a particular area of clinical research will help the

clinician be more knowledgeable about treating clients with associated concerns.

Other Roles

So far we have discussed four major roles commonly undertaken by clinical psychologists: psychotherapist, diagnostician, consultant, and researcher. Because clinical psychology is such a multifaceted field in both training and professional practice, clinical psychologists engage in various other kinds of work. For example, many clinical psychologists are teachers or administrators. These, of course, are roles that are shared by other kinds of psychologists as well. However, the content of their teaching and the settings for their administrative work differentiate clinical psychologists from their nonclinical colleagues.

In the realm of teaching, clinical psychologists engage in forms of teaching that are distinct from that done by most other psychologists. For example, clinical supervision involves teaching trainees how to conduct psychotherapy. Usually, clinical supervision takes place in a one-to-one context that involves attention to the trainee's acquisition of skills as well as the trainee's personal development as a therapist.

Clinical psychologists who engage in adminstrative work customarily work in mental health settings. They may be administrators of mental health clinics, treatment centers, or units in larger health-care facilities. Clinical psychologists are often hired for such positions because it is assumed that they have knowledge and experience in several relevant spheres. For example, a clinical psychologist may be hired to be the chief administrator of a community mental health center where the job description calls for a professional who is knowledgeable about psychopathology, psychotherapy, research, and organizational issues.

Advantages and Disadvantages of Clinical Psychology

Advantages

As you have read this chapter so far, I hope that you have found the work of clinical psychologists to be interesting and challenging. Clinical psychologists are offered a variety of opportunities and seemingly countless possibilities. Whenever I am about to con-

clude that I have done most of what I can think of doing in this field, a new opportunity seems to come along. For example, I was recently contacted by a university colleague to collaborate in the establishment of an innovative academic program. This professor from the "plant and soil" department asked me if I would help develop a program to train horticultural therapists, paraprofessionals who would work with institutionalized individuals teaching them the care and nurturance of plants. It struck me as an intriguing and very challenging opportunity.

In addition to the personal enrichment that most clinical psychologists find in their work, clinical psychologists have numerous opportunities for being positive influences. Their professional endeavors can positively affect the lives of individuals, groups, organizations, and society. Often this influence is immediately observable. A very good feeling results when we know that our interventions have had a positive impact on others.

Disadvantages

As is the case with any field, clinical psychology has some unpleasant aspects. For anyone considering this field for a career, it is particularly important that these disadvantages be evaluated. Two primary stresses have emerged in the lists of clinical psychologists who have been surveyed about job satisfaction: the emotional toll of the work and the increasing pressures to engage in clinical psychology as a business rather than a helping profession.

Despite all the comments so far about how interesting and challenging clinical work can be, it is important to realize that it can also become boring and emotionally draining. The extent to which clinical psychologists experience these negative aspects relates to several factors such as their own personality, their work setting, and the populations with which they work. The nature of the field dictates that the clinical psychologist is always dealing with problems, whether the problems belong to an individual, family, or organization. Consequently, the clinician is often dealing with unhappy or troubled people. Clinicians have different ways of coping with this reality; some are able to maintain an effective distance from their work so that they are concerned with but not consumed by their work. Others find that the diversification that is possible in the field helps them maintain their own emotional equilibrium.

The second problem is one of recent origin. The health-care marketplace has changed markedly during the past decade. Many clinicians who entered the field because of idealistic aspirations to help people now find that they are competing in a business atmos-

phere to stay afloat financially. New approaches to health care—such as health maintenance organizations, group practices, and contracting with businesses to provide mental health care for employees—have nearly obliterated the solo private practitioner from the mental health scene. Clinical psychologists must now consider using marketing strategies to attract new clients and developing new specialties to differentiate themselves from other professionals. In addition, like all other health-care providers, clinical psychologists have become the targets of liability suits that were previously unheard of in this field. They have also been confronted by a myriad of new laws that affect clinical practice, for example, regulations about confidentiality and the duty to warn possible victims of an assaultive client.

CASE STUDIES

CASE ONE: THE PSYCHOLOGICAL ASSESSMENT OF JONATHAN
Jonathan is a 26-year-old construction worker who was referred to me for psychological testing by a social worker colleague. Jonathan had recently sought professional help following an arrest for selling cocaine. Jonathan had told the social worker that he needed counseling because he was so depressed and anxious. He tried to convince his therapist that he had gotten into drug trafficking with the intention of saving enough money to return to college, from which he had flunked out in his freshman year. He stated with great sincerity that his goal was to become a social worker devoted to helping adolescents who were involved with drugs. Jonathan admitted to extensive drug use over an eight-year period, involving daily use of several substances including alcohol, marijuana, cocaine, amphetamines, and hallucinogens. Jonathan swore to his new therapist that his days of drug use were history and that he was committed to abstinence. My colleague presented me with two referral questions: (1) Was Jonathan sincere about his commitment to reform or was he manipulating the system in order to look good for the court trial? (2) Had Jonathan sustained any brain damage from his long-term substance abuse?

I conducted a personal history interview and administered the WAIS-R, the MMPI, and the TAT. Jonathan's history was one of multiple clashes with the law but not a single day in jail. In Jonathan's words, he had always managed to engage in "good public relations" with the judge. His smooth interpersonal style, his sad stories, and his vows to rehabilitate consistently kept him out of jail. Jonathan's MMPI profile showed him to be an individual with high energy that

he characteristically invested in self-destructive pursuits. His TAT stories were filled with themes of trickery and manipulation. Thus, the answer to my colleague's first referral question was clear: Jonathan had an antisocial personality, and he was using the mental health system in a manipulative way.

The WAIS-R provided clues to the second referral concern. Preliminary findings suggested that Jonathan had sustained some significant organic damage from his extensive substance abuse. He had developed a slight tremor that interfered with his eye–hand coordination, and he had deficits in attention, memory, and concentration. Although there might be some improvement should Jonathan completely abstain from substance use, it seemed likely that some of his impairments were permanent. In writing my report, I recommended that Jonathan's therapist present him with the very troubling diagnostic picture in the hope that the seriousness of Jonathan's psychological and physical problems might bring him to his senses. I also recommended that Jonathan be referred to a neuropsychologist and a neurologist for a comprehensive assessment of organic damage. ♦

CASE TWO: CONSULTING TO A
DEINSTITUTIONALIZATION PROGRAM

The administrator of a local deinstitutionalization program recently asked me to serve as a consultant for this program that managed ten clients in community residences following their discharge from lengthy hospitalizations at the state psychiatric hospital. She asked me to assist the program in dealing with two particular concerns: (1) assist the staff in developing a treatment program for a woman with a history of nonsuicidal self-cutting behavior, and (2) assist the program administrator in dealing with poor employee morale and staff turnover. My contract with this agency called on me to provide two hours of consultation on a weekly basis for six weeks.

In my initial meetings with the six staff members, I set about doing an assessment. Because I was presented with two problems, it was necessary to undertake separate but related assessments of the client and of the staff. I needed to find out as much as possible about the particular client, including the nature of the client's pathology, her life history, current emotional status, the specific factors that have usually been associated with her self-cutting behavior, and the reinforcements in her life.

In my early work with the staff, our efforts were exclusively devoted to developing a better understanding and treatment program for this client. However, while engaging in these discussions, I

also had the opportunity to develop an understanding of the staff—their strengths, difficulties, frustrations, and interpersonal issues. Although I informed them at the outset that we would later discuss ways to improve their employment experience, I made it clear that our first priority was to develop an effective intervention program for the client. Beginning my work with the staff by focusing on the client proved to be beneficial, because it provided the staff with a context within which to get to know me as a collaborator rather than as someone who was coming in to shake things up.

Regarding the client, the staff and I developed a comprehensive treatment plan with a behavioral focus. We developed a treatment plan that is often called a *token economy*. In such a plan, the client is rewarded with some form of token for engaging in socially appropriate and constructive behaviors and must forfeit tokens if she engages in inappropriate behaviors such as self-mutilation. At certain intervals, the client cashes in the tokens for a particular reward, such as money to go to the movies. We were very specific, going so far as to reward the client with a token for each meal that she was able to handle a dinner knife without brushing it against her skin.

Regarding the staff's problem, it soon became evident to me that there were several organizational problems. The most notable problems were the scheduling of work shifts and insufficient opportunity for staff input regarding administrative and clinical issues. Work shifts changed on a weekly basis, sometimes necessitating an employee to work an all-night shift followed immediately by a day shift. Consequently, employees were often disgruntled about the fact that they could not plan other commitments for more than a week in advance, and they were often too fatigued to work efficiently or enjoy their off-hours. The problem was readily resolvable, because improved work schedules could be instituted. The more challenging problem was facilitating staff input. It quickly became apparent to me that the employees needed regularly scheduled staff meetings that would encourage collaborative problem solving. Weekly meetings were instituted, and I attended the first two in order to help the staff develop agenda and procedures for dealing with their concerns. ♦

CASE THREE: RESEARCH ON ATTITUDES
ABOUT PSYCHOTHERAPY
It is a commonly known fact in the clinical field that people do not like the idea of entering psychotherapy, even if they are considerably distressed. Several reasons have been documented, the most

common of which is that people perceive psychotherapy as carrying a stigma. Some people believe that entering psychotherapy is a statement to themselves and others that they are unable to solve their own problems and that they are somehow defective. Time after time in clinical interviews conducted in the university's Psychological Services Center, therapists have heard new clients speak of how embarrassed they felt to be entering psychotherapy.

The issue intrigued me, and I wanted to develop a way to better understand attitudes about obtaining professional psychological help. In order to assess these attitudes in the population of interest, students at the university, I developed an attitude scale that I administered to several hundred undergraduates. I was particularly interested in understanding why an individual who had a clinical problem, such as depression, would resist seeking professional help. In addition to the attitude scale, the research participants completed a scale that assessed the possible presence and depth of depression.

I separated those subjects who were indeed depressed and studied the reasons they gave as to why they had not sought professional help to deal with their depression. I found that these subjects had several strong beliefs about psychotherapy that pertained to issues of stigma, autonomy, cost, and trust in the professional.

By understanding the specific beliefs that were keeping distressed individuals from seeking help, I was able to undertake two endeavors geared toward dealing with these concerns. The first involved community education, and the second involved discussion of such potential concerns with prospective clients who were considering entering psychotherapy at the Psychological Services Center. Community education took the form of writing an article for the campus newspaper in which I discussed the phenomenon of emotional distress, particularly depression and its prevalence. I also briefly described what psychotherapy involves. Based on my research findings, I discussed some common beliefs and misconceptions about psychotherapy and gave practical information about how professional help could be obtained on campus. Second, I established a protocol in the Psychological Services Center in which intake clinicians would discuss with prospective clients some of these same matters. A follow-up study demonstrated positive results attributable to both educative interventions. ♦

Becoming a Clinical Psychologist

Assuming that you have not been scared off by the disadvantages to being a clinical psychologist, there is yet another challenging aspect that pertains to the attainment of such a career goal. Admission to clinical psychology graduate programs, particularly those in Boulder model university departments, is very competitive. It is common for each of the accredited university graduate programs to receive hundreds of applications for a dozen or fewer admission slots.

Undergraduates who intend to be one of this select group should set their course early and engage in certain activities that will enhance the likelihood of being admitted to one of these programs. Remember, however, that the Boulder model programs emphasize research training to some extent. For many, extensive research training and involvement is neither appealing nor relevant to career goals, and they should consider some of the alternatives to Boulder model training. The most commonly chosen options in the field of psychology would be the pursuit of a doctorate in professional psychology, counseling psychology, or school psychology. Admission to these programs is usually less competitive than would be the case in Boulder model programs, but if the program is accredited by the APA, there is assurance that it meets important educational criteria.

Although there are psychology jobs for people with bachelor's and master's degrees, all states require a doctorate in order for a person to be licensed as a psychologist. Without a license, psychological activities would be limited and would have to be conducted under the supervision of a licensed psychologist. An individual who is intent on becoming a mental health professional but adverse to the idea of pursuing a doctorate should consider the field of psychiatric social work. A person with an M.S.W (Master of Social Work) is eligible for licensure and is often trained to engage in psychotherapy activities.

To get admitted to a clinical psychology doctoral program, whether in a university-based Boulder model program or in a professional school of psychology, applicants need to prove themselves in several contexts. Because there are usually so many applicants for a limited number of slots, admissions committees often look at quantitative criteria first—grades and scores on the Graduate Record Examination (GRE). For example, a grade-point average

that is below 3.0 will knock an applicant out of the running at most schools. Similarly, low GRE scores will put an applicant at a distinct disadvantage. The higher a person's grades and scores, the greater the likelihood of making the first cut.

Second, admissions committees usually look for some demonstrated commitment to clinical work. An applicant should have had the opportunity of testing out the field, even in a paraprofessional role as an intern or mental health worker.

Third, it is usually advantageous to have had some research experience. This is particularly true for the Boulder model programs. Having worked with professors on research projects is quite beneficial. If a student has played a substantial role in a research project, perhaps even co-authoring a published research article, that applicant's chances for admission will be enhanced considerably. An additional benefit of this kind of involvement is that the student will very likely receive a strong letter of reference from a professor who will be able to attest a knowledge of the applicant that exceeds what is usually possible in a classroom relationship.

Fourth, applicants must give attention to the manner of self-presentation in correspondence, completion of application materials, written personal statement, and interview. Successful candidates are usually those who are able to demonstrate maturity, professionalism, and a healthy degree of self-understanding.

Once an individual is admitted to doctoral training, he or she will engage in at least four years of graduate courses and clinical practica. Programs that are accredited by the APA usually require four years of work on campus followed by a year-long internship at a health-care facility with a training program that is also APA accredited. On-campus studies will involve the completion of various courses that generally represent the whole field of psychology and specifically cover the primary areas of clinical psychology. General psychology courses may include the topics of statistics, personality, and physiological, social, and developmental psychology. Clinical psychology courses will include topics such as assessment, psychopathology, and psychotherapy, probably accompanied by practicum experiences.

Additionally, the student is involved in research to varying degrees depending on the philosophy of the doctoral program. At one extreme are a few Boulder model programs with a primary commitment to research training. These programs require that the student complete various research courses and research practica that

culminate in a master's thesis and a doctoral dissertation. At the other extreme are a few professional schools that have virtually no research requirements. Most programs fall somewhere between these two extremes.

The internship year is a time during which the trainee becomes fully immersed in clinical work. There are various kinds of internship opportunities. The most competitive and prestigious internship placements are at major medical schools, where the psychology intern is trained alongside trainees from many other health fields. There are also internships in community mental health centers, college mental health facilities, and so on.

Following completion of the doctorate, the clinical psychologist must become licensed in order to practice. Licensing laws differ from state to state, but most states require a minimum of two years of full-time supervised work in one's field, at least one year of which must be postdoctoral. Therefore, even after clinical psychologists have completed their doctoral degrees and their internships, they must acquire at least one more year of supervised training in order to practice clinical psychology without supervision. Licensing examinations also differ from state to state. Most state psychology boards administer a standardized examination in general psychology. This is supplemented in many states by a second testing component, which may be an oral examination, a clinical case presentation, or an essay examination.

The field of psychology provides many career possibilities, and within the particular field of clinical psychology there are various training and career possibilities. The distinction between the traditional Boulder model programs, with their emphasis on scientist-professional training, and the professional programs, with their heavier emphasis on the development of clinical skills, is a particularly important consideration for any aspiring clinical psychologist today. It may have bearing on the kind of career opportunities that will be accessible once the doctorate is received.

When advising undergraduates who are struggling with a decision regarding the kind of graduate training to pursue in clinical psychology, I advise them to carefully evaluate their personal interests and goals. Usually, the best way of undertaking an informed evaluation is through experience. In addition to clinically relevant undergraduate courses, clinical practica and research practica can provide ideal opportunities for evaluating the particular training options and career routes within clinical psychology.

SUGGESTED READINGS

BOHART, A. C., & TODD, J. (1988). *Foundations of clinical and counseling psychology.* New York: Harper & Row.

FRETZ, B. R., & STANG, D. J. (1980). *Preparing for graduate study in psychology: NOT for seniors only!* Washington, DC: American Psychological Association.

HALGIN, R. P. (1986). Advising undergraduates who wish to become clinicians. *Teaching of Psychology, 13,* 7–12.

KORCHIN, S. J. (1976). *Modern clinical psychology: Principles of intervention in the clinic and community.* New York: Basic Books.

LOUIS COSTA

Louis Costa is Professor of Psychology and Dean of Social Sciences at the University of Victoria. He is a graduate of the Clinical Psychology Program at Teachers College, Columbia University, and has taught at the Albert Einstein College of Medicine and Queens and City Colleges in New York City. Dr. Costa is a diplomate American Board of Clinical Neuropsychology of the American Board of Professional Psychology (ABCN-ABPP) in clinical neuropsychology and has served as president of the Division of Clinical Neuropsychology of APA, president of the International Neuropsychological Society and Chairperson of the Section on Clinical Neuropsychology of the Canadian Psychological Association. He has contributed empirical, theoretical, and professional articles to the neuropsychology literature and edits the Journal of Clinical and Experimental Neuropsychology. ♦

5

The Clinical
Neuropsychologist

Kevin had been a good student; he graduated near the top of his high school class. In fact, high school had been a breeze. He could achieve A grades in math and science without spending endless hours cracking the books. That left plenty of time for socializing. He had saved enough money to buy a moped. So he had wheels. He took one last summer fling before going off to engineering school in the fall.

Kevin was found unconscious in a ditch off a quiet suburban road. His crumpled moped was 20 yards away. He was probably hit some time during the night by a passing motorist. Fortunately he was wearing a helmet; otherwise he surely would have been killed. As it was, he was in a coma due to a severe concussion. He also had a broken collarbone, but that would mend easily.

After three days, Kevin regained consciousness and was moved from the intensive care unit to the neurology service of his local hospital. X-rays had shown no skull fracture and his parents were assured that he was out of danger. Nevertheless, his progress in the hospital was slow. Kevin could recognize his family and friends but he seemed confused. He would often lose track of simple conversations, could not recognize his doctors or nurses, and seemed to have little idea of what time of day it was. He couldn't remember his accident or, for that matter, anything that had happened after dinner on the evening of the accident. In a week or two his confusion lifted slowly. He was more aware of his surroundings and, although he felt more tired and irritable than usual, he was eager to come home.

Six weeks later the accident seemed like a bad memory—or nonmemory, since he still couldn't remember the actual event. It was already mid-August and time to begin thinking about engineering school. Kevin had become short-tempered with his parents and sister and didn't see as much of his friends as before. But he was sure all that would settle down once he started work at University.

Kevin enrolled in five courses: calculus, physics, chemistry, and two basic courses in engineering. It was a complete disaster. He was unable to concentrate in class and couldn't bring himself to do his homework in the evenings. Each week he fell further behind and each week the pressure built up. By November he was a nervous wreck, snapping at anybody in sight over the most trivial things. In the evenings, alone in bed, he cried.

Kevin was eventually persuaded by a friend to seek help at the student counseling service. The counselor, who had seen several cases of this sort, quickly referred him to the clinical neuropsychologist who worked at the medical school at his university. Kevin was interviewed and given a complete battery of neuropsychologi-

cal tests. In addition, a follow-up neurological evaluation was scheduled with the neurologist who had seen him after his head injury. A *neurologist* is a physician specializing in the diagnosis and treatment of nervous system disorders.

Kevin had little difficulty with most of the neuropsychological tests he was given. His language comprehension and his ability to solve complex perceptual problems were excellent. No sensory or motor deficits were found. What was observed, however, was that Kevin had a serious attention and concentration deficit. He could repeat only three numbers backwards (e.g., "7-2-5" repeated as "5-2-7") although normally bright persons his age can do five or more.

When given a test requiring sustained attention, the Paced Auditory Serial Addition Test, he again did poorly. This task requires the patient to add pairs of randomized digits so that each is added to the digit immediately preceding it. If the examiner says 5, 8, 3, 9 the appropriate responses are 13, 11, 12. The digits are presented rapidly, at rates of about one per 1.5 seconds. Kevin's performance fell apart completely as the rate of digit presentation was increased.

In addition, Kevin showed much more difficulty than would be expected of someone of his intelligence on tests of concept formation and of recent memory. He was unable to sort common objects into categories such as use, size, and color. He could not learn a list of 12 unrelated words on ten trials and had difficulty remembering and repeating a short story when tested 45 minutes after it was first read to him.

It was clear to the neuropsychologist after evaluating all her data that Kevin was suffering from a postconcussion syndrome, characterized by difficulty with speeded tasks, higher order concept formation, and memory, plus increased irritability and low frustration tolerance. It is interesting to note that his neurological exam, at this time, was essentially normal.

The impact of Kevin's disabilities on his school performance was devastating. Faced with five courses in which lecturers rapidly presented complex information, he was completely unable to keep up with the masses of information to which he was exposed. As lectures built concept on concept, his memory deficit prevented him from retaining the basic information needed to follow the instructor's reasoning. The experience was basically foreign to him; he had rarely experienced these difficulties in high school. Now he felt quite threatened and angry at himself and his teachers.

The first step in Kevin's therapy involved an explanation of the problem by the clinical neuropsychologist as she saw it. She

The formboard test can help identify the location of brain damage. (Courtesy of the editor, Robert Gifford.)

pointed out many of the difficulties that he was experiencing in terms that he could understand. She attributed most of his problems to his head injury and pointed out that such problems were not infrequent in head injury patients. Through her intervention Kevin was permitted to withdraw from his courses without penalty. Kevin was able to recognize his concentration and memory deficits and willing to start a rehabilitation program to work on these disabilities. He made sufficient progress to enroll in a single course the following semester. He and his cognitive rehabilitation therapist, a clinical neuropsychologist specializing in treatment, worked together weekly developing techniques to improve his ability to concentrate, to retain information, and to study effectively given his residual disabilities. The following year he was able to take a full course load and although not as sharp as before his accident, he was well on his way to significant recovery.

Kevin's case is repeated thousands of times per year in North America. Most often the effects of head injury are less severe and more transient, clearing up in a matter of hours or days. In other cases the symptoms are more severe and permanently alter the lives of those involved.

What Is Clinical Neuropsychology?

Neuropsychology in its broadest sense involves the study of the relationships that exist between the nervous system and behavior. Human neuropsychology focuses primarily on cognitive functions most developed in humans and their relationship to the central nervous system. Clinical neuropsychology involves the application of neuropsychological knowledge to practical problems with patients.

Clinical neuropsychologists are psychologists who specialize in the identification and treatment of the *behavioral* consequences of nervous system disorders and injuries. In Kevin's case, as we have seen, while his behavioral difficulties stemmed from a head injury, he was considered medically recovered by his neurologist at the time his school performance was severely impaired. This discrepancy underlines the need for persons with psychological training to deal with the behavioral aspects of neurological disease or trauma. Often, physicians lack the sensitivity, skill, or time to deal with them effectively.

The Background of Neuropsychology

Physicians in ancient Greece and Rome made occasional references to behavior which had changed as a result of head injury. Since the middle ages, careful historians have documented descriptions of the relationship of neurological disease to alterations in language, sensory, and motor functioning. It was not, however, until the last half of the nineteenth century that interest in neuropsychology grew significantly as a result of the findings by Paul Broca and by John Hughlings-Jackson that most language functions were mediated by the left cerebral hemisphere. That is, if injury or disease affects the central part of one's left hemisphere, deficits in speaking, reading, writing, and aural comprehension are a frequent result.

Between 1860 and 1940 many investigators, mostly neurologists, attempted to relate the effects of neurological disease to behavior using the psychologies of that era. Only with the development of modern approaches to psychological measurement (e.g., test construction, scaling, etc.) could psychologists equip themselves with tools that enabled them to contribute significantly to neuropsychological knowledge. Constructs derived largely from cognitive

testing (e.g., verbal, arithmetic, spatial abilities, sensory, and motor skills) provided reliable and valid instruments which could be used to examine patients with injuries to localized parts of the brain. This has taught us much about brain-behavior relationships.

By the early 1960s a small number of clinical neuropsychologists with good backgrounds in neuroanatomy and clinical neurology were able to use behavioral tests well enough to predict where in the brain tumors were located, strokes had occurred, or other disease processes were focused. In an era where specialized neurological x-ray techniques were often dangerous and inconclusive, this neuropsychological detective work was invaluable. It also provided the core of basic knowledge about the relationship between cognitive and affective behavior and the nervous system on which modern clinical neuropsychology is based. Throughout this period, and even to the present day, the focus of clinical neurological activity has been on assessment and diagnosis more than on intervention and treatment.

Gradually, for several reasons, the tide is turning. Most importantly, understanding the psychological effects of neurological disorders is of little aid to patients and their families unless it can help in decision making. Does grandma have the capacity to continue to live alone and maintain herself after her last stroke? Does an accountant have enough judgment to resume his business after the removal of a benign frontal lobe tumor? Is Kevin ready to return to school after his head injury?

In cases where cognitive deficits are found to persist after neurologic disease, what can be done to alleviate them or enable the patient to circumvent them? Can patients with severe memory deficits learn to improve their memories? Can they be taught to use external devices as memory aids? Can others with perceptual problems, such as inattention to the left side of visual space produced by a right hemisphere stroke, relearn to pay attention to the left side of this environment, and thus to read properly again?

Nowhere is the connection between assessment and treatment more closely linked than in the area of learning disabilities. In this field clinical neuropsychologists, together with educational psychologists and speech pathologists, identify the type of learning disorder exhibited by a child and implement therapeutic procedures designed to facilitate learning.

Finally, clinical neuropsychologists often are asked to do individual and group counseling with spouses, parents, and children of patients with neurological disorders. Often these relatives have little information about the behavioral effects of the

patient's disorder and require assistance in coping with difficult behaviors as well as in reordering their own lives as the family attempts to adjust to the patient. Clinical neuropsychological therapies are in their infancy. Many offer promise but their development and evaluation will challenge the field for years to come.

As in all applied fields of psychology, most practitioners are concerned with improving their skills and techniques. Thus, all clinical neuropsychologists are trained to do clinical research and for some research is their primary professional activity.

Clinical neuropsychologists work in a variety of settings among the most common of which are neurology, neurosurgery, psychiatry, and pediatric services of large hospitals. In these settings they see ill, hospitalized inpatients but also practice in hospital clinics (e.g., patients with seizures, sleep disorders, genetic disorders) in which outpatients are seen. Other clinical neuropsychologists work in hospitals, centers, or clinics devoted entirely to special populations: rehabilitation facilities, geriatric centers, residences for the mentally handicapped (formerly called mentally retarded). Some clinical neuropsychologists work in special schools for learning disabled children or in special units within public school systems. An increasing number are in private practice, many dealing with legal issues relating to compensation for injuries, or responsibility for alleged crime on the part of their patients. Some clinical neuropsychologists specialize in adult or child cases exclusively, others limit their practice to particular types of patients (e.g., those with epilepsy and related disorders), while many work in settings which require expertise with all types of patients.

It is difficult to determine the number of clinical neuropsychologists at work in North America at present. It would be fair to estimate though that assessment and treatment of neuropsychological patients is the major professional activity of about 2,000 psychologists.

The Scope of Clinical Neuropsychology

Head injury patients are a small, but increasing, fraction of cases seen by clinical neuropsychologists. Many other cases stem from neurological disease, which may be produced by infection, metabolic disorder, tumor, degeneration of nervous system tissue, and by diseases of the vascular system supplying blood to the brain.

The causes of some neurological diseases are unknown (e.g., multiple sclerosis).

In all cases, central nervous system disorders produce changes in behavior which may affect the capacity of the patient to work effectively or even to function independently. Some neurologic diseases produce acute disabilities from which the patient recovers completely. Others leave patients with chronic long-term disabilities to which they must adjust; still others are progressive and may result in total incapacitation and death.

It is probably conservative to estimate that there are about one million *new* cases of neurological disease in North America each year, many of which should be seen by a clinical neuropsychologist.

In recent years, it has become evident that clinical neuropsychologists can contribute to the understanding of the behavioral consequences of other medical conditions affecting the nervous system indirectly (e.g., alcoholism, AIDS, cardiovascular disease). Furthermore, neuropsychological models are applicable to the understanding and treatment of learning disabilities. Indeed, one grandiose future forecaster (Costa, 1983) has predicted that the twenty-first century will see the discovery of the physiological bases of aptitudes such as mathematical, musical, or administrative abilities and this, combined with advances in genetic engineering, will make the problems faced in Huxley's novel *Brave New World* appear trivial.

Clinical Neuropsychological Practice: An Overview

Typically, patients are referred to the clinical neuropsychologist by other professionals in the settings in which they work; although referrals by lawyers, teachers, family, and even self-referral is not uncommon. In all referrals from nonmedical sources, the competent clinical neuropsychologist should make sure that concurrent medical illness is evaluated and treated by appropriate medical personnel.

Clinical neuropsychological assessment focuses on the major areas of ability needed by all individuals to function in society. These include the understanding and expression of language in verbal and written form, attention, concentration and memory, as well as visual, spatial, auditory, and somesthetic perception. Concept formation and judgment are assessed as well as the patient's ability to form and execute plans involving ordered sequences of behavior. Personality

measures round out the picture, particularly in cases with elements of psychiatric as well as neurological disorder.

The Strategy of Assessment

The Deficit Model

Normal individuals vary on many of the abilities measured in a clinical neuropsychological assessment. Factors such as age, education, and intelligence influence test performance. A clinical neuropsychologist looks for areas of deficit performance as an indicator of neurological disease but is always faced with the question as to whether the performance observed is a true deficit or simply a variation of normal behavior.

Fortunately, there are several ways around this problem. Occasionally, as in the case of Brian (see Case Three), patients are tested both before and after a head injury or the onset of disease. More often one must infer what the patient was like prior to the onset of the disorder. This is done in three ways. First, one can make assumptions about a patient's previous level of ability from his or her educational and occupational level. Second, certain achievements of people are remarkably resistant to neurological disease. Old rote learning and one's fund of factual information, for example, tend to remain unimpaired while other abilities decline. Third, interviews of the patient and relatives often provide significant information about what the patient was like before the onset of illness or injury.

Once an estimate of the normal functional level for a given patient is obtained, the test results can be examined to see what patterns of behavioral deficit exist. Different kinds of neurological disorder produce different patterns of deficit. For instance, the difficulties in attention, concentration, memory, and personality change seen in the case of Kevin are among a cluster of symptoms frequently seen after severe concussion. A frequently occurring pattern of deficits in damage to the central part of the right hemisphere involves:

1. impairment of fine manual skills such as placing small pegs in a pegboard, and loss of ability to identify common objects by touch with the left hand only;
2. impairment of spatial organization;

3. inattention to visual stimuli occurring on the left side of the body;

4. difficulty in putting on clothing properly.

Once the clinical neuropsychologist has identified the pattern of deficits exhibited by a particular patient, a whole series of questions can be examined. Sometimes the focus is diagnostic, as in the case of a patient referred by a neurologist with the question "Does this patient have early Alzheimer's disease? Neurological tests showed nothing." At other times the patient's medical condition is well diagnosed and emphasis falls on devising plans or interventions to help the patient and his or her relatives understand and overcome the disabilities.

Some illustrative cases are presented here.

CASE STUDIES

CASE ONE: STEFAN

Stefan was a physician who emigrated to the United States from Hungary shortly after the uprising in 1956. His adjustment was quite successful, in part because he was good at languages and knew a significant amount of English on his arrival. He quickly got his medical credentials in order and after a brief period was granted a license to practice medicine in New York State. He opened a private general practice in a Hungarian neighborhood in New York City and was quite successful.

In the spring of 1976 his wife died. He appeared to adjust well to this loss; however, several weeks later he was mugged on the way home from work. Although he was hit over the head and knocked to the ground, he did not lose consciousness and sustained no apparent physical injury.

Stefan became depressed after the mugging incident and within a week was unable to work. He expressed fears about going out alone and also about his ability to continue to take care of his patients. A trial of antidepressant medication failed to lift his depression and eventually he was hospitalized. The psychiatric staff felt that the double blow—the loss of his wife and a brutal mugging—was certainly sufficient precipitating causes for depression in this 60-year-old man but it was decided to refer him for neurological and neuropsychological evaluation to rule out other possible factors in his case.

The neurological results were difficult to interpret. He had a normal clinical neurologic exam (e.g., reflexes, cranial nerve exami-

nation, sensory and motor exam) except for the evaluation of his mental status. The neurologist found him to be reasonably alert, quite cooperative, well oriented to time and place and capable of his own good judgment. But he was clearly depressed and also surprisingly vague about recent events in his past history. X-ray technique (a brain scan) showed very mild cortical atrophy of the kind seen occasionally in normal 60-year olds.

In clinical neuropsychological testing, although he was depressed, he was quite cooperative. He worked hard on all the tests given him. Intelligence testing revealed the superior performance that one would expect of someone of his occupational level. His performance was somewhat slow but this is commonly seen in depressed patients. No evidence of sensory (visual, auditory, and tactile) disturbance, or of motor (strength of grip, or fine motor coordination) was found. Stefan's performance on perceptual tests was about average for his age level and a bit below what one might expect from estimates of his optimal level of functioning.

The first indication of serious difficulty came on tests of verbal fluency. When asked to state as many different words as he could beginning with the letter F he could manage only 5 in 60 seconds which was well below expectation. He complained that several Hungarian words came to mind but he didn't mention them because they wouldn't count. He was next asked to name as many different animals as he could. His score was in the bottom quarter of his age group, a further indication of verbal fluency loss commonly seen in cases of damage to the left frontal areas of the cerebral cortex. His performance on tests of verbal and visual memory was also poor. The rest of his exam was within normal limits.

I noted that disturbances in recent memory as shown in neuropsychological testing, and also in his vagueness on the mental status exam conducted by the neurologist, are often among the earliest signs of Alzheimer's disease. Impairment in verbal fluency is another common manifestation of this disease although in this case the fact that English was his second language complicated the picture. I informed his psychiatrist that there were possible signs of early Alzheimer's disease in Stefan's case and that he should be reevaluated in one year to see if his symptoms had progressed. In the meantime, supportive psychotherapy for his depression was suggested.

Four months later Stefan's daughter convinced him to give up his apartment in the inner city and live with her and her family in the suburbs. Once there Stefan's disabilities became more apparent. Deprived of his familiar surroundings, he was unable to orient him-

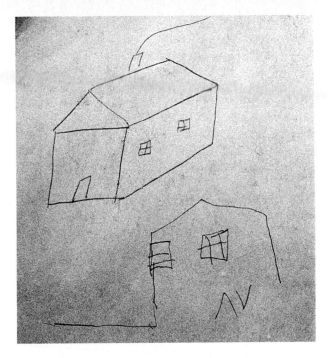

A 61-year old man made the lower drawing when asked to copy the upper one. The drawings are part of a test that was used in his case to make an early and correct diagnosis of Alzheimer's disease. (Courtesy of the editor, Robert Gifford.)

self in his new environment. He could not find his way home from the neighborhood shopping center and frequently got lost. He had great difficulty in learning the location of common objects in his daughter's household. As time passed, his daughter noticed that Stefan occasionally would completely forget conversations that he had had with her only hours previously.

Follow-up evaluation in 1977 revealed a progression of Stefan's cortical atrophy and further deterioration on neuropsychological tests. At that time a diagnosis of Alzheimer's disease was made. Stefan lived for three more years with his daughter but by then his behavior had deteriorated so significantly that she was no longer able to care for him. He died in a nursing home in 1982.

This case illustrates several difficulties often faced in neuro-psychological assessment:

1. Often patients show symptoms (in this case depression) which may result from a psychiatric disorder instead of, or in addition to, neurological disease. Was Stefan's depression due to the loss of his wife and the mugging incident or did it reflect his increasing awareness of his diminished cognitive capacity?

2. It is sometimes difficult to determine whether a given behavioral deficit is a direct consequence of neurological disease or normal variation in ability or experience. Stefan's low scores on verbal fluency tests might have been attributed to the fact that his native language was Hungarian. On the other hand, he was a bright man who quickly learned to speak good English shortly after his arrival in the United States.

3. Some neurological diseases are of slow onset with the earliest signs being subtle behavioral changes. Follow-up examination may be necessary before a diagnosis can be made or ruled out. ♦

CASE TWO: MARY

Mary, a 45-year-old telephone switchboard operator for a large company, was referred to me by her general practitioner. He felt that she had a memory deficit and was concerned that she might have Alzheimer's disease.

On testing, Mary turned out to be a woman of average ability. Her scores on memory tests and on all other tests in the neuropsychological battery were within the normal range. Personality testing with the Minnesota Multiphasic Personality Inventory (MMPI) revealed an anxious, withdrawn, self-deprecating woman who had significant difficulty with social relationships. Mary was asked to give an illustration of her memory problems. She said that recently the old switchboards had been replaced by new ones. She had been given brief instruction on the new switchboard by a supervisor who expected her to learn quickly and efficiently. The switchboard operator then stood behind her while Mary tried to route incoming calls. She was extremely nervous and was unable to use the new machine. Humiliated by the experience, Mary went home in tears. In the following weeks, although she adapted to the new switchboard, Mary experienced other events in which learning something new was difficult and anxiety producing. She became

convinced that she was losing her mind and had half convinced her doctor that this was the case.

Mary was reassured that her test results were normal. A neurological evaluation revealed no disease. She was referred for counseling to help control her anxiety and help her to build self-esteem. She was scheduled for a one-year follow-up exam, but when the time came she cancelled her appointment, stating that she was feeling much better and that she saw no need for further neuropsychological evaluation. She was probably right.

Mary's case demonstrates that not all cases seen by clinical neuropsychologists turn out to have neurological disease. A practicing clinical neuropsychologist must be familiar with a broad range of personality and psychiatric disorders. She or he must have sufficient clinical skills to use interview techniques effectively in eliciting relevant information from patients and others.

In the two cases presented here, the primary focus was on assessment. The essential question was "What is going on with the patient to account for the behavioral symptoms observed?" In many other cases the cause of the patient's behavioral problems is clearer and the primary focus shifts to intervention or rehabilitation. That is the focus in the next case. ♦

CASE THREE: BRIAN

When Brian was 12 he was injured in an accident on a construction site. He and some friends were exploring the foundation of a new house when a piece of heavy scaffolding came loose and hit Brian, causing a skull fracture and brain contusions.

Brian was hospitalized for several months, during which he was sent to me for a neuropsychological evaluation. Since the issue of negligence on the part of the construction company would undoubtedly arise, it became important to determine whether Brian had suffered any permanent disability as a result of the accident. To do this, it was important to get a clear picture of Brian's level of functioning *before* the accident. I contacted his school to obtain copies of their records.

Brian, it turned out, had done poorly in school for several years and had been diagnosed as having a learning disability. His intelligence test scores were in the low-average range and he was reading and spelling at third grade level. Verbal and visual memory were low-average for his age and tests of linguistic ability showed mild impairment. His parents reported that he had been an active child

with many friends and that he really enjoyed tinkering with old bikes in his father's bike shop.

When tested in the hospital, Brian was rather passive and apathetic. He had little insight into his own condition. Surprisingly, his IQ test results were almost identical to those obtained prior to his accident, and his scores on reading and spelling achievement tests actually showed some slight gains since his first evaluation. Neuropsychological testing revealed poor performance on tests of concentration, verbal and visual memory, and of language functioning. All these deficits had been present to some extent prior to his injury.

I referred Brian for a speech pathology evaluation, recommended not only that he receive tutoring, but also that his family be seen regularly by a social worker who could aim them in assisting Brian to develop the skills necessary to maintain an independent adjustment in adulthood. At that point it was unclear what the long-lasting effects of Brian's head injury would be. I couldn't honestly say to what extent his deficits were a consequence of his head injury or his preexisting learning disability.

I heard nothing of Brian for eight years. It was that long before his parents' lawsuit against the construction company was scheduled to come to court. Brian's lawyer asked me to see him again to establish the extent to which Brian's head injury had affected his behavior.

Before testing Brian I found out what had happened since I had seen him last. Brian had gotten none of the help I had suggested. He had remained in school for three years without making any significant progress and then left. Most of his school friends lost interest in Brian and drifted away. For a time Brian worked for his father in the bike shop but he was so passive and forgetful that he was of virtually no help. Brian sat around the house most of the day watching television. He showed little interest in social activities, in part because he couldn't follow other people's conversations easily. About a year before I saw him again he met a girl named Marsha. They started spending time together, and a few months later Brian moved in with her. He had become totally dependent on her. She worked as a file clerk and spent her remaining time taking care of him.

When I saw him for testing, Brian spoke very short sentences in a flat, quiet voice. He asked no questions and showed no evidence of spontaneity. He described himself as being unhappy and experiencing difficulty in thinking. He had no plans but indicated that he expected to remain with Marsha. The interview and subsequent

clinical neuropsychological evaluation brought out the following deficits:

1. Poor insight and low motivation.
2. Inability to initiate and maintain behavior.
3. Impaired attention, concentration, and memory.
4. Impaired language and reading comprehension.
5. Lack of social skills and the ability to manage money.

The construction company hired its own neuropsychologist who did an independent evaluation of Brian. Although for a while they tried to maintain that all his symptoms could be attributed to a prior learning disability, eventually they had to concede that Brian had sustained a severe head injury and that changes in his personality (in lack of ability to sustain behavior, loss of interest and lack of ability to plan, poor attention, and memory) were attributable to frontal lobe damage. They settled the case out of court.

Although sufficient money was held in trust for Brian to assure him a moderate income for the rest of his life, it was evident that it would be difficult, if not impossible, for Brian to function as an independent adult without significant therapy. A program was worked out with a clinical neuropsychologist who specializes in cognitive retraining. It included counseling sessions aimed at helping Brian to gain insight into his situation and increase his motivation for independent behavior.

In addition, a variety of training techniques, some using computerized programs, were instituted to help Brian circumvent or overcome his cognitive difficulties. Treatment is still underway and to this point, about one year since I saw him last, Brian has made modest gains. He continues to live with Marsha, an otherwise isolated woman who clearly enjoys nurturing Brian and playing a dominant role in their relationship. ♦

Becoming a Clinical Neuropsychologist

Training

What does a clinical neuropsychologist need to know to practice in an applied setting? It is commonly agreed that he or she is first and foremost a psychologist. Thus, training at the undergraduate and

graduate level in several substantive areas of psychology is necessary—for example:

1. Biological bases of behavior.
2. Cognitive and affective bases of behavior.
3. Social bases of behavior.
4. Individual differences.

Any psychologist should have some exposure to all of these fields. Clinical neuropsychologists in particular require training in the following areas:

1. Basic psychology.
2. Basic neurosciences.
3. General clinical psychology.
4. Clinical neuropsychology.
5. Clinical neurology and related disciplines.

This kind of training requires a doctoral degree, almost always the Ph.D.

Division 40 (Clinical Neuropsychology) of the American Psychological Association has collaborated with the International Neuropsychological Society to develop a set of guidelines for doctoral training programs in the United States, which are reproduced here. These guidelines have been approved by Division 40 but have not, as yet, been approved by the APA as a whole. APA has been slow to move toward specific specialty designation for newly emerging fields such as clinical neuropsychology. For a detailed discussion of the issues involved see Costa, Matarazzo, and Bornstein (1986). The guidelines presented here should, however, give you a good feel for what graduate training in clinical neuropsychology should include.

Guidelines for Doctoral Training Programs in Clinical Neuropsychology

Doctoral training in clinical neuropsychology should ordinarily result in the awarding of a Ph.D. degree from a regionally accredited university. It may be accomplished through a Ph.D. program in clinical neuropsychology offered by a psy-

chology department or medical faculty or through the completion of a Ph.D. program in a related specialty area (e.g., clinical psychology) which offers sufficient specialization in clinical neuropsychology.

Training programs in clinical neuropsychology prepare students for health service delivery, basic clinical research, teaching, and consultation. As such they must contain (a) a generic psychology core, (b) a generic clinical core, (c) specialized training in the neurosciences and basic human and animal neuropsychology, and (d) specific training in clinical neuropsychology. This should include an 1,800-hour internship which should be preceded by appropriate practicum experience.

(A) Generic Psychology Core

1. Statistics and methodology
2. Learning, cognition, and perception
3. Social psychology and personality
4. Physiological psychology
5. Life-span developmental
6. History

(B) Generic Clinical Core

1. Psychopathology
2. Psychometric theory
3. Interview and assessment techniques
   i. Interviewing
   ii. Intelligence assessment
   iii. Personality assessment
4. Intervention techniques
   i. Counseling and psychotherapy
   ii. Behavior therapy/modification
   iii. Consultation
5. Professional ethics

(C) Neurosciences and Basic Human and Animal Neuropsychology

1. Basic neurosciences
2. Advanced physiological psychology and pharmacology

3. Neuropsychology of perceptual, cognitive, and executive processes

4. Research design and research practicum in neuropsychology

(D) Specific Clinical Neuropsychological Training

1. Clinical neurology and neuropathology
2. Specialized neuropsychological assessment techniques
3. Specialized neuropsychological intervention techniques
4. Assessment practicum (children and/or adults) in university-supervised assessment facility
5. Intervention practicum in University supervised facility
6. Clinical neuropsychological internship of 1800 hours. Ordinarily this internship will be completed in a single year, but in exceptional circumstances may be completed in a two-year period.

(E) Doctoral Dissertation

It is recognized that the completion of a Ph.D. in clinical neuropsychology prepares the person to begin work as a clinical neuropsychologist. In most jurisdictions, an additional year of supervised clinical practice will be required in order to qualify for licensure. Furthermore, training at the postdoctoral level to increase both general and subspecialty competencies is viewed as desirable.

In Canada, Section 23 (Clinical Neuropsychology) of the Canadian Psychological Association (CPA) represents clinical neuropsychologists. This body, together with the section on brain and behavior, has presented a set of guidelines to CPA for its approval. Although quite similar to the U.S. guidelines, the Canadian guidelines differ in the following respects:

1. Social psychology is deleted as a requirement. Other aspects of the generic core, e.g. physiological psychology, are moved to the neurosciences category.
2. An intervention practicum in a university-supervised intervention facility is not required.
3. Students are required to complete 1800 hours of practicum-internship. Three hundred hours of basic assess-

ment practicum within the University are required. In addition the student may choose a full year clinical neuropsychology internship *or* 1,500 additional hours of practicum experience of which no more than 600 hours will be devoted to research.

Cripe (1988) has compiled a list of U.S. doctoral programs that are in conformity with the Division 40 guidelines. Because no formal accreditation mechanism exists, these programs have not been formally evaluated by an accrediting agency. In Cripe's words "It is suggested that students become aware of the guidelines for training, contact the various programs, and check for themselves to see if their training needs will be met" (p. 14).

Getting Started

Many undergraduate psychology departments in North America offer a course in general neuropsychology. Although such beginning courses appropriately concentrate on basic neuroanatomy, neurology, and theory of brain-behavior relationships almost all draw on clinical material and elaborate on the issues exemplified in the case studies in this chapter. Students seeking more detailed descriptions of patients with neuropsychological disorders and the theories which have arisen in an attempt to understand their behavior should read *The Shattered Mind: The Person After Brain Damage* by Howard Gardner (1975). *Left Brain, Right Brain* by Springer and Deutsch (1981) offers a readable introduction to the area of hemispheric specialization. This book integrates clinical and research data in treating many problems of interest to neuropsychologists.

SUGGESTED READINGS AND REFERENCES

COSTA, L. (1983). Clinical neuropsychology: A discipline in evolution. *Journal of Clinical Neuropsychology, 5*, 1–12.

COSTA, L., MATARAZZO, J. D., & BORNSTEIN, R. A. (1986). Issues in graduate and postgraduate training in clinical neuropsychology. In S. B. Filskov & T. J. Boll (Eds.) *Handbook of Clinical Neuropsychology* (Vol. 2.) New York: Wiley.

CRIPE, L. I. (1988). Listing of training programs in clinical neuropsychology. *The Clinical Neuropsychologist, 2,* 13–24.

GARDNER, H. (1975). *The shattered mind.* New York: Knopf.

Reports of the International Neuropsychological Society-Division 40 Task Force on Education, Accreditation and Credentialing (1987). *The Clinical Neuropsychologist, 1,* 29–34.

SPRINGER, S., & DEUTSCH, G. (1981). *Left brain, right brain.* San Francisco: Freeman.

CYNTHIA D. BELAR

Cynthia D. Belar received her Ph.D. from Ohio University in 1974 after an internship at Duke University Medical Center. From 1974 to 1984 she was on the faculty of the Department of Clinical and Health Psychology at the University of Florida's academic medical center and currently serves as Director of the Clinical Psychology program there. From 1984 to 1990 she served as Chief Psychologist and Clinical Director of Behavioral Medicine for the Kaiser Permanente Medical Care Program in Los Angeles. She has also served as Chair of the Education and Training Committee, APA's Division of Health Psychology; Chair of APA's Graduate Education and Training Committee; Chair of the Executive Committee, Association of Psychology Internship Centers; and Chair of the Arthritis Health Professions Research Committee of the Arthritis Foundation. Her research has been in the area of pain, stress management, and biofeedback. She is the co-author of a recent book, The Practice of Clinical Health Psychology. ♦

6

The Health Psychologist

Last week, I saw a patient who had been referred to me by an orthopedic surgeon. This patient, a 52-year-old truckdriver, had had back surgery one year ago but was still suffering from severe back pain that prevented him from resuming his occupational activities. He had seen numerous neurologists, orthopedic surgeons, and physical therapists, and had received multiple medical treatments, none of which were successful in relieving his pain. He was quite upset about the changes in his life due to his pain problem; he had become less sociable, more irritable, and more dependent on analgesic medication. There had also been an increase in conflicts with his wife, who now was forced to work in order to provide additional income. Nevertheless, he was reluctant to see me because he feared that seeing a psychologist meant that people would think that his pain was "imaginary" or "all in my head." However, his family physician urged him to meet with me for at least one consultation.

I was able to reassure this patient that over the past 10 to 15 years psychologists had become very involved in providing consultation and treatment services to chronic pain sufferers. The *gate control theory* of pain (Melzack & Wall, 1965) led to a shift away from viewing pain as a purely sensory event. I pointed out that through both scientific research and clinical practice it had been discovered that the experience of pain was affected by numerous emotional, cognitive, and behavioral factors in addition to the specific noxious stimulation resulting from a disease process. We talked for some time about the possibility of some pain becoming "conditioned", just as other physiological processes can be learned. I gave him the example of the image of a lemon being cut open and the juices being squeezed out. Many patients will salivate as I describe this example; then they really understand how bodily processes can become learned, and thus respond to purely psychological stimuli. I informed him that psychological factors were involved in *all* chronic pain problems, not just his, and that the view of pain as being "in the head" *or* "in the body" had been discarded by modern science. I also explained that a number of psychological treatment methods had been developed to facilitate coping with pain, adjustment to lifestyle changes and self-management of painful sensations. I then proceeded with a psychological evaluation to determine whether I might be of help to him with his own particular pain problem.

What Is Health Psychology?

Health psychology is "the aggregate of the specific educational, scientific, and professional contributions of the discipline of psychology to the promotion and maintenance of health, the prevention and treatment of illness, and the identification of etiologic and diagnostic correlates of health, illness and related dysfunctions" (Matarazzo, 1980, p. 815). Given the breadth of the field, health psychologists engage in a wide variety of activities. In fact, probably very few health psychologists do exactly the same thing.

In the previous example I was functioning as a clinical health psychologist direct service provider. However, many other health psychologists are currently engaged in activities related to this man's problem. A colleague of mine directs a large pain clinic and through his administrative activities ensures comprehensiveness and quality of rehabilitation treatment efforts. Other health psychologists conduct research on the psychophysiological aspects of pain (i.e., what factors mediate the perception of and tolerance to painful stimuli? How can people learn more tolerance for pain?). Other health psychologists train physicians and health care providers to understand, identify, and manage the psychological aspects of chronic pain and illness.

Some health psychologists design prevention programs so both the general population and specific high-risk populations (e.g., secretaries, truck drivers, laborers with lifting duties) have the opportunity to learn how to modify their behavior to prevent back injuries. (Back pain is a very costly national health problem, both in terms of money spent and the patient suffering experienced. In fact, chronic pain of all types is estimated to cost $90 billion per year in the United States.) Other psychologists are working at the health policy level, trying to ensure that governmental funding is allocated to both research and clinical services in this area, and that certain safety precautions are available to workers on the job. In general, the activities in which health psychologists engage include:

1. clinical practice (diagnosis/assessment, consultation, intervention/treatment),
2. research,
3. teaching,

4. administration,

5. program development,

6. health policy formation.

Some health psychologists focus exclusively on one or more activities; others engage in some of each.

The field of health psychology has mushroomed within the past decade. In 1978 the American Psychological Association (APA) established a Division of Health Psychology in response to members' growing interests. Current membership is approximately 3,000 psychologists from many different subareas of psychology (e.g., clinical, counseling, school, industrial, physiological, experimental, neuropsychology, social, developmental, experimental). It is estimated that nearly 50% of these health psychologists are engaged in some direct patient contact at least some of the time. Guidelines for education and training in health psychology were developed at a national conference in 1983 and are described more fully later in this chapter. Stone's *Health psychology: A discipline and a profession* provides a comprehensive overview of issues in this rapidly growing field (Stone et al., 1987).

Sometimes there is confusion about the terms *health psychology* and *behavioral medicine*. All health psychologists work in the area of behavioral medicine. However, behavioral medicine is much broader in that it is an *interdisciplinary* field made up of many different disciplines, of which psychology is only one. The Society of Behavioral Medicine provides a scientific and professional forum for physicians, nurses, epidemiologists, health educators, public health specialists, nutritionists, dentists, physical therapists, and others who are committed to the integration of behavioral and biomedical sciences as they relate to health and disease.

The Background of Health Psychology

Interest in the psychological aspects of health is not new. In Western culture, the Hippocratic school of medicine viewed health as a natural balance of physical and emotional aspects, mediated by a harmonious mixture of the humors (for example, phlegm and choler). Writers throughout history have referred to the need for a healthy mind in order to maintain a healthy body. However, "mind" and "body" were often described as distinctly separate entities. With the

development of psychoanalysis came theories of how specific illnesses were caused by specific emotional conflicts. For example, some psychoanalysts believed that chronic pain sufferers were really suffering from guilt for a perceived misdeed, and that pain was a form of self-punishment. Ulcers were thought to be the result of unresolved feelings concerning dependency on the mother.

As the biobehavioral sciences moved toward more scientific rigor, some very interesting studies began to document the effect of psychological stress on bodily functions. For example, it was noted that people tended to show an increase in blood pressure when they were angry or upset. Later it was learned that people could use psychological methods to control their own blood pressure—something which previously had been believed would be impossible because blood pressure was mediated by the autonomic nervous system and thus not thought to be subject to voluntary control.

Overall, the past three decades have been marked by an increased focus on psychological, social, and biological determinants of health, illness, treatment, and prevention. One need only to review the recent reports of the Surgeon General of the United States to understand how *behavior* (especially eating, drinking, utilization of seat belts, drug usage, smoking, and exercise) has been implicated in many significant national health problems. Many disciplines have been involved in developing this body of knowledge, and psychology—as the science of behavior—has made very significant contributions. Although a review of these contributions is outside the scope of this chapter, a brief summary of some of the basic concepts in health psychology is given below. An excellent text by Feuerstein, Labbe, and Kuczmierczyk (1986) also provides an introductory review of basic knowledge in the field.

Basic Concepts in Health Psychology

Stress and Illness

The term *stress* is utilized by many people other than health psychologists, often in many different ways. For the purpose of this discussion, let us consider that stress has two components: *stressors* and the *stress response*. Stressors are those stimulus events that require some form of adaptation or adjustment. Stressors can be external physical or psychological stimuli (e.g., heat, cold, crowding, marital conflict, loss of loved one, job pressures), or internal physiological or psychological stimuli (e.g., pain, hunger, thoughts, feelings). Stressors may be *either* positive or negative in nature, and

are defined by whether or not they elicit the stress response in an individual. That is, not all people respond with the stress response to a particular stressor; stressors are often specific to individuals. However, there are some general stressors identified by Holmes and Rahe (1967) that many people will respond to (e.g., divorce, personal injury, marriage, retirement, change in residence, vacation), and in looking at data gathered from large groups of people, the accumulation of these stressors has been associated with increased incidence of illness.

The stress response has emotional, cognitive, physiological, and behavioral components. Physiological components include activation of the sympathetic and parasympathetic branches of the autonomic nervous system. Epinephrine and norepinephrine are released, as are hormones such as ACTH (adrenocorticotropic hormone) and endogenous morphine-like substances known as endorphins. Emotional responses include despair, fright, and joy. Cognitive components include the perception of the situation, concentration difficulties, and coping styles such as ignoring and distraction. Behavioral components may include withdrawal, avoidance, aggression, or facial expressions. Obviously the stress response itself is a very complex one, and the relation between stress and health or illness is even more complex.

Although there are many theories about the effects of stress in the etiology, exacerbation, and maintenance of disease, findings are often inconsistent, and more research in these areas is needed. These inconsistencies probably occur because so many different variables potentially mediate an individual's stress response (e.g., sense of personal control, positive attitude, social support), and because there has been considerable reliance on correlational research designs in the field.

At present, one of the most exciting areas in all of modern science is that of psychoneuroimmunology. For example, researchers Janice Kiecolt-Glaser and Ronald Glaser (1988) have completed studies documenting the effects of stress on the functioning of the immune system. It is also known that certain psychological treatment techniques (e.g., relaxation training) can enhance aspects of the immune system, although the relation of these findings to actual disease states is not yet understood. Continued research is required in order to identify the actual mechanisms through which psychological factors affect health.

Health psychologists are aware that illness itself, and the associated treatments, are also stressors for patients. Thus there is a great deal of focus on *coping* with illness. Lazarus and his

colleagues define coping as "the cognitive and behavioral efforts necessary to manage environmental and internal demands and the conflicts among them. These cognitive and behavioral actions, or efforts, are directed at mastering, tolerating, reducing, and/or minimizing environmental and internal demands and conflicts that strain an individual's resources" (Feuerstein et al., 1986, p. 162). As a result of her studies with female cancer patients, Taylor (1983) postulates that in the process of adaptation to illness, the patient makes an attribution about its cause, makes efforts at mastery (e.g., control of side effects of treatment, avoidance of recurrence of cancer), and engages in self-enhancing activities to restore self-esteem. Training in coping skills have become the focus for many interventions in health psychology.

Health Behavior

Another important concept in health psychology is health behavior. These behaviors may be preventive (e.g., dental checkups), avoidant (e.g., no smoking or drinking, avoidance of air pollution), or a reflection of specific health and safety practices (e.g., wearing seatbelts, having a first-aid kit, sleeping enough, watching weight, exercising, or complying with medical regimens).

One model used to understand health behavior is known as the health belief model (Becker & Maiman, 1975). This model has been useful in predicting participation in cancer screening, compliance to medical regimens and other health behaviors. Major aspects of the model include the individual's (1) belief in his or her susceptibility to an illness and (2) perception of the severity of the consequences of having the illness. Whether perceived health threats result in health-oriented behavior depends on the individual's analyses of the relative benefits and costs of the health behaviors involved. For example, an individual with hypertension who does not believe it to be a serious health problem, who experiences no immediate symptoms of the problem, and who does experience negative side effects of prescribed antihypertension medication is not likely to adhere to the prescribed treatment regimen.

Health behaviors have received more national attention since the 1979 Surgeon General's Report (Califano, 1979) provided convincing data indicating a strong relationship between personal habits and seven of the ten leading causes of death in the United States. This report provided an impetus for growth of the area of *behavioral health* within health psychology. Much effort has been devoted to methods for the modification of health behavior (e.g., smoking cessation, weight loss, dietary change to reduce sodium or

cholesterol) given research findings such as the direct relation between smoking cessation and reduction of risk for coronary heart disease, respiratory disease, and some kinds of cancer.

Illness Behavior

Another basic concept in health psychology is illness behavior. Patient responses to symptoms and illness vary considerably. Maladaptive illness behavior, such as a preoccupation with bodily symptoms, is often associated with overuse of the medical care system (which escalates national health costs) and negative emotional impact on the family. An organic basis for some patients' physical complaints cannot be found and their illness is thought to represent a "conversion" of a psychological problem to a physical one (conversion reaction).

The Scope of Health Psychology

By now it should be clear that health psychologists deal with a broad range of problems related to health and illness. In this section, we shall take a closer look at the range of activities involved. Several cases illustrating the kinds of methods utilized by the health psychologist will be described in more detail later.

Health psychology focuses on both experimental and applied problems. Research attempts to understand interactions among biological, psychological and social factors in health and disease (the biopsychosocial model) in order to (1) construct an accurate scientific model via creating new knowledge, (2) develop new methods of clinical practice, and (3) design new programs aimed at health enhancement and disease prevention. For example, health psychologists study how hormone levels affect mood states, how airport noise influences health, how psychological factors facilitate or impede recovery from a heart attack, or how addictions can be overcome. Applied health psychologists solve specific problems presented by individuals or consumer groups. Their activities include lobbying for legislation that affects health, treating individual patients and their families, or consulting to industry about job stress to decrease absenteeism.

As an example, one of my colleagues directs a hospital unit devoted to the care of children with diabetes, a disease that requires much behavioral self-management and compliance to medical

regimens. She has studied methods to help children learn to give their own injections of insulin; she also provides counseling to parents and pediatricians regarding the child's care (e.g., how to maximize compliance with the prescribed diets).

Another pediatric health psychologist I know has developed special films that can be shown to children before they go to the dentist so they will be less fearful while undergoing dental procedures. She also provides services to children who enter the hospital for surgical procedures. Such interventions result in less fear and anxiety on the part of the child, which in turn facilitates the provision of medical care without behavioral disruptions. I am aware of one case in which physicians could not perform a needed medical procedure (a spinal tap) on a young boy because he was so disruptive. After behavioral treatment, the child tolerated the procedure more calmly, and with much less pain, and the physicians were able to obtain the data they needed in order to make a diagnosis.

One health psychologist I know consults with industry. He provides special programs at the work site (including stress management, smoking cessation, and weight reduction) in an effort to improve workers' health. Many companies are interested in such programs because they know that healthier workers are more productive workers, and everyone can win by their provision of these services. Another health psychologist who consults with industry has a special contract to see employees through employee assistance programs (EAPs), which are now commonly found in companies. She provides confidential, individual consultation to employees in an attempt to resolve crises and identify needs for additional health care.

Other health psychologists apply their research and applied skills to real life problems such as:

1. Helping physicians to communicate more clearly with their patients.
2. Designing health-care systems to meet the needs of various ethnic groups.
3. Increasing women's skillfulness in detecting breast lumps through self-examination.
4. Providing psychological interventions for the nausea and vomiting that often accompanies chemotherapy for cancer.
5. Helping to develop a smoking prevention program for use in a local grammar school.

6. Assessing whether an elderly person is significantly depressed, suffering from an organic brain syndrome (e.g., Alzheimer's disease), or both.

7. Teaching patients how to cope with pain.

8. Helping nursing staff cope with their feelings about the death of a patient.

9. Training patients with memory problems in various strategies to improve memory.

10. Helping AIDS victims cope with their disease and its impact on their families.

Obviously, the specific methods utilized by the health psychologist will depend on the nature of the problem. However, whatever the methods utilized, the health psychologist usually gives consideration to the interplay among biological/physical, psychological, and social factors with respect to the individual patient, his/her family, and social network, the specific health-care system and the broader cultural context.

A special feature in health psychology is the need to cooperate with other professions and disciplines in order to provide adequate care or to conduct relevant research. The service provider interacts with numerous medical and surgical specialists, as well as with other health-care professionals. The researcher often depends on biomedical researchers for expertise concerning the measurement of disease. The prevention-oriented psychologist often interacts with public health officials and educational specialists. The health policy psychologist may spend substantial time interacting with personnel in governmental agencies and with elected officials. Some health psychologists interact with all of these groups.

CASE STUDIES

CASE ONE: PRESURGICAL EVALUATION

There are many men who have lost their ability to maintain an erection sufficient for sexual intercourse. This happens sometimes due to diseases that cause changes in the blood vessels, or because of side effects of medications, such as for high blood pressure. Since sexual functioning is such a basic part of human life, this can be very distressing to many men, and to their partners. However, medical technological advances within the past decade have made it possible for a urologic surgeon to implant a penile prosthesis. This

apparatus permits a man to have sexual intercourse using his own penis.

Every few weeks I provide consultation to someone who is considering this procedure. The surgeon who performs the operation requires that all such patients be seen prior to surgery for the purpose of psychological evaluation. This surgeon is very aware that sexual functioning can be affected by a number of psychological as well as medical factors, and that a successful technical surgery does not guarantee a successful behavioral outcome. This particular surgeon not only wants his patients to have successful outcomes, but also wants to avoid getting sued by unhappy, angry, dissatisfied customers! Let me tell you a little about Mr. B.

Mr. B., a 66-year old retired engineer, developed erectile failure gradually in association with his diabetes. He stated that he and his wife of 25 years had enjoyed a happy sex life until four years ago when his problem began. They had not had intercourse for over two years when I saw them. Prior to seeing Mr. B. I reviewed his medical record and spoke with the surgeon. I was informed that medical evaluation had revealed significant damage to his nerves, which would prohibit a natural erection in the future. The penile prosthesis was this man's only hope for intercourse. I decided to interview Mr. B. alone first.

Mr. B. was quite worried about seeing a psychologist, since he had never done so before and came from a generation and a culture in which people did not talk openly about sexual functioning and private matters. In addition, since it was acknowledged that my report had some bearing on the surgeon's decision about whether to operate, I was a potential "roadblock" to his perceived future happiness. Establishing rapport was a high priority, because this is critical to being able to conduct an adequate evaluation.

I elicited Mr. B.'s concerns about the evaluation and then communicated that I understood his perspective and was sensitive to the difficulties this posed for him. I also conveyed a perspective of my role that was broader than being a "roadblock"; I suggested that we might discover together ways in which his sexual functioning could be facilitated with or without the prosthesis. In any case, he needed to recognize that his physicians know that sexual functioning is as much psychological as physiological, and that I was part of the professional team that worked with all patients considering this surgery. He was not being singled out. In addition, I assured him that it was important for him to have a full understanding of the nature of the procedure, about which I would ask him many questions.

During my interview, which lasted over an hour, I asked Mr. B. about his understanding of what would actually happen to him and how it would affect him physically, emotionally, and behaviorally. I asked him what his understanding of the surgery was, how painful he believed it would be, what the period of recuperation would be, what he thought sex would be like afterward, what changes he expected in his penis, what experience he had had with illness or surgery before, how he felt about the surgeon, what questions were yet unanswered, whether he felt he would like to talk with a previous recipient of an implant, how he expected his wife to react, what he might do if the surgery were unsuccessful (or the implant malfunctioned at a later date), plus numerous other questions.

My training as a clinical psychologist before I became a health psychologist gave me the skills to conduct these interviews in a manner that provides reliable data. However, my training as a clinical psychologist did not cover the information I needed to conduct these evaluations, because I must also know the realistic answers to the questions I ask! Overall, my training and experience have honed my skill at observation, how to follow up on important leads, how to interpret specific data in the context of other data, and so on.

I had three major goals during this interview: (1) to assess how realistic Mr. B.'s expectations about the surgery are; (2) to determine whether he has any psychopathology or emotional problem likely to interfere with the outcome; (3) to determine which behavioral factors might interfere with hospitalization or recuperation (e.g., anesthesia anxiety, compliance). I have seen patients who were convinced that the prosthesis would provide a cure for their marital problems, ensure a larger penis, or help them function as they did in their early twenties.

Research in this area has shown that patients with unrealistic expectations are more likely to have significant problems after the surgery. In addition, patients who are significantly depressed are at higher risk in any surgical procedure; for these patients elective surgery is often best postponed until the depression has been treated. The level of intellectual functioning in other patients, in combination with their interpersonal passivity and intimidation by physicians, may result in a lack of knowledge concerning surgical risks and need for planning for recuperation. These patients, without additional counseling, are not able to give full informed consent to the procedure.

Mr. B. had read quite a bit about the procedure; in addition, he had visited the library and watched numerous TV programs on the subject. He knew that some of the information he had obtained

from TV was sensationalized. Overall, he appeared to have a realistic understanding of the procedure itself and his probable capacities for postsurgical sexual functioning. I did not find evidence of significant emotional problems, nor did I have concerns that he would not be able to comply with the medical regimen or deal with the need for recuperation.

Because I also interview the patient's partner, I asked Mrs. B. to enter the interview after the first hour. The three of us met for an additional hour. It turned out that Mrs. B. had not really discussed the surgical procedure with her husband, telling him merely to "do as he liked." Although she initially expressed support for him, it soon became clear that she was quite anxious and upset about the impending resumption of sexual activity. Sex had not been very pleasurable for her, because it tended to be something that was organized around his needs (although she had never directly expressed hers). Since the decrease in ability to maintain erections, other sexual activity had ceased as well, and she was somewhat relieved to no longer have the demands for sex that she had experienced from him in the past. In fact she was quite angry about having to deal with sex again "at my age," and threatened to withhold opportunities from him, telling him he could "get it elsewhere."

Mr. B. was surprised by his wife's attitude. Surgery was postponed pending completion of a trial of counseling sessions which were conducted in the absence of the potential for intercourse. Mrs. B. was helped to express her emotional and sexual needs. Mr. B. was trained to provide alternative means of sexual stimulation and satisfaction. The couple's communication pattern was identified and problem areas noted. Later surgery resulted in a successful technical and psychological outcome; indeed, Mrs. B. reported that she enjoyed sex more than she had in their previous 25 years of marriage, and had significantly revised her attitudes about sexuality and aging.

It is especially noteworthy here that even when the purpose of a professional encounter is assessment, the process of assessment is itself an intervention that can upset a seemingly stable situation. The clinical health psychologist is sensitive to these issues, and ready to provide therapeutic interventions where needed. This case required data concerning biological, sociocultural and psychological processes in order to adequately diagnose and treat. In this case I relied on medical experts and self-report of *both* the patient and his spouse. I did not find it necessary to conduct more formal psychological testing or behavioral assessment (other ways to measure behavior and to obtain data), although in some cases these might be

necessary if the psychologist's hypotheses about the nature of the problems are not well supported from interview data alone. ♦

CASE TWO: EVALUATION OF A HEADACHE TREATMENT PROGRAM

I am currently working on the evaluation of the headache treatment program we developed some years ago. This treatment program is based on current psychological research demonstrating the effectiveness of psychological methods such as biofeedback, cognitive behavioral therapies, and relaxation training in the treatment of chronic migraine and tension headache. Headache is one of the most frequent reasons for seeking medical care, and a number of psychological methods have been found to be very effective in treatment.

One method of treatment for both tension and migraine headache is that of *biofeedback*. This treatment involves making information concerning specific biological processes available to the patient through the provision of precise feedback about a particular physiological variable. Many different kinds of biofeedback (blood pressure, rectal sphincters, temperature) are used for different problems. A specific muscle group is thought to be related to tension headaches (i.e., the frontalis muscle in the forehead). Electrodes are placed on the skin above this muscle and muscle tension is measured with electromyographic recordings. When the patient is provided with information on the exact levels of tension in this muscle, he or she can learn how to control the muscle, relax it much more fully, and thus eliminate muscle contraction-related pain. The rate of improvement with this treatment averages around 50 to 60%, although some clinics report significantly higher rates of improvement (Andrasik & Blanchard, 1987).

A broader and increasingly more effective headache treatment method is cognitive behavioral therapy. This treatment more explicitly considers the emotional, cognitive and behavioral aspects of headache problems and trains the patient to identify stimuli associated with increased headache (triggers), to identify adaptive and maladaptive coping responses to these triggers and to engage in more adaptive coping behavior.

The headache treatment program in our setting functions in the context of a large health maintenance organization (HMO), the most rapid growing method of health-care delivery in the United States. We have provided both individual and group treatment services to a number of headache patients and have been very satisfied with the results. In fact, the consulting psychiatrist, who had no prior experience with these kinds of treatments, has been very

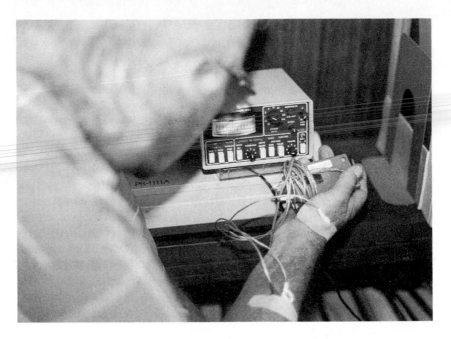

This man is receiving visual biofeedback that will enhance the precision of his muscle control. (Courtesy of the editor, Robert Gifford.)

impressed by the clinical progress of the patients. He was aware that most of these patients have long histories of not responding to previous psychiatric and medical treatments. Research on the effectiveness of the current psychological treatments has been done, but our program has only "testimonial" evidence of its success in our setting. This kind of evidence is very common in health-care settings, and the *scientific* basis for the effectiveness of the intervention is usually established elsewhere (e.g., a university research setting).

Because our HMO setting is a prepaid health-care system, there is an incentive to find the most *cost-effective* methods of treatment for various problems. For example, if headache could be treated equally effectively with either individual or group treatment, we would choose to offer the group treatment whenever possible. Historically, researchers in university settings rarely consider treatment time, effort, and cost as variables in clinical outcome research. In fact, the more expensive the procedure, the more money the health-care provider might make! However, given the escalation of health-care costs and society's inability and unwillingness to pay

the price, there is more and more incentive to examine treatment-related costs. A prepaid managed health-care system is an ideal place to study such issues; in fact, future health-care management teams will require such evidence in order to allocate resources to specific programs.

In order to undertake a cost-effectiveness study of our own headache program, we need data on (1) how patients were doing prior to treatment, (2) how they are doing after treatment and at least one year later, and (3) the costs of providing the health psychology treatment. It is also important to know the cost of providing other health-care services to the patient for a period of time prior to treatment and after treatment. These latter data are usually called medical utilization data. Previous research has demonstrated that decreases in medical utilization often offset the cost of providing psychological services themselves, but medical utilization cost offset data in regard to health psychology services are less well documented. This is an important issue for the development of health policy, because the most cost-effective treatments will receive more of the health-care dollar in the future.

It is also interesting that the federal government is undertaking a study of the *quality of care* given to medicare recipients by 300,000 individual physicians. These data will be made public, with the expectation that they will guide consumers' choices of physicians in the future. Although similar evaluations of applied psychology have not yet been undertaken, health-care psychology may be the first area studied. The future of our profession depends on our ability to compete successfully in this arena. The industrialization of health care has already occurred.

To accomplish our program evaluation, we use standard information obtained from every clinic patient. This information is available because we utilize a patient-completed questionnaire to help guide our interviewing. We can easily extract data concerning headache, including duration, intensity, frequency, associated symptoms, location, and nature of pain. Patients also report the amount of interferences with work, recreational, and family activities that their headaches cause. At the end of treatment we often ask the patients to complete a follow-up questionnaire with many items identical to the pretreatment survey. We also have information from the clinical progress notes, as well as patient diaries that are kept as part of program participation. However, we have been less consistent in gathering follow-up data in a *formal* manner. Thus another survey of all patients who have completed the pro-

gram is needed to have the kind of data that we can submit to statistical analyses.

Our most difficult problem will be to accurately assess "medical utilization." We have decided to count visits to physicians, radiologic studies and hospitalizations. Tracking the amount of medication consumed would be impossible given the information available in medical charts (and patient self-reports in this area are notoriously unreliable), so we have decided to forego it for this study. However, we are considering how to better capture this information for future program evaluations. The management of our organization will be able to provide cost estimates for physician visits, radiographic procedures, hospital stays, and so on.

Using statistical techniques we will analyze our data to assess patient improvement (effectiveness) and cost. We will also work toward the similar analyses for headache patients who receive other kinds of treatments to compare and determine cost-effectiveness of various treatments. Given the limited amount of funds available for health on a national level, many health psychologists believe we must learn which treatments or procedures return the "biggest bang for the buck". ♦

CASE THREE: TREATMENT OF CHRONIC PAIN PATIENTS

The treatment group I conduct for patients who suffer from chronic pain is oriented toward helping patients learn to cope with pain, to control their own pain where possible, and to maximize their daily functioning in the face of pain. Medical or surgical approaches have not helped these group members. Most have suffered for five years or more. They are not in a psychologist's group because it is "imaginary pain." Their pain is related to medical problems that cannot be cured. Nevertheless, as noted in the introductory example, psychological methods can still be useful.

The group sessions last approximately ten weeks after which there is a follow-up group for "alumni" to meet once a month to support others' progress and continuation of self-control methods. Patient referrals come from neurologists, physiatrists (rehabilitation medicine specialists), neurosurgeons, orthopedic surgeons, and mental health professionals. Some pain problems include postsurgical pain (e.g., post-mastectomy for cancer), low back pain, neck pain, and post-herpetic neuralgia. We do several different things in each session. In the educational component, I provide information about self-management or about psychological factors

that affect pain. In the psychotherapy component we analyze patients' individual situations; and, in the skills training component, patients practice methods of self-control or problem solving to help cope better with their pain.

One topic might be *relaxation response*. This response, which is the opposite of the fight-or-flight response, is associated with lower blood pressure, decreased muscle tension, lower respiration, increased hand temperature, lower heart rate, and a number of other signs of lower physiological arousal. There are many different methods of learning the relaxation response, and relaxation training is one of the most useful tools of the clinical health psychologist. We know that more physiological arousal is associated with greater experience of pain; relaxation is associated with a diminished experience of pain. In a session, patients actually practice one of the relaxation methods currently used—autogenic training. To measure how each person is doing, small temperature monitors are held by each person. Many patients increased their fingertip temperature over 5°F during their first attempt! They were very impressed by the influence their behavior could have over their physiology, and how this relaxed state was one of more comfort and less pain. They agreed to practice twice daily for the next week.

Other methods used in the group include appropriate goal setting, diary keeping, biofeedback training, discussion of family interactions, analysis of emotions and their effect on pain and suffering, discussion of how to deal with the health-care system, review of issues in medication usage, and mutual emotional support. Sometimes family members attend for consultation on how to deal with related problems. Many members say that the group has provided an opportunity to interact with others with similar problems, and that for them it was the first time that they felt understood. As group members learn, they become very helpful to one another in identifying when someone's behavior may be increasing pain habits or suffering. There is substantial peer pressure to maximize healthful activity and to avoid taking on the role of an invalid.

My role is to provide information and specific skill training and to manage the group process in a therapeutic manner. I must be alert to the possibility of "psychological casualties," and use my clinical skills to continually assess individual problems. I use elements of various theoretical frameworks, including cognitive behavioral, social learning, and psychodynamic approaches.

Some people do not benefit from this group; they tend to drop out early. However, others make dramatic changes that are attested to by family members and manifested by significant increases in

occupational and recreational activities. Mr. F. no longer uses a cane to walk and has stopped complaining continuously about how bad he feels. In fact he now feels more chipper and has started part-time work. Mrs. C. has resumed favored activities that she had avoided before because of embarrassment over her disabilities. Mr. S. no longer takes so much pain medication that he is "drugged out" most of the time.

Most patients report that the group participation was extremely helpful, although for different reasons. Some indicate that the relaxation training was the most useful component, and that it gave them a sense of control over their pain. Others report that keeping a diary allowed them to plan their activities better, and helped them become more self-observant about their own behavior. Some felt better able to deal with their depressive feelings after the group experience. Others corrected long-standing family problems that they believed had made their pain problem worse. Because most patients, to some extent, want to please me by telling me how much I've helped, I try to verify behavior change through multiple sources of data, and encourage participation in the follow-up group to promote maintenance of treatment gains. ♦

Becoming a Health Psychologist

In 1983, leaders in the field of health psychology met for a five-day national conference at Arden House, New York. These leaders developed a set of recommendations to guide the development of education and training for future health psychologists, some of which are summarized here. The doctoral degree was acknowledged as the entry level into the profession.

There is wide agreement in the field that education in the *broad* discipline of psychology is fundamental to health psychology. This includes knowledge and skills in: statistics, research design and methodology, psychological measurement, history and systems of psychology, biological bases of behavior, social bases of behavior, cognitive bases of behavior, affective bases of behavior, individual differences, scientific and professional ethics, legal issues and professional standards. "Learning how to learn" is a major goal, and is psychology's only protection against obsolescence.

Core education in health psychology includes the attainment of additional knowledge and skills, specifically in the social, biologi-

cal, and psychological bases of health and disease, health policy and organization, health measurement, and research methods pertinent to specific areas (e.g., epidemiological methods, biostatistics, and clinical trials). The depth of focus on specific content areas and the particular research skills taught will vary across programs depending on the student's focus within health psychology. An overall goal is the integration of biological, psychological, and social aspects of health and disease.

An essential component in the education of health psychologists is the exposure to the health-care system itself. There must be opportunities to develop skills in working with other health-care disciplines (e.g., physicians, nurses, public health officials), and to learn about political and economic aspects of health care and how they might affect psychological research and practice. For example, discharge from the hospital is sometimes determined by insurance coverage, not disease status. Using hospital discharge as a measure of disease status could then lead to false conclusions. Furthermore, there are certain customs associated with the health-care culture that health psychologists must be aware of, or they may be excluded from participation! Fundamental to education and training in health psychology is the availability of psychologists who can serve as role models in the student's area of training. These role models serve as mentors, without which the educational process will be inadequate.

If someone wants to become a practitioner of health psychology (i.e., provide health psychology services), even more additional training is required. These psychologists need knowledge, skills, and supervised experience in assessment, intervention, consultation, and evaluation. The specific skills will vary, of course, depending on the context (individual patients, consumer groups, industrial settings, communities, legislatures, etc.) but they must be *broad* in nature, extending along the whole continuum of behavior (both "normal" and "abnormal"). A one-year predoctoral internship (supervised applied experience) is also required and a postdoctoral training experience is recommended if one wishes to practice independently.

While a survey of doctoral programs in health psychology was completed some years ago (Belar, Wilson, & Hughes, 1982), the most current information can be obtained from the Society of Behavioral Medicine[1] which recently conducted a survey of education and training opportunities in the area. Another source of information is the Division of Health Psychology, which can be reached through the American Psychological Association (APA). As yet, there is no

accreditation process (i.e., external quality assurance by the APA) for training programs in health psychology as there is for clinical, counseling, and school psychology, although many APA accredited clinical psychology programs have an emphasis in health psychology. In the future, there may very well be accreditation for clinical health psychology programs as well.

Health psychologists are employed in a variety of settings. Earlier surveys have found that universities, medical centers, and private practice account for approximately 60% of health psychologists (Morrow & Clayman, 1982). Other opportunities exist in managed health-care systems, government agencies, nonhealthcare industries, and private research groups. As the trend toward increased accountability for the expenditure of health-care dollars continues, more opportunities are likely to become available, as many health psychologists will possess a unique blend of both applied and research skills that will increase value to managed health-care systems. In addition, as scientific study reveals more knowledge about the interaction among psychological and biological factors in health and disease, there will be more opportunities for direct clinical service provision in these areas (e.g., assessment and diagnosis, treatment and intervention, consultation, program development and evaluation). It is indeed a healthy field.

ENDNOTE

[1] P.O. Box 1277, Rockville, MD 20850

SUGGESTED READINGS AND REFERENCES

ANDRASIK, F., & BLANCHARD, E. B. (1987). The biofeedback treatment of tension headache. In J. P. Hatch, J. G. Fisher, J. D. Rugh (Eds.) *Biofeedback: Studies in clinical efficacy*. New York: Plenum.

BECKER, M. H., & MAIMAN, L. A. (1975). Sociobehavioral determinants of compliance with health and medical care recommendations. *Medical Care, 13*, 10–24.

BELAR, C. D., DEARDORFF, W. W., & KELLY, K. E. (1987). *The practice of clinical health psychology*. New York: Pergamon Press.

BELAR, C. D., WILSON, E., & HUGHES, H. (1982). Health psychology training in doctoral psychology programs. *Health Psychology, 1*, 289–299.

CALIFANO, J. A., Jr. (1979). *Healthy people: The Surgeon General's report on health promotion and disease prevention.* Washington, DC: Superintendent of Documents, U.S. Government Printing Office, 017-001-00416-2.

COHEN, F., & LAZARUS, R. S. (1979). Coping with the stresses of illness. In G. C. Stone, F. Cohen, & N. E. Adler (Eds.). *Health psychology.* San Francisco: Jossey-Bass.

FEUERSTEIN, M., LABBE, E. E., & KUCZMIERCZYK, A. R. (1986). *Health psychology: A psychobiological perspective.* New York: Plenum.

HOLMES, T. H., & RAHE, R. H. (1967). The social readjustment rating scale. *Journal of Psychosomatic Research, 11,* 213–218.

KIECOLT-GLASER, J. K., & GLASER, R. (1988). Psychological influences on immunity: Implications for AIDS. *American Psychologist, 43,* 892–898.

MATARAZZO, J. D. (1980). Behavioral health and behavioral medicine: Frontiers for a new health psychology. *American Psychologist, 35,* 807–817.

MATARAZZO, J. D., WEISS, S. M., HERD, J. A., MILLER, N. E., & WEISS, S. M. (Eds.) (1984). *Behavioral health: A handbook of health enhancement and disease prevention.* New York: Wiley.

MELZACK, R., & WALL, P. D. (1965). Pain mechanisms: A new theory. *Science, 150,* 971–979.

STONE, G. C., WEISS, S. M., MATARAZZO, J. D., MILLER, N. E., RODIN, J., BELAR, C. D., FOLLICK, M., & SINGER, J. E. (Eds.). (1987). *Health psychology: A discipline and a profession.* Chicago: University of Chicago Press.

TAYLOR, S. E. (1983). Adjustment to threatening events: A theory of cognitive adaptation. *American Psychologist, 38,* 1161–1173.

JOHN DURKIN

John Durkin worked for 14 years with young people in Toronto, Ontario, and in Victoria, British Columbia. Some of this work involved counseling young people contacted on the street or in other locations where young people meet. Other parts of it included providing youth programs and administering a large camp. He then completed his Ph.D. at the University of Victoria in physical education, specializing in the mental and social aspects of play, recreation, and sport. His graduate work won prizes from the Canadian Association of Sport Sciences and the Canadian Association for Psychomotor Learning and Sport Psychology. Dr. Durkin has published over 200 popular and academic articles plus a book and chapters in three other books. He has given numerous workshops in various courses in these areas, and hosted his own television show. He has a black belt in karate and maintains an active interest in the spiritual, mental, and physical aspects of martial arts training for both himself and those who train with him. ♦

7

The Sport Psychologist

A few weeks after I had given a workshop to a figure skating club, one of the senior skaters contacted me for help. She often let personal problems interfere with her performance and had considerable difficulty dealing with anxiety while waiting for her event to occur.

The skater's anxiety was combatted by teaching her relaxation and visualization techniques that could be used as either part of her training program or before her event, by teaching her to "park" her problems, and by establishing with her a fixed routine that she could follow before her competitions in order to give her time some structure.

The relaxation and visualization techniques used were similar to those discussed later in the chapter. After the skater had learned to relax, we worked together to develop a mental film of a strong performance. Producing a visualization sequence for this skater required putting together different aspects of several of her performances so that she had the feeling of an ideal event.

I told the skater to "park" the problems she could do nothing about at the time. She formed an image of wrapping them up in a tidy bundle and putting them at the bottom of her gym bag. She did not have to worry about losing the problems since she could always go and unwrap them again when it was time to deal with them. On the other hand, she might eventually want to take the package and throw it in the garbage.

Establishing a fixed routine for the skater before and between events was the last phase of the program. This routine included a series of steps with a mental check-off list. While part of the routine involved the visualization procedure, mundane items such as food and water also were included. The skater understood that this routine would have to be changed depending on the amount of time that was available.

There were other dimensions of her skating that could have been worked on, but the athlete's funds were limited. Even the two or three new techniques she learned improved her performance and, more importantly from my point of view, her enjoyment of the sport.

Like this skater, all athletes have maximum levels at which they potentially can perform a certain activity. No one, including the people involved, knows what this level is but only that it is different for each person and is composed of physical and psychological factors. Physical training and conditioning attempt to develop the athlete in terms of strength, stamina, and suppleness. The responsibility of a sport psychologist involved in competitive athletics, on the other hand, is to develop the psychological or mental and

emotional resources of the athlete to reach further toward the maximum performance potential. Because most elite athletes are prepared well physically, the difference in results during a competition is often due to these mental and emotional factors.

Other sport psychologists are concerned with community-based athletics and recreation programs rather than with elite athletes. They are involved in helping both adults and children increase the physical, mental, and emotional benefits of their recreation experience. They might also be concerned with why people do or do not stick to exercise and weight-control programs.

Sport psychologists, then, deal with clients ranging from the world class athlete or team to those with an interest in physical activity for recreation or health reasons. They can help all athletes to improve mental skills for better performance or devise ways of enhancing mental and emotional satisfaction from the sport or recreation activity. These approaches are not mutually exclusive. A mental trainer working with elite athletes tries to ensure that these athletes benefit psychologically from their performances and one dealing with community recreation teaches techniques to improve athletic performance.

The following three examples should help to illustrate the different types of approaches that a sport psychologist might take. In the first case, a figure skating club asked me to help deal with the difficulty that some skaters encountered in completing certain jumps and with the stress of competition. Some routines in figure skating involve controlling fear and anxiety about falling. As well, the figure skater must often wait a considerable length of time before his or her routine starts. This waiting leads to high stress levels for many.

The club initially wanted to know if I could come and speak about psychological techniques that they could use to help them with their problems. They were hoping that a two-hour session would give them the skills that were necessary. I had to tell them that this would not likely happen as learning mental skills takes practice in the same way that learning physical skills does. I agreed, however, to speak to them about the kinds of things that could be done.

In the second case, a martial arts club approached me about how their members could obtain more of the mental rewards that supposedly occur in the martial arts. They felt that their club was missing this aspect of their training in that they were practicing their techniques and kata (routines) but were not seeing the types of psychological changes they expected.

This club was prepared for long-term involvement and knew that I had a black belt in a martial art and considerable experience in the area. They nevertheless wanted to meet with me as a group to discuss the kinds of programs and skills I had to offer. In addition, I detected a certain amount of anxiety from the sensei (club leader or teacher) that I might usurp some of his authority.

In the third case, a man approached me with difficulties in controlling his weight and maintaining an exercise program. He wanted to know if any of the techniques used by sport psychologists would be of help to him. Again he was looking for a quick fix and was surprised to find that learning either the mental or behavioral techniques he needed would involve some effort on his part.

What Is Sport Psychology?

Sport psychology is a relatively new field. As a result there is not a good definition of what is included and what is not, but most sport psychologists focus on one or all of three aspects: (1) motor learning, (2) mental and emotional processes, and (3) social relations. From a motor learning point of view, people want to know about the conditions that promote or retard the learning of a motor skill. An example of a strong motor learning approach is a recent advertisement for a position in human motor performance. Areas mentioned for possible research included biomechanics, neurosciences, engineering, ergonomics, and cybernetics.

Other sport psychologists are more interested in the mental and emotional factors that influence performance and the psychological outcomes of physical activity. They also might study what children learn in play or what value individual people obtain from their recreation. Often they are interested in how the psychological make-up and training of the athlete influence performance. Typical concerns for this group would be stress control, visualization, and centering. This approach to sport psychology, the main focus of this chapter, started to become a distinct discipline from motor learning in the 1960s. The process is still continuing.

The third group of scientists look at sport from a more social point of view. They are interested in questions such as violence in sport, reasons for engaging in particular sports, the role of the spectator, and the overall character of particular sports.

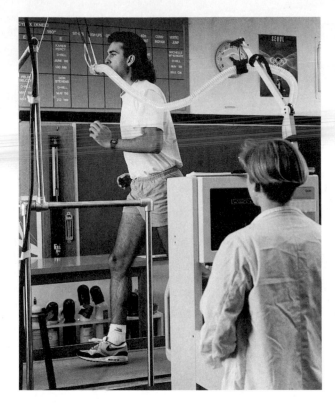

Analysis of physiological output during treadmill exercise improves understanding of athletic performance. (Courtesy of the editor, Robert Gifford.)

While three areas have been distinguished, many sport psychologists are involved in at least the teaching of all areas and may have research or training involvement in more than one.

Background of Sport Psychology

People who work in the area of sport psychology are divided about when the field began. Some see the beginning of sport psychology in the mental training techniques that were used by athletes and soldiers throughout history. Perhaps the best known of these is the training of the samurai in traditional Japan. In addition to high

levels of physical skill, these warriors were taught techniques to relieve stress, focus attention, control their own pain and thought processes, and other skills used today in psychological training for sport.

The importance of samurai training methods should not be exaggerated, however, because many people tend to attribute to mental training the kinds of powers that border on the occult. In fact, effort rather than magic is required. In addition, ethical sport psychologists would not use techniques that have the potential to damage the athlete and certainly would not agree to the sacrifice of self in commitment to the team that appears to have been expected of the warrior.

In an academic sense, the field of sport psychology is usually described as starting with articles produced just prior to 1900. This early material is best illustrated by Coleman Griffith's reports in the 1920s and 1930s. He studied the nature of psychomotor skills, motor learning, and the relationship between personality variables and motor performance. He published books such as *The Psychology of Coaching* and *Psychology and Athletics*. Other authors working at the same time wrote about motor learning and coaching. From the beginning there seems to have been a split into psychomotor learning and a more psychological approach to sport.

Many of the studies before the 1920s also were interested in the psychological benefits that could be obtained from regular sport and fitness activities. These benefits ranged from the ability to concentrate and work longer periods of time to the development of leadership and group identity. Sport was praised because of its contribution to society and not because it was fun. A few researchers at the turn of the century examined psychomotor topics that are still of interest today. These included reaction time, perception, and the transfer of learning from one sport to another.

From the 1930s to the end of World War II there was little interest in sport psychology. In the late 1940s, however, interest in courses and research in motor learning and sport psychology grew once more. Studies of the effect of psychological conditions on sport activity, the psychological benefits of sport, and psychological factors involved in motor learning and control were done again. Most people involved in this research and in the formation of organizations related to sport psychology had a physical education background rather than psychology. This continues to be the situation today.

The International Society of Sports Psychology grew out of the First International Congress of Psychology of Sport held in Rome in 1965. At this meeting, a group of North American researchers interested in sport psychology and motor learning decided to organize a group for Canada and the United States. This occurred before a meeting of physical educators held in Chicago the next year when the North American Society for the Psychology of Sport and Physical Activity (NASPSPA) was formed.

During the Second International Conference of Sport Psychology, held in Washington in 1968, several Canadian researchers began forming the Canadian Society for Psychomotor Learning and Sport Psychology (CSPLSP). This organization met under the auspices of the Canadian Association for Health, Physical Education, and Recreation from 1969 until 1977, when it became a separate society. CSPLSP is now developing closer ties with the Canadian Association of Sport Sciences.

Before 1970 it was possible to keep track of all the major publications in sport psychology throughout the world, but this has not been true since; indeed there has been an explosion of books related to sport psychology. Some are designed for those involved in the training of athletes and are the most detailed in terms of their descriptions of procedures and results. Others have been developed for the athletes themselves and contain strategies that can be used without the benefit of someone trained in the area. There also are a number of audio- and videotapes that fit in this category. A few are designed for anyone interested in sport and the training of athletes.

Finally, in the 1980s there have been several popular writers who have jumped on the sport psychology bandwagon with books and tapes that are supposed to extend the principles of sport psychology to all areas of life. Often these books describe the performances of elite athletes and imply that these results can be obtained by anyone through the use of some psychological technique. The books usually do not mention the tremendous physical effort these athletes make to condition and train their bodies, nor do they emphasize that learning mental skills takes as much effort and dedication as the learning of physical skills. Because of lack of success with the techniques people come to doubt the value of mental training and lose the opportunity to incorporate very valuable techniques into their lives.

The Scope of Sport Psychology

Breadth of Field

Sport psychology comprises a broad range of topics. Salmela (1979) conducted a content analysis of research in sport psychology for the years 1969 to 1979 and found that the most frequently occurring topics were the effects of personality factors, attitudes, competitive anxiety, and achievement motivation on sport. More recently the emphasis has been on sport performance enhancement with a great increase in research on self-control, imagery, concentration, relaxation, and cognitive skill development. The focus on elite athletes also has been broadened to include youth sport and recreation activities (Salmela, 1982).

Psychological Foundations in Sport (Silva & Weinberg, 1984), a text often used in undergraduate sport psychology courses, is a good collection of articles written by a number of prominent sport psychologists. This book, which tries to cover most of the field, has eight sections:

1. evolution of sport psychology;
2. personality and performance in sport;
3. anxiety, arousal, and performance;
4. motivation;
5. aggression and sport;
6. group dynamics in sport;
7. issues in sport socialization;
8. exercise and psychological well-being.

The breadth of the field also is indicated by the tables of contents of journals. Volumes of *Journal of Sport and Exercise Psychology* for 1988 and 1989 for instance carried articles on topics ranging from imagery theory through stress management and gender differences in attribution to group cohesion and psychological factors related to athletic injuries.

Sport psychologists use a number of different types of measuring devices to evaluate psychological conditions among athletes under different conditions. Some of these tests were developed for a specific study and may not be suitable for other conditions. Others have shown good levels of consistency when used repeatedly with the same subject as well as agreement with other accepted indi-

cators of a particular psychological state such as anxiety. Examples of the more accepted tests include the Sport Competitive Anxiety Test or SCAT (Martens, 1977), the Profile of Mood States or POMS (McNair, Lorr, & Droppleman, 1971), and the Test of Attentional and Interpersonal Style or TAIS (Nideffer, 1976).

The SCAT is designed to measure specifically the anxiety a person generally feels in a competitive sport situation. It has been used in studies such as the one which showed that those junior high school athletes who had high SCAT scores reported more frequent evaluation and performance worries and more anticipated negative feelings when they anticipated playing poorly (Rainey, Conklin, & Rainey, 1987).

The POMS is a measure of an individual's mood state at a particular period of time. It has the six subscales of tension–anxiety, depression–dejection, anger–hostility, vigor–activity, fatigue–inertia, and confusion–bewilderment. An interesting result of this test is the so-called "iceberg effect" (Morgan, 1980): High-level athletes tend to show lower levels of tension, depression, anger, fatigue, and confusion than the general population but higher levels of vigor.

The TAIS has six measures of attentional style, two measures of behavioral and cognitive control, and eight measures of interpersonal style. The six scales on the attentional style component of the TAIS are probably the ones that have received the most attention. Three of the scales, broad-external, broad-internal, and narrow focus indicate components of effective focusing while the other three scales, external-overload, internal-overload, and reduced focus, indicate ineffective focus. Nideffer (1985) used the concepts of width of focus (broad versus narrow) and direction of focus (external versus internal) to present what he considered to be the best area to attend to during different activities. Although studies such as the one done by Reis and Bird (1982), which showed that broad attenders had faster reaction times than narrow attenders under conditions of low anxiety with the reverse being the case under conditions of higher anxiety, support aspects of the TAIS, but the validity of the attentional style scales has been questioned in terms of their prediction of how visual information is processed (Dewey, Brawley, & Allard, 1989).

Research Approaches

As well as a broad range of interests, those who study sport psychology also differ in their approach to research. One approach involves

controlled studies in a laboratory environment. For instance, a sport psychologist might want to know whether visualization practice helps in learning to shoot baskets from the foul line in basketball. The researcher using the controlled approach might have four groups. The members of each group would be tested initially to see how many baskets they could score out of 50 throws without any training. The control group would then be told not to practice any basketball until the final test was made in six or eight weeks. Group B might spend 15 minutes, three times per week practicing shooting baskets. Group C would also practice three times per week but half of their practice sessions would involve only visualizing the shooting of baskets. A fourth group, Group D, would do only the visualization and would not do any physical practice.

Visualization on the court during practice. (Courtesy of the editor, Robert Gifford.)

Typical results from such experiments show that the control group does not improve very much, the group that only used visualization improves somewhat, and there is no significant difference between those that spent all of the practice time actually shooting baskets and those that spent half of the time shooting baskets and half of the time in visualization. In other words, physical practice was necessary but visualization was as good as actually shooting baskets, provided a certain level of physical training also was maintained.

Other researchers question the validity of these types of studies as indicators of a player's performance in an actual game setting. In the game, there is much more pressure on the athlete than in the controlled study where there are no crowds and no pressure from other players. These researchers would prefer to do "field" studies that involve actual athletic activity.

These researchers might measure the foul shooting percentages for all the athletes during a number of games before any of the experimental conditions began to get some baseline data. They would then have four groups as in the previous study except that now results would be measured in terms of shooting percentages in actual game situations.

Initially, the second method might seem to be the only way to go, but it also has some difficulties. The major one is its lack of control over the other factors that might influence shooting percentages. For instance, in the earlier games there might be less pressure than in later games, so percentages might be lower in later games. Also it is hard to control the level of practice outside of experimental sessions of athletes who are involved in competitive sports.

You may have recognized that one way to get around at least part of this difficulty is to use the scores of the control group. Provided the control group has the same game experience as the experimental groups, then we could expect that any changes that might occur in control group scores would also occur in the other groups and change the experimental groups' scores to reflect this difference.

There are many questions in sport psychology that reflect this controversy about the superiority of one experimental approach over another. For instance, does improving reaction time by teaching athletes to control anxiety result in improved performance during competition? Or does teaching concentration techniques lead to better results in target shooting?

Relaxation, Concentration, and Visualization

Relaxation, concentration, and visualization are important components of all approaches to mental training for sport activity. A person who wants to use many of the sport psychology training tools that are available must first be able to relax. Actually, relaxation involves concentration and, in cognitive methods, visualization as well; so all three skills usually have to be developed together. Let's look at relaxation first.

The two general methods of relaxation training are distinguished by the extent to which they use visualization. I will give you brief examples of each approach; you might want to try them out. I have found the methods work best if a set of instructions or suggestions are written out and then read into a tape recorder. Read the instructions slowly and stop for approximately five seconds between each step of the procedure.

The first approach does not involve very much visualization but rather requires you to ask different parts of your body to relax. Get into a comfortable position in an easy chair or lying on the floor. Lying in bed usually is not a good idea because we associate beds with going to sleep and you want to be very awake but relaxed when you are finished.

Start by asking your feet to relax, then your calves, and so on, up your body. Picture each part of your body or concentrate your attention on it and allow it to relax. The trick is in the allowing, not ordering. Do not contract your muscles or move your body in any way. Be particularly careful of your shoulders, neck, face, and head. Try to really feel them relax.

Because you probably have never truly relaxed, don't be fooled by initial efforts. Try repeating the exercise two or three times per session to see if you can deepen the relaxation. As you practice, you will become more and more relaxed.

Cognitive relaxation techniques involve greater amounts of visualization. These methods do not rely on thinking about the body, although I have found it particularly effective to have people use a physical method a couple of times at the beginning of a session and then switch to a cognitive one. An example of a simple cognitive technique that I use with children involves pretending that you are a cat lying in the sun. Feel the warmth on your body and your muscles relaxing. A variation on this approach asks you to see or feel a golden light moving down over your body from head to foot.

As the light passes a part of your body, that part becomes totally relaxed and healthy. Actually, these methods include aspects of both physical and cognitive methods.

A more sophisticated cognitive method might ask you to imagine yourself walking through a field. You would be asked to feel the sun on your body, hear the birds singing, and smell the fresh cut hay. You would try to feel the ground you are walking on. Perhaps you would allow yourself to see a nice stream at the edge of the field. Allow yourself to go over and sit beside it. Look, listen, smell, feel, hear. Allow yourself to lie down by the stream. You are so relaxed; your body is completely relaxed.

Biofeedback is not specifically a relaxation technique, but it can be used for this purpose and often produces a feeling of relaxation. Biofeedback training uses instruments or other monitoring techniques to help people learn to control some aspect of their involuntary nervous system. Taking your pulse or listening to your heart with a stethoscope are examples of monitoring the responses of your body. Although there is some debate as to the amount of control over these involuntary actions that can be obtained by biofeedback, almost everyone can attain some degree of control. In the process people learn how situations and thoughts influence their bodies.

In addition to learning control, they also learn to relax and concentrate. For instance, an athlete who is having difficulty learning to relax might decide to learn to control his heart instead. He might use an electrocardiogram to monitor his heart rate and would then use different thoughts and visualizations to lower his heart rate. When the "feeling" of the lower heart rate as well as the appropriate techniques are learned, the machine can be removed. Although the changes might not be of medical significance, they are of psychological significance because in learning to control the biological function the athlete learns to control mental conditions.

When you are ready to end all relaxation procedures, it is best to arouse yourself and get up slowly, especially if you have been lying down. This gives your body an opportunity to adjust itself to the change in blood flow.

The use of relaxation techniques immediately prior to athletic events may not be suitable for all athletes. Each athlete must determine the level of excitement that leads to the best performance. This is why it is necessary for elite athletes to keep accurate records of their feelings before and during events. If the level of stress is too low, performance will suffer; if the level is too high, performance also suffers. For each person and each event there is an optimal level for maximum

performance. In athletics, as in real life, it is not so much a matter of not having butterflies as of getting them to fly in formation!

Becoming deeply relaxed is much more difficult than you might think. Many people will think about other things they should be doing or will let negative thoughts disturb them. Relaxation involves concentration. Learning to concentrate is one of the most difficult mental training tasks that the athlete faces. If people are not able to concentrate, they will be unable to benefit from many of the other mental training programs. This difficulty in learning to concentrate is one of the reasons why some of the experiments and field studies conducted by sport psychologists do not obtain positive results. For instance, it may often take an athlete up to a year just to learn to relax and to concentrate, but many sport psychology studies are completed in two or three months and often do not include training in the difficult area of concentration.

You may think that everyone can concentrate. Try it. Imagine an orange. You may see the orange on a screen in front of you; others may see it inside their heads; and some may not actually see an orange but will still have an impression of an orange. Have someone keep track of the time while you try to hold this image for one minute. You will probably find that after a few seconds other thoughts and images start to intrude. On the other hand, a person who is trained in concentration skills could hold the image as long as desired.

It is difficult to teach concentration skills well in a book because each person has different problems. Some general principles may help however. Most people find it easier to see the orange as if it were on a screen in front of their forehead. They watch the orange on the screen rather than making any effort to project it there. In other words no effort is made, just watch. It also is easier if the orange is visualized in as much detail as possible. Note its color. Is it a uniform color or are there some spots that are a different shade? See the texture. Rotate it. Is the orange round or some other shape? Can you smell it? The combination of relaxed observation and attention to detail should make the exercise easier.

The next and final step—the one that is most useful in actually mental training—involves the process of visualization. In order to visualize effectively it is necessary to be able to relax and concentrate. To experience how visualization works, imagine the orange again, but this time peel it and break it into sections. See the sections of the orange clearly and the juice squirting out as you break it into sections. Can you smell the orange? Now take a piece of the

orange and put it in your mouth. Does anything happen in your mouth? You may notice the production of saliva.

Athletes use visualization in a number of ways. They may see themselves performing the action as if they were a spectator or they may actually try to experience all the sensations of performing the activity. They may alter time in that they visualize an action that takes a long time such as a marathon race being completed in a manner of minutes or they may take a brief action such as a jump and slowly analyze it. They may also visualize the action in real time. One of the athletes I worked with was able to imagine his swim performance in a time that was very close to his real time. He could feel the water on his body, count the number of strokes he took to complete an event, and feel the sensations inside his body. He was there in a real sense.

In all of this, you may be having trouble getting any image of the orange, let alone cutting it or eating it. Don't worry about this; practice helps. Also remember that not everyone gets a visual image. Some people experience more of a *feeling* of the object or procedure.

Ethics and the Sport Psychologist

Those who are working with the mental training of athletes or using mental training techniques for general recreational situations must be very aware of the ethical issues involved in their activity. Two of the most important of these involve claiming expertise or knowledge that one does not have and compromising the welfare of the athlete.

Many of us in sport psychology are not registered clinical psychologists or psychiatrists. We are involved in education and perhaps some level of counseling. We do not perform psychotherapy. Although I have considerable training in counseling and have a Ph.D. that included courses in psychology, sport psychology, and physical education, I always refer clients with serious emotional difficulties to the appropriate experts.

The second ethical dilemma can arise when the sport psychologist is working for a team. Considerable pressure may be placed on the person doing the mental training to teach techniques to the team or to individuals that he or she feels uneasy about. Examples of this can range from aggressive affirmations to the demand to patch up an athlete who may be under a lot of strain.

It can also go the other way. When sport psychologists work

with an athlete, they may find out something about an athlete that might endanger the athlete's chance of being selected for a particular team or winning a scholarship. The team is presumably paying the sport psychologist, so the question of responsibility arises. The answer is that the sport psychologist is responsible to the athlete rather than to the team. All disclosures that might affect an athlete must be authorized by the athlete. The only exceptions are ones that are needed to protect an athlete. For instance, if an athlete expresses serious thoughts of suicide, the mental trainer must get some help for the client. This may not mean approaching the team however. A clinical psychologist or parents may be more appropriate. Then let these significant others, along with the athlete, make a decision about contacting team officials, because they are not so likely to have a conflict of interest.

Many other ethical issues are involved in the practice of sport psychology. Some of them, such as concerns about methods of advertising, may not be immediately obvious. Those who want to practice sport psychology and who have the necessary training and experience should join the sport psychology association for their country or area. In Canada, the group is called the Canadian Association for Psychomotor Learning and Sport Psychology. Those living in the United States could contact the North American Society for the Psychology of Sport and Physical Activity. People in other areas usually can find the appropriate group by phoning a university with a physical education department and asking to speak to the person involved in sport psychology.

CASE STUDIES

CASE ONE: FIGURE SKATERS

In the first case, a figure skating club approached me in the middle of the summer. The coaches and skaters were holding a camp in a nearby town and wanted to discuss mental training with me. As I already mentioned, they were hoping that they could get me to come and speak to them for a couple of hours with the expectation that they would then understand mental training. Part of the reason I was asked involved a serious concern about the training of the skaters, but I am sure another reason was to expand the program at the camp a bit by bringing in a guest speaker. Those in the area of sport psychology get used to being treated as a bit of a sideshow. Many coaches and athletes feel that the *real* training involves physical skills but that mental training should at least be mentioned because there is so much hype about it. In addition, some

coaches may be threatened by an outside expert and not be willing to really commit time to mental training.

This time the coach phoned me and wanted to know how much I would charge to come to the camp. I told her that I had a speaking fee but that it would be impossible to really teach many skills in a group session over such a short length of time. All I could do would be to tell the club members about the kinds of things they might learn and give a few demonstrations. The coach agreed to this, but I still felt that the coach thought she could take what I said in the speech and apply it herself without having to contact me again.

When I got to the arena, all of the skaters were off the ice and getting ready for their meeting with me. Their approach was quite casual; they seemed to feel that this was time off. I spent two hours doing demonstrations similar to those already described and discussing different approaches to some of the problems that skaters encounter. I also talked about skaters, such as Brian Orser, who use sport psychologists.

If the coach had asked me to continue with the group, it would have been necessary to go through some very definite steps in order to define the nature of my relationship to the club. There are both ethical and practical issues involved. The ethical issues were discussed earlier. Practically, I would have had to discuss with the coach and the skaters both what was expected and what would be the likely outcome of a training program. This might have involved several meetings to ensure that everyone understood what was going on and to help the skaters realize that I was there to help them improve their performance and not to "look between their ears." Fees also would have had to be discussed; how these were going to be paid and the access that individual skaters would have to me would have needed to be understood clearly right from the beginning. At the end of this discussion a detailed service contract would have been drafted and signed by me, the coach, and officials responsible for the club. ◆

CASE TWO: MARTIAL ARTS

The second case was most interesting to me for a number of reasons. It combined my interest in sport psychology with more than 20 years of involvement in the martial arts. In addition, club members were not so much interested in using mental training techniques to improve their performance as in finding ways to obtain the maximum amount of psychological benefit from their activity.

I decided to start my involvement with the club with a couple of

demonstrations. I first asked the sensei (club leader or teacher) to stand as firmly as he could on the floor and for one of the students to come up and try to push him aside. Even though the sensei tried to resist, the student pushed him aside relatively easily. I then asked the sensei to relax his body and to imagine that roots were growing out the bottom of his feet, through the floor and into the ground below. These roots held him solidly without effort on his part. The student had much more difficulty pushing him aside this time.

Another demonstration involved one of the students bracing his right arm while another student tried to bend it. This was done with relative ease. The student was then asked to relax his arm and to imagine that a beam of energy was going from his body, through the arm to the wall. This beam of energy could not be bent. The student then tried to bend the arm again. This time it was almost impossible to do so.

The other students in the club were impressed. I told them that whether they believe the beam of energy or the roots actually existed or not was irrelevant. They had only to pretend that these conditions existed. The differences in their performance could be explained by changes in the center of gravity and muscle tension in the body brought about by the visualization exercise. This may not be true for the exceptional abilities exhibited by some advanced martial artists.

Some club members pointed out that relaxation and visualization training may work in a controlled situation, but wanted to know if they could be used in an actual sport context. I answered that the process of transferring the learning was called *automating the relaxation response*. This involves programming the mind during the training phase to give the same relaxation response when, for example, the fingers are held in a particular way or when a certain phrase is used by the participant, regardless of the particular conditions.

An example of this is *centering*. The athlete trains in a noncompetitive situation to center, that is, to bring attention back to the body and to the present. One type of centering procedure begins by having the athlete stand with his or her feet a comfortable distance apart. The weight is centered over the feet so there is a feeling of balance. When breathing out the athlete concentrates on the feeling in the abdomen. The athlete feels this center lowering and deepening. The knees are bent slightly. On the next inbreath the athlete maintains the lowered feeling and on the outbreath feels again the center lowering. This is done three or four times. By centering with the breath, the athlete learns to associate each outbreath with a feeling of being centered and can intensify the feeling during competition by increasing

the strength of the outbreath. Centering combines a feeling of relaxation with balance and strength.

Within a couple of weeks there was a noticeable difference in the dojo (school). The aggressive edge that had characterized the club was gone and students were much more intent on their mental and physical condition during their activity. Many of the students reported that they adapted the routines from class to their personal life and found them to be very useful. The sensei was very pleased with my work because I never threatened him and always tried to explain to him what I was going to do before the class. Indeed, when it was possible for the sensei to explain the routine himself, I encouraged him to do so. ♦

CASE THREE: WEIGHT CONTROL

I immediately identified with the third case, the man who was having trouble controlling his weight. I love food, especially a good dessert. "Why it won't amount to anything," I say to myself. "I'll just climb a few stairs and take it off again." The problem is that it is much more pleasant to eat the dessert than it is to climb the stairs, so there is a tendency to put off climbing the stairs.

When the man approached me, he had already obtained a complete medical checkup and had tried several exercise programs. He also had a diet that was approved by his physician. Although I don't think that special diets are necessary or that it is necessary for everyone to obtain a physician's checkup before engaging in physical activity, this man was 45 and quite overweight—at least by the jiggle test. That is, if you jump and something jiggles that shouldn't, you are probably overweight.

I tell my clients that weight loss and staying with exercise programs are not really a manner of will power but rather of reinforcement for behavior change. The basic problem in weight loss or exercising, as in all activities that we would like to put off, is that at any given time it is probably easier to eat or not exercise than it is to not do so. Imagine that there is a piece of cake in front of you. It certainly seems to me more pleasant to eat it than not to eat it. The reward for eating is immediate, but the reward for *not* eating may not show up for the months or years it takes me to reduce to the weight I would like to have.

Thus, the first step in working with the man involved establishing realistic exercise and weight loss goals for him. The two really must go together for maximum health. One of the best ways I have found to start the process involves giving the client a copy of a

little book called *The Phacts of Life* (Collis, 1984). This book has divided bits of exercise and avoidance of snacks into 25 calorie units called phacts. These phacts can be accumulated by combining the exercise and avoidance of snacks.

All of us have a basal metabolic rate or amount of energy required to maintain normal body activity during rest. This rate varies from individual to individual and tends to decrease with age. Exercise burns more calories than sitting because activity increases our metabolic rate. A good measure of our metabolic rate is the amount of oxygen we consume. During exercise we increase our oxygen consumption, of course, but these increased levels of oxygen uptake continue even after we have finished our activity. Wenger and Chad (1988) for instance found that the times for oxygen levels to return to normal after 30, 45, or 60 minutes of exercise were 128, 204, and 455 minutes respectively. Not only did higher metabolic rates continue after exercise but longer exercise durations resulted in proportionately greater increases in time spent at higher oxygen utilization or calorie consumption levels. This means that exercise uses more calories than indicated on the standard calorie chart.

I worked with the man to establish a realistic goal for each day and week as well as a progression that could be undertaken. The number of phacts earned each day were recorded. It was immediately obvious when levels fell below the goal for the day. Instead of some long-term goal, the man had only to meet the requirements for each day to ensure that he would lose weight and have a suitable exercise program.

While meeting goals for the seven days of the week and having a perfect graph are very reinforcing for most clients, I plan to expand this behavior modification program in the future by contracting with clients to meet their goals for the day and week or be required to pay some penalty that we would agree on at the beginning of the program.

This man also had a very poor image of himself and there was a good chance that this image would find a way to defeat the whole program. We tend to act in accordance with how we perceive ourselves. His self-perception was as fat and undisciplined. To help him overcome this image, I taught him how to use a visualization technique and developed some positive statements or affirmations that he could use. The image used in the visualization technique was of the client in good shape and full of energy as well as happy and confident in his ability to deal with all areas of his life. The client came up with the two affirmations, "Day by day I am getting more and more health" and "I can stick to my phact goal for today."

The man lost the weight he wanted to and went on to become quite involved in athletic events. Unfortunately, not all clients work out so well. The immediate appeal of that TV and piece of cake is so great! I have to resist taking a break for a bite to eat right now! ◆

Becoming a Sport Psychologist

Training

Students who wish to specialize in sport psychology are faced with a difficult choice. In many jurisdictions, the word "psychologist" or any word that uses psychology or a derivative of it cannot be used unless the person using it is a registered psychologist. Some government funding agencies will only give money for sport psychology to those with clinical psychology accreditation. On the other hand, graduates of psychology departments account for only about 15% of those who are working or involved in the area of sport psychology; most of the rest were trained in physical education or sport science departments. The majority of the positions that I have seen advertised in the field of sport psychology have asked for a physical education background.

The word *sport* of course is not restricted, so any psychologist could call himself or herself a sport psychologist, even with no background in sport or perhaps in any type of psychology that involves working with people. Some psychologists may believe that their training in psychology equips them to be a sport psychologist, but this is untrue. Sport psychology is a broad field with its own extensive research literature. No one can ethically describe himself or herself as a sport psychologist without being familiar with this literature. Certainly most, if not all, sport psychologists have an extensive background in sport and athletics.

The problem for the student then, is finding a way around this "Catch-22." The best way probably would involve a program that includes courses and an internship in psychology and physical education that would meet requirements for accreditation by the provincial or state psychological association. Such programs are not common; it would probably be necessary to contact many universities before a suitable program could be developed.

The other approach that students can take, the most common by far, involves earning a Ph.D. in physical education with a specialization in the area of sport psychology. Several universities

in Canada and many in the United States and Europe offer such an alternative. The difficulty, as already described, is that the graduates of such programs cannot advertise themselves as psychologists without the danger of prosecution by psychological associations who are quite vigilant in protecting the name. However, words such as counselor, therapist, and mental training consultant are not protected and most of the people working in the area use these terms or the word educator, which I use and consider myself to be.

Accreditation

In addition to training programs, those planning to enter sport psychology should be aware of the accreditation program that has been or is in the process of being implemented by the sport psychology organization in their area. For the most part, these programs are voluntary in that people working in the field can choose to belong or not.

While registration is voluntary, it is very valuable because these organizations hold meetings where different approaches can be discussed, publish a newsletter, and provide a code of ethics that helps to ensure proper approaches to clients. Those interested in the exciting field of sport psychology must make every effort to improve constantly their knowledge and skills if they hope to offer clients the best possible service.

Employment Prospects

There are only a limited number of opportunities in the sport psychology field and obtaining one of these depends on a combination of ability, training, luck, and a considerable amount of self-promotion. Graduates from sport psychology programs can expect that a few positions will be available each year at universities throughout the world. Successful applicants for these positions will be expected to teach other courses in addition to those in sport psychology and will be able to spend only a limited amount of time in the actual practice of sport psychology.

Those with an entrepreneurial flair may choose to take their training and experience to the marketplace. Success here will depend on a combination of value of the services the sport psychologist is able to offer and skill in marketing these services to individuals and teams. While both the challenges and rewards of

the entrepreneurial route are exciting, the risks are large. Freelancing is definitely not for those who are looking for security.

As well as opportunities in sport, those with sport psychology training are better qualified than most to pursue a career in business. They offer an employer skills in areas such as goal setting, motivation, stress control, and planning, in addition to the traditional benefits of an academic education.

SUGGESTED READINGS AND REFERENCES

Butt, D. S. (1987). *The psychology of sport: The behavior, motivation, personality and performance of athletes.* (2nd ed.). New York: Van Nostrand-Reinhold.

Collis, M. (1984). *The phacts of life.* Markham, ON: Fitzhenry & Whiteside.

Cratty, B. J. (1984). *Psychological preparation and athletic excellence.* Ithaca, NY: Mouvement Publications.

Cratty, B. J., & Pigott, R. E. (1984). *Student projects in sport psychology.* Ithaca, NY: Mouvement Publications.

Dewey, D., Brawley, L. R., & Allard, F. (1989). Do the TAIS attentional-style scales predict how visual information is processed? *Journal of Sport and Exercise Psychology, 11* (2), 171–186.

Harris, D. V., & Harris, B. (1984). *Sports psychology: Mental skills for physical people.* New York: Leisure Press.

Martens, R. (1977). *Sport competition anxiety test.* Champaign, IL: Human Kinetics.

McNair, D., Lorr, M., & Droppelman, L. (1971). *Manual for the Profile of Mood States.* San Diego, CA: Educational and Industrial Testing Services.

Morgan, W. P. (1980). The trait psychology controversy. *Research Quarterly for Exercise and Sport, 51,* 50–76.

Nideffer, R. M. (1976). Test of attentional and interpersonal style. *Journal of Personality and Social Psychology, 34,* 394–404.

Nideffer, R. M. (1985). *Athletes' guide to mental training.* Champaign: IL: Human Kinetics.

Orlick, T. (1986). *Psyching for sport: Mental training for athletes.* Champaign, IL: Leisure Press.

Orlick, T., & Partington, J. (1986). *Psyched: Inner views of winning.* Ottawa, ON: Coaching Association of Canada.

Rainey, D. W., Conklin, W. E., & Rainey, K. W. (1987). Competitive trait anxiety among male and female junior high school athletes. *International Journal of Sport Psychology, 18,* 171–179.

Reis, J., & Bird, A. M. (1982). Cue processing as a function of breadth of attention. *Journal of Sport Psychology, 4,* 64–72.

SALMELA, J. H. (1979). Psychology and sport: Fear of applying. In P. Klavora & J. V. Daniel (Eds.), *Coach, athlete and the sport psychologist.* (pp. 13–21). Toronto: University of Toronto.

SALMELA, J. H. (1982). Sport psychology. In J. J. Jackson & H. A. Wenger (Eds.), *The sport sciences.* (pp. 81–88). Victoria, BC: University of Victoria.

SILVA, J. M., & WEINBERG, R. S. (Eds.). (1984). *Psychological foundations of sport.* Champaign, IL: Human Kinetics.

WENGER, H. A., & CHAD, K. E. (1988). The effect of exercise duration on the exercise and post-exercise oxygen consumption. *Canadian Journal of Sport Sciences, 13,* (4), 204–207.

DONALD J. BAUMANN

Donald J. Baumann's area of interest is understanding and solving social problems. He received his Ph.D. from Arizona State University and currently teaches at Trinity University in San Antonio, Texas. He has published articles, book chapters, and technical reports on topics as diverse as altruism, citizen involvement with the police, alcoholism, acquaintance rape, migrant farmworkers, and the homeless. He has consulted to numerous public and private organizations. ♦

CHARLES J. HOLAHAN

Charles J. Holahan is Professor of Psychology and Associate Director of the Community Psychology Program at the University of Texas at Austin. He has been a Visiting Faculty Member in the Department of Psychiatry at Stanford University. He has published more than 50 scientific articles and chapters and two books dealing with his research on environmental stress and the factors that keep people healthy during stressful periods. He is a Fellow of the American Psychological Association and has served as a consultant to governmental, educational, and medical institutions. ♦

8

The Community Psychologist

Recently, the Housing Authority of a major city became troubled about residents' discontent, fear for personal safety, and vandalism in a low-income housing project. They turned to our team of community psychologists for help in evaluating the project. What they needed most, they explained, was an in-depth understanding of day-to-day life in the setting. To answer their questions one of our team members, a courageous young woman named Anita, moved into the project as *participant observer*.

During the year Anita resided in the project she compiled a detailed record to document its quality of life. Her findings demonstrated how difficult life in the project was. Few residents made friends in the setting. Most distrusted their neighbors so completely that they remained barricaded behind locked doors. Residents also distrusted the Housing Authority. They felt alienated from the political process and isolated from normal patterns of urban life. Anita's findings played a central role in encouraging the Housing Authority to improve its low-income housing program, including opportunities for resident participation in housing policies.

Of course, the influence of the social context on people's lives is not restricted to low-income housing. Have you ever stopped to think about how the social context in which each of us lives and works can affect the quality of our lives? For example, a college student's day may begin unhappily in a dormitory that is too noisy to foster positive social relationships. The way he or she thinks, feels, and behaves, may also be shaped by this temporary home. Another kind of social context involves public places—streets, sidewalks, alleys—places where the homeless temporarily reside. When these public places begin to deteriorate, incivility is a natural outcome, and this affects all of us, homeless and nonhomeless alike (Wilson & Kelling, 1982). Sidewalks are not repaired, litter and garbage collect on the street, windows remain broken, and, ultimately, social rules are not followed.

Because such places have become detached from the fabric of our communities, we are fearful and distrustful of them. We ask that the police intervene to enforce the rules that were once easily monitored by citizens when these public places were civil. Recently, citizens working with the police have been used to help reestablish rules, belonging, and a positive quality of life. Some social contexts, however, may have too many rules or rules that are not flexible. A large mental hospital is one example. Here, isolated people sitting in rows are surrounded by cold, colorless walls, glaring corridors, and locked doors.

Surprisingly, traditional psychology has neglected the way in which contexts such as these affect our lives. Recently, a special branch of psychology has evolved to address this oversight—community psychology.

What Is Community Psychology?

Community psychology attempts to improve the quality of life of individuals through prevention at a social systems level. In practice, it favors modifications in features of the community system itself, rather than treatment of the individual client. This approach is based on the realization that the problems individuals face are often caused by conflicts and pressures from the social settings—family, school, workplace, neighborhood—where they live and work. Moreover, the community psychology approach is based on the recognition that if social settings are part of the problem, interventions aimed at changing social settings need to be part of the solution.

Community psychology is characterized by a concern with applying psychological knowledge in attempting to improve the quality of people's lives. Since its inception, community psychology has been an inherently applied discipline with a social intervention focus. Community psychology emerged largely as a reaction to limitations in the perspective and practice of clinical psychology. Community psychologists have been critical, for example, of clinical psychology's focus on deficits rather than health, on treatment instead of prevention, and on individuals in contrast to social settings.

More specifically, community psychology has three key defining characteristics: (1) an intervention *goal* that focuses on quality of life, (2) an intervention *target* that encompasses social processes at a variety of levels, and (3) an intervention *method* that relies on primary and secondary prevention (Holahan & Wandersman, 1987). These defining characteristics merge aspects of clinical psychology, social psychology, and public health, respectively. Community psychology's focus on quality of life stems from its roots in clinical work. Its social process orientation applies research knowledge and research methods from social psychology. Its reliance on prevention reflects developments in the epidemiology of physical disease and public health models of disease prevention.

The Background of Community Psychology

The roots of this new approach can be traced to the history of the community mental health movement. The publication in 1961 of the federally supported *Joint Commission Report on Mental Illness and Health*, brought a new awareness that the community offered a strategically greater treatment potential than previous methods of intervention that focused on the individual client. This idea was given a powerful boost through the Community Mental Health Centers Act of 1963, which represented a partial implementation of the report and established a framework for a national network of community mental health centers.

In 1965, this idea was strengthed further when clinical psychologists, who had gathered for a conference in Boston, began to focus attention on community systems as a more appropriate way of thinking about people's quality of life than individual illness. The old intrapsychic individual therapy model began to give way to a new notion of the community as a social support system, and of the idea that many psychological problems could be prevented through such a system. Social system interventions that attempt to go beyond the individual client were the natural result.

This conceptual redefinition of mental health was refined further in 1975 at the National Conference for Training in Community Psychology in Austin, Texas, where psychologists reconceptualized the bonds between the individual and social systems in ecological terms. This ecological analogy, borrowed from biology, helped psychologists to understand that the interrelationships between people and the various social systems where they live and work are complex, two-directional, and constantly changing. In addition, the Austin conference gave psychologists an opportunity to reflect on and to articulate the values that underlie community psychology. Two values emerged as central to the community movement—a broad concern with *human welfare* at a societal level and a commitment to *social justice* in the distribution of society's resources.

The Scope of Community Psychology

Community psychology emphasizes social processes at a variety of levels, from small groups to neighborhood networks to whole com-

munities. Community psychology examines the ties between the individual and the broader social context, and employs social systems interventions to effect behavioral change. Community psychology strives to bring a societal awareness into psychology, as well as a psychological appreciation to the conventional study of societal processes. The community psychology perspective represents a domain of inquiry where psychology meets sociology and political science, where the individual interacts with society.

The approach to social intervention that characterizes community psychology reflects an underlying concern with prevention. Cowen (1980) cites two major factors that have encouraged an interest in prevention among community psychologists: "(1) The frustration and pessimism of trying to undo psychological damage once it had passed a certain critical point; (2) the costly, time-consuming, culture-bound nature of mental health's basic approaches, and their unavailability to, and ineffectiveness with, large segments of society in great need" (p. 259). *Primary prevention* attempts to prevent the occurrence of risk factors, while *secondary prevention* efforts are initiated when initial coping attempts have been unsuccessful, and are directed toward helping individuals cope with continued stress.

Consistent with this commitment to prevention at a social process level, the issues traditionally studied by community psychologists focus on implementing and evaluating preventive interventions with groups at psychological risk. Community psychologists are involved, for example, in health and social policy planning for children, minority and economically disadvantaged persons, and the elderly. They try to help these groups through preventive programs in areas such as education, housing, criminal justice, public health, and social welfare. To achieve these broad objectives community psychologists typically work collaboratively with experts in other disciplines, including educators, psychiatrists, social workers, social policy planners, public health workers, city planners, and criminologists.

Two Ways Community Psychologists Solve Problems

The social systems approach of community psychology combined with the social values that underlie the field lead community psychologists to be especially interested in solving social problems. In general, two processes guide community psychologists in their

selection of the particular social problems they try to solve: (1) *curiosity* about situations that, although not yet identified as social problems, have potential of becoming social problems and (2) *responsiveness* to identified social problems where the expertise of community psychologists is explicitly sought.

Sometimes phenomena are of interest in their own right. Community psychologists become curious. They stop what they are doing, ask questions, and gather information; uncertainty is reduced, and what was unknown becomes known (Reich, 1982). The first pair of cases in this chapter are examples from our own work as community psychologists that illustrate how curiosity can lead to an exciting quest for an answer, and how the individuals on the journey—faculty and students alike—can learn from their explorations. One example involves coming to understand how citizens can participate with the police. Another involves changes in a university dormitory that helps to promote supportive bonds between neighbors. Both these cases involve three basic steps: (1) asking the right questions, (2) gathering the information, and (3) reducing uncertainty.

Responsiveness to an expressed societal need also can lead the community psychologist on a journey to solve a social problem. In this case, the questions are often known, and the task of the community psychologist is to find a methodology through which they can be answered. So we wait: ideas in hand, skills in pocket, for the opportunity to use our knowledge. The second pair of cases in this chapter are additional examples from our work as community psychologists that illustrate how the application of social support theory helped solve two different types of identified social problems, one involving homelessness, and the other, a psychiatric hospital. The third and fourth case studies focuses on: (1) preventing an existing problem, (2) gathering data, and (3) collaborating on a solution to the problem.

CASE STUDIES

CASE ONE: THE POLICE AND CITIZEN INVOLVEMENT
Police officers perform vital functions in the community. The most visible of these functions are law enforcement and crime control activities; less visible are duties related to social regulation. As a consequence of witnessing their involvement in a myriad of these situations, our evaluation group, consisting of a number of students and one faculty member (Baumann), came to understand more fully the complexities of policing in America. But first, we became

curious. Consider the following circumstance a student in our group witnessed riding with a police officer:

> Responding to a call from a distraught woman, an officer and a student encountered a family fight which had apparently been going on for some time. The woman wanted the police to remove her husband from the premises and the situation was hostile. The husband did not wish to leave. The officer calmed the situation and brought order by establishing a temporary truce between the couple. The husband was allowed to stay. The student's report suggested that the situation was an emotionally difficult one, and that the officer's behavior was appropriate to the circumstances. He was calming, reassuring and, at the same time, was able to find a solution to the immediate problem and quickly bring order.

In riding with other officers, it became very clear to all of us that incidents involving both law enforcement and social regulation occur with great frequency and directly affect lives. We wondered how citizens might help police officers perform what to us appeared to be an overwhelming task.

Asking the Right Questions. We did what anyone does when they become curious: we asked questions, although in a very systematic way.

Two immediate tasks were: (1) locating the critical elements (or variables) in the question, and (2) stating the relation between these elements in a testable way. We turned to the history of American policing for an answer. We discovered that citizens in colonial America were expected to help in community emergencies and to raise the alarm in response to events disruptive of the public order. It was only at the turn of the twentieth century, as the political climate and crime rates changed, that citizens were removed from their working relationship with the police. Recently, however, it has become clear that without citizen participation with the police the tie to the flow of information for effective law enforcement is lost. Thus, citizens are again being asked to help, but it is unclear what their role should be.

We asked what should be the first goal of citizen participation. History suggested that because citizen involvement developed out of the desire for more effective law enforcement, that should be our point of departure. We then realized that one law enforcement goal of citizen involvement was the key to unlocking several others: time

spent by the police in certain types of crisis police calls. We speculated that this time could be lowered by citizen participation because the police would be free to leave the scene to respond to other calls. However, our observations suggested that time would not always be saved because some police calls might be perceived as more dangerous than others. We would not expect officers to leave citizen participants alone in these types of calls. We therefore hypothesized that the presence of citizen participants in police calls results in a direct time savings to police officers in non-dangerous police calls.

Gathering Information—Finding the Right Method. We now had to gather information to answer our question. In general, the nature of the question dictates the method used to answer it. We had a naturalistic observational study, and it seemed to us that an appropriate method was a naturalistic experiment. It was naturalistic because we could not conduct a true experiment with control over the relevant variables and random assignment, yet it was similar to an experiment because the way in which calls were assigned to the citizens was approximately random. Four categories of crisis intervention police calls were considered: public welfare, mental health, victim assistance, and domestic dispute.

Public welfare calls were those that involved checking on the personal welfare of citizens, and included police calls officially labeled "check welfare" and "missing juvenile" (e.g., someome lost, ill, or intoxicated). *Mental health* calls were those that involved responding to a need for psychological services in victimless crimes (e.g., police calls officially labeled *insane person, overdose,* and *attempted suicide*). *Victim assistance* calls were those that dealt directly with the single victim of a crime perpetrated by another (e.g., *reported rape*). The final category, *domestic dispute,* involved altercations between family members (e.g., calls labeled *family fight* in police records).

Two comparison groups were established for each of the four crisis intervention call categories. The experimental data were derived from those crisis intervention calls in which the citizen participants were available and were used by police officers. Comparison data were derived from crisis intervention calls responded to by participating police officers when they were not able to use citizen participants because they were unavailable (e.g., they were on another call, out of radio range, etc.). Such calls were identified by officers on their personal log sheets and verified by official records. Dispatcher-recorded police time spent in response to calls within

each category was the principle outcome measure and officer related dangerousness was the secondary measure.

Reducing Uncertainty—Making the Unknown Known. We collected data for a one-year period. At the end of the year, we learned, as we had hypothesized, that police time was saved in all crisis intervention calls that were nondangerous. Domestic disputes were the lone exception. However, even here our pursuit of an answer yielded results. Police time in the form of repeat calls appeared saved by citizen involvement. We were very excited. We shared our data with the citizen participants and the police. Their response? We want more! Translate this to policy. What does it mean? We translated time to dollars, calculating citizens' savings to the taxpayer and the police. We discovered that such a program could save a city of roughly one million people $750,000 per year (Baumann, Schultz, Brown, Paredes, & Hepworth, 1987).

Furthermore, our observations suggested to us a theory about police-citizen involvement. Consider the two circumstances of law enforcement and social regulation that police officers deal with. In the first, an aggressive, forceful response is required, while in the second, an empathic, calming one is required. Theoretically, the two responses are likely incompatible, especially under conditions of high arousal. The result, one would expect, is that the more well-learned response is likely to be displayed, regardless of the situation. If the individual is well trained to handle calls involving the empathic provision of aid to citizens (most police *calls* are like this) he or she could err when facing a situation requiring an aggressive response by *under*reacting. If the individual is well trained to handle calls involving aggressive responses (most police *training* is like this), he or she could err when facing a situation requiring the empathetic provision of aid by *over*reacting. We believe this to be an important theoretical insight from our study, and the idea is currently being investigated at a police training academy. In addition, the students working on the project received a special benefit: They were part of changing the unknown to the known through science, a rare kind of excitement and one that is not easily forgotten. ♦

CASE TWO: DISTRESS AND DORMITORY LIFE
Students, too, live complex lives. They must adjust each semester to new schedules, are under pressure to continually perform well, and often must adjust simultaneously to a badly designed living setting. This last issue became apparent when I (Holahan) was counseling students as a part of my work as a university teacher. I began to

notice that a large number of students I spoke with were more than normally distressed. I became curious; I began asking questions.

I found that these students came from the same environment and had a common complaint: The focal area of concern was a high-rise dormitory on campus, which had become a socially isolated setting rather than one rich in social interactions. The high-rise dormitory housed over 3,000 students, and vandalism, the institutional environment, and social isolation, as well as a lack of privacy were common complaints. Through a collaborative planning session it became clear to all involved—myself, a graduate student, the dormitory staff, and student representatives—that a systems level intervention was the best approach to improving social contact in the dormitory. Our task was to design and evaluate such an intervention.

Asking the Right Questions. Our first step was to ask the right questions. During the first six months of the intervention we held

Dormitory life can be stressful or not, depending on the quality of social support and even the building's design. (Courtesy of the editor, Robert Gifford.)

weekly meetings with the director of the high-rise dormitory setting and the assistant director in charge of student activities. These sessions resulted in a commitment from all of us to the goal of improving the quality of life of students who resided in the setting. Our objective was to provide flexible policy and environmental design solutions that would both enhance students' opportunity for social interaction, while also affording the opportunity for privacy.

During the next three months of the intervention staff were asked for their views and they were trained in skills relevant to assessing and dealing with the impact of institutional change. Through discussions with dormitory staff, along with discussions with student residents, we learned that for individuals new to campus life an important coping strategy involved the establishment of close and easily accessible friendship networks. This reinforced our initial hunch concerning the psychological significance of the social isolation of the high-rise dormitory. Perhaps, the design of the high-rise dormitory inhibited the formation of these supportive friendship networks. In order to answer this question confidently and thereby design a successful intervention, we needed more information from those individuals most affected—the student residents of the dormitory.

Gathering Information—Finding the Right Method. We decided to systematically evaluate two types of dormitories for comparative purposes: low-rise and high-rise settings. In addition, the role of floor level was examined. We developed a scale that measured students' satisfaction or dissatisfaction with their living environment. The separate items in the scale measured: satisfaction with meeting people, making friends, recreation, opportunities and places for personal conversation, comfort, privacy, student influence in policy decisions, physical layout, overall feelings of satisfaction, and help or support for personal problems. A second measure was also developed: level of friendship networks in close proximity to the resident's room. This measure was oriented toward measuring friendship at different levels of intimacy. The method used to administer these measures was a 15-minute survey questionnaire that students could complete on their own and return to us anonymously.

Making the Unknown Known: Reducing Uncertainty. The results of this student survey indicated that residents of low-rise dormitories were more satisfied than residents of high-rise dormitories. The social atmosphere of the high-rise dormitory also

differed from that of the low-rise dormitory. Relative to low-rise students, students in the high-rise dormitory felt less commitment toward fellow students and felt less affinity with and control over the formal organization of the dormitory. Additionally, within the high-rise dormitory, high floors were rated more poorly on the same characteristics than low floors (Wilcox & Holahan, 1976).

We used our findings to provide feedback to campus adminis-trators who could make a difference in dormitory policy. Collabora-tive feedback sessions were held with staff and administrative personnel in the high-rise dormitory. First, findings from the sur-vey were presented and discussed. This was followed by a brain-storming session oriented toward generating a range of solution alternatives. Finally, possible solutions were reconsidered in the light of administrative priorities, financial constraints, their likely success, and the time period necessary for implementation. The solutions that emerged from this process were then accepted as workable strategies for improving student satisfaction which could be implemented over a relatively short-term period.

The particular change strategies that were developed were of two types: (1) administrative policy revisions oriented toward facilitating students' adaptive coping efforts with existing environ-mental realities and (2) decisions concerning physical remodeling in areas where minimal financial input might generate optimal behavioral benefits. Policy revisions included:

1. resident-assistant training programs based on the study's findings,
2. a special orientation program for students new to the high-rise dormitory environment,
3. an emphasis on increased social contact between students and residence hall staff at all levels,
4. increased dormitory social functions organized at the floor level to facilitate the establishment of proximate friend-ship networks, and
5. greater administrative responsiveness to students' requests for specific roommates or roommate changes.

Physical design changes included construction of attractive par-titions in the huge, open dining area to facilitate group contact and social interaction, and refurnishing of the badly deteriorated lounge areas on each floor to encourage social participation and friendship formation. ♦

CASE THREE: THE HOMELESS AND SOCIAL SUPPORT

The homeless are now a visible social problem. When I (Baumann) began to study the problem of homelessness in the early 1980s, our society was just becoming aware of the issue. Where I lived, cities were changing; downtown areas were being redeveloped. Old buildings were torn down and new ones lodged in their place; small parks replaced the rubble of warehouses and alleys. Well-dressed men and women began to frequent the shops, boutiques, and clubs that dotted the new city scene. However, they literally ran into a social problem—the homeless. Removed from the destroyed single-room-occupancy hotels, flushed from the alleyways, trash bins, and other niches they occupied, the homeless stood visible to all: disheveled and uncivil against the stark and fresh backdrop of the gentrified cityscape.

Knowledge of Prevention. The city had a problem. Local papers were filled with solutions that ranged from "run them out of Dodge" to regulating the problem in a kindly and understanding manner. We knew that the city had an even more serious problem; it had no

The homeless represent one important challenge for community psychologists. (Courtesy of the editor, Robert Gifford.)

data or theory on which to base solutions. Furthermore, the solutions offered did not attempt to prevent the problem, but only to manage it. We saw this as a golden opportunity. Armed with a history and knowledge of prevention, my students and I believed we could help. Armed with the belief that homelessness is a process—the homeless were likely once housed—we were ready to start considering alternatives to static-endstate solutions. We argued that data were needed to understand the *process* of homelessness—why and how it occurred—and that without this, an effective solution was not possible. Things do change and knowledge of how and why they change at least allows an attempt at altering their course.

We argued that social support theory might provide an especially useful framework for understanding homelessness: social support is a theory of affiliation, and homelessness is a theory of disaffiliation. We believed that the process of homelessness involves three stages of loss of support, followed by the attainment of another type of support—that of other homeless people. Entrenchment in homelessness results in the *first stage*, when family support is lost. Family support is critical to an individual's overall sense of well-being and for the provision of essential resources. When family support is weak, absent, or lost, individuals turn to friends. In this *second stage*, a loss of support from friends is also critical. Friends may not have the resources to provide protection against the loss of a house, but they protect against the loss of home—the sense of psychological belonging. A *third stage* of loss can also occur—loss of community support. Too often the community support needed for personal survival is unavailable to individuals with no permanent residence, no proof of a job, and no means of transportation. Another part of the homeless process—disaffiliation—has started (Bahr, 1968). In the face of the inability to gather sufficient resources to reverse the tide, and with survival at stake, the homeless tend to drift further and further from traditional relationships and institutions, and often turn to other homeless individuals to regain a measure of support.

Obtaining Data. Armed with this theory, we then sought to collect data through interviews with homeless people. These data were hard to obtain. They required that we consider how to randomly sample a population with guaranteed anonymity and without duplicating an interview. Another issue was trust; would the homeless tell us the truth? Furthermore, our aim was to collect data over several problem domains: physical health, mental health, employ-

ment, housing, the law, and social support. This takes time, and lengthy interviews can be taxing.

In the end, we chose an interview of moderate length, and paid the homeless for their help. We solved our problem of double counting by marking the hand of people we interviewed with dye used by the blood bank. It is colorless, odorless, nontoxic, and shows only under a black light. All that remained was trust. To our surprise, we were not only trusted (our interviewers were extremely familiar with the street) but the 500 homeless we interviewed were quite willing to tell us about themselves and their lives.

We learned several important things:

1. The homeless have problems in several domains and those problems are more pronounced than those of the non-homeless.
2. The homeless underestimate the magnitude of their problems as a function of their entrenchment in homelessness.
3. Additional costs of entrenchment appear to be increased arrest due to increased visibility.
4. The benefit of the support of other individuals is psychological—those with social support are more psychologically functional than those without support (Baumann & Grigsby, 1988).

Collaboration. We turned in our report and waited for the community to act. They did not. What was wrong? Although we were the experts on homelessness, we did not have the power to implement what we knew. The community leaders had this, and collaboration with these leaders was the only answer. We mounted a collaborative effort aimed at making experts out of those community leaders who could make a difference in planning and policy.

The data collection phase had taken a year, and we presumed the planning phase would take another. Further, part of the data collection team were no longer available, and new and more team members were needed. The city was approached and agreed to the amount we requested for the project. To no one's surprise, key players and politics made this a rather effortless accomplishment. So too was teaching these individuals what we had learned. Theory and data made this possible. They had been assembled as a task force to solve the problems and they were our client.

Once these leaders understood the process of homelessness

and its consequences, several solutions emerged. All these solutions had to do with enabling homeless individuals to obtain self-sufficiency through the reestablishment of community, friend and family support. They also contained the potential for prevention by shoring up existing support networks. We created a five-step plan that included the provision of:

1. basic services (food, hygiene, clothing, etc.),
2. health care (physical and mental),
3. shelter services,
4. employment (to include job necessities such as day care, transportation, job preparation, and job training), and
5. transitional housing.

Each step required the inclusion of some form of social support. The reestablishment of family (or surrogate family) ties was offered for those in need of alcohol treatment. Housing programs with buddy systems, whereby intact support groups from the street could become self-sufficient were also available. We provided funds for each possible program combination. Ultimately presented to the city as a two-volume report, the five-step plan was to cost $2 million dollars and $1 million each year thereafter (Baumann, et al., 1986a, 1986b).

We are gratified that funding for major components of each step of our plan has been provided to agencies that proposed solutions within the guidelines of the social support-based five-step plan. Outcome research will ultimately determine whether our plan was effective. ♦

CASE FOUR: A PSYCHIATRIC WARD AND SOCIAL SUPPORT
Another disturbing, though less visible, social problem is the plight of patients in psychiatric hospitals. Many psychiatric hospitals present patients with an institutional environment that is more likely to worsen than to alleviate their distress. For example, many such settings are overcrowded, with physical facilities that are poorly maintained and in deteriorated condition. While I (Holahan) was working as a postdoctoral researcher in New York, I was provided the opportunity to substantially improve the environment on the admitting ward of a major mental hospital. City University of New York, where I was housed, was extremely supportive of efforts to solve real-world social problems. With the encouragement of the university, I decided, along with William Ittelson and Susan

Saegert, to plan, conduct, and study a large-scale physical remodeling on a psychiatric ward of a New York City hospital.

Knowledge of Prevention. Because psychiatric hospitals can adversely affect the healing process, they provide a unique opportunity for preventive interventions. The combined influences of an institutionalized atmosphere, crowding, the disruption of ongoing social relationships, and the inherent dependency of the patient role can exacerbate existing illness and subject individuals to new threats to their psychological health. Overcoming features of the hospital environment that exacerbate existing illnesses or thwart the recovery process is the beginning point for secondary prevention efforts. Eliminating factors in the hospital environment that can precipitate new health problems, such as depression from the loss of personal control that often characterizes the patient role, represents a unique opportunity for primary prevention.

The remodeling was intended to encourage social support, involvement, and cooperation among patients and to discourage the social withdrawal that had become typical of the ward. A private sector was created in the bedrooms by installing six-foot-high partitions, creating a number of two-bedroom sections in each dormitory. A table and two comfortable chairs were installed in a screened-off area of each bedroom to allow for private conversations. Small group interaction was encouraged in one dayroom, where new tables and chairs were arranged in small social groupings. Larger group socializing could occur at large tables in the dining room.

Obtaining Data. The demands of the setting will dictate the appropriate research design, the appropriate research tools, and the appropriate research measures. Part of the excitement and creativity of being involved in community psychology is precisely this confrontation with a new setting, which, because of its physical characteristics, history, and people, demands to be dealt with in a unique way. The experimental design we used was a response to the particular parameters of the situation we were dealing with. For example, because there was a second ward within the hospital that was similar to the ward we wanted to change, we could have a control condition. In addition, because the hospital already randomly assigned patients to all their admitting wards, we could use a true experimental design.

We particularly wanted to gather behavioral data that would offer a reliable picture of what would happen on the ward after the remodeling. One concern was that existing behavioral techniques

would likely influence the activities in a ward—they would be too reactive. So we developed techniques in which we became a part of the daily routine on the ward, but changed the natural, ongoing processes as little as possible. Measures of change were begun six months after the remodeling was completed to allow sufficient time for enduring ward routines to become established. Data were collected for five weeks, using a time-sampling recording of patients' behavior.

Consistent with our goals for the remodeling, we found that after the remodeling, patients on the remodeled ward engaged in more social behavior and were less passive and withdrawn than patients on the unchanged control ward. The level of social activity on the remodeled ward was almost two thirds greater than on the unchanged control ward. In contrast, isolated passive behavior was almost 50% more prevalent on the control ward compared to the remodeled setting. The improvement in social activity after the remodeling was dramatic, and included socializing among patients, between staff and patients, and between patients and hospital visitors (Holahan & Saegert, 1973).

The remodeling also qualitatively improved the atmosphere on the ward. Patient interviews demonstrated that patients on the remodeled ward perceived the ward as significantly more attractive and tended to feel more positive toward the ward than did patients on the control ward. Moreover, openness to change at one level provided an impetus for a simultaneous openness to change at other levels. As the remodeling was being completed, ward staff began meeting on their own initiative to discuss for the first time the development of a ward treatment philosophy. As a result of these meetings, staff members began to perceive the previously ignored needs and frustrations of the patients on the ward.

Collaboration. Several things, beyond the encouragement of the university, made it possible for us, as outside investigators, to plan and direct this preventive remodeling. First, there was a long history of trust and confidence between the university and the hospital system of the City of New York. Second, the university was prepared to deliver $5,000 to the hospital to remodel the ward. This exchange was important because it demonstrated that we had something we were willing to give to be involved. Third, we were willing to be patient and work with staff and administrators in their own time frame, ensuring that they had some control over the entire process. Finally, key players in addition to the investigators, grantee, and hospital administrators were necessary to implement the project.

We were able to use the benefits of friendship: the architect working on our team was a personal friend of the ward director. Furthermore, we were able to enlist the confidence and support of two staff members who were critically important to our understanding of what was happening in the hospital environment: From the start these staff members gave us an insider's view of the ward and which problems we would encounter. ♦

Becoming a Community Psychologist

Education

Graduate education is necessary to become a community psychologist. Two types of graduate programs exist for training in community psychology: community programs and clinical-community programs. These two types of programs exist in approximately equal numbers. *Community programs* require no coursework in clinical content areas; instead their coursework entails subjects such as program evaluation, community organization, and social policy. Students in community programs typically engage in field placements in research and policy institutes, criminal justice facilities, and public health facilities. *Clinical-community programs* require additional coursework in clinical content areas such as psychological assessment and psychotherapy. Students in clinical-community programs typically engage in field placements in community mental health centers, child and family services, psychiatric facilities and schools (Godin, Elias, Dalton, & Goldstein, 1988).

Employment

Community programs prepare students to work in the areas of program evaluation, action research, and social policy analysis, with little emphasis on clinical practice. Graduates of community programs are most likely to obtain employment in applied research/program evaluation positions, community-based treatment facilities, and academic positions. *Clinical-community programs* prepare students to work in the areas of basic research, program evaluation, and action research, as well as in clinical practice. Graduates of clinical-community programs are most likely to obtain employment in academic positions and in community-based treatment facilities (Godin et al., 1988).

SUGGESTED READINGS AND REFERENCES

BAHR, H. M. (1968). *Homelessness and disaffiliation.* New York: Columbia University Bureau of Applied Research.

BAUMANN, D. J., & GRIGSBY, C. (1988). *Understanding the homeless: From research to action.* Austin, TX: Hogg Foundation for Mental Health.

BAUMANN, D. J., GRIGSBY, C., BEAUVAIS, C., BISHOP, S., GREGORICH, S., OSBORNE, M., & NELMS, D. (1986a). *Taskforce on the homeless, Volume I: Program plan and projected budget.* City of Austin, Austin, TX, July 1, 1986.

BAUMANN, D. J., OSBORNE, M., BEAUVOIS, C., GRIGSBY, C., GREGORICH, S., BISHOP, S., & NELMS, D. (1986b). *Taskforce on the homeless, Volume II: Supplement to the final report.* City of Austin, Austin, TX, August 1, 1986.

BAUMANN, D. J., SCHULTZ, D. F., BROWN, C., PAREDES, R., & HEPWORTH, J. (1987). Citizen participation in police crisis intervention activities. *American Journal of Community Psychology, 15,* 4, 459–471.

BRODY, J. G. (1986). Community psychology in the eighties: A celebration of survival. *American Journal of Community Psychology, 14,* 139–145.

COWEN, E. L. (1980). The wooing of primary prevention. *American Journal of Community Psychology, 8,* 253–284.

GODIN, S., ELIAS, M., DALTON, J., & GOLDSTEIN, S. (1988). Masters and doctoral level programs in clinical-community and community psychology: An empirical comparison. *The Community Psychologist, 21,* 15–20.

HOLAHAN, C. J., & SAEGERT, S. (1973). Behavioral and attitudinal effects of large-scale variation in the physical environment of psychiatric wards. *Journal of Abnormal Psychology, 82,* 454–462.

HOLAHAN, C. J., & WANDERSMAN, A. (1987). The community psychology perspective in environmental psychology. In D. Stokols and I. Altman (Eds.) *Handbook of environmental psychology.* New York: Wiley. (pp. 827–861).

LEVINE, M., & PERKINS, D. V. (1987). *Principles of community psychology: Perspectives and applications.* New York: Oxford University Press.

REICH, J. W. (1982). *Experimenting in society: Issues and examples in applied social psychology.* Glenview, IL: Scott-Foresman.

WILCOX, B. L., & HOLAHAN, C. J. (1976). The social ecology of the megadorm in university student housing. *Journal of Educational Psychology, 1976, 68,* 453–458.

WILSON, J. Q., & KELLING, G. L. (1982). The police and neighborhood safety. *The Atlantic Monthly,* March, 29–38.

ROBERT SOMMER

Robert Sommer is Professor of Psychology and Director of the Center for Consumer Research at the University of California, Davis. Started in 1976, the Center conducts consumer-interest studies for nonprofit organizations, including local and governmental agencies and voluntary organizations concerned with consumer issues. In addition to his work on consumer issues, Professor Sommer is the author of several books, including Personal Space, Social Design, *and* A Practical Guide to Behavioral Research *(with Barbara A. Sommer).* ♦

HOWARD G. SCHUTZ

Howard G. Schutz is a Professor of Consumer Sciences at the University of California at Davis. He received his B.A. (1950) from the University of Illinois; his M.S. (1952) and Ph.D. (1955) in Psychology from the Illinois Institute of Technology. Schutz has worked at the Quartermaster Food and Container Institute (1951–57), Battelle Memorial Institute (1957–1962), and since 1970 has been at the University of California at Davis, where his research interests cover the general area of consumer behavior. He teaches an undergraduate course in consumer behavior and a graduate course in consumer research methods. Dr. Schutz is a Fellow of the American Psychological Association's Division of Consumer Psychology and a member of the Association for Consumer Research, the American Council of Consumer Interests, and the American Marketing Association. He has been a Visiting Scientist at the California Department of Consumer Affairs and the Norwegian Institute for Consumer Research. ♦

9

The Consumer Psychologist

"Will consumers accept oranges grown with a lower amount of pesticide? The oranges are likely to have minor cosmetic blemishes but this will not affect flavor, juiciness, or nutritional quality." This question was brought to us by an agricultural researcher. If the answer were positive, it would encourage farmers to use smaller amounts of chemicals. Our task as consumer psychologists was to investigate the willingness of shoppers to buy oranges that are not cosmetically perfect.

What Is Consumer Psychology?

We are all consumers of goods and services. No matter what we do for a living, there is no way to be totally independent of the marketplace. We buy products, buy or rent housing, and use services such as medical and dental care. The study of consumer behavior is important to virtually every segment of society. Industry wants to know what people buy, who buys, why they buy, the influence of advertising, how people use the product, and what they do with it after they have finished with it. Government agencies, with responsibilities for promoting safety and health, need to present public messages effectively. Purchasers have a stake in learning about their own consumption patterns and how these are influenced by advertising, product design, store layout, and so on. Students of human behavior cannot disregard an activity as widespread and important as consumption. Consumer behavior is a vast testing ground for the laws and principles of general psychology, and a unique and important area of study in its own right. Research on consumer satisfaction cuts across other branches of applied psychology. Whether one is discussing counseling, teaching, or human factors (person-machine relationships), one can ask about the level of user satisfaction with the product or service.

Psychologists have become professionally involved in consumer behavior in different ways. Some are employed by firms selling products to consumers; others work for government agencies or private organizations devoted to consumer education and protection, and others study consumption as a special type of behavior. In advancing knowledge about consumers, the researcher contributes to the overall pool of knowledge about human behavior.

Consumer psychology is by definition a subfield of psychology. Consumer psychologists study motivation, perception, and

learning, the major topics of academic psychology, in order to better understand consumer decision making and behavior. Consumer psychology supplies many of the theoretical underpinnings of *marketing* which involves those business activities that direct the flow of goods and services from producer to consumer or user. *Consumer behavior* is a cross-disciplinary field that draws its concepts and methods from many different disciplines, including psychology, sociology, cultural anthropology, and economics. Consumer behavior includes the decision-making processes involved in acquiring, consuming, and disposing of goods and services (Mowen, 1987). This covers the study of what people consume, where, how often, and under what conditions (Engel, Kollat, & Blackwell, 1973).

The Background of Consumer Psychology

Consumer behavior is relatively new as a separate field of study. Most writers trace its origins to the 1950s, a period of relative affluence with an abundance of goods in the marketplace. Firms realized that they could sell products more easily if they could identify in advance what consumers wanted to buy. While it was possible to create demand artificially, it would be more beneficial to identify demand in advance and respond to it. The focus on consumer needs and wants became known as the *marketing approach* and provided the impetus to seriously study consumer behavior (Schiffman and Kanuk, 1983). Other factors contributing to the development of the field were the rapid pace of introducing new products (many of which would not be successful), shorter product life cycles (planned obsolescence), the identification of different subgroups among consumers, and an increased interest on the part of government agencies and private organizations in consumer protection (Schiffman & Kanuk, 1983).

The Scope of Consumer Psychology

The way specialists in consumer behavior approach problems depends on their training and professional orientation. Psychologists tend to emphasize basic processes such as perception and learning (e.g., How does a label acquire name recognition? What

kinds of colors and patterns have pleasant associations?). Sociologists are likely to emphasize the influence of family, class, and organizational memberships on what people buy and how products are used. Sociologists also study the process by which products are accepted by the public. Not all people adopt a new product when it is introduced. Some people adopt it quickly while others wait longer, and still others never make the change. Economists are likely to look at the effects of market and demographic factors on the demand for goods and services.

Most of the time, purchases are made by individuals, but sometimes they are made by more than one person, as when a couple selects a wedding ring or hires a painting contractor. Consumption is a process rather than an act, starting sometimes with an information search, such as reading back issues of *Consumer Reports*, followed by comparison of available items, purchase, use, and finally recycling, resale, or disposal of the item. Each aspect of the consumption cycle has been studied by researchers. There have been investigations of consumer search behavior and comparison shopping. Researchers have studied recycling—what types of people are most likely to recycle, what motivates them, and the types of appeals and incentives that are most likely to encourage recycling.

Much of consumer psychology rests on the application of basic psychological processes to consumer issues. Here are some lessons for advertisers based on social psychological studies undertaken in the laboratory:

- ♦ Messages attributed to high status, popular individuals will be more likely to influence attitudes than statements attributed to unknown individuals. Associations with celebrities can "rub off" on products.
- ♦ When a sports announcer has been linked to exciting events for years, pairing the announcer with a product is likely to convey a feeling of excitement to the product.
- ♦ An actor associated with so-called tough guy roles will bring this quality to the viewer's mind when paired with a specific product.
- ♦ Group discussions followed by group decisions are more influential in changing attitudes than printed information or a lecture. If advertisers can get satisfied customers to discuss products with others ("Alpha Beta, tell a friend"), the result is likely to be increased patronage.
- ♦ Observing another person performing an act which has

favorable consequences (buying a product and expressing satisfaction) is likely to increase the response pattern through modeling. This approach can be used to encourage people to use products correctly, e.g., recycle aluminum cans rather than discard them.

In a similar vein, psychologist S. H. Britt (1955) describes how principles of learning can be applied by advertisers:

- ◆ Order of presentation is very important. Information presented at the beginning or end of a message will be better remembered.
- ◆ Uniqueness is important. In a magazine with all full-color ads, a black-and-white advertisement will stand out.
- ◆ Since the rate of forgetting tends to be very rapid immediately after learning, repetition of the message is important.
- ◆ Learning is aided by active practice rather than passive listening. Encouraging listeners to participate in a message by sending in a coupon or filling in the blanks in a slogan (Smokey the Bear declaring, "Only you . . .") increases the likelihood that the message will be remembered.

Support for Research

Some research on consumer behavior is supported by industry as part of a marketing program. Other studies, often described as *consumer interest research*, are funded by government agencies who want to learn the best ways to present safety messages to consumers. A third category of research is value-neutral, in that it aims at understanding consumer behavior without trying to influence it directly. This type of research usually takes place at universities and examines theories of cognition, perception, and social influence as they relate to consumer decisions.

The source of support for research influences the questions asked and what is done with the results. Working for industry imposed many constraints on a researcher. Often the information collected is proprietary, i.e., it belongs to the client and cannot be published in technical journals. However, market researchers who work for industry may have access to sources of data and funds not generally available. Researchers who work for government may find themselves limited by bureaucratic rules in their choice of ques-

tions and methods. Some issues may be out of bounds to researchers working for one agency because they are officially classified as falling under the mandate of another agency. Relative to researchers working for industry or government, those teaching at universities enjoy more freedom in their choice of topics and methods but may be limited in funding and removed from sources of data.

In practice, research undertaken for industry, government agencies, and at universities is not always clearly separated. University faculty who develop models of consumer decision making may serve as consultants for industry or government, and those psychologists employed full time in private marketing firms are occasionally hired by nonprofit organizations to promote public service activities.

Organizations and Journals

The professional organizations and the journals show the range of activities that take place in consumer psychology. Division 23 (Consumer Psychology) of the American Psychological Association (APA) is the primary professional organization of consumer psychologists. Division 23 publishes a newsletter and the edited proceedings of the annual meeting. The Association for Consumer Research (ACR) is composed primarily of marketing psychologists, but overlaps considerably with Division 23. The organization is one of the co-sponsors of the *Journal of Consumer Research* and supplies many of the editors. Another major publication outlet for its membership is *Advances in Consumer Research*, the proceedings of the annual meeting. The American Council on Consumer Interests (ACCI) is an interdisciplinary organization devoted primarily to public interest issues. ACCI publishes the *Journal of Consumer Affairs* in addition to the proceedings of the annual meeting. The American Marketing Association (AMA) attracts psychologists working in industry or teaching in business schools and sponsors both the *Journal of Marketing* and the *Journal of Marketing Research*. There is an International Association for Research in Economic Psychology in Brussels, Belgium, and several international journals in the field, including the *Journal of Economic Psychology* published in Holland and the *Journal of Consumer Policy* edited in Denmark.

Psychologists who study how products are used (e.g., automobiles or appliances) may belong to the Human Factors Society and publish in journals such as *Human Factors* and *Ergonomics*.

Additional journals in which articles on consumer behavior can be found are the *Journal of Applied Psychology, Journal of Retailing, Journal of Psychology and Business, Psychology and Marketing,* and *Journal of Advertising Research.*

Depending on the issue studied, articles on consumer behavior are found in specialized periodicals in applied fields. The researcher undertaking a study of consumer satisfaction with legal services, for example, has the option of publishing the findings in a consumer-oriented journal, or in a periodical directed to the legal profession. A study of consumer attitudes toward food additives could be directed either toward an audience concerned with consumer protection or toward the food industry. The variety of publication outlets is an attractive feature of consumer research.

Market Segmentation

Manufacturers and marketers think of a *market* as composed of subgroups with different *demographic factors,* such as age, income, gender, and region, and *psychographic factors,* a term referring to the analysis of attitudes, values and activities. *Life-style research* attempts to describe how consumers live, think, and behave, by combining demographic information (age, education, gender and other population statistics), with attitudes, values, and interests. It has also been called AIO for activities, interests, and opinions (Wells & Tigert, 1971). Activities refer to how people spend their time, interests to their preferences, and opinions to their expressed attitudes. A combination of demographic and psychographic information yields profiles of those consumers likely to purchase products or use specific services (McNeal, 1982). Some consumer psychologists see this as an intermediate form between large-scale survey research which gets at surface opinions, and motivational research with small samples that tries to go beneath the surface.

A recent demographic trend in North America with implications for the food industry, has been the increase in two-earner households, i.e., families in which both husband and wife are employed outside the home. Two-earner households do not have an abundance of time for food preparation, leading to more interest in take-out items, rapid preparation techniques, and food eaten outside the home. To reach two-earner households, marketers emphasize the convenience of products. The increased number of elderly and retired people leads to the use of mature models in advertisements,

larger type on labels and advertising messages, and products specifically designed for this age group.

When used in advertising, psychographics is intended to determine the target (to whom the message should be aimed), the content of the message, and the most suitable medium (newspaper—if so, which one? or TV—what time of day and which program type?). Psychographic analysis was used to characterize accident-prone motorists. Relative to the accident-free drivers, those who had two or more accidents within the past five years were more likely to be impulsive risk takers, optimistic, cosmopolitan, and adventurous (Mehrota & Wells, 1977). This portrayal of the accident-prone driver may provide useful information to government agencies concerned with highway safety to the insurance industries in setting rates.

Methods of Consumer Research

Consumer psychologists employ a variety of methods that differ widely in the number of people included, the time and cost of the procedure, the format, and the depth of the questions. Describing these techniques should give you an idea of what consumer psychologists do, how they do it, and the type of training needed to enter the field. Most of these methods have been adapted from other fields of psychology, but some new ones have been developed.

Survey research is used to gather information about people's beliefs, attitudes, and values. The basis of a survey is the *questionnaire*, a series of written questions on a topic about which the respondent's opinions are sought. There are two general types of questionnaires: self-administered, which people fill out themselves, and interview-administered, in which a professional interviewer asks questions and writes down the answers. The self-administered form is more economical in time and cost.

Consumer researchers devote considerable effort to pretesting the questionnaire. If the questions are confusing and unclear to the respondents, the information received will be of little value. Most of the questions have multiple-choice answers which are easy to classify and analyze statistically. Open-ended questions, which leave the respondent free to respond in any way that seems relevant, are much more difficult to interpret, score, and analyze statistically. They are useful when the researcher does not know all the possible answers to a question, when the range of potential answers is so vast that the question becomes unwieldly in a multiple-choice for-

mat, or when the researcher wants to avoid suggesting answers. Multiple-choice questions are best when there is a large number of people in the survey, when the answers are to be machine-scored, and when the responses from several groups of individuals will be compared.

The questionnaires used in consumer surveys may also accompany products or services. The self-administered questionnaire left on a restaurant table or motel dresser for customers to fill out will not achieve a random sample, but it is a very economic and efficient way for a company to receive feedback from its customers and identify consumer problems before they become serious. You have probably filled out questionnaires that accompany warranty cards for a newly purchased camera or stereo. The manufacturer wants to know where the product was purchased and how you heard about their brand. This information is used by the company in its advertising and marketing programs.

Instead of a self-administered questionnaire, a survey may use an interview format. The key element of an interview is the verbal give-and-take between two people in that the format of the questions is set beforehand. Another way of describing an interview is as a "conversation with a purpose." Interviews can be done with an individual or a group, in person, or on the telephone. Interviewers can ask consumers where they shop, what items they buy, and what product attributes are important to them. This is a straightforward approach, similar to a public opinion survey, and does not require a great deal of interpretation or elaboration. If a certain percentage of the respondents say that they shop at a particular market because its prices are lower or that the quality of the fruits and vegetables is higher, this information is accepted at face value and marketing programs are built around it.

A *focus group* is a small number of consumers in a target population (the group that the firm or agency wants to reach) brought together with a trained facilitator for a several-hour discussion of an issue. Typically people are paid an hourly rate for their participation. A session is held in a special interview room containing a table, chairs, microphone, and sometimes a video camera for recording interactions. The format is left unstructured to allow a free flow of ideas and opinions. The facilitator may demonstrate products or distribute samples to stimulate discussion. Group interaction is likely to produce new ideas and viewpoints.

Some researchers want to approach the issue at greater depth by identifying connections between consumption and values. The *depth interview* can be a fruitful approach in the exploratory

phase of product development when little is known about how consumers will respond to a new item. Considerable use is made of follow-up questions. The interviewer follows the respondent's answer with requests for more information at an increasingly deeper level. Such interviews are expensive and time-consuming, and require a highly trained psychologist. This type of analysis is only as good as the skill and intuition of the interviewer.

Tauber (1972) employed depth interviews to find out why people shopped. At first glance, the answer is obvious, i.e., people shop because they need to purchase something. However, Tauber reasoned that there were other motives operating, some of which were unrelated to the actual buying of products and that an understanding of these other motives could lead to better shopping strategies for consumers and marketing approaches for retailers.

Tauber conducted individual depth interviews with 30 shoppers in Los Angeles. He asked people to recall their most recent shopping trips, discuss their activities while shopping, and what they enjoyed most and least about each trip. Individual answers were probed with follow-up questions. Among the shopping motives that came out of the interviews were the desire for diversion, self-gratification (buying something nice for oneself), learning about new trends and styles, the need for physical activity, and sensory stimulation. For motives which lie beneath the surface, depth interviewing is probably a better approach than a questionnaire or standardized interview. Since the depth interview tends to be time-consuming, often taking an hour or more per respondent, sample size tends to be small relative to public opinion surveys.

Motivation research describes a wide range of qualitative techniques for getting beneath the surface of why people act as they do, not at the surface level of immediate response, but at a deeper level connected with motivation, emotion, hope, fear, and so on. Ernest Dichter (1964), Director of the Institute for Motivational Research, is generally considered the originator of this technique which draws heavily from clinical psychology and psychoanalysis. The skills involve a combination of a public opinion researcher with those of a clinical psychologist. Many corporations use motivation research to design and pretest advertising messages.

Psychological tests are used to identify the types of consumers likely to purchase products or services. When the research employs *standardized tests* such as the MMPI (a personality test) or the Edwards Preference Inventory (a vocational interest test) for which detailed norms are available, the responses of people buying the product can be compared against the norms for the general

population to learn, for example, if people who buy sports cars are likely to be adventurous or fun-loving.

To study personality at a deeper level, the researcher can use *projective tests* which present people with incomplete or vague stimuli. It is assumed that people fill in the details by projecting their personal concerns and experiences. Often the nonverbal aspects of the response (e.g., hesitation or embarrassment) are as important as the verbal content. The following are examples of projective techniques.

On the *word association test*, the respondent is told a specific word and asked to respond with the first word that comes to mind. This method can be used to study associations to products, brands, or corporate names. Does a proposed brand label for outdoor equipment suggest freedom and exploration, as the manufacturer hopes? With the *sentence completion test*, the respondent completes a partial statement like, "When I eat pasta . . . ." Responses such as ". . . I am happy" or ". . . I meet friends" would be indicative of the social nature of the product. Responses to the incomplete sentence "People who shop at the supermarket after midnight . . . ." could identify motives for and barriers to late-night shopping. On the Thematic Apperception Test, the respondent is shown blurred or vague pictures and asked to tell stories about what is happening. In adaptations for marketing research, the scenes show people shopping or using products.

The *semantic differential* can be included in written questionnaires. This technique was developed by psychologist Charles Osgood and his colleagues to measure the meaning of concepts (Osgood, May, & Miron, 1975). When applied to marketing, people are asked to rate a product or service along a series of scales with divergent adjectives at either end. The adjectives can be tailored to suit the specific topic.

Example: Rate espresso along each of the following scales:

Strong . . . . Weak
Expensive . . . . Inexpensive
Excitable . . . . Calm
Friendly . . . . Unfriendly

The method can be used to develop a profile of products or brand names. The technique is easily administered to large numbers of respondents in a standardized manner and produces quan-

titative responses that can be compared across samples. Some researchers feel that the technique is useful for providing ideas that can be explored more fully using motivation research.

Experimentation is used by researchers working for the food industry who conduct flavor comparisons in which attributes such as sweetness or saltiness are systematically varied. Consumers rate each item tasted. When the labels and other identifying information are removed, this is called a *blind taste test*. Allison and Uhl (1964) recruited (without great difficulty) 326 beer drinkers to sample beer with and without identifying labels. When the labels were left on, the respondents expressed a strong preference for their favorite brands. When the labels were removed, there were no significant differences between brands. The researchers concluded that product differentiation among these major brands of beer arose primarily through the perception of the label rather than the taste of the beer.

A *consumer panel* is a group of consumers selected according to certain characteristics, such as age, education, or background, that is brought together on a continuing basis to evaluate products. When a marketing firm needs someone of a particular age or background, they look in their files and recruit someone from the list. Panel members might be asked to rate various brand names for a new product in terms of excitement or clarity, ease of remembering, and so on. By bringing the same people back on repeated occasions, the panel method allows the researchers to see how responses change over time. For example, can people remember the brand name of products evaluated a week earlier?

Consumer researchers may systematically *observe* people in retail settings to learn how purchase decisions are made. To what degree do people read product labels or safety information? How much time is spent in comparison shopping among similar products, or do consumers head directly to a favorite brand? Observation may also be used to determine how products are used. Researchers observed customers at salad bars in order to identify potential health and sanitation problems. Most observation is done unobtrusively without customers being aware of it. This is easier in a public setting such as a supermarket or restaurant than in private homes. *Participant observation* involves a researcher who becomes part of a setting in order to study it. A researcher using this approach might become a clerk in an auto showroom or clothing store in order to study shopping habits. A variation of participant observation is the *pseudoshopper* technique in which a researcher impersonates a customer. This method is used by government agencies to investigate consumer fraud. The researcher might drive

an automobile requiring only minor adjustments to various auto repair shops and obtain diagnoses and repair estimates. Estimates that were grossly out of line might be regarded as abusive or fraudulent and require action on the part of a regulatory agency.

CASE STUDIES

CASE ONE: STOVE TOP DANGER

I sit alone in my cubicle in the psychology building preparing the morning lecture for the consumer psychology course. As one of only a handful of applied psychology courses, the class is popular with students from different majors. Students in business, nutrition, textiles, and engineering take the class to learn about psychology, while students in psychology and sociology take it to learn about applied research.

The telephone rings, interrupting my train of thought. The caller is the secretary to Lori Davidson, the Director of the State Department of Consumer Affairs. I know her from an earlier project on deceptive advertising. A fruit juice manufacturer made claims about the vitamin C content of its product that the agency suspected were misleading. I led focus groups to learn how consumers interpreted the advertisements. The interviews showed that consumers drew incorrect conclusions about the product from the advertisements. Based on this information, the Department of Consumer Affairs persuaded the company to modify its ad campaign.

Lori had been a liberal arts major and then had gone to law school. After law school she took a job in the Fraud Division of the Consumer Affairs Department. When the governor appointed her director, this was welcomed by the agency staff who had feared the governor might make a political appointment. "We've been receiving complaints about the new Smith oven," Lori declared. "People can't tell when the front heating elements are lit, and if they put anything on the rear elements, they are likely to burn themselves. The manufacturer claims that people aren't reading the instructions and considers the letter writers to be a few cranks unrepresentative of their thousands of satisfied customers. Is there some way our agency can find out if the problem is widespread? I don't want to wait for the federal government to act. It will take months for them to get around to even looking at the issue."

By coincidence, I was familiar with the Smith product. I had been considering a new oven earlier in the year and had inspected the available models. When I first saw the sleek design of the Smith countertop, I wondered vaguely if purchasers would notice the

small warning light indicating the front burners were lit. On the basis of the comparison given in *Consumer Reports*, I had decided to purchase the top-rated Jones oven which was more economical in terms of gas and had the best maintenance record, but the image of the white unbroken Smith countertop had stuck in my mind.

I scheduled the meeting with Lori for the following week in her office. I enjoy occasional trips away from campus to learn what consumer agencies are doing. Several others attended the meeting. I brought my associate, Kathy, who handled the technical details of survey research. Accompanying the director were the head of the consumer complaints division and a staff attorney. As a result of the meeting, I received a contract to survey recent purchasers of Smith ovens. Under pressure from the agency, the Smith Company agreed to supply its records of all purchasers for the past three years.

The survey had several objectives. The primary one was finding out if other users, including those who had not made formal complaints, had experienced problems. Were there people who had been burned who had not made formal complaints, or who had received near burns that hadn't resulted in either injuries or complaints? The second goal was to identify more clearly the source of the problem and who was experiencing it. Did people read the instructions that came with the oven? Were people paying attention to the warning light that the manufacturer felt should have eliminated the problem? What were people cooking when the accident occurred? The project would also provide information for Henry's research program on consumer perceptions of product quality. Although the survey was directed toward a specific product, it would be an opportunity to collect additional data on consumer satisfaction.

From previous surveys on safety aspects of appliances and from agency files of written complaints, Kathy and I designed a questionnaire covering safety aspects of ovens in general, features of the Smith oven in particular, the respondent's level of satisfaction with products available in the marketplace, plus a few standard demographic items such as age, gender, education, and income that would be useful in interpreting the responses. Kathy drew a random sample of 400 households from the list of recent purchasers of the Smith oven. She estimated that approximately half of the delivered questionnaires would be filled out and returned. Each questionnaire was accompanied by a cover letter from Department of Consumer Affairs and a stamped self-addressed return envelope.

The questionnaires went out in early November. Undeliverable envelopes came back immediately. Two weeks later, Kathy sent a

reminder postcard to nonresponding households asking them to please fill out the questionnaire and send it in, or request another copy if they had lost the original. By mid-December, 53% of those surveyed returned their questionnaires. This return rate was sufficient to undertake a statistical analysis of the replies. As the data were being entered into the computer, Kathy phoned ten nonresponding households to estimate the degree of nonresponse bias. If the nonrespondents were similar in their views and demographic characteristics to the people who had returned the questionnaires, the nonrespondent bias would not be considered serious.

The survey turned up many other customers who had experienced problems with the Smith oven, including injuries that had not been reported to the state agency, and some near-misses that could have been serious. With the new information, the agency director called the manufacturer. Given the widespread nature of the complaints, the manufacturer agreed to withdraw the new model and take corrective measures.

A demographic analysis of the complaint letters showed that they tended to be written by the more educated and affluent purchasers. Kathy and I included this finding in a paper on consumer complaints published in the *Journal of Consumer Affairs*, the top journal among researchers working on consumer-interest issues. ♦

CASE TWO: WHITE BREAD BLUES

Profits were falling at the Acme Baking Company. Customers were no longer buying the glutinous white bread that had been the staple of the company's line of baked goods. The president of the company summoned to his office the head of the research department that creates new products for the company and the head of the marketing division that tests public acceptance. The president believed that a two-pronged attack on the problem was warranted, first to identify sources of consumer dissatisfaction with its white bread, and, second, to identify new products that would enable the company to increase its market share.

The research director was delighted to discuss some new items his staff had been working on. Several different bread products were being developed and he was eager to test-market them nationally. The marketing director was also aware of the problem. For years he had maintained that the consumer's romance with white breads was coming to an end. Children still liked the way that the bread wadded up in the mouth like chewing gum, but adults

were shifting to fuller-bodied breads with more fiber content. On the basis of the discussion, a fast-track research plan was devised.

Consumer panels would be used to compare Acme breads with those of competitors. The plan would require six months and an additional $50,000 budget allocation for the marketing division.

The marketing director who had been assigned responsibility for the project decided to subcontract the consumer tests to an outside marketing firm. Johnson Marketing Company was selected to be the subcontractor since the firm had offices in the major cities served by Acme Baking. District managers of Johnson Marketing were given responsibility for assembling focus groups of consumers representative of the Acme market. These individuals had previously volunteered to serve on consumer panels and would be paid $25 an hour each for their participation.

The sessions took place in testing rooms rented by Johnson Marketing in shopping centers. A videotape recording was made of each session. The facilitator began the session by asking the participants to taste and compare samples of unlabeled white bread and discuss their reactions. Then the participants tasted pieces of whole wheat and rye breads, also without brand names. Finally, the participants compared the white breads with the whole wheat and the rye breads in appearance, texture, body, and flavor. These dimensions had been identified by the marketing firm as important to purchasers of baked goods.

The group sessions revealed that Acme white bread was seen as less nutritious than the darker whole wheat and rye breads. Even though there was no actual basis for this difference, since Acme routinely enriched white bread to bring it up to government nutritional standards, the perception was widespread that darker color was associated with more flavor, body, and higher nutritional value. Especially for health-conscious consumers, the white color was associated with an absence of flavor and nutritional value. Depth interviews with a few selected consumers confirmed these impressions.

That there was no factual basis for these beliefs meant little to the company. If consumers were avoiding its products, there was a problem. The marketing director presented the company president with several options. Option A would involve more effective promotion of the company's present white bread through an emphasis on its nutritional value. However, the results of the focus groups and depth interviews showed it would be difficult to overcome the widespread perception that white bread contains "empty calories." Option B, which the marketing director recommended, involved the company promoting new whole wheat and rye breads under a

European-sounding name. It was felt that the previous image of the company's glutinous white bread would be so strong that the Acme label would be unsuitable for the fuller-bodied breads. Option B would also allow the company to retain its youth market who preferred soft and chewy white breads for sandwiches.

Option B was accepted by the company. They made enormous profits on the new line of European-style breads. The marketing director was given a promotion, the company president a large bonus, and the company stockholders received increased quarterly dividends. ♦

CASE THREE: COSMETICALLY IMPERFECT ORANGES
A group of researchers using integrated pest management (IPM) came to our offices seeking assistance. They wanted to know if consumers would be willing to purchase oranges grown with a minimal use of chemicals. The oranges would sometimes have minor cosmetic scarring but no decrease in flavor, juiciness, or nutritional

Some shoppers will choose only unblemished oranges; others are more concerned with the fruit's origin, freedom from pesticides, or price. (Courtesy of the editor, Robert Gifford.)

value. The issue is important to farmers considering ways of reducing their dependence on chemicals. If consumers are willing to accept produce with minor blemishes, farmers will be more willing to adopt the IPM approach.

The study was carried out at 14 supermarket locations and involved 409 shoppers. Each shopper was shown photographs of cosmetically perfect oranges alongside photographs of similar oranges with two levels of blemish (minor black scarring on the surface of the orange).

Initial acceptance of the blemished oranges was very low. Over three quarters of the shoppers were less willing to purchase a blemished orange relative to the perfect orange. Acceptance rose dramatically after information was provided about reduced pesticide use. With the explanation, the majority of customers, regardless of initial level of acceptance, became *more* willing to purchase the cosmetically imperfect orange than the standard orange. The shift in attitude was most apparent among younger, well-educated shoppers, and among women. The results showed the need for a consumer education component as part of an overall strategy to reduce farmers' dependence on agricultural chemicals. ◆

Becoming a Consumer Psychologist

Reflecting the interdisciplinary nature of consumer behavior studies, professionals can be trained in a variety of fields, including all of the social sciences and business and marketing programs.

Those whose fields are more narrowly focused on consumer psychology tend to use one of three available pathways into the field. The first is formal training in applied psychology at the undergraduate or graduate levels with emphasis in human factors, organizational behavior, or applied psychology. A second route is through a conventional program in experimental psychology followed by a shift into more applied studies. The third pathway into the field is through a degree in business or marketing with a heavy emphasis on psychological factors. Some universities, such as the University of Florida, UCLA, and Purdue University, offer graduate programs in psychological aspects of consumer behavior and marketing. Interested students should check catalogs for courses and programs of study. Further information on graduate programs

and careers in consumer psychology is available from the Division 23 Membership Chair, American Psychological Association.[1]

Some undergraduate courses are particularly relevant to consumer behavior. A course in personality will be useful in constructing *psychographic profiles* of consumers likely to buy certain types of products. From a class in experimental psychology, students can learn how to conduct preference tests or make flavor comparisons among competing food products. Research methods courses can teach the basics about questionnaire design and survey research which is used widely in consumer psychology. Training in clinical psychology can assist in conducting unstructured interviews with emphasis on qualitative information.

Courses in consumer behavior are often taught in university departments of family and consumer sciences, home economics, business, and economics. Courses taught in home economics or family studies tend to emphasize consumer education and protection: How can people be educated to spend money wisely on goods and services? How can the public be assured of product quality and safety in the marketplace? Courses offered in business schools tend to follow a marketing perspective: How can you sell goods and services to consumers?

A student who graduates with a B.A. degree may obtain an entry-level position in a marketing firm and receive on-the-job training in consumer behavior. Some firms prefer students to receive a general education at a university and leave the specific job-related training until later. Entry-level jobs may be in marketing research or corporate development in a consumer goods company. In addition, graduates may also work for advertising agencies or market research firms which service the corporate sector. A student interested in consumer psychology should seriously consider applying for internships to experience the practical aspects of this field. Opportunities for internships may be found in consumer affairs agencies associated with city, state, or the federal government, in the marketing departments of corporations, or in specialized market research firms or advertising agencies. The classified section of the telephone directory in your city will probably contain listings for firms doing marketing studies. Internships can involve paid employment on a full- or part-time basis interviewing consumers in shopping centers or other public locations, helping to conduct focus group discussions, or assisting in the myriad of

[1] See Chap. 1 Endnotes.

details connected with survey research. Student assistants are usually very welcome on these labor-intensive projects.

In conclusion, consumer psychology is a young and exciting field. There are only a few formal training programs, but it is possible to study other specialty areas of psychology and supplement this with on-the-job training in industry or government.

SUGGESTED READINGS AND REFERENCES

ALLISON, R. I., & UHL, K. P. (1964). Brand identification and perception. *Journal of Marketing Research, 1,* 80–85.

BRITT, S. H. (1955). How advertising can use psychology's rules of learning. *Printer's Ink, 252,* 74–77, 80.

DICHTER, E. *Handbook of consumer motivation.* (1964). New York: McGraw-Hill, 1964.

ENGEL, J. F., KOLLAT, D. T., & BLACKWELL, R. D. (1973). *Consumer behavior* (2nd edition). New York: Holt, Rinehart, & Winston.

MCNEAL, J. (1982). *Consumer behavior.* Boston: Little, Brown.

MEHROTA, S., & WELLS, W. D. (1979). Psychographic and buyer behavior. In A. G. Woodside et al. (Eds.), *Consumer and Industrial Buying Behavior.* New York: North Holland, p. 60.

MOWEN, J. C. (1987). *Consumer behavior.* New York: Macmillan.

OSGOOD, C. E., MAY, W. H., & MIRON, M. S. (1975). *Cross-cultural universals of affective meaning.* Urbana: University of Illinois Press.

SCHIFFMAN, L. G., & KANUK, L. L. (1983). *Consumer behavior* (2nd Ed.). Englewood Cliffs, NJ, Prentice-Hall.

TAUBER, E. M. (1972). Why do people shop? *Journal of Marketing, 36,* 46–49.

WELLS, W. D., & TIGERT, D. J. (1971). Activities, interests, and opinions. *Journal of Advertising Research, 4,* 27–35.

LOREN EDWARD ACKER

Loren Edward Acker received his Ph.D. from the University of California, Los Angeles, in 1966 and, with receipt of an international overseas fellowship, continued his work in behavior analysis and development through the University of London. He has since taught and done research in both applied and experimental behavior analysis in Canada at the University of Calgary and, currently, at the University of Victoria. His academic and research activities, supported by federal and provincial grants, have culminated in numerous scientific publications and the graduating of more than a dozen doctoral students.

Dr. Acker has been active in both the professional practice of applied behavior analysis and in the public dissemination of behavioral principles through television, radio, computer, and other media. But Dr. Acker insists, whether asked or not, that he owes his knowledge and convictions in the natural science approach to human behavior to his parenting of his four absorbing daughters (Becky, Lori, Kasey, Kelly). His very patient wife Sandy, his daughters, parents, and friends, to whom his behavioral analyses are most frequently directed, all know that though vexations at times, they always reflect his concern and caring. ◆

10

The Applied Behavior Analyst

I'm going to tell you about a client who enjoyed flashing. He was referred to me by the courts because he needed help with his sexual and social behaviors. It was either get help, or prison! But first, who am I and . . . ?

What Is Applied Behavior Analysis?

Applied behavior analysis is a technology popularly called behavior modification: this behavioral technology, not unlike the technology of engineering, for example, involves the application of basic facts and principles that arise out of countless laboratory experiments on animal, including human, performance—i.e., behavior analysis. Applied behavior analysts are usually psychologists, like me, who are interested in helping people change and strengthen their behavior by the application of these basic, laboratory derived principles. We are not, however, exclusively comprised of psychologists. Over the past two decades, an increasing number of sociologists, geographers, economists, political scientists, physicians, nurses, social workers, teachers, parents, and even kids have become trained in the principles or laws that govern behavior. Consequently, applied behavior analysts, as a group, have become greatly enriched in numbers and in kind. Many of these people have, to the benefit of the profession, published their efforts in professional journals to share their accomplishments and techniques.

Psychologists who are applied behavior analysts generally have three goals in the pursuit of our work. One goal stems from our roots in the *experimental* analysis of individual behavior (i.e., the general area of behavior analysis); that is, we are attempting to extend the reliability and generality of principles discovered in many laboratory experiments on human and other species. Another goal, which we share with nonpsychologists, is to help individuals acquire and maintain new and better ways of behaving which will prove beneficial to both the individuals seeking help and the people in their lives. A final goal, and a goal shared by all people, is to succeed at what we're doing so that we can make a living, earn the praise and respect of those around us, and generally enjoy the benefits of being a productive member of society. In fact, this last goal honestly reflects one of the most important and general principles that all behavior analysts assert so enthusiastically; namely, behavior—our own behavior included—is governed by its consequences, its success, its rewards, or payoffs.

As an applied behavior analyst, as a husband and parent, and as a friend and a professional resource to others, I have developed a very deep respect for the importance of the *consequences* which follow on behavior—whether it is my behavior, the behavior of my wife and kids, or the behavior of my friends, acquaintances, and clients. So it shouldn't be surprising that when a judge ordered a young adult male to seek therapy for his inappropriate sexual behavior ("flashing"), and that young male arrived at my office, I immediately considered the *consequences* for the young man of his flashing.

The young man, whom we'll call Tony, provided me with a very reasonable and likely description of the immediate consequences for his behavior—it felt good; it was arousing. This was likely the payoff! In fact, applied behavior analysts have found that people can often identify the rewards for their own behaviors, and Tony's remarks did not seem unreasonable. They were certainly unpalatable to me personally but partial nudity, in the presence of an unknown woman, could reasonably be arousing to Tony (and frightening to the woman!).

It is perhaps instructive to note here, that when I asked Tony why he flashed, he came up with some rather involved and complicated "reasons" which had to do with how he must have hated his mother and unconsciously disliked women in general. His words sounded like they had come out of a traditional, classic textbook in clinical psychology. Not coincidentally, Tony had been "treated" by several other professionals through the years. Being a behavioral psychologist, however, I was more impressed with the immediate consequences or rewards for his flashing as possible current reasons for it. I was less interested in historical matters; especially when the role of these types of variables (e.g. unresolved childhood conflicts) has never really been confirmed in laboratory experiments.

The effects of sexual arousal, and other very biologically based consequences to behavior, however, have a long history of identification as determinants of behavior—in both human and other species. Thus Tony, for the first time in his life, was confronted by a psychologist who was not going to delve into his childhood or his expressed attitudes toward his mother, women in general, or sex. This psychologist was primarily interested in noting that Tony got pleasure from his acts and this psychologist was about to launch Tony on a path of learning other behaviors—that is, other more acceptable ways of obtaining sexual arousal and, in addition, *mutual* gratification with women.

Tony seemed almost relieved to hear that no one was going to

try to deny him his pleasures. Many people have the mistaken belief, mainly from films, so-called slick literature, and from the actual practices of some clinical psychologists (who may be novices in applied behavior analysis and who are seeking badly needed and improved forms of therapy) that behavior modification primarily consists of punishing undesirable behaviors. Not so! Punishment, at best, only temporarily weakens behavior and, not surprisingly, clients quickly learn to avoid painful therapies—they stop coming back! Remember: Behavior is sensitive to its consequences.

Tony and I sat down to work out the details of his therapy. What were the more acceptable sexual behaviors? What were the acceptable situations in which mutual sexual gratification could be pursued (standing in dark alleys with his pants pulled down was not one!). What other social behaviors must he learn as preliminaries to sexual involvements with women (friendship and caring? dating? congenial talking? dancing?—what else would you consider as being appropriate romancing?).

It is especially instructive to note here how applied behavior analysis often involves sitting down with the client in the role as a coresearcher into the effective acquisition of new skills. Tony and I would keep records of his behaviors, analyze data together, and change our therapeutic procedures as the data dictated. Applied behavior analysis, then, is very often a cooperative endeavor rather than an authoritarian one. The applied behavior analyst, above all else, respects the fact that behavior is sensitive to its consequences and to ignore the desires or goals of the client is to ignore the client's rewards. And to ignore the client's rewards is to eventually doom the continuance of the therapy itself. In fact, in a broader sense, Tony and I were both embarking on a mutually dependent, professional relationship that could continue only so long as we were *both* achieving successes with it.

Many details of Tony's therapy must go unmentioned here. Briefly, Tony had to learn how to talk with women in mutually satisfying ways. He had to learn how to get his nerve to ask a woman out on a date. He had to learn a number of social skills that were obviously weak or lacking altogether in his behavioral repertoire.

Most importantly, he had to learn how to keep records and graphs of his improvements. This meant that his newly acquired and fragile social skills could be assessed by both of us, and that he could be rewarded by his own perception of improvements.

While Tony was learning the preliminaries to mutual sexual enjoyment with women, we had to be very careful that old, inappro-

priate ways of sexual gratification were avoided. I walked the streets many times with Tony, late at night when flashing was most likely to occur. Under these conditions, I would encourage him to *walk away* from possible flashing situations, to keep a count of his successes, and to graph them for later consideration.

Fortunately for Tony, we found an effective reward for his successes. Unfortunately for me and my wallet, the reward was a rebate on part of the fees. In addition, and as a means to immediate sexual gratification, Tony was encouraged to develop masturbatory techniques to the fullest and to discount the myths he had learned over the years about self-stimulation being harmful. Of course, one natural consequence for his failure to stay out of flashing situations was the court's threat to return him to prison where the incidence of knifings and beatings of sexual offenders is high. The fact that this delayed and punitive consequence had been so ineffective in the past (Tony was already a two-time loser) was recognized by both of us and so my wallet became a source of supplementary rewards for nonoffensive behavior. (It's sometimes hard to make a living if your only source of income is doing *effective* behavior modification.)

How did Tony do? Follow-up data showed that he managed to stay out of prison, acquire social and sexual skills, and eventually develop a close relationship with a woman-friend. And to this day I lose not one moment of sleep pondering the question as to whether he and his mate might, in the seclusion of their own living quarters, flash to one another for mutual sexual gratification.

The Background of Applied Behavior Analysis

The history of behavioral psychology is, perhaps, as old as the living beings on this planet. Though not a systematically pursued science until around the turn of this century, some of its major principles or laws were understood by our great-grandparents and by most of our ancestors for tens of thousands of years before them.

One of our central principles, the *law of effect*, which states that behavior is strengthened or weakened according to the consequences it produces, was certainly understood by the first parent who patted his offspring on the head after a good hunt or whacked the hand that attempted to steal food from him. In 1969, the *Journal of Applied Behavior Analysis* printed a two-century old letter

by Benjamin Franklin in which he advised a churchman to increase attendance among his parishioners by giving regular participants tasty treats. In short, ever since living beings first congregated in groups, they have learned that *behavior is controlled by its consequences.* All living creatures, in one way or another, wield the whip or the carrot, the sneer or the smile in affecting the behavior of others. This has been good, it has been bad, it has built happiness, it has brought sadness, but most of all it has been as natural as nature can be. The law of effect reflects the adaptability of living beings to their environments: behavior that succeeds gets stronger, and behavior that fails, weakens.

The history of behavioral psychology, as a natural science, is a recent one. It began early in this century as a systematic study of what our parents, and generations before them, knew about behavior in a less formal and much less exact way. The groundwork had been laid by the end of the 1800s by developments in the natural science of biology. The proponents of evolutionary theory, for example, observed that species of living beings were biologically evolved according to the successes of the species in biologically adapting to their environments.

It was a small but significant step to assert, in the decades to follow, that the behavior of individual members of species may also adapt, behaviorally, to their physical and social environments. Thus, within the life span of any individual, those behaviors that were successful in promoting the well-being of the individual would grow stronger while unsuccessful ones would grow weaker.

To assert, in the early twentieth century, that the biological characteristics of species evolved according to their success at adaptation and that the behavior of individuals, within their lifetime, were also governed by adaptive outcomes, was a heresy to many—especially in the case of behavioral adaptation. Nonetheless, behavioral psychologists began emerging who would bring the tools of laboratory experimentation to bear on the topic of behavioral adaptation in living beings. For example, Edward Thorndike demonstrated, in a series of classic experiments, that cats efficiently learned to escape puzzle boxes and their solutions were determined by what had succeeded for them in the recent past. He formulated the controversial behavioral law of effect in which many behaviors were seen to be determined, primarily, by the effects or consequences they produced from the environment (i.e., successful or unsuccessful adaptation).

By the 1930s, psychologists had begun to systematically and painstakingly investigate the generality of this law of effect on many

other living creatures, including human beings. By 1953, B. F. Skinner had published *Science and Human Behavior* and the path had been cleared for the large-scale experimental analysis of individual human behavior. And as this *experimental* analysis of behavior produced reliable findings, an increased number of behavioral psychologists turned their attention to the application of the emerging behavioral laws to problems of individual human beings; that is, the field of applied behavior analysis took root.

Scope of Applied Behavior Analysis

Not Just Flashing

Not all applied behavior analysts work with flashers. In fact, we don't all work with clinical problems. A great many behavior modification programs have been undertaken for such diverse problems as increasing litter pick-up, increasing bus ridership in urban areas, increasing energy conservation, increasing the use of safety equipment in work situations, increasing healthful exercise, increasing student learning in the classroom, and increasing just about any behavior that people want to increase in themselves or others. The key term here is *increase*.

From comments I have already made, it should be clear that applied behavior analysts favor the use of rewards or, as we call them, *reinforcers*, as a consequence for behaviors to be strengthened. Noxious consequences can be used to weaken behavior, but no one really enjoys giving spankings and threats, and no one really enjoys receiving them; so effective and ethically sounder behavior modification procedures tend to rely more on *reinforcers*.

Littering

How do we increase litter pick-up in movie theaters? We have actually made free tickets available for a certain number or weight of bags of litter. We have reinforced litter pick-up. As an applied behavior analyst you, sometime in the future, might be consulted by a theater chain to install and monitor such a program.

Automobile Addiction

How do we increase bus ridership in a crowded urban area? We have paid people to ride buses—not with money, necessarily (although

why not!), but with vouchers for discounts at local businesses or free drinks with a purchased hamburger.

You, as a behavior analyst, might be consulted by government to implement such a program as part of an energy conservation or antipollution program. Of course, you'll have to know what to suggest when the data begin showing, as actually happened, that the increased ridership consists of middle-aged people who used to walk rather than people who used their automobiles. In other words, you might discourage people from walking who should be exercising without having any impact on reducing gasoline consumption, exhaust emissions, or traffic congestion. You will have to know enough about changing behavior and assessing the changes to modify the program.

By the way, the involvement of community merchants for providing reinforcers is a mutually agreeable practice to both government and commerce. My students and I find that merchants are eager to use vouchers as reinforcers for "good" community behaviors because it gets consumers into their stores. And governments love it because they don't have to use tax money to pay for "good" behavioral changes.

Energy Wasting

How do we increase energy conservation? A good deal of experimentation on entire neighborhoods has shown that pleading for conservation through advertisements or local community groups may change how people talk (i.e., their expressed attitudes), but it doesn't change their actual use of electric power. However, a proportionately large cash rebate on an electric bill contingent (i.e., dependent) on reduced consumption during peak periods when brown-outs are likely, reduces the actual behavior of energy consumption.

You, then, could be approached by lower power utilities to develop and evaluate similar conservation programs.

Carelessness

How do we increase the use of safety equipment in work situations? Research indicates that office memos or displayed posters are of little benefit. Even special seminars or workshops, when their effects are actually measured, appear grossly inadequate (although they certainly earn money or status for the so-called leaders). When reinforcers such as bonuses and extra time for coffee breaks are used contingently, however, safety related behaviors change and the economy of reduced injury becomes apparent in bottom-line

figures. But, again, all this depends on data and on improving our techniques as the data dictate.

Self-Destruction

How do we increase healthful behaviors? This is a relatively new area of application and the results are not yet complete for long-term effects. However, over shorter periods of several months, exercise and improved eating habits can be increased through both social and material reinforcers administered by spouses and other family members. Gloomy or deathly predictions by physicians, public health officials, or family members seem of little benefit (with their presumed effects being seldom, if ever, documented).

Ineffective Teaching

How do we increase student learning in the classroom? In this case, almost 20 years of controlled studies on tens of thousands of students in classrooms across the continent suggest that students can be taught more effectively. With the systematic use of various reinforcers, students learn in much less time, at a much higher level of mastery, with greater enjoyment, and with a lessened likelihood of dropping out of school. Reinforcers such as food, praise, simple cash, or merely immediate performance feedback are used in association with academic materials that have been carefully arranged in order of increasing difficulty for each individual student. Most importantly, the academic skills, themselves, are specified in terms of observable behaviors (i.e., in terms of what the student actually must SAY or DO).

Better Living through Experimentation

Have you noticed a common element of *experimentation* in all of these problems and the attempts to solve them? Aside from what we have already learned, namely that reinforcers are used to increase desirable behaviors, there is ongoing experimentation in applied behavior analysis.

Experimentation is what you do when you're not sure or you simply don't know the answer to the question of what causes what. Psychology is a very young science and thus we are often in this predicament. So, when we set out to implement behavior modification programs, we try to obtain credible conclusions—i.e., that what we did caused the observed results. We not only want to walk away from

the project with a sense of having helped each client, we also want to have an increased sense of scientific understanding about the events we were working with—what caused what! This, apart from all else, gives merit to the work of applied behavior analysts. I (and YOU if you want a career in this area) must know how to record and analyze data and design programs in such a way that the analyses will yield answers as to what is likely causing what.

Don't Let Data Scare You

Now don't get scared at the mention of data, analyses, and experimental designs. Behavior analysis, as a natural science, relies less on large-scale, massive studies, which often require sophisticated statistical treatment, than does psychology, in general, as a social science. In fact, many behavior analysts question the need for the use of statistical methods and involving more than a few participants or subjects in any behavioral experiment (see Sidman, 1960).

The analyses of many of our experiments rely heavily on graphic and other pictorial presentations of data. This is like many experiments in biology and even the physical sciences in which numerous repetitions (replications) of experiments are preferred to one-shot, statistically analyzed studies. Also like many experiments in the natural and physical sciences, the design of our experiments is more a matter of simple logic than the meeting of statistical requirements.

For example, if you want some evidence that free movie tickets, given for bags of litter, causes cleaner theaters, then:

1. At a Saturday matinee, collect and weigh the amount of litter before you make tickets contingent on collected bags of litter.
2. At the next Saturday matinee, announce the contingency between tickets and litter and measure the effect.
3. Cease the contingency at the third Saturday's matinee and measure the effect.
4. Resume the contingency for a fourth Saturday's measure.

We would expect to find that the theater is cleaner for those matinees in which there is reinforcement of litter pick-up. Do you know how to weigh litter? Can you graph the numbers in a presentable fashion? Can you understand the logic of doing the experiment in the order of the events just specified? If you can say a

tentative yes to these questions, then you're on your way to understanding the basics of doing research as an integral part of applied behavior analysis. Of course, there are more details to this than I have mentioned, but the logic and skills are very much the same. There should be nothing in all this scientific endeavor which should scare you away from a career in applied behavior analysis.

CASE STUDIES

The great variety of problems to which applied behavior analysts can bring their skills and interests was just barely touched on in the preceding section. In fact, any social, political, economic, or personal problem which has people behaving in one way or another, can be one in which an applied behavior analysts could play an important role in the solution. It makes sense that if one is concerned with people's screaming behavior at rock concerts, politicians' decision behaviors at a cabinet meeting, consumers' purchasing behavior in the supermarket, or a child's academic or disruptive behaviors in a classroom, then the scientist who has special training in the principles of behavior is needed. Thus, a career in applied behavior analysis likely means a readiness to respond to behavioral questions in a wide variety of problem areas.

Perhaps I can give you a further appreciation for the breadth of involvement one must expect from a career in applied behavior analysis by recounting three instances in which my expertise in the analysis of behavior has been useful to others.

CASE ONE: PROBLEMS IN CHILD REARING

I often teach courses in child psychology at my university. I could, however, be teaching these same courses at a college, a community center, or a public school in the evenings. The fact that I AM teaching is not a coincidence; many applied behavior analysts have teaching as their main source of income and, as we'll see, use teaching as their major tool in doing behavior modification.

Almost always, in teaching a course in child psychology, I am fortunate to have a number of parents as students who are currently up to their ears in child rearing. I say I am fortunate because the parents reinforce me for keeping my course material at a practical and down-to-earth level and the remaining, as yet childless students, seem to appreciate a less theoretical, less ivory-tower approach. My courses, then, are usually well attended and larger than most. The upshot of all this is that I have no shortage of

students who approach me every term with dilemmas about misbehaving kids—either their own kids or the children of others.

One typical and recurring child-rearing problem has to do with getting a young child to quietly stay in his or her crib or bed at night once the lights-out call has been given, and to manage this in a way that will leave the parents (or other attending adult) in a decent enough frame of mind to enjoy the rest of the evening. Unfortunately, there are many young children who, once in bed, seem to use the bed as only a temporary base for continued action: "Tuck me in"; "I wanna glass of water"; "Mommy . . . uh . . . uh . . . Daaaaaaady . . ." Many minutes or even hours will pass in which the adults must engage in counteractions to protect their time for adult leisure from kiddy corruption.

This one simple but potentially devastating problem contains several interesting points about behavioral control. First, in any attempt to modify behavior, a behavioral analysis should reveal the minimally acceptable, good behavior that the person (in this case, the child) is *currently* producing. Second, a pathway or avenue, lined with reinforcers, must be charted *from* the current, minimally acceptable behavior *to* the most desirable behavior. Third, a seemingly large amount of time and energy must be initially devoted to the process if a long-term solution is to be realized.

As an applied behavior analyst I was obliged to tell these adults (parents, nannies, and babysitters alike) that they must put down their guns, clubs, knives, and threats, put a smile on their face and be ready to use up to an hour of praise, pats, and hugs on each of several nights of intensive parenting.

Remembering the three points I just listed, the procedure I've convinced others to try goes like this. First, determine the number of seconds in which the child is likely to stay nestled down, under the covers and without fussing, after the adult has turned and started to leave the room (we call this a *baseline* and, in severe cases, it quite often turns out to be a rather small number like four or five seconds). Second, divide this number in half and ask the adult to leave the child for only this number of seconds, returning to praise, pat, or kiss (i.e., reinforce) the little one for having behaved properly. Note how I ask them to start with the minimally acceptable yet likely behavior, i.e., just a few seconds of quiet silence from the child. Third, ask the adult to repeat this last step, increasing the interval between reinforcements by only 50% each time.

Usually, within a half-hour or so, the child will be asleep before the next reinforcement and the whole procedure can be repeated on subsequent nights, increasing the starting value by 50% on each

occasion. The adults have started with the currently occurring, minimally acceptable good behavior and literally walked a pathway, lined with reinforcers for them and the child, toward the most desired behavior. Within a week, the problem should be solved. The adults are then free, usually for life, except for a few intervening and short retraining sessions, to enjoy their evenings in peace and quiet—a peace that they typically have not had for the last several months or more before having consulted with an applied behavior analyst.

Of course, I would never have prescribed such a procedure if I hadn't already found it to be quite successful with each of my own four daughters and the children of many next door neighbors in apartments with tissue-paper thin walls.

This example, from my own practice, has a feature which is common to many behavior modification programs. I call this feature the unpretentious or direct approach. Before considering a career in this area, and even before going on in your reading of this chapter, you should be clear on what one gives up, as a professional, in entering the field of applied behavior analysis. What one gives up is that professional mystique in which you might enjoy basking when practicing other kinds of therapy. For example, if you were asked to treat the child management problem which I just outlined, you might find it more exciting to query the parents about their "real" feelings toward their child, the child's possible insecurities and fears, and more of the psychological, mental, or otherwise *unobservable* but supposedly more "meaningful" aspects of human relationships.

If you think you'd enjoy this type of role in the lives of your clients, then you may find it hard to accept that a career in applied behavior analysis denies you this mysticism and the worship from clients that it can bring. Quite often, instead, you will simply be considering and counting observable behaviors (screaming, getting out of bed, head knocking on the crib or wall) and prescribing rather *direct* and (initially) time-consuming actions for your clients. In fact, you'll be putting the "therapy" most directly into *their* hands. Not all clients will initially appreciate this!

As you teach them to start at their child's current level of acceptable behavior (merely a few seconds worth in the example we've just been considering) and to increase their demands very, very slowly while being generous in their use of reinforcement, you'll find yourself being more a teacher than a traditional therapist—a teacher of basic principles of behavior. We will see this role of teacher again in the coming examples and I would ask you to not be disappointed with the prospect of giving up a more typical

therapist role in favor of a more behavioral one. The personal satisfaction that comes from helping people to successfully solve behavioral problems can often outweigh any thrills from being mystical. ♦

CASE TWO: GENTLENESS AND AFFECTION
The occurrence of aggression in its milder forms of shoving and kicking among kindergarten kids or more violent behaviors among older children and adults has received more attention by all kinds of research psychologists than almost any other social behavior. It shouldn't surprise you, then, that being a behavioral psychologist who insists that we must focus on building positive behavioral repertoires through reinforcement rather than weakening behaviors through punishment, I would become interested in the flip side of this social question; namely, the encouragement of gentleness and affection.

Applied behavior analysts tend to be mavericks in psychology. If everyone else is studying hitting and kicking then, perhaps, the important thing to look at is hugging and patting behaviors. Whether we are just professional nonconformists or nonconformists in our profession is a topic for another time; suffice it to say that there is good reason to study the other side of aggression.

To begin, however, let's look at the conventional wisdom for studying aggression. If our interests in aggression are primarily for applied and social reasons, as opposed to being mainly academic in nature, then understanding the causes of aggression could have two benefits. First, it could allow us to avoid inadvertently teaching the harsher forms of aggression to our children. Second, it could allow us to more effectively suppress antisocial forms of aggression in those who have already learned it.

In both of these cases, however, we will have ignored the more fundamental question of what people could be doing *in place of* aggressing toward each other; the more humane forms of social interaction and problem solving for our kids and ourselves. We have no shortage of ways to counter aggression in others by using punishment (itself an aggressive act); our history as a species testifies to this. A very challenging question for our species, however, is the question of how to build and maintain the gentler behaviors in a spirit of cooperative and constructive problem solving and social interaction. Toward this end, the applied behavior analyst, supported by much research on both animal and human learning, advances the proposition that we profit, in the long term, by building or strengthening good behaviors through reinforcement. We

naturally turn to the option of the development, the construction, the maintenance of pro-social, gentle, and affectionate behaviors rather than to the punishment and suppression of aggression.

Some teachers and parents ask me how to reduce aggression in their children. Such questions should be immediately reformulated in their positive form; namely, how can we encourage gentleness and affection in our children?

Over the years of having done basic laboratory and field studies on gentleness and affection, my students and I have developed reliable measurements by counting the frequency of such behaviors as pats, hugs, kisses, and gentle touching. Behavioral measurement, above all else, is a prerequisite to doing any applied behavior analysis. Thus, when a local school approached me with a request to discourage aggression (i.e., encourage gentleness) in their students, we were set to go.

To deal with this request, we tried to use current, common practices in the classroom in an effort not to disrupt normal routines. In the grade school years, kids spend a significant amount of time listening to stories read by teachers and parent volunteers. It is generally assumed that such stories provide an enrichment and broadening of experience. More specifically, it is assumed that the content of such stories has some effect on the behavior of the children. Working on this assumption, we read a classroom full of children a story in one of several different ways and looked at the subsequent effect on their play behavior with toys and with each other. We sought to create a story reading situation that could be used easily within school classrooms and that would encourage gentle forms of subsequent interaction.

One might expect that this procedure would be rather straightforward and easy. One simply reads stories, to kids, which contain little or no aggression and lots of gentleness and then one sits back and lets the printed media do its work. Isn't it generally believed that the media (TV, books, films, and other forms of entertainment) effectively teach our children ways of behaving? This is the popular wisdom. It may not, however, be this simple!

We wrote two stories concerning a child's visit to the local zoo. One story, called the *gentle story*, contained a variety of instances in which the child was affectionate, caring, and gentle with various animals he encountered. The other story, called the *control story*, was identical in content but lacked any mention of nice interactions.

The *gentle story* was read by the teacher in one of three ways to each of three groups of children. To one group, it was simply read, with feeling, but with no embellishments. To another group, it was

read but the teacher also demonstrated, with the aid of stuffed animals, the various affectionate, caring, and gentle behaviors which the child in the story engaged in. To a third group, the story was read in a participative way, with the teacher demonstrating the various nice behaviors, but also asking each child, in turn, to demonstrate to the class, with a stuffed animal, the nice behavior just described. Immediate verbal praise (reinforcement) was given for the child's participation in the story.

The results were clear. When we counted the incidence of gentle, caring, and affectionate behaviors in the children's play, later in the day, with toys and with each other, only the third, participative way of reading the story had a positive effect (compared to that of the control story). It was not sufficient merely to read a nice story, nor to read and demonstrate for the children the nice behaviors in the story. The only way to increase the children's nicer interactions was to read the story, demonstrate the nice behaviors, and then ask them to practice some nice behaviors during the reading. This made them more affectionate with their toys, gentler with each other during their free play period and, most interestingly, *less aggressive* to each other too!

It's provocative to speculate that it may be what children are asked to *do*, rather than what they are asked to *see*, that more strongly affects what they do later. I do not suggest that there are no effects of the media on our children. I ask that we temper our beliefs about the magnitude of these effects and perhaps concentrate more on what we directly teach our children to do in their every day interactions with us. This can be a tough pill to swallow, as parents and teachers, because it suggests that our time *alongside* our kids, which takes more of our time, may be more important than their time merely in our presence.

One consequence of this applied behavior analysis study, aside from stimulating additional experiments, was that some teachers from other schools became interested in doing participative story reading with their classes. Did we succeed in some small way in developing a technique for encouraging gentle behaviors which could be easily incorporated into current grade school practices of story reading? More importantly, did we succeed in some small way in refocusing the efforts of adults away from a strategy of weakening aggression through threats and punishments to a strategy of encouraging gentleness through reinforcement? I sincerely hope so.

The causes of behavior are not always what the popular wisdom would have us believe. Simply letting kids passively listen to

and watch stories (or passively submit to other media) may not be as influential as having them participate in their learning. Applied behavior analysis has often enough produced data that challenge currently accepted truths. So be warned! A career in applied behavior analysis, if not in any scientific endeavor, may put you at odds with the general community on more than several occasions. Be prepared to be different; be prepared, if necessary, to buck the popular wisdom. ♦

CASE THREE: APPLIED BEHAVIOR ANALYSIS ON THE CAMPUS
The environment that is closest of all to many applied behavior analysts is the environment in which their major income is earned—the university or college campus. In my case, I have been on salary at three universities. I spend a good deal of time teaching university students. The behaviors I have to encourage or build in my students (or should we call them clients?) are their reading behaviors and their verbal behaviors both on written exams and orally in class. Of course, they interact with me in many other ways, some quite pleasant and some not so pleasant, but their academically oriented behaviors are what I'm paid to assist. Therefore, if there is anything to the technology of behavior modification, I should, as a trained professional in this area, be able to create more effective teaching to enhance the learning of my students (i.e., clients!).

If you choose a career in applied behavior analysis, you will likely be teaching too, whether in a community mental health center, a hospital or institutional setting, a school or college, or even in private practice. You may very likely give reading assignments to your clients or students so that they can understand how to count and graph behaviors, how to take baselines with their spouses, children, or themselves, and how to use reinforcement contingencies and many other specialized techniques to change behavior. In short, if you are an applied behavior analyst, you are a teacher.

You might think that you already know how teachers should be teaching. After all, you've been in school for more than a few years yourself. Don't however, be misled by your own experiences. The use of behavior modification techniques in the classroom is not yet commonplace. Though they are very widespread across the world, they are likely unknown to you; they are still no match, numerically, for conventional, traditional teaching. You have likely not experienced mastery learning, personalized systems of instruction (PSI), contingency management, direct instruction, or precision teaching, a few examples of current behavior modification programs being used in classrooms. Some details about the kind of teaching you

could be doing as an applied behavior analyst are given below.

One common problem is that students or clients often fall behind in their reading assignments. This is not an outrageous assertion, is it? You may not have kept up on reading the chapters in this book. (Quite frankly, when I was a student, I procrastinated too.) Reading academic material, for reasons well known to applied behavior analysts, either can't compete with more pleasurable events or is too often aversive and people avoid aversive, punishing events.

An excellent way to encourage steady progress in reading assignments is to provide frequent exams or quizzes, up to three times a week, and to demand at least an "A" test performance which, if met on the first quiz, gets you off the hook for the rest of the week. In addition, let's not use up time with lectures—after all, you could use this time for reading. Not that lectures can't be fun and be made to seem very valuable. I personally enjoy lecturing. But lectures are a relatively poor way to transmit much information efficiently. Lectures can be painless, if they are coated with humor and decorated with audiovisual aids, but learning is usually an active process— the student should engage in the behaviors to be learned; that is, the student should write or talk or otherwise *do* the subject matter. Sitting comfortably in a room playing the roll of a passive sponge is hardly learning as it should be.

What remains, then, is a course in which the student has three chances each week to pass a quiz on the week's reading at an *A* mastery level. In addition, there are no lectures except for one "enrichment" (fun) lecture at the end of the week for those who have passed the quiz. Thus, with this system, students can receive more immediate feedback (reinforcement and further instruction) for their reading efforts and, thus, should keep up better than ever before. (By the way, your grade for the course is determined by the number of chapters or units you pass at an *A* level; that is, what you decide to learn, you learn well or you don't bother at all!)

How well does this work? According to our published results (Acker & Goldwater, 1975) it's a very effective system. You are much more likely to get an A in the course, you retain the information longer and better than when taught by traditional lecture methods (as checked one year later). You are also more likely to continue taking psychology courses and you state that you've greatly enjoyed the experience. It's called mastery learning and it comes in various sizes, forms, and flavors—some more successful than others. And it's occurring, in one form or another, in a growing number of universities, colleges, community health centers, public schools, and other places where people have something to learn in the way of

new behaviors. As an applied behavior analyst, you may someday be using it, in much more refined and effective forms, on your clients (i.e., students!).

But be clear, your role as a teacher will be more as a behavioral engineer, creating an environment to optimize learning, rather than as a guru or philosopher-king with students or clients sitting in awe at your feet. Again, we see that a career in applied behavior analysis may lack a certain mysticism and "pizzazz." But take it from me, there's a lot of reinforcement for you that comes from being *successful* at increasing desirable behaviors.

Students or clients should *perform* behaviors in order to learn them. What if your goal is to have students or clients read only limited amounts of material but be able to fully understand and relate their understanding to others? The behavior modification technique for this goal is similar—namely, reinforce students for talking intelligently about what they're reading. My students and clients, both, must learn the basic principles of behavior. And, more specifically, they must show me that they can communicate the material to others because education OR therapy is a communal enterprise which demands the involvement of others. So if you're considering a career in applied behavior analysis, you should consider the kinds of techniques you may be using to get people to talk the subject matter.

Students in my advanced courses, rather than being passive sponges in a lecture situation, earn points for talking, answering questions, debating with others, and generally participating in their learning. Thus their grade, in part, depends on how many times they have spoken up in class. Likewise, clients taking night courses in parenting have been reinforced for speaking up in my classes, for talking the subject matter, for saying how they'll take a baseline, how they'll administer reinforcement, and how they'll measure the outcomes. Their grade or praise from me is contingent on their speaking up.

You might ask, at this point, whether this at all guarantees that the students or clients have prepared enough to be able to say intelligent things. You should suspect, however, that most adults have learned that opening their mouths and having gibberish come out can be socially painful. Our schooling has usually taught us that there are no shortages of classroom vultures waiting to pounce on the carcass of nonsensical, ill-prepared words. In fact, this may account for the reluctance to speak out in class. By adding a reinforcement contingency, however, to speaking out (by making grades or approval contingent on it or even by throwing out candy

bars to students who speak, which I have sometimes done) the likelihood that the students will adequately prepare, judging by the content of their discourse, dramatically increases. That is, if you can get people to open their mouths you'll find that they don't punish themselves by failing to prepare their words. For adults, at least, speaking in public on well-defined topics almost seems to guarantee adequate preparation.

As I've said before, therapy and teaching are very difficult to differentiate in applied behavior analysis—they are much the same thing to us. In working with students in the smaller, more advanced courses where their verbal behaviors are being targeted for strengthening or change, an occasional student surfaces who has an intense fear of talking aloud in class. Here, any distinction between therapy and teaching seems to completely vanish. You are trying to get the student to acquire new concepts (words and syntax). Your efforts to do so must deal directly with his or her fears about talking in class.

Here again, I'll show you the direct, frontal approach to this problem which addresses the educational goal and the fear at the same time. In short, the student is instructed to see me before a class meeting, present his written expression to me for critique, to take the improved written concept to class and read from it when called on (only the first several words if that's all he can manage), and then to sit back and enjoy my very positive reaction to his contribution. This particular technique, in various forms, has worked with every student who has come to me for help. By the time the term is half over, most of these initially fearful students are easily contributing in oral participation in class.

Therapy and education have shared goals. In the case above, you would not want to cure a fear of speaking out without assuring that he or she will have something appropriate to say. Likewise, you can't teach someone to say appropriate things if they have a fear of talking out. Both problems, the therapeutic one and the educational one, have to be addressed, simultaneously.

Your career in applied behavior analysis, if you're put into some kind of formal educational role, which is quite likely, will often entail individualized therapy programs like the one described. People you will be dealing with in a classroom, whether at a university, college, community health center, night school or other agency, will be individuals in need of behavioral change—many different kinds of behavioral change—and you'll be the person best equipped to do it.

Let's return, now, to the teaching of verbal skills in a classroom situation. You can get as specific as you want about the verbal skills

that the students or clients are to learn. I have reinforced them for just simply stating, in their own words, the ideas they've read. I have reinforced them for criticizing the content of their readings. I have reinforced them for defending their readings from the intellectual criticisms of other students. In short, I have tried to reinforce them for actively involving themselves, verbally, in the material to be learned. But none of it could have been done, on any scale at all, without grades, approval (or even candy) as reinforcers.

Does this all sound a bit childish? Students sometimes complain, when presented with behavior modification techniques, that they're old enough not to need "spoon feeding" or other such crutches. My experience and data have shown me, however, that this sort of objection quickly vanishes as they find themselves doing things which they had not expected to be able to do (such as getting first class marks and speaking out, intelligently, in class). A career in applied behavior analysis can, unfortunately, subject you to some initial disbelief or reluctance from students or clients. You've got to be prepared for this and to ride it out until the behavioral changes begin occurring. And then nothing succeeds like success! ♦

Becoming an Applied Behavior Analyst

Education

It's never too late to begin an appropriate educational pathway to becoming an applied behavior analyst. However, there are easier and harder ways to do it. The harder ways are very numerous, as you can imagine, and I need not detail them here—we all seem to readily stumble across the many hurdles that wind up in our paths. So I will propose one of the more direct and ideal pathways. This will be a pathway for you to anchor your plans to and for you to deviate from as the needs arise and, indeed, they will arise.

Your educational pathway should begin by selecting an appropriate university for the initiation or continuation of your undergraduate training. I recognize that many of you may be economically prohibited from having a wide range of institutions to pick from. I suggest, however, that you follow the logic of my recommendations and modify the specific details to suit your own situation. At worst, you'll only be able to satisfy one or two of my recommendations, but you'll at least know what some of the critical

factors may be and you may be able, at a later time, to make up actual deficiencies in imaginative but practical ways.

Let me repeat that the relationship between psychology and behavior analysis is volatile. Some behavior analysts, both applied ones and those solely in basic research, have made explicit statements, at international conferences on behavior analysis, that they do not feel at home in psychology or other social science departments. Some have suggested the operation of separate programs at the undergraduate and/or graduate levels. Whether these rumblings will eventually culminate in a parting of the ways, as has already happened at a few universities, is anybody's guess. For the immediate future, you will likely not be affected—just be forewarned and understand the recommendations that follow in light of this unrest.

Consult the Behavioral Literature

Start with the most recent issues of the *Journal of Applied Behavior Analysis* (available in your library) and look for studies on topics of your own interest or simply for titles that look interesting. There are other good journals but I strongly urge you to limit your energies and time, for the present purpose, to the best! Collect a sample of a dozen or more of these studies on your topic (e.g., treatment of the retarded, classroom behavior, organizational or business applications, medical applications, deviant behavior, depression, self-control, etc.) and start noting who the authors are and where they are currently teaching. Certain educational institutions will begin to stand out as having active and publishing applied behavior analysts.

Consult University Catalogs

From the institutions you have selected, get information about an undergraduate major in psychology, or better yet, in applied behavior analysis if such an undergraduate specialization is offered. Many colleges and universities keep collections of catalogs from other schools in their libraries or counseling centers. If your favorite school has a major in applied behavior analysis then your job is simple—apply for admission. If, in the more likely case, there is only a major in psychology which is offered, then you've got to do some digging. Keep your eyes open for an experimental psychology orientation that offers more than a couple of courses in animal and human conditioning or learning. Look also for the offerings of physiological or comparative psychology courses or any courses

with a more biological focus. (Along this line, take a look at offerings in the biology department and in computer science to note whether there are special courses for students in the social sciences—these two areas are excellent complements to your planned career.)

You may wonder why I have not mentioned courses in the more applied or mentalistic areas of psychology (e.g., abnormal psychology, clinical psychology, child or adolescent development, cognitive psychology, personality, psychometrics or psychological testing, clinical neuropsychology, and others). I strongly believe that you'll be wise to get as strong a background in animal and human conditioning (or learning) as possible along with the appropriate complements already noted. You only have so much time and room to fit in the needed most courses. I have no fear that the seemingly meatier looking offerings will seduce you at times and that their topics may look like a more direct route into your *applied* interests. Spare them too much involvement and get a good foundation for graduate school. (Note that I would give almost this same advice, as regards to the meatier looking courses, to any undergraduate psychology majors, no matter what their area of interest, if they were planning to do graduate work!)

Talk with Those Who Really Know

Talk with students who are currently enrolled as undergraduate majors in psychology. Seek out the more involved ones who are likely active in undergraduate psychology societies or clubs. You may not find many who are planning careers specifically in applied behavior analysis but that's OK. What you want to find out now are some things that official university catalogs don't tell you. What are the satisfactions and dissatisfactions with the program? What are the professors like? What seems to be the real orientation of the department (e.g., behavioral? cognitive? clinical?). Are the faculty effective in their instruction of students? Are they considerate and supportive of student needs? Of course, you could go to the faculty with these questions but why not ask the consumer of the product rather than the seller?

Carefully Consider the Textbooks

Look at course textbooks, on an initial visit to campus and on the start of each term, to find out exactly what the content of the various courses will be (don't trust in possibly outdated or inaccurate university catalog descriptions—course contents can be very changeable as faculty play musical chairs in their hiring and firing).

Challenge the Rules when Necessary

University rules are not engraved in stone. Careers in applied behavior analysis are usually not easy to pursue without bending rules. In addition, curricula usually do not recognize or provide for differences in the study skills or interests (sources of reinforcement) of individual students. Sometimes counseling centers, on campus, will provide services to help you "adjust." Look for applied behavior analysts on their staff. But in the meantime, when you find yourself, for example, overwhelmed in a particular course and unable to get out of it because the official drop date has passed, bring pressure and good argument to bear on administrators—all the way to the top, if necessary. You bought the product, and it's expensive these days, so you should try to have it customized to your changing needs as much as possible. Rules can't be considered as more than being able to cover the average case—if your case seems special, challenge the rules. Surely, especially at an institution for higher learning, ideas (rules) should be capable of challenge and debate.

Keep an Eye toward Graduate Schools

Start going through a process somewhat akin to the first three recommendations noted earlier regarding the selection of a graduate school.

Once you've selected a couple of possibilities, get information from them to help you make constructive choices in relevant, current courses to take and relevant community agencies to volunteer for in your spare time. Not too long down the road you'll be wanting to convince a selection committee that you've taken, and done well in, the important courses and that you've gotten your feet wet out in the real world, too!

In addition, and not just in your last year, you must consult with your favorite behaviorally oriented professors. They should know you by name and, ideally, one should have already hired you as a research assistant. They'll know where the good graduate schools are for your interests. And, most importantly, you'll be wanting them to write letters of recommendation for you. That's the least they can do for your months of dedicated service to their research program. Also, they should have some friends in key places; if they value your work, they should be glad to send a known quantity, YOU, to a colleague and friend.

Graduate Training

If you're wondering whether to go this far, the answer is simple—DO IT! Though graduate students are far from rich, monetary support

in the way of fellowships, teaching and research assistantships, and part-time community work is better than at the undergraduate level. Also, you'll likely be more employable at a better salary when you're finished, and graduate training gets you closer to research and the skills that make applied behavior analysts unique and valuable. You'll learn how to do research as an integral part of behavior modification programs on individuals. No one else in the field of psychology gets the intensive training that enables single-subject, individual research to be done. Without this tool for evaluating the effect of your individualized programs, you will be offering little more than your subjective or clinical impressions or case histories as proof of your worth. We're quickly entering an era in which clinical judgment alone will just not suffice or be tolerated in the helping professions.

In addition, graduate training will provide you with other research and analysis skills (e.g., program evaluation and cost-benefit analysis techniques) which again reflects the growing demand for accountability from the helping professions. There's no escaping the fact that as world economies become more threatened, and the end to threat seems nowhere in sight, governments, corporations, and individuals will be demanding more for their dollars. The era when a psychologist could simply hang a shingle out on the street (with fancy initials attached) as a means of earning a living off of the misfortunes of others is drawing to a close. You'll need to be tooled up with more than the latest fad cure from the mystical domains around you. In short, you'll need to be practicing a technology with its roots in a firm foundation of science as well as continually contributing to it.

Employment

Where you'll be working depends on what you want to do so we've just about come around full circle. If you're interested in the non-clinical type applications, such as urban problems of transportation, waste recycling, energy conservation, pedestrian safety, speeding and seat belt usage, safety equipment in the workplace, management of classroom behavior, or numerous other examples of problems involving the right behavior at the wrong time or the wrong behavior at any time, then you'll very likely have to be on salary at an academic institution. From this base, and with the help of government grants at a university or college, you'll be available to consult with various agencies in the community and you'll have a

cadre of students to do some of the legwork of applied behavior analysis and its associated evaluative research.

If you are interested in medically related problems such as reinstatement of motor skills after strokes (e.g., biofeedback), or exercise after heart attacks, or patients taking their prescribed medication, or the control of vomiting, urinating, or soiling, or the reduction of fear toward medical and dental procedures, then you may work in a major hospital setting, either university or government based.

If, however, your interests are more traditional and you want to have an impact on such problems as anxiety, depression, psychotic behavior, phobias, and sexual dysfunctions then you could also get certified by an appropriate board to practice privately or through a mental health agency.

But in all the possible settings where you could be working, those of us who have trained you will be hoping that you'll be evaluating the progress that you and your clients will be making by doing the analyses that are so much a part of applied behavior analysis.

May the contingencies of reinforcement benefit you.

SUGGESTED READINGS AND REFERENCES

ACKER, L. E., & GOLDWATER, B. C. (1975). Instructor-paced, mass-testing for mastery performance in an introductory psychology course. *Teaching of Psychology, 2,* 152–155.

LUTZKER, J. R., & MARTIN, J. A. (1981). *Behavior change.* Belmont, CA: Wadsworth.

MARTIN, G., & PEAR, J. (1988). *Behavior modification: What it is and how to do it.* Toronto: Prentice-Hall, Canada.

SIDMAN, M. (1961). *Tactics of scientific research.* New York: Basic Books.

SKINNER, B. F. (1953). *Science and human behavior.* New York: Macmillan.

PAUL HOFER

Paul Hofer is a research associate at the Federal Judicial Center in Washington, DC. He received the J.D. (1986) and Ph.D. (1987) from the joint programs of the University of Maryland and Johns Hopkins University. He has served as a consultant to attorneys and is interested in home confinement, legal reasoning, computerized presentence reports and testing, and the development of standards. ♦

11

The Lawyer-Psychologist

People face many problems today. The list is long and often seems to be growing—the danger of crime, the lost human potential caused by inadequate education or employment discrimination, hazards in the workplace, family conflicts involving child support or domestic violence. It may seem that problems like these are so great that there is nothing we can do about them. The problems cause difficulties for *individuals*, but solutions cannot be found working individually or even with the help of only a counselor or therapist. These are *social* problems that require legal or political solutions. They require that our laws be properly written, effectively enforced, and fairly implemented. Clearly, one of the most important influences shaping our lives and controlling our behavior is the law and the legal system.

Many professionals study and work within the legal system, notably economists, political scientists, sociologists, criminologists, and of course, lawyers. All these disciplines bring to the law special methods and theoretical perspectives. Psychology—as one of the oldest, most diverse, and most methodologically sophisticated of the social and behavioral sciences—is especially well equipped to apply its tools to a wide variety of problems in the law.

Here's an example from my work.

Business entrepreneurs have recently developed small battery-powered electronic transmitters that emit a radio signal in a 100- to 200-foot radius. The transmitters are so small—about the size of a pack of cigarettes—that they can be strapped to a person's leg without seriously interfering with movement or clothing. The radio signal can be detected by a special receiver/dialer device that plugs into normal telephone wires. The receiver/dialer can continuously monitor the radio signal and determine if and when a person wearing a particular transmitter leaves the 100- to 200-foot radius area. The receiver/dialer can be programmed to automatically call a central computer periodically to report that the person has stayed within range, or to call immediately whenever the person leaves range. The transmitter also sends a special signal if the person wearing it tries to tamper with it or remove it.

Given the problems with crowding found in many prisons, and the great expense of new prison construction, many people are interested in exploring whether these electronic monitoring systems might be used to punish and control criminal offenders as part of parole or probation supervision outside of prison. Offenders might be sentenced to a type of home confinement—just as parents might send children to their room as a form of punishment. The central computer can be programmed to recognize periods of each

day that the offender is required to stay within range of the receiver, and periods when they are allowed to leave, perhaps to go to work, to attend drug treatment programs, or religious services. If the person leaves when he or she isn't authorized to leave, the central computer immediately alerts the police, parole, or probation officers responsible for supervising the person and a search for them can begin. In some jurisdictions, offenders who can afford it are charged up to $15 a day to use the electronic equipment. The state no longer has to use tax money to feed and house the criminal; the convicts pay for their own room and board and their own electronic monitoring as part of their punishment.

When people hear of this technology, they often have strong reactions. Some feel it is a dangerous step toward an Orwellian world, where "Big Brother" could monitor our every move. Others think it is a humane alternative to prison that allows convicted criminals to stay with their families, keep their jobs, and pay for their own punishment. The more one thinks about the idea, the more one realizes that we should not jump to conclusions based on our own limited knowledge and assumptions. There are too many intriguing possibilities and unanswered questions. Instead, we need careful analysis and research to decide if home confinement could help solve problems in our criminal justice system.

Federal judges have been interested in home confinement as a new sentencing option, an option that is more severe than simple probation but less severe than prison. The judges want to proceed cautiously and with as full an understanding of the technology's implications as is possible. As a lawyer/psychologist working for the federal courts, I was asked to analyze the issues, review the research literature and the relevant law, and to report what we know about home confinement, what we need to find out, and how we can learn more. Then the courts can decide whether home confinement is a good idea and how it should be used.

The monograph *Home Confinement: An Evolving Sanction in the Federal Criminal Justice System* (Hofer & Meierhoefer, 1987) helped alert parole, probation, and prison officials, as well as judges, to the potential of this new technology. Pilot programs were established in 12 federal districts to explore the practicality of the equipment. An evaluation plan was developed to gather data on the number of escapes, the number of new crimes, the amount of money earned by offenders while in the program, the amount paid in fines and restitution, and other relevant factors necessary to assess whether the benefits of home confinement outweigh its costs. If the pilot programs are successful, thousands of nonviolent offenders

could be diverted from prison or released from prison earlier than their normal release date. The offenders would serve their remaining time under home confinement, leaving more room in the prisons.

What Is Law and Psychology?

As you have learned in your reading so far, the discipline of psychology encompasses a broad range of methods, theories, and subject matter. Sometimes it seems the only thing psychologists have in common is their interest in understanding human beings and solving human problems. The subspecialty of law and psychology is also diverse. It is not defined by a single method or general theory, but instead by its subject matter—the law and legal system in all its forms. Psychologists working in the legal field often focus on one or two aspects of the system, such as the jury, eyewitness testimony, or the insanity defense. Many fields of study are so new that an enterprising professional can carve out a specialty, perform the needed policy analysis and empirical research, and become an expert proposing solutions to one of the many problems in the administration of justice.

The Scope of Law and Psychology

Three broad areas of psychological work in the law have emerged. The first involves psychologists serving as consultants or expert witnesses in trial courts. Research psychologists who specialize in polygraph tests or hypnosis may work with the police during their investigation. Researchers in perception may testify about the factors affecting the accuracy of eyewitness identification. Experts on persuasion may work with attorneys to refine the lawyers' presentations of evidence and arguments before the jury. Clinical psychologists may testify at trial or sentencing about a person's insanity, about their competency to stand trial, or about their future dangerousness. This type of law-related psychology is sometimes called *forensic psychology*. Clinical psychologists in private practice or in government agencies such as state mental hospitals or prisons may specialize in forensic psychology.

The second area is the use of psychology in appellate advocacy,

where judges on an appeals court are asked to clarify the law or to interpret the Constitution. Psychologists may provide information to judges sitting on these courts as they decide some of the most important and controversial issues of the day. Often this information is presented in *amicus curiae* briefs—also called "friend of the court" briefs—filed by professional organizations such as the American Psychological Association. Amicus curiae briefs tell the judges what the psychological literature says or does not say about the issue. For example, the APA has recently filed briefs informing the U.S. Supreme Court about the current findings on homosexuality and the effects of sodomy laws on psychosexual development. It reviewed the research literature on the capacity of mature adolescents to consent to abortion. It explained the findings on the effects of sex stereotyping on employment discrimination. When such briefs on issues are being prepared, an expert panel including the original researchers who did the relevant studies may be formed to advise the lawyers.

The third broad approach in law and psychology is the study of law and legal institutions from outside the system. Psychologists engaged in this area do not work on a particular case before a court, but instead study the law as an ongoing social and psychological process. They may study how children are socialized into being obedient, or disobedient, to the law. They may study how various actors in the legal system function, such as how police decide to intervene in domestic conflicts or make an arrest. They may study the interactions of prosecutors, defense lawyers, and defendants in plea bargaining. Or they may analyze how litigants negotiate and resolve their conflicts before going to court. Psychologists engaged in this type of research are often located in universities with legal studies programs, or in government or private think tanks devoted to the analysis and improvement of the justice system.

These examples illustrate many problems that confront psychologists working in the law. Many of us are trained both as lawyers and as psychologists. Many are psychologists who have focused on the legal system as their primary subject of study. Regardless of the topic or the training of the investigator, the problems facing lawyer-psychologists typically require skills in both *legal* and *empirical* research. The unique talents that psychologist-lawyers bring to the problems they tackle include both this broad range of research skills and also a comprehensive approach to analyzing problems. This approach could be called the *psycholegal perspective.*

The Psycholegal Perspective

Facts and Values

Legal research involves working with the complex indexing and reference system found in law libraries to locate statutes, cases, regulations, and other materials that can identify legal questions posed by a problem, and then using legal reasoning to find or propose answers. *Empirical* research involves identifying scientific questions raised by an issue, and then conducting the experiments, surveys, or other scientific study needed to answer them. The facts discovered through science are sometimes called empirical findings. Identifying empirical questions and finding empirical answers is the most important skill of the lawyer-psychologist. This type of research and reasoning is called *empiricism*.

There is not complete agreement on the meaning of the term empiricism. Some people consider empirical knowledge any knowledge that is gained through experience rather than through logic alone. Scientists define empirical knowledge more precisely. It is knowledge that we get through our senses; knowledge of the world we can all see, hear, touch, taste, and smell. To study a problem scientifically we must define and measure our concepts using observable data. For example, consider the problem of prison crowding. We may all have opinions about the effects of crowding and about whether prisons are more crowded than they should be. We may even disagree on the definition of crowding. These opinions are based on common sense and on our own values. But to study prison conditions scientifically, we can count the number of people per cell, the average square footage available to each inmate, and the per capita number of violent incidents among inmates. These readily observable events cannot be disputed if we define our terms precisely and measure carefully. With this data we can *describe* prison conditions. We can study the relation between crowding and violence to see if violence increases as space for each prisoner decreases, as would be the case if crowding was a cause of violence.

The law needs to describe people and problems too. But the primary function of the law is to *prescribe* how people *should* act and what government *should* do to solve social problems. Whether prison crowding has increased is an empirical question; but whether it has increased too far, and whether government should spend money building prisons rather than on defense, housing for the homeless, or other problems, is a *value* question. There is not an empirical answer to value questions. Our eyes alone cannot tell us if the prisons are too crowded; we must also exercise moral and ethi-

cal judgment. We have political methods such as elections and court decisions to resolve issues involving values. Scientists can describe, but they have no special legal authority to prescribe.

When psychologist/lawyers confront a problem, they must carefully separate the scientific questions from the value questions. Their scientific training gives them special expertise on factual questions. They are skilled at developing tests, defining variables, and calculating statistics. They may be able to predict how many people are likely to be in prison next year better than a layperson, by using statistical projections of crime rates. But do you think they are in a better position to say who should be in prison? Or for another example, they may be able to predict how a person is likely to vote in an election, but are they better able to say how they *should* vote?

This philosophical distinction between the *descriptive* and the *prescriptive* underlies the psychologist-lawyer's approach to a problem. When confronted with questions such as the proper role of electronic monitors and home confinement in the criminal justice system, we must begin by identifying the factual questions. For example, are most people with only an electronic monitor able to abide by the rules and stay at home? Can we predict who will succeed and who will fail? Are people who get home confinement less likely to commit additional crimes than those who go to prison? Are they more likely to find work and continue employment after their sentence? These questions have empirical answers. We can design research studies that compare offenders who are given home confinement with similar offenders who are sent to prison. Then finding the answer is just a matter of calculating the results.

But the facts alone won't tell us if home confinement is a good idea, or if it is being used fairly. For example, it may be that psychologists could give a personality test that measures impulsiveness and identify some people who are more likely to try to escape from home confinement. Is it fair to send some people to prison and some to home confinement—even if they committed the same crime—just because of a personality difference such as this? What if the personality difference was the result of genetic or environmental factors over which the person has no control? Or what about the ancient belief that "a man's home is his castle?" Is it a violation of the right to privacy in the home and the right to be free of unreasonable searches and seizures for the government to force a person to wear an electronic monitor 24 hours a day? These are value and legal questions, and scientific training does not help us answer them.

Matching the Tools to the Problem

A psycholegal analysis must match the research tools of psychology with the questions those tools can answer. For example, if we want to know if home confinement is more likely than prison to reduce recidivism (i.e., new crimes) among criminals, we can pose an empirical question: Do offenders who receive different forms of punishment have different rates of recidivism? To answer this, we could design a two-group experiment. The form of punishment becomes the *independent variable* in the experiment—the factor whose effects we want to study. Each group will get a different form of punishment but must be similar in all other ways. The rate of recidivism is the *dependent variable*—the factor that fluctuates depending on the effects of the independent variable. Other factors

An electronic monitoring device. (Courtesy of John Colville, Victoria Times-Colonist.)

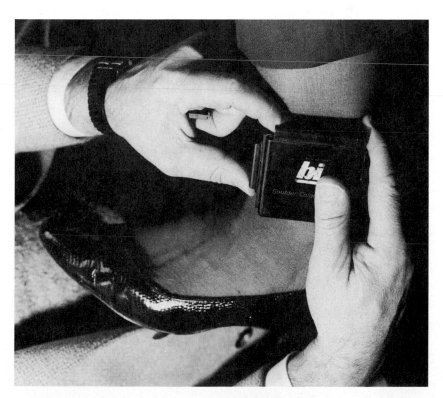

that might account for differences in rates of recidivism need to be *controlled*.

First, we need to create groups that are as similar to each other as possible. We could do this either by finding matched pairs of similar offenders, and putting one of each pair in each of the groups. Alternatively, we could randomly assign a group of offenders to one of the two options. The randomization would help ensure that there were no systematic biases between groups (e.g., offenders with the worst criminal records all in one group). The differences that did exist would tend to even out in the long run. Next, we would study the groups for several years, keeping track of which group committed the most new crimes, who had the better employment record, and so on. Finally, we would analyze our data using inferential statistics. If the study is designed correctly, a comparison of the two groups would resolve the question of whether the difference in recidivism rates between the groups is statistically significant, i.e., not likely to be random variation. It would help us decide if the difference was caused by home confinement, or could have been due to some other factor.

Empirical research requires careful design and planning, as well as careful use of statistical analyses. Lawyers are generally unfamiliar with research design. They will not know how to form control groups, or how to decide the number of people that are needed in a study to get statistically reliable conclusions. Nor will they be able to define the variables, design the database on the computer, or calculate the needed statistics. These skills are what make psychologists especially valuable. Anyone interested in conducting research in legal settings or on legal problems must be thoroughly trained in research design and statistics. I believe no other area of study is more important to a psychologist-lawyer. Once research skills are mastered, they can be applied to a wide variety of problems.

Nonempirical Questions

It should be clear that value judgments are not empirical questions that can be answered with scientific methods. But are all the questions asked of forensic psychologists empirical questions? When I tell people that I am a psychologist and a lawyer, they often immediately assume that I spend most my time working on issues of criminal responsibility. They think I evaluate defendants and decide if they were supposedly insane at the time they committed their crimes.

Some forensic psychologists do evaluate the mental status of

defendants for the purpose of testifying in court or reporting to the judge. There is considerable dispute, however, about how far a psychologist should go in giving an opinion on the ultimate issue—whether the person is criminally responsible and should be punished. Psychologists and psychiatrists draw a clear distinction between *mental illness*, which they regard as a descriptive medical term much like the diagnoses of other diseases, and *insanity*, which is a legal term that includes a value judgment that the person should not be punished. Many people argue that the scientific skills of the psychologist are no help in deciding whether a person is criminally insane.

You may be able to see why this issue is so controversial. First, the issue of responsibility raises difficult philosophical questions. Science generally assumes that people's behavior, like the rest of the natural world, is *deterministic*. Behavior is the product of genes, hormones, disease, environmental influences, and other forces that are ultimately outside a person's control. Is it fair to punish people for behavior that is caused by something beyond their control? Law, on the other hand, assumes that most behavior is the product of free will. Your actions are the product of your voluntary choices, and the major cause of these choices is you. If you choose to do evil, then you deserve punishment. Do you think that psychologists' training will help them decide these difficult questions?

Even if we assume that people sometimes have control over their behavior and sometimes do not, is there any way we can use our eyes and ears to tell if a person was out of control when they committed an illegal act? In other words, is the question of responsibility an empirical question? We can see how they behave. We can ask them to tell us what they were feeling and thinking. We may see them express regret over what they have done. But we know that some people are good actors; they can lie or pretend. If you have ever tried to judge whether someone was telling the truth, or if they were sincerely sorry for their behavior, you know that you can't see into another person's mind. You can only infer what is going on in someone's head by what he or she does. This evidence is not as foolproof as is the counting, correlating, and comparing that is typical of purely empirical research. Many people believe that laypeople, such as those on a typical jury, are as capable of making these judgments as are psychologists. The trial of Bonnie Garland's killer, described in the first case study, shows how difficult these questions can be.

Legislation-Oriented Research

Lawyers fill many different roles in our legal system. They are legislators, litigators, judges, and advisors to clients. The kind of psychological information that a lawyer needs depends on the role of the lawyer in the system. For example, legislators need to predict the likely effects of new laws they are considering. In the United States, many states have recently debated whether the speed limit should be increased from the former national limit of 55 miles per hour to some higher limit. Some states have raised the speed limit to 65, but others have left it at 55. Psychologists can contribute to this debate by studying and describing the psychology of compliance with the law, by designing educational materials to promote highway safety, and by analyzing accident rates and types before and after speed limit changes or among states with different limits.

Evaluating the Effects of Laws

The variation in traffic and other laws among the states has often been called a natural laboratory. If two states have different laws, we can investigate whether this legal difference—like an independent variable in an experiment—causes other differences, such as different accident fatality rates. As another example, consider capital punishment. Legislators considering whether to add or remove capital punishment from their criminal codes often want to consider the deterrent effects of the death penalty on the crime rates in their states. Because some states impose the death penalty for serious crimes and others do not, we can use this variation to study the effects of capital punishment.

A natural experiment such as this one requires great methodological care to decide whether the difference in the law is what *causes* any differences in crime rates. In a real experiment, groups are made as similar as possible in every way except for the independent variable under investigation. The scientist *controls* for all other factors that might affect the outcome. These potentially *confounding* factors are either held constant or are randomly distributed between the treatment and control group. In the real world, this degree of control is impossible. The difference in death penalty laws between the states is like an independent variable; crime rates make a good dependent variable. But there are many other differences among the states—in addition to the difference in capital punishment laws—which we can't control. Perhaps the states that have

capital punishment also have stricter law enforcement in general. Perhaps they are culturally more conservative, or have a generally older population. These factors may also account for a lower crime rate in those states. There are some methods for simulating the control found in a laboratory using quasi-experimental research designs. Researchers compare states that match as closely as possible on all relevant factors besides the independent variable, or they try to equate states using sophisticated statistical techniques.

If careful records have been kept, we might be able to use a *time series* evaluation design which compares crime rates before and after imposition of a new law. Since with this design we are comparing rates within the same state, we eliminate the problem of confounding differences among states. But before/after research designs also have limitations. Factors other than the new law may change at the same time as the law. For example, economic conditions might change, or the addition of capital punishment may be part of a larger crackdown on crime. Again it will be difficult to attribute any reduction in the crime rate to capital punishment per se. If capital punishment is not an independent cause of lower crime rates, other states can't lower their rate by changing merely this one law.

Resistance to the Use of Social Science

You may think that with so many methodological problems, doing this kind of research is more trouble than it is worth. Many politicians and legislators don't have much interest in serious social science. In part, this may be because they don't understand scientific methodology or because they don't like to have their authority to decide what is best for the state challenged by so-called experts. In addition, developing an opinion on a difficult and emotional subject such as capital punishment is uncomfortable if we feel there is a lot of uncertainty in our decision. We don't like to think that we could be wrong or make a mistake on a life-or-death issue. If someone points out all the errors in your thinking or all the problems with your evidence, you may resent it. Few like to admit that they could be wrong or that the opinions they held in the past were mistaken.

You may also have heard that "you can prove anything with statistics." The U.S. Supreme Court once described statistical analyses as "numerology." Many people use statistics if the data support their conclusions, but then ignore it if it supports the conclusion of their political opponents. Statistical analyses can be complex; it takes years of training to be able to recognize whether an

analysis was done accurately and fairly. With empirical data and proper statistical analysis, however, research cannot be used to prove anything any more than a census can prove that Canada has more people than China.

Research provides crucial information to political decision makers. It can expose the errors and assumptions in common sense and reduce the uncertainty in our decisions. To be accepted by politicians and lawyers, social scientists must maintain their objectivity and stick to the facts. They must explain their analyses in common language and teach their methodologies to the lawyers with whom they work.

Litigation-Oriented Research

The popular image of the lawyer is that of an articulate litigator who takes cases to court. Few lawyers are actually trial lawyers, but among those who do go to court, many have recently been using scientific litigation techniques to improve their chances of persuading juries and winning their cases. Jury selection, the presentation of evidence, and the lawyer's opening and closing arguments to the jury have all been the subject of psychological research. Let's outline how a psychologist might assist a lawyer as a case proceeds through trial.

Jury Selection

Jury trials begin with the formation of a panel of prospective jurors, usually drawn randomly from the list of registered voters in the jurisdiction. Sometimes it can take several days in court to select the final jurors from this list, because lawyers recognize that getting a jury that is favorably disposed to their client's position is a crucial component of trial strategy. Although a juror's decision is theoretically based on the evidence presented at trial, research has demonstrated that the preexisting attitudes of the jurors toward the parties in the case or toward the issues that will be raised can affect voting. If one of the parties in the trial is a large corporation, the attitudes of jurors toward corporations is likely to influence their sympathy with the corporation's case. Some cases receive much pretrial publicity and jurors have preexisting beliefs about the guilt or liability of a defendant. Judges ask the jurors whether they are able to decide the case impartially. Sometimes they admit they cannot and are excused from service. But even if they believe that they can be impartial, unconscious biases may affect their decision.

Lawyers have turned to psychologists to help them decide which prospective juror is most likely to be predisposed in favor of the lawyer's client. Psychologists cannot interview the actual prospective jurors to uncover these biases. But they can conduct surveys of registered voters in the community where the trial is to be held to determine whether certain types of people are more likely to have attitudes that could affect their verdict. For example, a survey in the town where the trial will be held might show that unfavorable attitudes toward corporations are most common among women, blacks, or blue-collar workers. Lawyers choosing from the panel of prospective jurors can use the survey results to infer what the attitudes of the women, blacks, and blue-collar people on the panel are likely to be. The corporation's lawyers may then seek potential jurors who fit the anticorporate demographic profile removed from the panel.

Lawyers can challenge *for cause* any juror who demonstrates or admits bias when interviewed by the lawyer or the judge. These biased jurors are then eliminated from the panel. Lawyers are also entitled to exercise *peremptory challenges* that allow each side to eliminate a certain number of prospective jurors without demonstrating that there is a particular cause to doubt their impartiality. By carefully using the preemptory challenges to eliminate the panel members least likely to be sympathetic to their client, they can create the jury most predisposed in their favor.

Arguments to the Jury

Once the jury is formed, the litigator's attention shifts to the opening argument—each side's the initial statement to the jury describing what they intend to prove and outlining their theory of the case. Psychologists may help evaluate the persuasiveness of the argument by forming focus groups of people similar to those on the jury and testing the argument on them before it is presented to the real jury. The focus group listens to the argument in a courtroom setting and are asked to describe their reactions to the argument: What was confusing? What was most convincing? Sometimes electronic devices are used to register their positive or negative reactions during the argument delivery. The lawyers can study these reactions and refine their speech until it has the maximum impact.

Where millions of dollars are at stake, parties will sometimes go to extremes to persuade the all-important jury. One of the most expensive and sophisticated litigation research methods is to use a *shadow jury*. The real jury cannot talk to the lawyers during the trial. To get feedback on how the presentation of evidence appears to

the jury, people similar to those on the jury are paid to sit in the courtroom (in the visitor's gallery—not the jury box) and listen to the trial. At the end of each trial day, psychologists interview the shadow jury to learn their reactions to the day's testimony and argument. The psychologists may learn that a crucial piece of evidence was misunderstood, or that the jurors found a witness unpersuasive, or that an argument that did not seem important to the lawyers struck a responsive chord in the jury. Then, later in the trial, the lawyers can seek to clarify possible misunderstandings or reemphasize the most persuasive points.

What do you think of these litigation strategies? Do you think it is fair to use shadow juries, or to try to select the jury most disposed in your favor before the trial even begins? Since this research is expensive, it adds to the cost of litigation and will be available only to parties who can afford it. The parties in a trial have always had different resources to hire expensive lawyers. Some lawyers are better at winning their cases and getting large monetary awards for their clients than others. Do you think the availability of litigation research to those who can pay for it adds still more unfairness to the trial system? Is there any better alternative?

Trial strategies have always been used by good lawyers to their client's advantage. There is a famous story about Clarence Darrow: He is said to have put a wire in his cigar to prevent the ash from falling. Then, when his opponent was presenting his case, he smoked the cigar. The jury's attention was diverted from the opposition's evidence to the ever-lengthening cigar ash. Scientific litigation research is a more explicit manipulation of jury selection and juror opinion than these home-spun techniques. But it may not add a significantly greater degree of unfairness than has resulted from varying abilities and strategies of lawyers.

The effectiveness of scientific litigation techniques—and not everyone thinks they are effective—does seem to challenge some of our most cherished beliefs about the trial. We accept the judgment of a jury to resolve our legal conflicts because we think they are fair. We think that they base their verdicts on the evidence and on sound reasoning. Sometimes when real jurors are interviewed after a trial it becomes apparent that they misunderstood the evidence, or were persuaded by relatively unimportant arguments. But the legal system is very reluctant to overturn the verdict of a jury. Although the research shows that preexisting attitudes influence juror's decisions, and although there may be experts who are better trained than lay jurors to understand evidence in complicated cases, no proposal to replace the jury has ever won widespread support.

Lawyers know that when a case goes to a jury for a decision unpredictable factors can influence the outcome. This mystique may partly explain why jury decisions are generally accepted. If you don't know exactly how the verdict was reached, you can't be sure it was unfair! As psychologists learn more about juries, there will be opportunities to improve the impartiality of juror selection and deliberations. But there will also be the danger that this knowledge will be available only to parties who can afford it.

Settlement-Oriented Research

Law and psychology have many differences, but one of the most significant has been their basic approach to resolving conflicts. The legal system is a formal and adversarial system. Lawyers are under strict rules to represent only one party in a conflict and present the strongest case possible for their client. Evidence that is not relevant to the legal rules that apply to the case cannot be presented in court. Only one side can win. Clinical and counseling psychologists, on the other hand, are more inclined to seek informal procedures that allow each side to tell their whole story whether it is legally relevant or not. They work with both parties to find common ground and bases for cooperation.

You can see how different the two disciplines are when you consider their approach to marital conflict and divorce. People who are unhappy in their marriage and go to see a psychologist are likely to be encouraged to express their feelings fully. The psychologist will not always take their complaints at face value, but will often attempt to uncover hidden problems. The psychologist is likely to try to find common interests and to work with both parties to encourage reconciliation, if possible. The spouses may be asked to participate in joint counseling, where the psychologist will be careful not to appear one-sided.

A lawyer, on the other hand, will probably focus on the faults of the marriage that are relevant to the law and that may constitute grounds for divorce. A lawyer could not suggest a compromise that would damage the competitive interests of his or her client. Few lawyers have time for an in-depth examination of all the problems in the marriage or the hidden feelings that lie below the surface. If you have watched popularized television shows about the legal system you may have noticed how the judge focuses narrowly on the few legally important facts in the case, even though it may appear obvious that the real source of bad feeling between the parties lies

somewhere else. The lawsuit may be a weapon used by one party to punish the other for a problem that really has little to do with the legal issues in the case.

There is a growing trend in law schools and among practicing lawyers to learn more about counseling, negotiation, and settlement skills. Psychological skills for interviewing, such as active listening instead of narrow and leading questioning, can often elicit information that would otherwise be overlooked. The high cost of litigation has forced lawyers and their clients to seek out less expensive alternative dispute resolution strategies. Mediation of conflicts is sometimes mandated by a court before adversarial proceedings are permitted to go forward.

The number of cases that result in a full trial has declined steadily over the years. Today, only a small percentage of cases go to court. Eighty-seven percent of criminal cases in the United States were resolved through guilty pleas in 1982, usually as the result of a plea bargain. In most jurisdictions over 90% of civil lawsuits are settled between the parties before trial. Psychologists working for the U.S. Courts and for private research organizations such as the Rand Corporation have been interested in studying settlement because so many cases are filed each year that there are not enough judges to have a trial for them all. Research has shown that judges can influence settlements by carefully managing the cases assigned to them. They can schedule conferences with the parties and set firm dates for trial. They can make settlement recommendations or seek expert advice to reach an agreement. The more settlements that are reached, and the earlier they come in a case, the more taxpayer money can be saved. The second case study describes an innovative approach to case settlement.

Testimony-Oriented Research

If a case goes to trial, psychologists sometimes take the stand and present expert testimony to the finders of fact—the judge or the jury. Psychologists have testified on a wide range of issues: the accuracy of eyewitnesses, the battered wife syndrome, the mental competency of criminal defendants, or the results of lie detector tests.

Sometimes psychologists work for one side in a case. These psychologists often report that the adversarial legal system puts them under special pressure and can threaten the objectivity of their scientific testimony. Lawyers are interested in winning and they sometimes grow impatient with psychologists who want to

present an impartial account of the research instead of an account designed to put the lawyer's case in the best possible light. Scientists are taught to report all the data, even if it casts doubt on their claims. Lawyers try to ignore the evidence unfavorable to their side. Scientists are always open to a better theory that may replace their current hypotheses. Lawyers are committed to their own theory of the case and won't admit, at least in front of the jury, that they have any doubts. If the data support the lawyer's side, the psychologist can work with the lawyer easily. But if the data are equivocal, the psychologist may come under pressure to slant his or her testimony. Some psychologists avoid this dilemma by working for judges as court-appointed experts. The judge, like the scientist, is interested in uncovering the truth—not winning the case.

One area where psychological testimony is common is in litigation over employment discrimination. Under U.S. law, plaintiffs can use statistics to help prove that there is discrimination by an employer. The percentage of job applicants who are white, black, or members of other racial or ethnic groups is compared to the percentage of each group who are hired. If a much smaller percentage of the minority group are hired, the court will infer that there was discrimination against the group. The employer then gets a chance to prove that there is some additional characteristic that is related to job performance and that makes a disproportionate number of the minority group less qualified for the job.

A common criterion used to select employees is performance on a screening test of skills and abilities. Psychologists who develop these tests must take special precautions to ensure that they are not culturally biased and are fair to all applicants. In the days following legal segregation in the United States, some employers added intelligence tests to their employment screening practices as a pretext to exclude blacks from better-paying jobs. Tests that had no relation to job performance were added at the very same time that explicit racial discrimination was made illegal. It appeared that employers were trying to exclude blacks by adding a test that they thought the blacks could not pass. The U.S. Supreme Court ruled in the famous case of *Griggs v. Duke Power Co.* that unless a selection criterion was proven to be related to job performance, it could not be used. The Equal Employment Opportunity Commission (EEOC) later established guidelines to clarify the research that courts should examine to decide if a test is fair or if an employer discriminates.

Today, employers must keep records of the percentage of different racial and ethnic groups that pass their employment tests. They must conduct validity studies of any test that excludes a dis-

proportionate number of minorities, women, or the handicapped. *Validity studies* are meant to prove that the test measures a skill that is crucial to job performance. For example, validity can be established by correlating scores on the test with the average sales figures for store clerks. If people with higher scores tend to make more sales, then the test is considered valid and can be used.

Sophisticated research techniques are used to identify culturally biased test questions. If a test item is especially difficult for some racial or ethnic groups, it is eliminated. Psychologists who testify in employment discrimination cases are often given an opportunity to act as teachers for the lawyers and for the jury. They explain the purpose and the reasoning behind their research as well as the results.

CASE STUDIES

CASE ONE: THE KILLING OF BONNIE GARLAND

Richard, the valedictorian of his high school in a Los Angeles barrio, came to Yale on a tuition and expenses scholarship. He struggled with his studies and with the social demands of the prestigious Ivy League school. He was never able to get the good grades he was accustomed to getting in high school. And although he participated in the Catholic student group, he felt his social life was inadequate.

After two years without a lover, he decided to find a girlfriend. His first relationship was one-sided; he called his feelings "love," but the girl didn't want to "get like that." The friendship eventually grew into an arrangement of convenience for her in which Richard was available if no other date could be found. It was humiliating, but he needed desperately to prove that he could be successful as a man. Finally, he met Bonnie, who seemed to like him as he was.

Bonnie Garland, a large-boned but vivacious freshman, came from a wealthy family in Scarsdale, New York. She was a real Yalie; her father was an alumnus of both Yale and Harvard Law School. Bonnie and Richard met at a Beatles movie and discovered they were both music fans. That first night after the movie, a thumb wrestling match turned into horseplay on the floor, which turned into kissing and petting. A week later they were spending almost all their free time together. Richard found her beautiful and proudly held hands to let everyone know they were a couple. A few months later they visited her parents, who didn't entirely approve of the relationship. But that seemed a minor problem. They had intercourse for the first time in her bedroom in Scarsdale. Richard couldn't believe how his luck had turned.

But Bonnie had doubts about Richard within a month of their meeting. Gradually her ambivalence grew. She felt the relationship was stagnant and expressed an interest in seeing other men after summer vacation. Yet the next year they continued to sleep together, sometimes skipping classes and staying in bed all day. They seemed sexually compatible. If she talked about being unhappy with the relationship, Richard made her feel guilty. The next summer, he was accepted into a Master's degree program in Texas—providing that he graduated from Yale. They worked together to finish his senior thesis, Bonnie typing while Richard wrote. During the rush of his last few days in New Haven, Richard says they talked tentatively of marriage.

When Richard was gone, however, Bonnie started dating. They talked often on the phone and Bonnie came to visit Richard in Texas when he was depressed over continuing academic problems. But while Bonnie was on a trip to Europe, Richard got a letter from her. Bonnie had a new boyfriend. Richard panicked; he immediately decided to go back east to live near Bonnie. He canceled plans for more graduate school. And he says he began having thoughts of committing suicide if things didn't work out with Bonnie. He packed his suitcase, including a stuffed dog for Bonnie and a copy of *Sybil*, a book about a woman with a split personality.

When the plane landed, Richard went immediately to Scarsdale. When he got there Bonnie was gone, but her mother told him that she and her new boyfriend were staying there. He would have to find someplace else. A friend on Long Island put him up for the night and he called Bonnie the next day. She invited him to visit once her other boyfriend was gone. Richard came back to Scarsdale still full of hope. But slowly over the next few days it become clear that they were no longer lovers, even though she had not yet slept with her new friend. Richard worried secretly that once Bonnie slept with someone else he would lose her forever because she would discover that Richard's penis was small. Finally, after a few days of trying to be nice, Bonnie said that her mother wanted him to leave the next day.

That night, Richard stayed awake after Bonnie went to sleep. He became obsessed with fantasies of the two of them lying in bed with their wrists slashed. "That was it for me. There was no point in going on. Bonnie was there so she was going to die too." With a strange lack of emotion, his mind began wandering to possible weapons: a glass mug in which they had shared some milk, the rope he had packed in his suitcase. He went downstairs past the kitchen knives to a workroom. On the wall was a claw hammer; he took it up to Bonnie's room. "I lifted it over my head the way a lumberjack

would raise a hammer. I hit her once around the temple. . . . Her body jerked . . . I cradled her head and called her name. . . . There was no response, so I laid her head back down. The next blow did break the skin and break the skull."

Richard left the house and drove toward the mountains north of town. He thought of taking the car on a mountain road so he could drive off a cliff. After several hours, he stopped at a church and fell asleep in the doorway. The next morning he knocked on the rectory door. A priest answered and Richard told him he had just killed his girlfriend and wanted to turn himself in. Later, the priest remembered that Richard appeared to be very agitated as he stood at the door. He was wearing no clothing except a pair of trousers, not even shoes or socks.

Five psychiatrists and clinical psychologists testified at Richard's trial, two for the defense and three for the prosecution. Based on their examinations, the defense team argued that at the time of the killing Richard was suffering from a disorder termed transient situational reaction that the defense claimed was severe enough to be called psychotic. The idea to kill Bonnie, the defense team argued, originated from Richard's unconscious, where a considerable amount of repressed anger was stored up. They said Richard acted like a robot, with no feelings. The prosecution team defined psychosis as "the inability to think, the inability to communicate, usually manifested by delusions, by hallucinations, disorientation." Their experts found no evidence of psychosis, of mental illness, or of extreme environmental stress. They noted that he was careful to avoid detection at the house and was able to drive a car immediately after the killing.

The jury had three options: Convict Richard for murder, acquit him on the basis of insanity, or find him guilty of the less serious charge of manslaughter. If acquitted he could go free; if guilty of murder he could get life in prison. If guilty of manslaughter the judge would choose a sentence ranging from a few years to a maximum of 8 to 25. How would you have voted? The jury found him guilty of manslaughter. The judge imposed the maximum sentence. Richard has said from prison that the judge should have taken his positive characteristics into account and given him a more lenient sentence. Richard said he had no previous arrests, had the capacity to be a productive citizen, and had a good personality. He said it was sad that Bonnie was dead, but there was nothing gained by wasting a second life.

The facts and quotations in this case study are from the book *The Killing of Bonnie Garland* by Willard Gaylin (1982). ♦

CASE TWO: ASBESTOS LITIGATION SETTLEMENT STRATEGIES

As early as the first century, ancient Greek observers noted sickness in the lungs of slaves who wove asbestos into cloth. In 1900, a London physician discovered lung damage during the autopsy of a 33-year-old man who had worked in an asbestos textile factory. In the United States, knowledge of the danger of asbestos did not become public until recent years. But documents discovered by enterprising attorneys in early asbestos lawsuits showed that asbestos manufacturing companies had known of the danger for decades, and had failed to take the necessary steps to warn workers of the risks. This crucial discovery proved that the companies were negligent and legally liable for damage to workers injured by asbestos dust. Juries began awarding workers suffering from mesothelioma, cancer, and other lung disease money damages for medical bills, for lost earnings, as well as punitive damages meant to discourage other companies from being so negligent in the future.

When word got out that these lawsuits for negligence against asbestos manufacturers could be won, lawyers from around the country rushed to file cases for their clients. Some courts, especially those in regions with industries that relied heavily on asbestos, were flooded with thousands of lawsuits. In case after case, juries have found companies negligent. Even though a major issue in these cases—manufacturer liability—is well established, asbestos trials are considered to be time-consuming and repetitive. Asbestos cases have added to the court backlog. It sometimes takes so long to schedule a trial that workers die before their case comes to court.

To deal with this flood of litigation some judges appointed experts, called special masters, to help manage the caseload. The masters began searching for ways to settle more cases soon after they were filed instead of waiting for a trial. Upon investigation, it became apparent that the major obstacle to settlement was disagreement over how much money each case was worth. Some victims had only minor health problems and received small damage awards, others had fatal illnesses. If the lawyers for both sides could agree on how much each plaintiff deserved, a trial could be avoided.

Psychologists worked with the court-appointed experts to find a method for estimating case worth that would be quicker, cheaper, and perhaps more reliable than a jury verdict. It was crucial that the method earned the confidence of the lawyers; it had to be compatible with the way lawyers themselves think about case evaluation. First, expert lawyers experienced in asbestos litigation were interviewed and asked to "think aloud" when they evaluated cases. It

became apparent that a limited number of factors played the leading role in case evaluation. These included the type of disease, the amount of exposure to asbestos, the plaintiff's age at the time of death or illness, the amount they earned before becoming ill, and whether they also smoked cigarettes. (Cigarette smoking was judged a contributing factor in the lung diseases.) When lawyers negotiated with each other over how much money was needed to settle a case, these factors were the main issues.

Legal reasoning is sometimes said to be based on precedents. Lawyers argue that a current case should be decided the same way as previous similar cases. Settlement negotiations appear to be another example of reasoning by analogy. If a previous case involved a nonsmoking shipyard worker who died of lung cancer in his midthirties, lawyers are willing to accept the outcome of that case as a precedent for a new case with similar characteristics. Once this fundamental feature of legal reasoning was found to apply to settlement negotiations, it could be used in settlement conferences called by the judge.

Data on settlement-relevant factors was collected from several hundred closed cases that had already gone to trial or reached settlement. Each closed case was scored on these *predictor* variables. The actual money awarded to the plaintiffs in these cases was also known, and this became the *outcome* variable. Statistical studies were done to determine which factors were actually correlated with damage awards and how important each factor was. A formula—technically known as a *multiple regression equation*—was developed to estimate the worth of a new case based on its score on the predictor variables. In addition, the data bank of several hundred closed cases could be used to find precedents that matched many if not most of the features of almost every new case. Could this data be used to facilitate settlement? Would lawyers accept the estimate as valid?

Judges ordered plaintiffs in new asbestos cases to complete a questionnaire that described all the relevant facts in their case. This questionnaire was due before the settlement conference, which was held long before the scheduled date for trial. At the conference, lawyers were given a computer report based on a search of the database for the past cases most similar to the present case. The report lists the features that the cases have in common and the amount of damages awarded in each. These precedents serve as a starting point for settlement negotiations between the parties.

Since the computer program mimics the reasoning of the lawyers, but uses a larger database, it may actually improve the fair-

ness of the negotiation and prevent any lawyer from making unreasonable demands. Lawyers can concentrate on deciding whether there is anything unique about the new case that is not taken into account by the data in the computer. If something is unique, lawyers can argue that the case is worth more or less than the old ones. In routine cases, the computer does what the good lawyer tries to do: predict what would happen if the case went to trial, and decide how much money the case is worth.

This system has been successful in settling virtually all the new cases without the delay and expense of a trial. A similar approach is now being explored for use in other types of litigation. ♦

Becoming a Lawyer-Psychologist

The American Psychology and Law Society, Division 41 of the APA is the professional organization of lawyer-psychologists. Its members come from a wide variety of backgrounds and training. Many are psychologists who have chosen the law and legal system as their primary focus of study. After graduate training in clinical, social, cognitive, or some other subdiscipline of psychology—usually leading to a doctoral degree—they develop an area of research in which they become an expert. Any psychologist can become a law-oriented psychologist in this way. Clinical psychologists who focus on legal issues may become forensic psychologists and join organizations and gain accreditation for their specialized skill.

After initial exposure to a particular legal issue, many psychologists become intrigued with the legal system in general and want to do research on other law-related topics. At some point, they feel that they must learn more about the law if they are to adequately communicate with lawyers and tailor their research to the needs of the legal system. Several universities offer postdoctoral training in law and psychology with an experienced researcher. Often the postdoctoral student will take several courses in a law school on topics related to their research interests. This exposure to the socialization process undergone by lawyers is valuable for improving communication between the two disciplines.

A few psychologists decide that they want to complete law school and become full-fledged lawyer-psychologists who can move comfortably between the two fields. By going to law school, the psychologist stops looking at the law from outside the system and may become a participant as well as an observer of the political and legal

process. The perspectives of the two disciplines are so fundamentally different that it can be difficult to switch from one to the other. The leading universities that have pioneered psycholegal study have developed joint programs in law and psychology where graduate students receive simultaneous training in both disciplines. This way no one professional view dominates the student's thinking.

After graduate training lasting from five to seven years, it is time to find a job. Some lawyer-psychologists become practicing attorneys; others remain primarily psychologists conducting empirical research. Few manage to do both. Law firms, psychiatric hospitals, or university departments that hire either lawyers or psychologists do not usually have a role designed for a combination. Lawyer-psychologists often must be creative and carve themselves a niche in the available job market by taking a more traditional post as either a lawyer or a psychologist, and then expanding that role to utilize their broader training. Many traditional jobs benefit from both legal and scientific research skills, and the combination of skills make dual-degree applicants highly competitive.

Universities are large employers of lawyer-psychologists in their traditional academic departments. Academic jobs offer the freedom, beyond teaching hours, to pursue whatever research interests you want, especially if you can get grants to help pay for them. Academic psychologists often consult or give expert testimony in addition to their university duties. Law school professors teach and write and sometimes collect or analyze data to include in their law review articles. You might be interested to know that law schools generally pay higher salaries than psychology departments, presumably because law schools compete with high-paying law firms for the top students. Think tanks such as the Rand Corporation or the National Center for State Courts offer much of the freedom of academic departments without the teaching component.

Governments offer a rich source of employment for policy-oriented lawyer-psychologists. Many government agencies—such as state hospitals and prisons, legislative and judicial staffs, probation departments, or employment offices—need a combination of empirical, legal, and administrative skills. There the lawyer-psychologist can vitally contribute to the interplay of policy, law, and science.

Studying law and psychology is a challenging intellectual task. It forces one to search for a third perspective—the psycholegal perspective—that encompasses both legal and scientific reasoning. The disciplines are divided by different paradigms of evidence, different standards of proof and explanation, and different problem-

solving methods. Fundamental concepts such as free will, causation, and validity have different meanings in law and psychology. To orient yourself and switch comfortably from one way of thinking to another, you are forced to become an amateur philosopher. Only the language of philosophy is adequate to describe differences between the two professions.

I can think of few areas of study that give one as great a breadth of understanding as law and psychology. So many of the leading issues of the day involve psychology and the law, it sometimes seems like the newspapers are filled with potential research topics. For students who think of themselves as renaissance men or women, a career in law and psychology offers a unique and fascinating perspective on the world.

SUGGESTED READINGS AND REFERENCES

COOK, T. D., & CAMPBELL, D. T. (1979). *Quasi-experimentation: design and analysis issues for field settings.* Chicago: Rand-McNally.

GAYLIN, W. (1982). *The Killing of Bonnie Garland.* New York: Penguin Books.

HOFER, P., & MEIERHOEFER, B. (1987). *Home confinement: An evolving sanction in the federal criminal justice system.* Washington, DC: Federal Judicial Center.

HOROWITZ, I. A., & WILLGING, T. E. (1984). *The psychology of law: Integrations and applications.* Boston: Little, Brown.

LOH, W. (1984). *Social research in the judicial process.* New York: Russell Sage Foundation.

WRIGHTSMAN, L. S. (1987). *Psychology and the legal system.* Monterey, CA: Brooks/Cole Publishing Co.

LARRY M. COUTTS

Larry M. Coutts currently teaches and conducts research at the Canadian Police College in Ottawa. He received his B.A. degree from the University of Winnipeg and his M.A. and Ph.D. from the University of Windsor. He has taught at the University of Guelph and served a number of years as Chief of both the Test Development and the Assessment Services and Programs Divisions in the Public Service Commission of Canada. He has published several articles in the fields of social and organizational psychology. ♦

Most of us will participate in the workforce at some time during our lives. In fact, it has been estimated that we will spend about 10,000 days working in organizations over the course of our careers. Whether we are employed as clerks, managers, professionals, salespersons, politicians, or assembly line workers, during our working lives we will confront a wide variety of organizational issues and problems that demand and capture our attention.

If we phrased some of these issues and problems as questions, they might include the following: Whom should we hire? How do I increase the productivity of my staff? How should our project team decide on the best course of action? Why am I so unhappy in this job? Why is it that the most talented employees always seem to quit this company? How can we promote more cooperative relationships among the staff? Should I supervise my staff closely on this particular project or relax my control? Why do some of my colleagues have more influence and power than others? What kinds of training will help us be more innovative? Is the department organized and structured effectively?

Organizational psychologists attempt to provide answers to such questions. More accurately, through our research and consultation, we try to assist individuals and organizations in arriving at their own answers to these questions. Ideally, the consultation and advice we provide is based on established research evidence.

Perhaps, a personal experience will illustrate this role. Not long ago, a colleague and I were asked to serve as advisors to a Royal Commission of Inquiry established by a provincial government. The inquiry, composed of a team of lawyers and headed by a judge, was charged with reviewing the policies and practices of a large urban police force. It would do this through a series of public hearings. Although the inquiry focused on several areas, including race relations, alleged police misconduct, employee morale, and management accountability, our role was to review the hiring and promotion practices of the force.

Specifically, we were asked to focus on the following types of questions: Are the force's hiring and promotion methods similar to those of other police forces? Are these methods valid? Are they fair? Does favoritism occur in the promotion system? Should the force revise its hiring and promotion procedures?

In seeking answers to these questions, we used four approaches. First, we reviewed the force's documents which described its current hiring and promotion procedures. Next, we needed to know how these hiring and promotion procedures were actually implemented and how they were viewed by various interest groups

12

The Organizational Psychologist

within the force. This was accomplished by interviewing the chief, deputy chiefs, representatives from all other ranks within the force, senior executives of the police union, and the chairperson of the police commission.

We also conducted a questionnaire survey of several police forces across the country to obtain comparative data about selection practices. Finally, and most importantly, we used the vast body of existing personnel selection research to guide our evaluation of the validity and fairness of the hiring and promotion methods used by the force. Our findings were eventually compiled into a report which we submitted to the inquiry and presented at the public hearing.

What Is Organizational Psychology?

Organizational psychology can be broadly defined as the study of organizations and the people who work in them. It is concerned with the way organizations influence the thoughts, feelings, and actions of their members. It is also concerned with how individual members influence the performance and effectiveness of the organization.

As organizational psychologists, we describe and measure the behaviors of individuals and groups that are important on the job and, ultimately, attempt to understand these behaviors through the development of knowledge about the relevant influences that affect them.

How do we decide which job behaviors are sufficiently important for study? Typically, a behavior is considered to be of interest to the extent that it has some impact on the goals and objectives of an organization and the people within it. In practice, this means that we often focus our attention on behaviors such as performance, leadership, creativity, stress, absenteeism, and quitting, and the variables that relate to these behaviors.

Organizational psychology is a complex and interdisciplinary field. Its complexity is indicated by the increasing number of specialty areas within it—areas such as personnel selection and evaluation, management training and development, leadership, decision making, communication, work motivation, job satisfaction and organizational design. Organizational psychology is also interdisciplinary because psychologists are not the only professionals working within these areas. Many researchers and prac-

titioners in the field have received their university training in a variety of other social science and management programs.

Organizational Psychology as a Science and Profession

Organizational psychology is a science and a profession. Its scientific aspect provides the research-based knowledge that is prerequisite for professional practice. This knowledge can be in the form of theories or in the form of empirically determined relationships. In either case, such knowledge is frequently applied by organizations to address some of the human problems that inevitably arise.

The goal of the science of organizational psychology is identical to that of psychology in general. It seeks to identify the variables associated with various aspects of behavior. The difference, of course, is that organizational psychology focuses on matters within the domain of work such as the relationship between the level of one's performance and the types of rewards and incentives dispensed by the organization. Ultimately, the explanation of such relationships is pursued through the development of theories and the testing of these theories against empirical data.

Organizational psychology as a profession is concerned with the application of the knowledge and methods of the discipline to practical organizational problems. Some organizational psychologists concentrate almost exclusively on solving such problems. This often includes consulting (as in the example), individual evaluations, and program development. Typically, a consultant advises in some area of expertise, such as management development, treatment methods, or organizational change. In some cases, he or she may be called on to assist in the resolution of individual or organizational conflicts. In the evaluation domain, the psychologist might assess the aptitudes, skills, and abilities of individuals for specific positions, promotions, or assignments, or provide career counseling to employees. A psychologist in program development may be responsible for developing and implementing a personnel selection system or a training program.

The Background of Organizational Psychology

Like most branches of psychology, the roots of organizational psychology are based in experimental psychology. The general principles or laws of behavior established by experimental psychology enable us to describe and explain organizational behavior. The study of individual differences also has had an impact on the development of organizational psychology. Around the turn of the century, psychologists became interested in the identification and measurement of the ways in which individuals differ in abilities, skills, aptitudes, and personality traits. Their interest gave birth to the testing movement and its application to personnel selection, evaluation, and classification, particularly in the military.

Frederick W. Taylor, the founder of scientific management, developed four principles very early (Taylor, 1911). These were: (1) scientifically design work methods for efficiency, (2) select the best workers and train them well, (3) create cooperation between managers and workers, and (4) share the design and the operation of work between workers and management. Unfortunately, his research on increasing efficiency was perceived by some as worker exploitation and his other principles received less attention at the time. Fortunately, later organizational psychologists developed Taylor's other principles more fully.

During the 1920s and 1930s, organizational psychology was profoundly influenced by developments in industrial engineering, such as the design and arrangement of work and machines. Organizations were viewed as mechanistic entities and emphasis was placed on their machine-like precision. Indeed, a focus on the relative efficiency of various worker-machine combinations was a major preoccupation of organizational psychologists of the day.

Against this backdrop, the Hawthorne studies of the 1920s and 1930s initiated a major revolution in organizational psychology (Roethlisberger & Dickson, 1939). These studies, consisting of numerous field experiments carried out in the Western Electric Company, served to highlight the complexity of work behavior. They also provided impetus to the human relations movement and dramatically changed our view of organizations and how they were supposed to function. From this point on, the social relations, feelings, and reactions of workers became important variables for study. Later, the human relations movement was further strengthened by the work of Abraham Maslow and Carl Rogers who emphasized

values of personal growth and the realization of one's potential.

Ironically, the original interpretation of the Hawthorne studies was wrong. From a superficial reading of the findings, the belief arose that a little attention and consideration on the supervisor's part would work wonders for employee morale and productivity. Subsequent research was to show that this position was overly simplistic and often dead wrong.

Since the late 1960s, most psychology, including organizational psychology, has been heavily influenced by the theories and research of cognitive psychologists. Today, for example, motivation theories emphasize the inferential skills of the worker. A renewed interest in the relation between cognitive ability and job performance has resulted in major advances in the testing movement. In addition, to the benefit of us all, research on human information processing capacities is playing a major role in the design and enrichment of work environments and jobs.

The Scope of Organizational Psychology

As mentioned earlier, organizational psychologists focus their attention on those activities within an organization that are important in some way to the goals and objectives of both the organization and the individuals who work in it. The kinds of research questions and problems that we deal with vary considerably depending on the particular interests and expertise of the individual psychologist. Generally speaking, however, our level of scientific inquiry or professional practice focuses on either individual behavior (e.g., job satisfaction and performance), social behavior (e.g., group dynamics and leadership) or organizational processes (e.g., decision making, and organizational change).

Let's now look more closely at the kinds of activities and research engaged in by organizational psychologists and then illustrate some of these activities with two case studies.

Measurement of Jobs

Many organizational decisions and practices depend on the job information obtained from job analysis. For example, information about the nature of job duties and responsibilities is important for

decisions regarding compensation and pay equity, the development of fair and valid selection criteria, performance appraisal, employee training and development, and career counseling. Psychologists have developed a number of methods for analyzing jobs and research has centered on their comparative usefulness for the purposes cited above.

Personnel Selection

Personnel selection is a major aspect of organizational life. It is the procedure through which an organization hires and promotes its employees. It is obviously an important and consequential activity. In fact, studies suggest that productivity differences between poor and superior performers in an organization can amount to more than $20,000 per employee per year! Thus, an organization that selects its employees wisely can reap substantial benefits. Important tasks for organizational psychologists are to develop and validate personnel selection techniques and to consult with those responsible for personnel operations. Good selection techniques enable organizations to determine, prior to hiring or promotion, the likelihood that a job candidate will perform the job effectively.

The variety of selection techniques developed ranges from standardized paper-and-pencil tests of knowledge, skill, or ability, through innovative structured interviews and self-assessments, to highly sophisticated management assessment centers designed to simulate the complexity of an executive's position. I will have more to say about assessment centers in a later section.

Since the early 1960s, employment testing has been immersed in a sea of controversy and is increasingly scrutinized by special interest groups, government, and the legal system. The prominent issues usually involve concerns of test bias—the perceived unfairness of standardized tests for minority and ethnic groups. As some observers have noted, the issue of potential bias in testing is an emotionally volatile one becuase it involves the specter of racial differences in inherited ability as well as the provision of job opportunities for minority groups. Test development specialists have been very much involved in these issues—often as expert witnesses in court. Such legal challenges and the resultant research on test bias have led to noticeable changes in test development procedures in the last 20 years.

Performance Appraisal

Once the person is hired, we wish to evaluate how well he or she performs on the job. In virtually every work situation each person makes some type of judgment about the other persons involved. Supervisors and managers are no exception. They inevitably make judgments about their subordinates. Although these judgments are often made informally, most organizations have formal, systematic rating procedures. This is the domain of performance appraisal. Performance ratings can be used to determine whether the employee should be promoted, demoted, transferred, or fired. Organizational psychologists develop performance appraisal measures that are valid, reliable, free of bias, practical to administer, and acceptable to management and employees alike. Performance appraisal information can be used to help employees to reach and maintain effective job performance.

Personnel Training

People bring to their jobs an assortment of previously learned skills, knowledge, interests, motivation, and attitudes. The additional learning people acquire after they become employees can take place through on-the-job experience or training. For some jobs, actual day-to-day work experience is probably the most effective method for developing the required expertise. For many jobs, however, well-planned and executed training programs provide the most practical method to develop such expertise.

Organizational psychologists develop training techniques aimed at supporting some organizational end goal such as more efficient production, reduction of operating costs, or more effective management practices. Research involves theories and principles of learning, the determination of training needs, and the development and evaluation of training methods. The research methods might include programmed instruction, role playing, business games, lectures, and the case method. The importance of training is underscored by the fact that for many occupations, particularly those of a technical, scientific, and professional nature, the obsolescence rate of current knowledge is dramatic. For some professions, it is estimated to be between four and five years from the time one graduates from university.

Motivation

If you ask a group of individuals why they work, the answers are likely to be diverse and even inconsistent. Some work only for money; some work because they love what they are doing; others work because of the status they receive. Organizational psychologists are concerned with the development and testing of comprehensive theories of work motivation. We seek to understand the effort, persistence, and direction of work behavior. Currently, there are several major competing theories of work motivation, including those referred to as *need* theories and those referred to as *process* theories.

Need theories specify the kinds of physiological and psychological needs, desires, and wants people have and the conditions under which they will be motivated to satisfy them in an organizationally useful manner. You probably already know a little about

Job training, an important area of organizational psychology. (Courtesy of the editor, Robert Gifford.)

one major need theory—Abraham Maslow's hierarchy of needs. According to Maslow, our needs are arranged in a hierarchy, with some needs more basic than others. Lower order or *prepotent* needs include physiological needs (food, water, sex) and safety needs (a healthy existence free from threats). Higher order needs include those for belongingness (to be liked and accepted by others), esteem (to obtain recognition and to have a positive self-image) and self-actualization (reaching our full potential). Like all need theorists, Maslow believed that an unsatisfied need produces behavior that is intended to satisfy it, after which that need is no longer motivating. A unique feature of Maslow's approach, however, was his notion that our lower order needs must be satisfied before we can become motivated to satisfy our higher order needs.

Need theories attempt to describe what motivates individuals. In contrast, *process theories* concentrate on how motivation occurs. One of the most influential examples of a process theory is Victor Vroom's expectancy theory. In simple terms, this theory assumes that people will be motivated to engage only in those work activities that are attractive or can be accomplished. How attractive various work activities are depends on the extent to which the consequences of the activities are valued by the individual. Organizational psychologists are actively engaged in testing the competing theories of work motivation.

Job Satisfaction

There appears to be a growing social concern that many people dislike their work situations. Much of our current interest focuses on this problem. A great deal of research effort attempts to identify meaningful dimensions of job satisfaction and determine how best to measure them. Some dimensions include the nature of the work itself (difficulty, control over work flow, chances for success); job-related rewards (perceived fairness of pay, opportunities for promotion and recognition); job context (hours of work, quality of the workspace, benefits); the employee's values, skills, and abilities; supervisory style of managers; and the competence, friendliness, and helpfulness of co-workers. Many different scales have been used to measure job satisfaction over the last 40 years, the most popular being the *Job Descriptive Index* (JDI) developed by Patricia Smith and her associates. This scale measures employees' attitudes in five areas: work, supervision, pay, promotions, and co-workers.

Organizational psychologists have also investigated some of

the consequences of job dissatisfaction including absenteeism, turnover, and possible reduction in physical and mental health. Curiously, research has not supported the intuitive notion that job satisfaction causes better work performance. On the contrary, there may be greater support for the hypothesis that performance causes satisfaction. That is, good performance that is rewarded or recognized in some fashion by the organization may in fact result in greater job satisfaction.

More recently, two new constructs related to job satisfaction have captured the attention of organizational psychologists. The first, *job involvement*, is viewed as a state of psychological identification with the job that results from the satisfaction of the employee's most important needs. The second concept is *organizational commitment*, which is conceived as a psychological state that binds the individual to the organization. The components of this state may include an emotional attachment to the organization, a recognition of the costs associated with leaving, and/or a perceived obligation to remain. Research on these constructs has begun to yield interesting results and to provide a deeper understanding of the determinants and consequences of job satisfaction in the workplace.

Group Dynamics

Organizational psychologists as well as social psychologists are very much interested in group processes. In the workplace, some questions raised include: How do new members get socialized into the work group? Why are some work groups more tightly knit than others? How do groups influence their members? What are the consequences for performance? Answers to these questions involve a number of avenues of research including the learning of norms and roles necessary to function in a group or organization, the effects of threat, competition, success, size, and member similarity on group cohesiveness, and the consequences of conformity and "group think."

The study of group dynamics has yielded some interesting results counter to conventional wisdom. In a series of laboratory and field studies, Dean Tjosvold (1985) and his colleagues demonstrated that although controversy creates internal conflict and uncertainty, it can also increase the understanding, acceptance, and use of opposing views, all of which can contribute to higher quality group decisions. Tjosvold argues that skillfully managed controversy should be widely used in organizations.

Leadership

Leadership occurs when particular individuals exert influence on others toward the achievement of some goal. It involves status differences as well as role differences, and leaders are almost always granted higher status than those who serve as followers. But, what makes a good leader? Are there particular personality traits or behavior patterns that set great leaders apart from others? Are there particular follower behaviors that make other people seem to look good? Or, is it simply that a great leader is one who capitalizes on the opportunities presented by the situation? That is, perhaps the great leader is the person who sees which way the crowd is going and jumps out in front. Unfortunately, despite the great volume of research conducted, there is not perfect agreement about what constitutes effective leadership, in what circumstances, and with which followers.

Early studies of leadership attempted to identify physical, psychological, and intellectual traits that might distinguish leaders from nonleaders and good leaders from bad. The findings of these studies were inconsistent and rather discouraging. It turns out that while some traits are weakly related to leadership capacity, there are no personal traits or characteristics that guarantee effective leadership across various situations.

Following World War II, organizational psychology shifted its focus to the study of leader behaviors and their effects on group productivity and employee satisfaction. Two major classes of leadership behaviors were identified (Fleishman & Harris, 1962). One, called *consideration*, is the extent to which the leader shows personal concern for subordinates. The other, called *initiation of structure*, is the extent to which the leader is task oriented and concentrates on attaining group goals. Hundreds of studies tried to link these two leadership styles to leader effectiveness but the results were often contradictory. Leader consideration often resulted in more satisfaction with the leader but not necessarily more productivity. On the other hand, task-oriented leadership styles were not consistently related to either group satisfaction or productivity.

By the 1970s, the evidence seemed clear. The same leaders and/or the same leadership styles are not equally effective in all situations. Current theories of leadership recognize that the success of a leader is dependent on the interaction between his or her style and the nature of the situation. Two such major approaches, the contingency theory of Fred Fiedler (1967) and the path-goal

theory of Robert House (1971) attempt to explain the situations in which various leader behaviors are most effective.

Communication

Communication is essential for effective organizational functioning. It is vital for all other organizational processes. Without it, employees would not know the organization's goals and objectives and would often work at cross-purposes. Communication is also pervasive. Supervisors spend upward of 50% of their time in face-to-face communication; senior managers spend almost 90% of their time engaged in communication.

Studies of communication have addressed a variety of issues including the upward, downward, and lateral flow of information across organizational levels; the functions and characteristics of informal, or grapevine, communication channels; and the problems that impede effective superior-subordinate interactions. One of the

Informal communication at work is at least as important as formal communication. (Courtesy of the editor, Robert Gifford.)

most extensively researched topics is the communication network. Formal networks prescribe and limit the information flow among personnel within the organization. They should reflect the communication requirements created by the organization's functions, technology, and authority structure.

Not all organizations have effective communication networks. Some suffer from chronic communication problems such as the inability to provide accurate and relevant information to those who need it, when they need it. Different communication networks also have been shown to effect group performance, leadership, and member satisfaction within organizations. For example, centralized networks, in which responsibility is concentrated in a dominant leader, may be more effective when the task is highly structured; conversely, decentralized networks, in which responsibility for problem solving is shared by group members, are likely to be more effective when the task is more complex and creative.

Decision Making

Organizational psychologists have spent a considerable amount of time trying to understand the decision-making process in organizations. Apparently, very few executives know how they actually make the decisions that govern the fate of their organizations. The focus of research has been on decision-making by individuals, groups, and, in some cases, organizational decisions that involve many individuals and groups.

A number of proposed models explain the decision process. Some specify how decisions should be made in order to maximize gains; others attempt to account for the realities of human cognitive limitations and social constraints and describe how the decision maker typically selects a satisfactory solution rather than the optimal one; still others consider the causes and consequences of decision stress.

Researchers have also examined the conditions under which managers should involve subordinates in decision making. It turns out that effective managers do not always use participative decision-making techniques; nor are they always autocratic. Rather, they have learned to diagnose a problem and use the most appropriate technique dictated by the conditions at hand.

Organizational Design

Organizational structure is the manner in which an organization divides its labor and functions and achieves coordination among them. Management usually attempts to organize in a way that will facilitate the attainment of organizational goals. During the first part of this century, *classical* organization theorists argued that efficiency could best be achieved by dividing tasks into specialized roles, devising detailed rules and procedures, and establishing an authority hierarchy with elaborate controls to ensure adherence to these rules and procedures. The *bureaucracy* was seen as desirable.

By the 1950s and 1960s, however, *bureaucracy* had become a dirty word and humanistic theorists began to prescribe an organization with flexible roles, open communication, participative leadership, and decentralized decisions. However, research has shown that neither type of structure is appropriate for all organizations all of the time. We now know, for example, that if work is predictable and routine, the necessary arrangement for getting it done can be highly structured. On the other hand, if it is not predictable or routine and there is considerable uncertainty as to how to do the job, then managers are better advised to utilize design strategies that emphasize autonomy, temporary work groups, and multiple lines of authority.

CASE STUDIES

CASE ONE: THE DEVELOPMENT OF AN ASSESSMENT CENTER

A constant source of concern to both business and government is their ability to attract and develop qualified managers. The truly effective manager has always been a rather scarce commodity. By the 1970s, however, the increased diversity and complexity of the modern organization began to place an even heavier burden on the existing management population. There was a critical shortage of good managers and the traditional methods for identifying and developing the available talent were woefully inadequate to cope with the problem. As a result, many North American organizations undertook an extensive review of their personnel practices with the intent of developing new and dynamic human resource planning systems. The Government of Canada was one such organization

that looked closely at the state of its management training and development.

The result of various taskforce reviews was the creation of the government's Career Assignment Program (CAP)—an integrated education and development program designed for middle-level managers and specialists who have shown high potential to become executives. The purpose of CAP is to ensure a continuing supply of high quality managers and executives within the government. Participants in the program begin with a nine-week management course followed by a series of three or four job assignments extending from one to two years each. The assignments are located across different departments and functional areas in order to broaden each participant's management experience and perspective.

During the early years, selection of candidates to CAP was left to the discretion of each government department based on general criteria related to age, salary, career history, and job performance (i.e., "track record"). Over time, however, the different standards applied by each department created severe problems in the range of quality of candidates who were selected. These problems led to the perception that CAP was not attracting sufficiently high potential candidates and the opportunities for job assignments began to dwindle. The program was in danger of collapsing. A major review of these difficulties resulted in the decision to establish an assessment center as one means of providing standardized selection criteria for entry into CAP.

What is an assessment center? You might be surprised to learn that it is not a place but a process, and one that is used in a variety of settings including business and industry, government, and the military. Typically, it is designed to evaluate managerial talent and potential. In an assessment center, multiple techniques are used to evaluate candidates, and these can include problem analysis exercises, group presentations, group discussion exercises, interviews, aptitude and personality tests, and in-basket tests. This latter technique needs some clarification. An in-basket test requires a candidate to actually work his or her way through the day-to-day collection of memos, telephone messages, short reports, meeting notices, and other documents that might demand a manager's attention. Trained scorers evaluate the order or priority candidates assign to the various tasks and the way in which they respond to them (making telephone calls, delegating work, scheduling meetings, writing memos and letters, and so forth).

A key ingredient to any assessment center program is that performance in the management simulation exercises is observed

and evaluated by a group of assessors who have been specially trained in this evaluation technique. Usually, these assessors are senior managers.

The development of the assessment center for CAP was undertaken by three psychologists at the Public Service Commission of Canada with whom I had the pleasure of working for several years—Len Slivinski, Ken Grant, and Robert Bourgeois. The development process was to last eight months. Because the goal of CAP was to groom individuals for executive positions, the first level within the government's senior executive category was used as the reference point. The assessment center would be designed to simulate the kinds of situations and problems faced by first-level executives.

In developing the assessment center exercises, two fundamental questions had to be answered. First, what are the common tasks and duties performed by first-level executives across the various departments, units, and functional areas? Second, what are the important qualities and abilities these managers need to possess in order to effectively carry out these responsibilities? The answer to the first question would provide the raw material for the content of the simulation exercises. The answer to the second question would determine the dimensions of ability to be evaluated through these exercises.

A comprehensive picture of the work of senior executives also required answers to a host of other questions. How do executives carry out their responsibilities? What are their differing styles? How often and with whom do they communicate? How do they use their time? What are the varied environments in which they operate?

Answers to the above questions were arrived at through a variety of investigative methods. Initially, members of the research team conducted extensive reviews of the personnel literature and made several visits to other organizations throughout North America to gain insight into the current state of the art in identifying managerial potential through the assessment center method. Batteries of tests were then administered to CAP participants and senior executives to determine which tests and abilities possessed value as predictors of managerial performance. Elaborate job analysis questionnaires were also administered to over 400 executives in order to identify critical job functions and abilities.

Perhaps the most valuable information to the researchers came from their efforts to gain in-depth accounts of just what was involved in the work of an executive. Interviews were conducted with senior executives throughout the government, asking them to

describe the types of activities in which they were involved and the skills and abilities they felt were necessary to carry them out. The interviews confirmed the findings of the job analysis questionnaires in identifying job activities such as short- and long-range planning, personnel services, representing the department to the public, setting objectives, and allocating resources. Through these interviews, it was possible to obtain many concrete examples of the breadth and complexity of each executive's job.

The interviews also focused on the managerial abilities deemed important for effective performance. For example, executives were asked: "If you had the responsibility for selecting a person for your position, what qualities and abilities would you look for?" The list of desirable traits offered seemed to include just about every human virtue. Nevertheless, this information was useful in pointing out the variety of qualities that executives considered important for their success.

For most of the executives interviewed, permission was also obtained to have their secretaries keep a diary log on their activities each day for a week. Special forms and instructions were prepared for this purpose. The researchers also sought and obtained permission to review memoranda, reports, and letters either written or received by each executive. This material provided detailed information concerning how the executive spent his or her day—the number of meetings held, the number of contacts with superiors, subordinates, and peers, and the time spent on operational activities such as program and policy review, project proposals, and budgeting.

The responsibility for integrating the information gathered from these diverse sources rested primarily with the research team. However, an important role was also played by a special government committee of senior personnel. This committee served as a vital sounding board and final decision-making body for all issues related to the development of the assessment center. It was recognized that their expert judgment would be invaluable in helping to determine the future needs of the senior executive category.

The distillation of this vast amount of data into meaningful information required considerable analytic and conceptual skills on the part of my former colleagues. The end product of this process was the identification and definition of the following 13 attributes important for executive success:

Intelligence	Planning and organizing
Creativity	Delegation
Stress tolerance	Analysis and synthesis

Motivation	Judgment
Effective independence	Oral communication
Leadership	Written communication
Interpersonal relations	

Once these abilities had been described, the next step was to construct the appropriate measurement methods. Here the wealth of information concerning the duties and responsibilities of executives provided the clues. Analysis of this material led to the creation of five management simulation exercises that reflected the kinds of problems and situations experienced at the executive level and would serve as cues to elicit behavior relevant to the abilities listed above. Each candidate's performance in the simulations would be evaluated by three specially trained senior government executives.

The assessment center developed for CAP is unique in that the five simulation exercises are fully integrated. On arrival at the assessment center, each candidate assumes the role of a senior executive in charge of a particular unit within a recently formed government agency. He or she is provided with extensive written background material outlining the organizational structure, activities, and issues facing the agency. The candidate then proceeds to engage, over a three-day period, in a series of activities and meetings related to the functions of the agency.

Work begins with an *in-basket* task in which the candidate responds to the reports, memoranda, messages, and background material deposited for the executive's attention. Building on this material, the candidate is then scheduled to conduct a *staff meeting* with four subordinate managers in order to deal further with the problems and issues facing both the unit and the agency. During this meeting, the candidate has the opportunity to meet and interact with staff, direct and control the meeting, seek out additional information, and implement decisions through delegation. The roles of the subordinate managers are played by trained actors who possess sufficient background information to respond to the particular style and approach of each candidate.

Following the staff meeting, the candidate is given an opportunity to prepare for a scheduled *briefing* to the president of the agency. The purpose of the briefing is to inform the president (another trained actor) of the general state of the unit for which the candidate has assumed responsibility.

During the fourth simulation, the candidate is asked to make a *budget presentation* to two senior financial officers of the organization (also trained actors). In preparing for this oral presen-

tation, the candidate must synthesize a considerable amount of information prepared by the subordinate staff regarding the program plans and budget forecast of the unit for the next three years.

In the fifth and final simulation, the candidate is invited to join a *taskforce* established to study and recommend solutions to problems within both the unit and the agency as whole. During this exercise there are six candidates, each of whom has participated in the four previous simulations. Taskforce members are expected to organize their time and resources, attempt to reach a consensus, and prepare a summary report for the president.

As you might imagine, the three-day assessment program is certainly a stressful experience for the candidates. But does it provide a valid evaluation of their managerial potential? In a word, yes. Follow-up research has shown that those candidates who receive high ratings of potential at the assessment center have a much greater likelihood of becoming senior executives than those candidates who receive lower ratings. Moreover, it has also been found that the performance of candidates at the assessment center is highly correlated with supervisor ratings of job performance up to four years later. ♦

CASE TWO: COMMUNICATION IN POLICE FORCES

The local police force is a fairly visible organization in our cities, and as such, is subjected to all manner of research by social scientists. For example, during the past few years alone, researchers at the Canadian Police College have been involved with dozens of studies investigating topics ranging from the public accountability of municipal police forces to the job involvement of front-line police officers.

Our empirical interest in the police is not surprising, given their mandate for crime prevention, maintenance of order and law enforcement, while at the same time recognizing the individual rights of citizens in a democratic society. What is surprising, however, is that very little of this research has dealt with the nature of the communication process within the police organization.

This is a curious omission for several reasons. First, effective communication is vital for the success of any organization and most obviously of vital concern to the communities the police serve. Second, the limited research that has been done reveals that communication is a top-ranking problem in police forces. Of particular importance, however, are the implications for police management of the shift away from viewing organizations as machines or organisms to viewing them as interactive social systems and cultures.

This view of organizations as cultures suggests that communication plays a key role in the development of the beliefs and values that police officers share, many of which are often revealed in symbolic communication such as stories, rituals, specialized language, and behaviors that shape and mold the police culture. From this perspective, police managers are faced with creating meaning and identity in a manner congruent with the goals of their organization. At the same time, front-line police officers are seen as interpreting meaning and identity from various behaviors and events.

The role of communication in the transmission of values and beliefs in police forces was the focus of a study undertaken by researchers at Wilfrid Laurier University under the sponsorship of the Canadian Police College. Approaching the study from a cultural point of view, the researchers examined many processes that are not typically considered communication, but which could be seen as sources of significant meaning for police members. For instance, all of the activities, policies, procedures, decisions, and changes within the force contain significant communication content and, hence, make value statements to members of the force. In this study, communication was viewed from two perspectives: Professor Gene Deszca looked at how managers develop meaning for their force and Professor Raymond Adamson looked at how rank-and-file police officers make sense of these events. I will discuss only the latter.

Messages flow from many sources within an organization, but they usually originate from some form of management decision. Professor Adamson attempted to identify the major sources of these messages and examined the fit between their actual content and how they were interpreted by subordinates.

An example cited by Adamson nicely illustrates the potential discrepancy between a message's intent and its result. The patrol function is an important part of good police service to the community. However, police management often disciplines members of various other units within the force by reassigning them to uniformed patrol duty. The *intent* is to punish unacceptable behavior. The *message* to patrol officers is that the patrol function is held in low esteem by management and is synonymous with organizational punishment. Given that many police officers spend their total career on patrol and that patrol work is critical for police success, this message is dysfunctional. As you might imagine, the lower ranks within the force construct their own meaning from such messages—one that is not likely to further the goals of the organization.

Three police forces participated in this component of the

study. They were selected because each force had recently undergone some significant changes involving communication processes within the organization. Force A was a municipal force serving an urban population in a medium-sized city. Force B was a relatively small regional force that served both an urban and a rural population. The third force, C, was a larger regional force. It served a large geographical area and a combined urban/rural population. In each force, members were divided by rank into senior managers (inspector rank and above), middle managers (staff sergeants and sergeants), and front-line officers (constables).

Investigation of the communication process in the three forces included a variety of data-gathering techniques. The most prominent of these was an unstructured or open-ended interview conducted with managers and front-line officers. Interviews with management were used to get some idea of the intent of their communication activities and to identify the communication channels. The bulk of the interviews were carried out with the lower ranks. This strategy enabled the researcher to get a grass roots view of the communication process and to see how management's messages were interpreted by front line officers.

The questions for the senior officers were primarily aimed at discovering their hopes and plans for the force and the values they espoused for the organization. Specific questions were then asked about how they communicated these hopes, plans, and values to the lower ranks. Front-line officers were asked what they thought were the major messages that management was trying to convey through questions such as, "How and what does senior management tell you about their objectives for the organization, their views on policing, how you fit into this picture, and what they expect of you?" They were also asked to identify the various communication channels involved. All interview responses were aggregated to reflect the degree of consensus within and across the three forces.

Two other investigation methods were also used. In the first, force records were examined for their communication intent. These records consisted of planning documents, annual reports, operations manuals, policies and procedures, and daily orders. In the second, the researcher sat in and observed various formal and informal meetings and noted instances in which communication was initiated and interpreted. These meetings included patrol muster, patrol group meetings, and management committee meetings.

The methods used to gather the data prevented any precise quantitative conclusions about the nature of the communication processes across the three forces. In particular, open-ended inter-

views do not lend themselves to such precision. However, the study was exploratory and the open-ended interview is ideally suited to the kind of in-depth probing of responses that one wants in such research. As an aside, the use of a detailed questionnaire to supplement the interviews would have undoubtedly added meaningful and more quantifiable data. Unfortunately, police forces are so often asked by researchers to have their members complete questionnaires that there is (or should be) legitimate concern about the seriousness with which officers will fill them out. I recently spoke with one chief of police who, at that moment, had six requests to conduct questionnaire studies sitting in his in basket!

The findings of this study have helped us understand of where, when, and why police management communication does not achieve its desired objective. Without doubt, Adamson's work has provided needed insights into the difficulties experienced by senior police personnel in shaping values, beliefs, and commitment among front-line officers. In the following paragraphs, I will describe a few of his more interesting observations and conclusions.

Analysis of the interview responses, documentation, and meeting discussions led first to the creation of a general communication model characteristic of all three forces. In this model, important communication systems and their areas of overlap were identified. Specifically, police force communication permeates the management system with messages about operations, planning, and goals. This basic system has five satellite communication systems including structure (chain of command, the rank system, autocratic orientation), promotion, recognition, control, and decision making. Each system has its own set of unique, identifiable messages which often conflict with one another and hinder management's attempt to convey to members what the organization is about and what it values.

One of the striking characteristics of the management system, for example, was its almost total reliance on formal written communication for informing the troops of force rules, procedures, policies, and new directions. This was true for routine and important matters alike. For instance, changes in the law that dictated new street behaviors were given little more attention in the written system than were routine matters.

Senior management saw little need to communicate face-to-face with front-line officers. They believed their emphasis on formal written communication provided clear guidelines for efficient and consistent performance and acceptable behavior. The interpretation of the message by front-line officers, however, was quite dif-

ferent. In their view, the written communications were frequently ambiguous and they seldom received follow-up clarification from management.

As a consequence, the front-line officers tended to do nothing; they assumed that the communication must not be important in the first place. On many occasions, there was a perception that senior managers communicated only in an ambiguous written form because they themselves didn't really know how to handle a particular situation. Obviously, the meanings intended by management were not those construed by the lower ranks.

Within the control system, citizen complaints against the police and related disciplinary procedures generated some strong conflicting messages. Under the law, management had no choice but to allow complaints to go forward even though many were unfounded. They believed that to do otherwise would be seen as thwarting justice. To the lower ranks, however, a different message was received: management was withdrawing its support and deserting them by letting these unwarranted complaints proceed; hence, one couldn't count on management support. Unfortunately, management was often unaware of this unintended message and so did nothing to correct it.

The recognition system also produced some interesting examples of message conflict. In each force, management was attempting to move policing away from the traditional emphasis on crook catching toward a more proactive partnership with the community. The achievement of this goal involves not only transmitting the message to front-line officers, but also obtaining their commitment to the beliefs and values inherent in the new approach.

The recognition process seemed to undermine this goal, however. Formal recognition in the form of official citations was much more likely to be awarded for traditional behaviors, such as criminal apprehension, than for the less exciting patrol activities associated with community-based policing. Even the informal recognition system conveyed messages that served to reduce front-line commitment to management's goal. In the eyes of the patrol officers, their job had not really changed. Despite management's apparent enthusiasm for the new proactive community-based approach, few additional resources had been provided to implement it. Thus, the sense among patrol personnel was that traditional job expectations still remained and the new approach to policing was simply an add-on to an already over-taxing job.

Research undoubtedly contributes to our better understanding of the inner workings of organizations. Those in positions of

authority who strive for more enlightened leadership can directly benefit, assuming, of course, that the relevant research findings are made readily available to the appropriate audiences. In police-related research, studies are frequently reported in police science journals that are distributed to police forces worldwide. The Canadian Police College takes a more direct approach, by sponsoring a three- or four-day workshop where senior police managers are invited to actively confront the issues raised and consider ways to resolve them. ♦

Becoming an Organizational Psychologist

To function as an organizational psychologist it is necessary to complete graduate school training in the discipline. Although there are still some jobs open to those with Master's degrees, the doctoral degree is increasingly required.

Master's and doctoral degrees are offered by a number of colleges, universities, and professional schools throughout North America. These programs are described in *Graduate Training Programs in Industrial/Organizational Psychology and Organizational Behavior* published by the Society for Industrial and Organizational Psychology (1986). This document should be available in your university library and will give you an overview of the particular nature and emphases of each program as well as the entrance requirements. Your academic advisor may not have the answers to all your career questions but will be able to guide you to the appropriate information sources.

It is not always necessary to have taken courses in organizational psychology at the undergraduate level in order to enter a graduate program in the field. However, if available, these courses are certainly desirable. Relevant course work can also be obtained outside psychology departments since many of the areas within organizational psychology are addressed by other disciplines. For example, courses in organizational behavior, design, development, and change are frequently offered by faculties of business, management, and administration.

In addition to undergraduate and graduate course work, formal training within a particular program will likely include some combination of independent study, supervised field research, and/or an internship with a given organization. A well-supervised

internship program has several potential benefits. You will get a feel for the kinds of real-world issues and problems confronted by organizational psychologists. This will help you determine where the gaps are in your current knowledge and how you might fill them when you return to your formal study program. You might also acquire some appreciation for the difficulties that can arise when one attempts to satisfy both the needs of the employer and the scientific and applied research demands of the profession. Learning to balance these elements will greatly contribute to your future effectiveness as an applied organizational psychologist. Finally, an internship program can provide you with a realistic job preview. Knowing at least a little about how an organization functions, and the role of the professional psychologist within it, will be useful when you make an employment decision.

Organizational psychologists work in four major settings: government and industry, consulting firms, research institutions, and academe. The availability of jobs in each setting differs considerably. According to one recent survey, about 60% of organizational psychologists are employed by business, industry, and government and another 35% teach within educational institutions. Many who teach, however, also provide consulting services to a variety of organizations in both the public and private sectors. Conversely, many organizational psychologists employed in government and industry also teach part time at colleges and universities.

The domain of organizational psychology continues to expand as new questions are asked and research techniques and applications are designed to answer them. One's knowledge and skills must be continually enhanced through on-the-job training, professional workshops, and literature review. Attendance at conferences sponsored by the American Psychological Association, the Canadian Psychological Association, the Society for Industrial and Organizational Psychology, the Academy of Management, and the International Personnel Management Association is also highly recommended.

Organizational psychology is a dynamic area of study and its future holds many challenges and opportunities for the researcher and practitioner alike. Undoubtedly, there are many reasons for this vitality, but the most important, perhaps, was provided by Campbell (1982) when he affirmed that we deal with societal issues of fundamental importance.

SUGGESTED READINGS AND REFERENCES

CAMPBELL, J. P. (1982). Editorial: Some remarks from the outgoing editor. *Journal of Applied Psychology, 67,* 691–700.

FIEDLER, F. E. (1967). *A theory of leadership effectiveness.* New York: McGraw-Hill.

FLEISHMAN, E. A., & HARRIS, E. F. (1962). Patterns of leadership behavior related to employee grievances and turnover. *Personnel Psychology,* (1962), *15,* 43–56.

HOUSE, R. J. (1971). A path goal theory of leader effectiveness. *Administrative Science Quarterly, 16,* 321–338.

JOHNS, G. (1988). *Organizational behavior.* Glenview, IL: Scott-Foresman.

ROETHLISBERGER, F. J., & DICKSON, W. J. (1939). *Management and the worker.* Cambridge, MA: Harvard University Press.

SAAL, F. E., & KNIGHT, P. A. (1988). *Industrial/organizational psychology: Science and practice.* Belmont, CA: Wadsworth.

SOCIETY FOR INDUSTRIAL AND ORGANIZATIONAL PSYCHOLOGY (1986). *Graduate training programs in industrial/organizational psychology and organizational behavior.* College Park, MD.

TAYLOR, F. W. (1911). *The principles of scientific management.* New York: Harper.

TJOSVOLD, D. (1985). Implications of controversy research for management. *Journal of Management, 11,* 21–37.

RUTH M. HERON

Ruth M. Heron is an ergonomist who has been elected to the Professional Register of the Ergonomics Society. She is employed by the Canadian government. She received her Ph.D. in 1975 from the University of Calgary and has worked as a professor and statistician in addition to her current responsibilities. Her research interests have included missing children, video display terminals, transportation systems, and communication systems. ♦

13

The Ergonomist

To introduce you to ergonomics and to illustrate how an ergonomist might apply his or her craft, let me tell you first about a relatively simple project I worked on a number of years ago. This project involved development of a wheelchair-securement/occupant-restraint system for use in a paratransit van. The function of a paratransit van is to provide transportation for people who, because of some disability, are unable to use the public transportation system. When these vans first began to appear on the scene in the early 1970s, design considerations focused on how to get potential users of the system (mainly the wheelchair-bound) in and out of the vehicle. And so various lifts were developed.

Later it became obvious that wheelchair passengers were at risk of serious injury in the event of an accident because no provision had been made to secure the wheelchair or to restrain the person sitting in it. My involvement in the problem began when a friend of mine, an industrial designer, asked me to provide ergonomics advice as he carried out a contract with Transport Canada to design and develop a system that would provide wheelchair passengers the same degree of protection available to people riding in ordinary vehicles with lap and shoulder belts and headrests.

The system my friend designed eventually took the form of a floor-mounted stand against which the wheelchair was to be backed. Telescopic arms could be pulled out at an angle of 45° to the floor and clamped onto the wheel rims to secure the chair; a belt and headrest were provided for the passenger. During development, much of my input concerned the physical and mental demands involved in the vehicle driver's task of maneuvering the chair in and out of place, clamping the securement arms to the wheel rims and releasing them, and fastening and releasing the belt system.

Each operation had to be broken down into small elements so that I could observe the interaction between the driver and specific design features of the system. The methodological approach was in fact a form of systems-task analysis that I will discuss more fully later. Let me say now only that, by applying this technique, I was able to pinpoint system features that would bring about stress to the operator's muscles, tendons, ligaments, or joints, or that would tax his or her normal capacity to process information in the brain. The passengers, of course, were not forgotten. However, as they had no tasks to perform in connection with the system, their interactions with it were much more passive than those of the vehicle operator. In their case, then, what was of interest were certain human factors—such as the aesthetics of the system, sensations of movement, and feelings of security, comfort, and dignity. When the proto-

type was field tested, I carried out a full-scale ergonomics evaluation of it, the results of which provided the basis for various modifications that would render the system ergonomically sound.

What Is Ergonomics?

Ergonomics—a curious, coined word! And one bandied about quite often these days in ways that suggest confusion about the discipline. This is not at all surprising because, since the time the word came into being, the science it represents has been utilized mainly by the military and aerospace industry. Other industries and governments have only recently begun to recognize the advantages of including ergonomists on their project teams.

To broaden understanding of ergonomics, we can start with a simple definition derived from the Greek roots of the word. The first part comes from *ergon* meaning *work*; the other from *nomos* meaning *natural laws*. Putting the two parts together produces a word implying that *ergonomics* is a branch of science which encompasses natural laws about work behavior. *Human factors* and *human engineering* are terms often used instead of ergonomics in talking about the field, but my own feeling is that ergonomics is preferable, first, because the discipline was christened that way and, second, because its roots define its meaning so well.

Practitioners of this young discipline examine the way people interact with machines and other person-made objects in their environment. In doing so, they are trying to discover whether anything about the design of these objects might make it difficult, or impossible, for people to operate or use them. If design features like these are removed, or modified so as to be compatible with the capacities of the human operators or users of a person-machine system, then the system will be safer and more efficient.

Perhaps already the little account of the tiedown will have provided a flavor of what ergonomics is all about. Still, to set the stage for later discussion, it will be worthwhile to look back on it and draw attention to some of its significant portions. To begin the process, note how often the word *system* has been used. This word denotes a concept that is extremely important to the ergonomics approach: in a system, all parts are related to one another, and no one part can be understood without understanding all.

One application of the systems approach to the tiedown is

implicit in the fact that attention was given to the driver's task as well as to the passengers' reactions to the system. Some developers who ask me to evaluate technological devices of this kind appear surprised when I immediately begin to study what the operator of a system must do, rather than considering only the feelings and attitudes of the disabled passengers the system was meant to help! Some appear equally surprised when I talk of looking at the mental as well as the physical demands of an operator's task, and I frequently need to explain that ergonomics is very much concerned with how people process information from the environment in their brains. However, taking a systems approach involves much more than just including all types of persons that will interact with the object or system: it demands also that each aspect of the system must be examined in relation to every other aspect.

The term interaction has also been used a number of times in the account of the tiedown. Use of this word implies that there is some sort of two-way process occurring between persons and machine systems. Ergonomists certainly do not see persons as being controlled by machines. Quite the opposite, in fact, since even

One city's public transport system for disabled passengers. (Courtesy of the editor, Robert Gifford.)

the most automated system—although it may appear to have eliminated humans from the loop—has been designed and developed by persons, and it is persons who will program and, hence, control its operations. Moreover, even the disabled passengers I described as interacting in a somewhat passive way with the tiedown device can exercise options with respect to the machine, whereas the converse is not true.

In adopting an interactional perspective, ergonomists are somewhat like environmental psychologists. One difference that is perhaps clear from the account of the tiedown is that the former begin with a much narrower focus, looking at small elements of person-system interactions and studying ways in which each is associated with sensory, perceptual, cognitive, motor, and psychological limitations of humans. You may have detected, too, a technical machine-like tone that is not evident in descriptions of environmental psychology, this stemming from the fact that ergonomics deals largely with systems conceived by engineers, environmental psychology with those conceived by architects and planners.

We will explore these aspects of ergonomics more deeply after some background on the discipline is presented.

The Background of Ergonomics

Ergonomics is generally regarded as a very new science but, actually, a considerable amount of research regarding the effects of working conditions on human performance was carried out between the First and Second World Wars. Studies in this area increased rapidly during World War II when military technology became so complex that it was outstripping the ability of operators to use it. One such study (Fitts & Jones, 1947), revealed that 270 "pilot errors" they analyzed after interviewing 500 pilots were related to the design of the cockpit. These errors fell into six categories as follows:

1. Substitution errors, occurring when one control was confused with another or could not be identified in time, and due largely to the way controls were placed in relation to one another.
2. Adjustment errors such as moving a switch to the wrong position or operating controls too slowly or too quickly.

3. Forgetting errors—for example, forgetting to check, release, or use a control at some critical time.

4. Reversal errors, involving the movement of a control in a direction opposite to the one that would bring about an intended effect.

5. Errors involving the unintended activation of a control.

6. Errors due to the pilot's inability to reach a given control.

From a review of this list, the reader will gain an understanding of why use of the quotes around the phrase "pilot errors" originates with the authors: They meant them to convey that the

Cockpits are very complex person-machine systems that ergonomists have helped develop. (Courtesy of the editor, Robert Gifford.)

real problems had something to do with the *design* of the displays rather than with the pilots.

After the war, many investigators in many disciplines—supported by government funding and inspired by the need to fill the gap in scientific knowledge about human capacities and limitations in relation to work—continued their research activities on human performance, mainly in the context of military problems. Those in the United Kingdom became unified as an interdisciplinary group in 1949 when they met at K. F. H. Murrell's office in the British Admiralty and jointly formed the Ergonomics Society.

While this move established ergonomics as a recognized discipline that would proceed apace with technological development, its scope then—and for a short period after—was limited largely to the design of displays and control panels used in the military. Very soon, however, the field broadened beyond this "knobs and dials" era to include interests in transportation, manufacturing, and communication systems. A holistic, systems approach was taken to the design of person-machine systems, with attempts being made to optimize efficiency by intelligent trade-offs in the allocation of functions to human and machine. (Actually, the latter approach has not appeared to be workable and, now that flexibility is possible through the modification of software, the practice is to allocate as much as possible to the machine.) Today, well into the information age as we are, ergonomics finds extremely important applications in the development of systems utilizing artificial intelligence, knowledge-based systems, and robotics.

Over the past decade or so, ergonomics has also increasingly been embraced by unions, with the thrust here being to improve the quality of working life through better design of tools, work stations, and working environment. A whole new subdiscipline called *macro ergonomics* has built up around the need to organize work systems and the design of jobs within these systems in a way that does not bring about undue stress to the worker.

The Scope of Ergonomics

The Ergonomics Model and Its Implications

But now, to get us more deeply into the topic, a working definition is needed. For this, we can say that *ergonomics* is the study of person-

machine systems in terms of the limitations and capacities of the human operator or user. This definition is embodied in the theoretical model put forth by Taylor in 1957 and shown in Figure 13-1. According to this model, the person in the system obtains information about the state of the machine from displays, integrates this input to the brain with information from higher level systems and the environment, decides on a control response, and exerts this response, thereby changing the state of the system. Information about the changed state is fed back to the operator through the displays, and the cycle then repeats itself. More recent models incorporate (1) environmental factors such as noise, illumination, temperature, and air quality; (2) psychological factors such as attitude, personality, mental set, fatigue, and alertness; and (3) social psychological factors such as group composition, roles, and communication patterns.

Nevertheless, Taylor's model is sufficient for driving home a number of important ergonomics principles. First, it implies that,

Figure 13-1 The ergonomics person-machine system model. *Source*: Taylor, F. V. (1957). Psychology and the design of machines. *American Psychologist, 21*, 249–258.

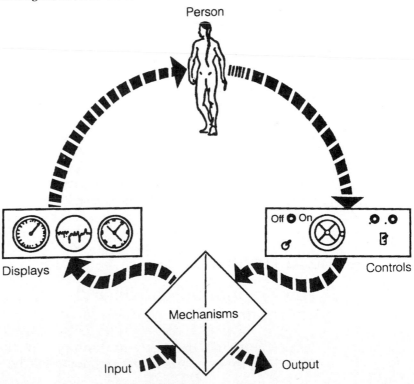

as mentioned earlier, ergonomics is systems-oriented. The operator and the machine are considered to be parts of one system and, therefore, a full understanding of a system cannot be gained by looking solely at the machine or solely at the person or solely at parts of either or both. The units of interest are person-system interactions, and an understanding of the system as a whole will be obtained only by examining *all* of these systematically and, because all parts of a system are interrelated, in an iterative fashion.

Second, Taylor's model sees the person and machine as constantly exchanging information. The person gives information to the machine through actions on control knobs, levers, and the like; and the machine feeds back information about the system through displays. However the person does have a special role because he or she picks up information from sources other than the machine displays.

For example, even before boarding a ship, the captain has already stored in his or her brain a considerable amount of information about the vessel's destination, the route that must be followed, environmental conditions likely to be encountered, and so on. Once on the ship, the captain refers to various charts, visually inspects environmental conditions, and receives radio and radar messages from land and airborne stations. Additionally, the captain receives messages about the actual behavior of the ship through visual, auditory, olfactory, and kinaesthetic cues. More explicitly, he or she can see how the ship behaves in interaction with the water or ice, can hear sounds and smell odors that may indicate abnormal conditions, and can feel, through nerves that tell the brain what is going on in the muscles, certain ship vibrations and ship/water or ship/ice interactions.

From this brief description of all the bits and pieces of information the captain of a ship receives, it should be clear that ergonomics regards the person in a system as a sensor and a processor of information. Many psychologists—Fitts, Posner, Broadbent, Norman, Keele, Welford, and Kahneman, to name only a few—have written a great deal about how people process information in their brains. Through their work, a model has developed which, to describe it in the most general terms, incorporates the following stages between the occurrence of some sort of event and a person's response to it: attention to the stimulus field, detection of the stimulus, discrimination of the stimulus from other events in the field, recognition, identification and interpretation of the stimulus pattern, decision regarding an appropriate response, and preparation for response.

Ergonomists must understand the processes corresponding

to each of the stages mentioned because, although we can only marvel at the fact that our brains accomplish such complex information-processing feats, their capacity to do so is limited in each case. Knowing the nature of these limitations enables the ergonomist to determine how design features of a display—or other parts of a machine involving use of sensory, perceptual, and cognitive capacities—affect system efficiency.

You will note that, while making my last point, I distinguished between sensory and perceptual capacities. We think of the former mainly in terms of reactions taking place when stimulus energy impacts on a receptor such as the eye or the ear, the latter in terms of a later process that ends when meaning is attached to the input. The distinction is important, because designers often think that, by providing a stimulus situation that is within the range of a given sense organ, they will get a certain behavioral result. However, we have only to look at some of the ambiguous figures appearing in introductory psychology texts (the one that can be perceived as either a pretty young or an ugly old woman is a favorite) to realize that, even though a perfect sensory message is received and sent to our brains, our perception of it may be quite different from what was intended by the sender of the message. This occurs because incoming information is combined with other information already stored in the brain.

Cognitive processes include the analysis of perceptual input, the integration of perceptions with other detail in long-term memory, decision-making regarding what to do about them, and preparation of the resulting external response. Humans were once thought to be single-channel processors, so that early in the chain of cognitive events things had to line up in the brain to be dealt with one by one. More recent models of human information-processing suggest that we do have some capacity for parallel processing, but this is very little and, in any case, there is always danger of overloading the system with ill-defined, ambiguous, or confusing data.

The ergonomist is constantly on the lookout for design features of displays that might bring about overloading effects. Can you imagine how important it would be to eliminate such features in the design of, say, a large nuclear power control room where the walls are covered with displays and where error-free information-processing by the operators is essential to avoid a disastrous accident? In their 1982 edition of *Human Factors in Engineering and Design*, McCormick and Sanders tell us that, in reference to the control room, the chair of the presidential commission investigating the 1977 Three Mile Island accident is quoted as saying: "It

looks to me like this is very bad human engineering." Daniel Ford's (1981) account of the incident provides ample justification for such a remark. The operators of the control room in question, albeit experienced and alert, did not activate a switch that would have closed a block valve and thereby closed a stuck-open pressure relief valve that was allowing cooling water to leak continuously from the reactor. The reason they did not take this action is because, although they knew how the block valve worked with respect to the pressure relief valve, there was nothing in the display system to tell them why the leakage was occurring. True, a special red light in the control room was *supposed* to provide information relevant to the status of the pressure relief valve. However the light was apparently an add-on device with only home-made labeling and, most importantly, with a circuitry such as to convey the *intent* of the electrical system to open or close the valve rather than the *actual position* of the valve. Apart from this critical design defect, Ford reports also that the more than 6,000 components of the control system in question were poorly organized in the 900 or so square feet of panel space, many in unreadable positions, and all spread out in a fashion that made it exceedingly difficult for the operators to synthesize information so as to gain an understanding of what was happening in the plant as a whole. On balance, then, it would seem that the control designers could have used a good ergonomist on their team!

Apart from being processors of information, persons in the Taylor model are also controllers of machines, and that means that they must exert motor responses. And so we get into another area in which persons have limitations. We can move each segment of the body only within certain ranges within certain planes, and our various muscle groups can take only so much weight against gravity as we perform activities involving complex involvement of the musculoskeletal system. Biomechanics and kinesiology cover these areas; anthropometry, the science dealing with the measurement of the physical characteristics of humans (particularly their sizes and shapes), is a related discipline. If we just stand or sit repetitively for long periods with parts of our skeletal structures out of alignment or stretched beyond normal range, we may subject muscles, tendons, ligaments, and eventually joints to stress that could result in permanent debilitating damage. For this reason, labor unions have become very concerned about the design of workstations, and designers then turn to anthropometry to determine what the dimensions of the various parts of these workstations should be. More specifically, a well known example of what is called repetitive strain injury (RSI) involves the swelling of the

interphalangeal joints of computer operators such as word processors and data entry clerks. The design of the QWERTY keyboard used by these operators did not take into consideration the differential strengths of the various fingers of the hands vis-à-vis the frequency of letter use in the English and French languages. The key for the frequently used letter *a*, for example, must be operated by the weakest finger, namely, the little finger on the left hand.

Even psychological factors are important to the model because personality, attitudes, emotions, moods, fatigue, and other internal states can affect how we process information and, hence, how the system as a whole behaves. If we compare how we feel on an ordinary day with how we feel on one following a night without sleep, or during which we've been involved in an accident, a family quarrel, or an unfortunate turn in an affair of the heart, we will quickly recognize that here, too, in the psychological domain, we have limitations.

Other factors that affect our capacity with respect to information-processing and external performance relate to environmental states such as lighting, background noise, temperature and quality of the air, and the aesthetic nature of our surroundings. In the next chapter, you will learn that the environmental psychologist is very much concerned with these factors as well, although in a more global context than the person-system interactions studied by the ergonomist.

Because so many different kinds of factors affect human performance, ergonomics is necessarily multidisciplinary. It draws its practitioners from medicine, anthropometrics, biomechanics, kinesiology, industrial and biomedical engineering, industrial design, environmental and other areas of psychology and, indeed, from any discipline whose body of scientific knowledge sheds light on the behavior of persons at work. A fully trained practitioner— who usually will work with engineers, industrial designers, architects, or other types of designers—should have at least general knowledge about *all* the disciplines that comprise ergonomics. However, because it is not possible to be an expert in every area, he or she will likely specialize in perhaps only one or two, calling in expertise in other areas whenever necessary. Specialty areas include biomechanics/kinesiology, process control or other situations involving complex inputs to the brain, control functions, workstation design, computer ergonomics, ergonomics for the elderly and disabled, transportation ergonomics, artificial intelligence, and expert systems, and many others. Regardless of the chosen area, proficiency in a variety of methodological techniques is also an absolute necessity, because it is important to know how to generate

information that will provide precise answers to questions posed for each different type of project.

Ergonomics in Laboratory and Applied Settings

Some ergonomists work mainly in laboratory settings, pursuing research activities related to the theoretical model described earlier, or to specific work problems such as the effects of repetitive muscular stress, noise, lighting, or temperature, the nature of video display terminal displays, or whatever. These people will wish to publish their work in scientific journals that appeal to academic interests. A colleague of mine at the University of Calgary has received international recognition for his research relating to road safety. He has done a great deal of work on traffic signs and is currently writing a book on the psychology of driving and safety.

Other ergonomists work mainly outside the laboratory on real-life problems. Generally, they are responsible to a client who usually has time and dollar constraints and, therefore, wants quick nonacademic approaches to his or her needs. Nevertheless, this sort of work can often be great fun as well as enriching and challenging and professionally rewarding. Let me try to put you in the picture about some of it. As one example, the applied ergonomist might be called on to assist with investigation of an accident, as was true in the case of the February 1986 train collision near Hinton, Alberta, Canada. Here, he or she would need to develop a strategy for assembling and analyzing all the facts surrounding the accident, some of which might relate to the sleep-rest cycles and general health of the persons involved, others to the design of the system, and still others to environmental conditions. All this activity would be done with a view to generating a set of factors that could have influenced person-system interactions in some adverse fashion and, thus, contributed to the probability of the accident. Recommendations might then relate to system design, procedure, policy, regulation—to whatever might be implicated in reducing the probability of a similar accident in the future.

Another type of applied problem an ergonomist might be invited to solve is one relating to a certain type of musculoskeletal stress—say, in the wrist—among factory workers. In this case, the ergonomist would likely look for work operations that require undesirable motions involving the wrist, especially on a repetitive basis, and perhaps against resistance. These task motions would, of course, be examined in terms of the design of the work environment

to which they related, more specifically, to the design of the tools used and of the workstations involved. It is hoped the ergonomist would be able to recommend design modifications to eliminate the undesirable motions and enable the workers to perform their tasks without undue strain to the musculature. For example, picking defective items off a conveyor belt and tossing them into a discard bin can bring about a very painful condition of the wrist. In this case, the solution might be as simple as moving the bin closer to the conveyor belt. However, solutions to repetitive strain injury problems in factory tasks can often be more complex. In the example I've mentioned, one that would bring about a whole new set of ergonomics considerations, and would likely be unpopular with unions, is the replacement of humans by a robotic system.

Frequently, ergonomists will be asked to participate in the development of some product. This work is very rewarding because, having watched and influenced the nature of a tangible system as it evolves through conceptual, drawing, mockup, and prototype stages, you feel you are part of something that makes the world slightly different from what it previously was. During these various stages, the ergonomist will provide ongoing consultation which assists the designer in making decisions about the product. Small-scale, in-shop, or laboratory tests might be carried out along the way to resolve some specific problem—for example, which of two forms of a display feature is more easily discriminated or more preferred, or which of two forms of a control device is more readily manipulated. Once the prototype is ready, it is taken to the field where the ergonomist carries out a full-scale systems analysis, as was done for the wheelchair tiedown described earlier.

And now after this glimpse at what applied ergonomists do, we can go on to the next section where descriptions of case studies provide greater detail, some of which concern relationships with the client and the all-important matter of methodological techniques for approaching problems.

CASE STUDIES

CASE ONE: A NAVIGATION AID WARNING SYSTEM

When I was approached about this system, it had already been developed to the prototype stage by a consulting firm of marine architects and engineers. With a microcomputer system at its heart, its intended function was to pick up information from strain gauges in the ship's hull after impact with ice and give immediate

and exact feedback to the navigator regarding the extent of stress to the hull.

The display system took the form of a small module that was to sit on the ship's navigating console. From the diagram in Figure 13-2 it will be clear that the mariner could receive information both from a system of red, yellow, and green lights and from a printer readout. The multilevel green-light histogram indicated tolerable levels of stress, the yellow lights indicated stress that was near the danger level, and the red lights indicated stress that could damage the ship's hull. You will appreciate from Figure 13-2 that the yellow and red lights were patterned so that information about the location of the impact could also be transmitted to the navigator. The printout gave the time and location of the impact, the strain gauge number, and a percentage indicating the extent of yield stress.

Why did members of this company come to me for help when they had already developed the device? Oddly, because they had also developed a questionnaire to evaluate how officers aboard the ship with the strain gauges reacted to the display system and, having heard that I had some skill with such instruments, wanted me to pass judgment on it! Frankly, I had to draw in my breath in preparation for a measured response.

Two major factors underlay my caution. On the one hand, the services of an ergonomist are most helpful if used *during* development rather than *after* when it is virtually too late to influence the design. Indeed, had I been called in earlier, the first step I would have taken would have been to conduct what is called a *task analysis*. The purpose here would have been to determine precisely what

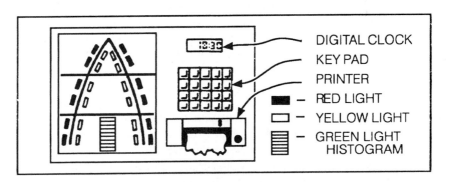

Figure 13-2 Display module of the navigation aid warning system.

information about hull stress the navigator needs to know, in what form this is best presented, and how the new task of monitoring the new display system could best be integrated with existing tasks. My strategy might also have included a method referred to as the *critical incident technique*. By asking a number of captains to describe experiences leading up to a critical ice navigation incident, I might have been able to obtain a more accurate picture of the kind of impact information they need during ice navigation.

The second aspect of the situation that gave me pause was that the prepared questionnaire was hopelessly inadequate for its intended purpose.

What I usually try to do in such cases—which are far from rare, I might add—is to explain the ergonomics of the situation as best I can, emphasizing that many processes occur in the brains of the users as they interact with a system, and that carrying out a meaningful evaluation of it requires careful design of instruments that will force the emergence of features of the system that might induce unsatisfactory outcomes of these brain processes. This is no mean feat, because people with superficial or no knowledge of ergonomics find it difficult to understand that brain processes could be important in evaluating an electronic device. Essentially, it is a matter of planting a seed of interest and nourishing it to the point of healthy confidence that you as an ergonomist have strategies capable of generating critical information about use of the system.

In the case of the navigation aid warning system, the magic appeared to work, and so I found myself redesigning the evaluation instrument. In its final form, it consisted of three sections. The first sought general information about the respondent, especially with respect to experience in ice. The second consisted of a series of probes related to (a) attentional factors; (b) the detectability, discriminability, recognizability, and interpretability of the lights, as well as the readability of the printout; and (c) the integration of the system monitoring, relaying, and interpretive tasks with existing tasks. The third section related to the use of information from the system in making navigation decisions.

In pretesting this instrument, I was fortunate in having access to a number of erstwhile ship captains who now held administrative positions. They were asked to review the items with a very critical eye as to their clarity, meaningfulness, and ease of completion. On the basis of their comments, I was able to make refinements that rendered the instrument clean, precise, and economical. It was

administered to the captain and his officers after about five days' experience with the system during one of the ship's voyages.

Inasmuch as no task analysis had been carried out before the system was designed, it was not surprising to learn from responses to the questionnaire that many modifications would be required before it could be regarded as ergonomically sound. In my technical report describing the evaluation and presenting these results, I made four recommendations. First, to increase discriminability of the lights, I recommended that the shape of either the yellow or red lights be changed, that the separation between them be increased, and that the thickness of the hull-shaped contour line be increased.

Second, as it was clear that many levels of the green-light histogram were not needed, I recommended that they be reduced to no more than five, a number well within the "magic number seven plus or minus two," which George Miller recommended in a famous 1956 paper on the number of items people are able to distinguish in various types of situations. Additionally, I suggested spacing out the different types of data on the printout in order to make it more readable.

The fourth recommendation was that the light display be separated from the printer and placed in a position closer to the captain. This suggestion followed from results indicating that the commander and the officers used the system differently. On the one hand, the commander was interested only in the light signals which he used mainly to confirm his own judgments about the thinness of the ice, or as feedback about how hard he was hitting the ice when ramming the ship through it. On the other hand, the lights appeared to be creating confusion with other officers whose kinesthetic cues often conflicted with those of the lights. (As it happens, their kinesthetic cues may sometimes have been more reliable than the light signals since, obviously, it was impossible to install strain gauges at every point at which an impact could occur and, therefore, signals did not always reflect the extent of impact with precise accuracy.)

Moreover, the tasks of monitoring the lights and the relaying of the relevant information to the commanding officer were not easily organized into their existing tasks and, in any case, increased the probability of delay or error in transmission of information. However, these other officers made use of the printout as a record of the ship's impact during the voyage. Perhaps by now you have inferred that the system in question, though intended as a warning device, could not be such since it is capable of providing the mariner with

information about an impact only *after* an impact occurs; the system is then perhaps more properly referred to as a *feedback* device.

As far as I know, only the last of my four recommendations has been adopted. Indeed, rather than reducing the number of levels of the green-light histogram, 10 levels of the yellow and red light colors were added, thus making 30 in all and, perhaps, creating a device that looks rather more like a Christmas tree ornament than an information display.

Now what is to be learned from this account? I'm sure you will have picked up from it a message to the effect that, among those for whom ergonomists perform their work, there may be a lack of understanding not only about what ergonomics is and how it can be applied to the development of systems, but also about the implications of its findings. As a consequence, ergonomists always carry the burden of carefully explaining their craft to prospective clients in terms that are neither academic nor preachy but that drive simply to the heart of the matter.

On the other hand, there is no need to hide the fact that becoming an ergonomist requires familiarity with and ability to interpret large bodies of scientific knowledge. Sometimes ergonomists are treated as though what they practice is just common sense or something that can be obtained from an elementary textbook. Patience wins here. But some form of certification, such as engineers and lawyers and even clinical psychologists have, may eventually serve our purposes even better.

Another aspect of being an ergonomist that is scarcely hidden in my account of the navigation aid system is that clients sometimes ignore recommendations that you consider exceedingly important. Alas, the ergonomist is *not* the decision maker; the designer or developer *is*! Sometimes there is opportunity for another kick at the cat (a gentle one, please), but often there is not, and the ergonomist must then simply live with his or her frustration. However, there is always a sunny side. Disappointing as it was to have most of my recommendations regarding the navigation aid ignored, the work I did was not without its rewards. People on the project steering committee, most of them former ships' officers, conveyed their great appreciation of the content of the report—at last, they said in effect, someone was looking at the human factors end of the navigator's tasks. The biggest lift, however, arose merely from doing the work, from working on a fascinating problem and believing that, through this effort, a system might become more efficient and easier for people to use. Ergonomics is fun! ♦

CASE TWO: A SYSTEM FOR COMMUNICATION-IMPAIRED TRAVELERS

The system I'm going to discuss now, called Communicaid, was developed for use by sight-, hearing-, and speech-impaired travelers in transportation terminals. I've chosen this particular project as a case study because my involvement in it was so different from that for the navigation aid device: In keeping with good ergonomics practice, it began right at the conceptual stage and carried on throughout the drawing, mockup, and prototype phases of development.

In its final form as a first-generation prototype, Communicaid was a cylindrical mesh kiosk which housed two computer workstations, one for travelers and one for a dialog agent. The traveler could use the computer in two ways: (a) independently, to obtain information from a menu-driven library about services within the terminal, and (b) in dialog with an agent, to obtain preliminary passenger-handling services such as flight assignment and seating arrangements.

During the development period of this system, most of my input was in the form of consultation that guided the designer. Many questions arose as the system evolved. How could the exterior of the kiosk be made recognizable to all the different types of potential users? A synthetic speech component was to be provided for the totally blind, but how could we accommodate the wide range of impairments between perfect sight and total blindness? Load on memory while reviewing menu categories would not be a problem for the speech- and hearing-impaired with sight because, in most cases, *all* the categories could be viewed on a single screen. But how could we design the synthetic voice menus so as to minimize load on memory of *blind* users? How could we best accommodate a population of users among whom many might need self-pacing, when all that was possible at the time was one speed of screen presentation? How could the design of the workstation, keyboard, and cursor control pad take account of the fact that many communication-impaired individuals also have motor impairments?

These questions represent only a few of the very many that required knowledge in the ergonomics domain and needed to be resolved. Were all resolved by the time the prototype was ready for field testing? Far from it! Actually, one of the purposes of putting a rudimentary prototype of a novel product into the field is to obtain information that will enable the designer to modify it to a form that eventually will be fully efficient and acceptable. For this reason, the

ergonomist has an important role to play in the field evaluation and, hence, must be prepared to apply highly effective methodological techniques to flush out the information the designer needs in order to proceed with either a second generation (Mark II) prototype or a production model.

A basic methodological tool for a field evaluation of a complex system such as Communicaid is some form of systems analysis. Engineers are familiar with this term which implies that the system will be broken down hierarchically into smaller and smaller subsystems until, through an analysis of how well the functions of these units are being met, all defects can be forced to emerge. However the engineer thinks of the system as consisting only of machine parts, whereas the ergonomist thinks of it as consisting of person-system interactions. Consequently the ergonomist must combine the systems analysis with some form of task analysis.

Now task analysis is somewhat of a generic term that subsumes many forms, and so careful thought must be given to the question of which one is appropriate for a given purpose. Rather than delve now into this complex topic, I'm simply going to say that, for the Communicaid prototype evaluation, I began with a form described by Berliner, Angell, & Shearer (1964). Some reasons underlying my choice were that it is suitable for a system design and development situation, it emphasizes communication and cognitive processes as well as sensory and perceptual ones, and it is very easy to use. Once I had modified it to suit my own purpose, it worked very well indeed.

Perhaps I can use one example to illustrate how all these considerations were integrated into an evaluation design. The Mark I Communicaid main menu screen, which was a feature of the subsystem meant to serve the hearing- and speech-impaired, will do very well for this purpose. Its function was to inform the user about the various categories of terminal information available. In interacting with the system while the main menu was in view, the test subjects had to perform the following tasks:

♦ Detect, recognize, discriminate, interpret letters and words.
♦ Store items in short-term memory.
♦ Decide whether to choose an information category, to return to the previous screen or the introductory screen, or to end the session.
♦ Move the cursor to the category of choice, or leave the kiosk.
♦ Press the hit button to make a selection.

My observations and subsequent interviews during the evaluation focused, first, on determining how successfully each subject was able to perform these tasks and, second, on pinpointing aspects of the main menu underlying any observed subject performance difficulties. Having carefully identified all the tasks for each part of the system beforehand, I was able to isolate design defects very easily.

As the main menu screen (as well as all the other screens) had been developed rather hastily without any ergonomics input, numerous problems surfaced during evaluation. One of the most serious in the main menu screen was that principles of perceptual organization had been ignored, so that subjects had great difficulty in quickly absorbing the material in the text and making sense of it. This problem was exacerbated by the fact that screen density was far too high (i.e., too many of the available screen pixels had been used for letters and symbols, thus making words and sentences difficult to discriminate from one another). The dimensions of screen characters were also nonoptimal, even for those with normal visual acuity, and brightness contrast was not great enough for certain users with some visual impairment.

These and other problems with the main menu screen, as well as those relating to each and every feature identified for the entire Communicaid system, were documented in a report which the designer was then able to use as a systematic and comprehensive reference for making modifications to the system. One of these modifications is worth a word or two. My evaluation had demonstrated that the dialog function did not work well because the agent, who had other duties in the airport, could not be permanently seated at the workstation. The agent had to be summoned by an auditory signal activated when a user selected the "Agent" option available at the end of each screen. Unfortunately, the agent was often either not within earshot of the signal or unavoidably detained. The drastic but altogether satisfactory solution to this problem was to retain only the information function in the Mark II version of Communicaid, and to incorporate the dialog function into an entirely new product designed for use at the ticket or check-in counters. The moral here is that it is important not to cling to a concept that proves to be ergonomically unworkable.

My participation in this project was very professionally rewarding to me, partly because being part of an endeavor that begins with only a vague idea and evolves through several stages until it is a novel and useful product fills me with wonderment and excitement, but also because my input was welcomed as necessary

to meet the goal of excellence toward which all members of the project team strived. ♦

Becoming an Ergonomist

Education

Because so many different disciplines comprise ergonomics, it is somewhat difficult to address the matter of preparatory education in a simple way. Certainly graduate study is required regardless of area of specialty; but, since very few North American universities offer an undergraduate program in ergonomics, the problem arises as to which undergraduate courses should be taken in preparation. In general terms, it can be said that you should acquire preliminary knowledge about how humans are structured and how they function in relation to their environment. Courses in perception, cognitive science, physiology, environmental and organizational psychology, anthropometry, and biomechanics are recommended. Because ergonomists frequently deal with engineers, a basic course in engineering is also a wise choice. Ergonomists must also have a well-stocked bag of methodological tools and tricks at their disposal; therefore courses in laboratory and field research methods, with emphasis in quantitative techniques, are essential. The value of these courses cannot be overestimated for those going into applied work, frequently requiring as it does innovative approaches to solving problems effectively despite time and money constraints.

In the United States, the State University of New York at Buffalo offers an undergraduate program in the Department of Industrial Engineering. In the United Kingdom, undergraduate programs in ergonomics are available at the following: University of Aston in Birmingham, University of Nottingham, University of Technology at Loughborough, University of Wales, and University College of Swansea.

In Canada, although many universities offer so-called human factors courses at the undergraduate level that are related to ergonomics because they deal with human life, you should try to obtain as many courses as possible that are legitimate ergonomics courses—that is, those that deal with how knowledge about human factors is applied to the design of products and systems in the working environment. Unfortunately, most of the latter are given through *several* departments rather than one that offers a fully

integrated ergonomics program. A list of Canadian universities that offer ergonomics courses can be obtained by writing the National Research Council, Ottawa, for an updated version of their 1986 report "Education for Ergonomics": National Research Council, Building M55, Montreal Road, Ottawa, ON K1A 0R6.

Plans to attend graduate school should begin well in advance by assembling as much information as possible about what sorts of programs are available. This information will not only help you decide which university you want to attend for graduate work, but also provide some guidance regarding courses that would be relevant during undergraduate studies.

In the United States, graduate study in industrial engineering is available at the State University of New York at Buffalo, North Carolina State University, and Louisiana State University. Graduate programs in human factors psychology are offered at over 30 universities in the United States. As with other graduate programs in all the areas of applied psychology, see APA's *Graduate Study in Psychology and Associated Fields* for locations and details. A very good and famous European school offering both undergraduate and graduate courses in ergonomics is Le Conservatoire National des Arts et Metiers in Paris, France.

In Canada, if you choose to go the route of industrial engineering, graduate study can be obtained at the University of Toronto and will soon be obtainable at the University of Montreal. The University of Waterloo offers a graduate program in system design engineering. The University of Calgary plans a graduate program in ergonomics in the near future.

Numerous possibilities for graduate study are available in the United Kingdom. These include the University of Technology, Loughborough (in the Human Sciences Department), University of Aston in Birmingham (in the Department of Applied Psychology), University of Birmingham (in Engineering Production), University College at the University of London (in the Ergonomics Unit), University of Wales College of Cardiff (in the School of Psychology).

For more information about graduate schools of ergonomics in Canada and other parts of the world, you might write to:

The Human Factors Society
P.O. Box 1369
Santa Monica, CA 90406

Human Factors Association of Canada/Association
Canadienne d'ergonomie,
1087 Myerside Drive,
Suite No. 5,
Mississauga, Ontario
L5T 1M5

Several journals that focus on ergonomics include the following, some of which might be available in your university library: *Ergonomics, Applied Ergonomics, Human Factors,* and *International Journal of Man-Machine Studies.*

Employment

An advertisement for an ergonomist in a newspaper, except perhaps in Europe, epitomizes the notion of a rare event! Still, employment opportunities for ergonomists are not entirely absent in North America and, in fact, are on the rise as governments and industry begin to follow the lead taken by the military and aerospace industry. More often than before, full-time ergonomists are being kept on staff of an industry concerned with occupational health and safety, or a government agency responsible for technological research and development, traffic safety, or health and welfare. Moreover, a sprinkling of ergonomics consulting firms is now dotting the large urban areas where industry and technological activity are concentrated. Requests for proposals for military projects, of course, often specify roles for ergonomists.

Freelance contract work could indeed keep an ergonomist rather busy these days, provided he or she is a willing and capable salesperson and learns how to produce results that meet the requirements of the client. The key here is, first, to ensure that you understand what the client's goals are, and then to explain in simple terms how ergonomics can be applied effectively toward meeting those goals. The savings in costs, due to improved safety and/or efficiency and the avoidance of retrofitting, is an argument that usually hits the mark. Once having built up a few contacts and won their confidence, you will likely find that more opportunities than you can handle begin to rise. A promising opportunity in this respect is provision of expert witness testimony in accident litigation involving product liability as well as traffic and industrial accidents. The difficulty then is that, to survive, you may need to take on work that is not professionally stimulating to you. A way out

of this, and one chosen by many ergonomists, is to combine your consulting practice with an academic career.

Students considering ergonomics as a path of study should not be discouraged by the current employment situation. There may not be many positions available, but neither are there many ergonomists to fill them. Moreover, all signs suggest that the market for ergonomists is becoming more favorable and that it should be quite good a few years hence.

SUGGESTED READINGS AND REFERENCES

BERLINER, C., ANGELL, D., & SHEARER, J. W. (1964). Behaviors, measures, and instruments for performance evaluation in simulated environments. *Proceedings of the symposium on quantification of human performance.* Albuquerque, NM: Electronic Industries Association.

FORD, D. (1981). Three mile island: Thirty minutes to meltdown. New York: Penguin.

FITTS, P. M., & JONES, R. E. (1947). Analysis of factors contributing to 460 "pilot-error" experiences in operating aircraft controls. Report TSEAA-694-12, Air Materiel Command, Wright-Patterson Air Force Base. Reprinted in H. W. Sinaiko (Ed.) (1961), *Selected papers on human factors in the design and use of control systems.* New York: Dover.

GRANDJEAN, E. (1988). *Fitting the task to the man: A textbook of occupational ergonomics.* London: Taylor & Francis.

KANTOWITZ, B. H., & SORKIN, R. D. (1983). *Human factors: Understanding people-system relationships.* New York: Wiley.

MCCORMICK, E. J., & SANDERS, M. S. (1988). *Human factors in engineering and design.* (6th ed.). New York: McGraw-Hill.

MEISTER, D. (1971). *Human factors: Theory and practice.* New York: Wiley.

MEISTER, D. (1985). *Behavioral analysis and measurement methods.* New York: Wiley.

MILLER, G. A. (1956). The magical number seven, plus or minus two. *Psychological Review, 63,* 81–97.

MURRELL, K. F. H. (1965). *Ergonomics: Man in his working environment.* New York: Wiley.

TAYLOR, F. V. (1957). Psychology and the design of machines. *American Psychologist, 21,* 249–258.

ROBERT GIFFORD

Robert Gifford is Professor of Psychology at the University of Victoria and president of Optimal Environments, Inc., a firm that specializes in planning and design research. He received his B.A. from the University of California, Davis, and his M.A. and Ph.D. from Simon Fraser University in British Columbia. He teaches environmental psychology and is the author of Environmental Psychology: Principles and Practice *(1987). He was the coordinator of the Environmental Psychology Section of the Canadian Psychological Association for several years, is the Special Issues Editor of the* Journal of Environmental Psychology, *and serves as a consultant to nonprofit and government agencies concerned with design for housing, schools, offices, the disabled, and outdoor recreation.* ♦

14

The Environmental Psychologist

The ultimate goal of most environmental psychologists is to improve the indoor and outdoor places where people live, work, and enjoy themselves. In practice, this often means helping to create buildings and parks that meet the needs of people who use them.

Here's one typical example. Two women from one of the larger religious denominations came to me one day. Their board had long ago taken on the responsibility of housing some of its elderly members. However, as sometimes happens when such a duty is gradually assumed, the first housing used for this purpose was far from ideal. It had been converted from another use and the board recognized that it was inadequate in many obvious ways. The board decided to construct a new building or thoroughly renovate an existing building to provide better housing for its senior citizens.

Until recently, the board might have gone directly to an architect for help. Gradually over the last 20 years, however, those who build or renovate buildings have come to understand the value of involving an environmental psychologist in the building design process. This is done either before or at the same time that the architect is engaged. (As we will see later, it is often done after the building is completed, too, to evaluate the project's success.) The environmental psychologist's contribution supplements rather than replaces that of the architect.

The two women had a specific question for me. Should the new housing contemplated by the board be built downtown or in a semirural area outside of town? They correctly realized that each location would have advantages and disadvantages for the elderly people living in it. The semirural location would provide more quiet, more fresh air, and greater proximity to nature. However, travel to amenities of the city such as shopping, cultural events, and hospitals would be more difficult. The downtown location offered the reverse version of this set of trade-offs. The women's subsequent questions concerned the design of the building itself. What makes an ideal building for senior citizens to live in?

What Is Environmental Psychology?

In practical terms, environmental psychology is the branch of applied psychology that answers these questions about the design of workplaces (especially offices), schools, hospitals, residences (especially multiple-unit dwellings), banks, resorts, libraries, and

many other buildings. Other environmental psychologists work on the design of outdoor spaces ranging from urban plazas to wilderness campgrounds.

Environmental psychology may be formally defined as the study of the transactions between individuals and their physical settings. The word *transactions* in this definition is very important, because it conveys the crucial point that individuals and environments influence and affect *each other*. Environmental psychologists are keenly aware that it is naive to consider only how the environment affects people. We are not blobs unilaterally shaped in predictable ways by blue walls, high temperatures, or windowless rooms. Instead, we often respond to these features of the environment, either before or after they influence us: We paint the walls another color, go for a cool swim, use another room. Furthermore, we often act first in our transactions with the environment: We litter, build a house in a previously undeveloped place, plant a garden, or put up a beautiful piece of art on a blank wall.

Environmental psychology is an interdisciplinary field. The successful practitioner will know something about architecture and organizational behavior, among other disciplines, although professional qualification in these fields is not necessary. It is important to know how to work with other specialists and with the wide variety of people who use (or will use) the building or park that is being renovated or newly built.

The Background of Environmental Psychology

A Capsule History

Psychologists have been concerned with the built environment for at least 60 years, but until the late 1960s the field had no widely accepted name. Some earliest studies in what eventually would be called environmental psychology were done at the Western Electric Company's Hawthorne plant, near Chicago. In a telephone assembly area, the effects of light, heat, and humidity on performance were investigated. In the Hawthorne studies, strong correlations between these environmental factors and productivity were found. However, even stronger correlations were found with certain procedural and managerial changes in the plant. Unfortunately, the investigators' conclusions emphasized these managerial influences, which we

might call social environment factors to distinguish them from the physical environment factors that are of primary interest in this chapter. The correlations between performance and lighting and temperature were overlooked. The result was that organizational psychology received a strong boost from the Hawthorne studies, but environmental psychology suffered an unwarranted setback.

World War II saw a renewal of interest in human behavior in relation to the physical environment. In England, the Parliament buildings were heavily damaged by bombs. Strenuous debate in the House of Commons ensued: Should the buildings be reconstructed as they were before, or should modern buildings be constructed? Winston Churchill strongly supported rebuilding in the old manner. He argued that a great democracy had been developed in the old buildings and that their very shape and form had played an important role in this process. His famous claim was this: We shape our buildings, and afterward they shape us. Churchill's arguments triumphed and the buildings were reconstructed as they were before.

The war also saw two other environments created with human behavior at the forefront of designers' concerns. The cockpits of fighter planes were increasingly arranged to match the pilot's body and perceptual and motor patterns. Such research into human factors or ergonomics research is at the border between environmental psychology and engineering psychology. The other wartime concern was the construction and reconstruction of hospitals. Great concern was expressed that certain designs might speed patient recovery but other designs might actually slow recovery.

In the late 1940s a discipline called *ecological psychology* was developed by Roger Barker and his colleagues in Kansas (Barker, 1968). They extensively investigated *behavior settings*—that is, small person-place interaction units such as the corner drug store, the high school basketball game, and the town council meeting. Barker showed that although the specific behaviors in these settings might vary from time to time, there is great consistency in the general pattern of activity and in the way that persons and places fit together to define the meaning and character of each behavior setting.

In the 1950s, the frontier of the field that was not yet called environmental psychology seems to have been in Canada. At Montreal's McGill University, the earliest experiments in what was then called *sensory deprivation* were carried out (Heron, Doane, & Scott, 1956). This tradition, now more accurately called *restricted environmental stimulation*, investigates the positive and negative

effects of placing individuals in settings that offer very low levels of perceptual information.

In Saskatchewan, an innovative psychiatrist named Humphrey Osmond became the director of a large, fortress-like mental hospital in the countryside. He assembled a team of progressive psychologists and architects who redesigned parts of the hospital with the particular needs and behaviors of the mentally handicapped in mind. This hospital project may be the very first instance in which environmental psychology was consciously applied to the design of a building.

However, only in the late 1960s did environmental psychology really become a distinct discipline. Early in the decade, two conferences were held in Utah under the label "architectural psychology." However, as the broader environmental movement grew stronger and some psychologists became interested in such nonarchitectural issues as pollution and the degradation of nature and its resources, the name environmental psychology became more accurate and popular. The phrase had been used first in print (in a slightly different context) by Egon Brunswik back in 1943, but it was 1967 or 1968 before the field, which now included ecological, architectural, and pollution concerns, settled on its present name.

The Scope of Environmental Psychology

By now, the broad range of problems attacked by environmental psychology should be clear: human behavior as it relates to the natural and built environments. In this section, we take a closer look at these concerns; later, three detailed case studies will be described.

As do most areas of psychology, environmental psychology has an experimental side to it as well as an applied side. University researchers are often interested in person-environment relations from a theoretical point of view; their immediate goal is constructing an accurate scientific model of how we interact with the physical environment.

One framework for this work is depicted in Figure 14-1. Environmental psychology is viewed from this perspective as being the simultaneous consideration of three sets of factors: characteristics of the *person* (e.g., male, female, old, young, American, Chinese, shy, outgoing); the *place* (e.g., classroom, bar, stadium,

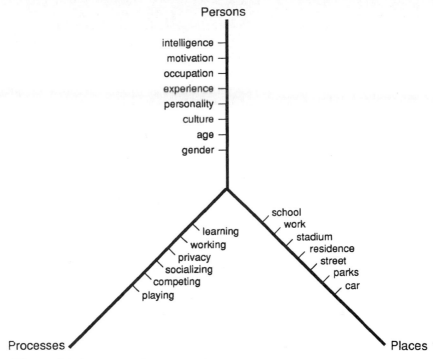

Figure 14-1   A basic framework for environmental psychology's elements.

bedroom, workplace); and the psychological *process* of interest (e.g., socializing, working, competing, learning, seeking privacy).

One environmental psychology textbook (Gifford, 1987) has organized these considerations into the following topics:

    I.   Individual Processes

        1. Environmental perception: How do we perceive our everyday surroundings?

        2. Spatial cognition: How do we orient ourselves as we make our way around a town or a building?

        3. Environmental appraisal: How do different people describe places and feel about them? Which places have particular meaning? Which settings are beautiful, to whom? Which settings' welfare are we especially concerned about?

        4. Environmental personality: How do individuals vary in the ways they characteristically interact with the

environment? How do these dispositions (e.g., to view the environment as a source of resources to improve life versus viewing it as an invaluable commodity to be conserved) help us to understand human behavior?

II. Interpersonal Processes

   1. Interpersonal distance: Why do we keep a certain distance from others? What distance do we select from which others in which circumstances and which places?

   2. Territoriality: Why do we claim various spaces for short or long periods? Who wants which territories for what purpose? How does having or not having a territory affect our behavior?

   3. Crowding: When there are many people around, what happens? The answer depends on who you are, who they are, and what you are trying to accomplish. High density does not always have negative outcomes.

   4. Privacy: Why do we sometimes want to be alone, sometimes we want to be with others? How do we balance these opposite needs? What happens when we can't?

III. Societal Processes

   1. Home and daily life: A few topics include: What is the effect of living in different kinds of dwellings? On the streets, how does temperature and weather affect crime and helpfulness? How do individuals respond to disasters such as earthquakes and floods?

   2. Learning: How do light, noise, temperature, and room arrangements affect classroom learning and behavior? How, outside the classroom, do we learn to deal with personal and global environmental issues competently?

   3. Working: How do noise, light, heat, air quality, and workspace design affect our performance, health, and satisfaction on the job? When we leave work for the evening or for a few weeks, how do we affect our destination and how does it affect us?

   4. Environmental design: What is the process by which buildings and outdoor areas are designed? How can all the knowledge gained from studying these topics be incorporated into design? What role do the everyday

users of places have in the design process? What role *should* they have?

5. Natural resources: What do we know about the psychological aspects of pollution? When do people help conserve forests, fuels, endangered species, and other limited resources, and when do they waste them?

Most of these questions are dealt with by the *applied* environmental psychologist as well as the *experimental* environmental psychologist. Their emphases, however, are different. The experimental approach is geared toward building valid theoretical models of person-environment interactions in general, but the applied approach is to solve an immediate practical problem brought by a certain client. These practical problems are likely to be local, specific, pressing, and not very amenable to solution by laboratory methods. The client may care little about the theoretical aspects of the problem; instead, effective (and often, quick) action is expected.

As an example, one of my graduate students is working with city officials on recycling. The officials may have some vague interest in theories about recycling, but their main concern is to get more people to participate in their program. They expect the environmental psychologist to know the theory and research and to translate this knowledge into practical recommendations that will actually increase recycling in the city.

As another example, environmental psychologist Ben Barkow was recently asked to judge the impact of renovating a large, old, ornate, well-known Toronto movie palace into six small, modern theaters. The client wanted to know several things. How much public support is there for renovating the theater? What behavior patterns occur in the existing theater? Which of these should be encouraged by the new design, if the renovation goes ahead? Which are unsatisfactory, indicating that the new design should improve the ease with which theater patrons can, for example, buy snacks or find their seats easily?

The environmental psychologist's job is to know which methods of gathering information will yield quality answers to these questions, and to use these methods well. Let us turn now to three environmental psychology cases that I can describe in more detail.

CASE STUDIES

CASE ONE: PLANNING A NEW BUILDING
I received a call one day from the Executive Director of the local Multiple Sclerosis (MS) Society. The society was thinking about a new

building. It was presently housed in three separate buildings that were not even in the same neighborhood. One held its administrative offices; the physiotherapy clinic was in another; its storage facilities were in the third. The society felt that the transportation and communication difficulties of this arrangement were not in its best interest. In addition, the offices and clinic were clearly inadequate in many ways. The executive director asked if I would give a talk to a meeting of the Board of Directors. We agreed that my topic would be "Creating Humane Buildings."

The meeting was attended not only by the board members, but also by some staff members and a few active society members. In the talk, I outlined the process by which a building could be created that incorporates many of the needs and preferences of building users. The talk was illustrated with examples of previous projects I had worked on.

Such presentations are a common feature in the life of the environmental psychologist. They serve a number of purposes. Potential clients are able to hear your ideas, views, values, and experience, and can judge whether they might wish to work with you on their cherished dream.

A few days later, the chairman of the board called. The board had liked the presentation and wished to negotiate a contract. Could we have a meeting, he asked, to work out the details of the agreement? The call was welcome for three reasons. First, I welcomed the opportunity to help design a building for a group of people with special needs. This was partly based on altruistic motives, but because a fee was involved, I was not acting entirely out of altruism. The second reason was that I knew the chance to design for an unusual group would be more interesting than designing a building for a typical group of able-bodied persons. This project would have definite and uncommon requirements, and I liked that idea.

The third reason was more personal, and it concerned the board chairman and something that happened at the presentation. During my talk, questions were asked and discussions ensued. At one point, the chairman, perhaps feeling that it was his duty to take charge of the situation, had rolled out a large sketch pad on a movable stand. He began drawing the existing building (a retail electronics store) and offering potential design solutions to problems he thought the society would face in the renovation. It seemed that everyone except him knew that these speculations were too early and presumptuous.

Finally, the executive director had the courage to interrupt him and say, "Isn't the purpose of this meeting to listen to our

speaker's views on the *process* by which design decisions might be made, rather than to make the decisions right now?" This was especially welcome to me, but perhaps painful for the chairman, because one point I had been emphasizing was that design decisions should clearly reflect the views of individuals who use the building every day—in this case, MS patients, their families, staff members, and volunteers. Of course, at this stage, the involvement of these groups was still weeks away.

After this episode during the presentation, I was concerned that the chairman might have taken this interruption personally, or at least that his attempt to make decisions immediately meant that he was opposed to involving patients and staff in the decision-making process. If so, he could easily have found a way to avoid further involvement with this environmental psychologist! Happily, the chairman later realized that his approach had been inappropriate. As the project progressed, he enthusiastically adopted the idea that building users should be consulted in the design process.

The methods we selected for this project were interviews and behavioral observations. Everyone in the society was given the opportunity to be interviewed either through a personal invitation or notices in the society newsletter. A few individual interviews were conducted, but most interviews were done with small groups within the society. More than 20 interviews with over 80 individuals were conducted. These groups included numerous patient groups, office staff, physiotherapy clinic staff, volunteers who help in the office and clinic, board of directors, and several support groups, which are composed of patients, family, and friends from different districts or who share particular interests.

Each interview ranged from one to three hours in length. The interview was sufficiently structured that we could be certain of covering each in a long list of building features, but unstructured enough to hear suggestions about building features that we had not thought to include in the list of features. The interviews produced a very large mass of information that had to be sorted, compared, reconciled, and integrated.

Certain themes emerged repeatedly in the interviews. One was a great concern for bathroom design. MS patients have difficulty with many standard bathrooms and were very eager to contribute their ideas on this matter. The case of the bathroom gives me the chance to make a very important point. The environmental psychologist must be very careful to separate proposed design *solutions* from design *goals*. An interviewee might say, for example, that we really *must* choose a certain kind of handle on the sink's taps. He

has that kind of handle at home and it is much easier to use than the usual handles are.

However, every proposed design solution is based on a design goal. In this case, the implied goal is to provide tap handles that are easy for MS sufferers to use. It may be that the handles in the interviewee's home are indeed the best design solution available, but it could also be that a new or different (and even better) design, unknown to the interviewee, is available. If the suggestion of a particular type of handle is accepted without further thought on the part of the designer, the better solution may be overlooked. Therefore, the design solution is noted—it might indeed be the best—but the environmental psychologist tries to determine, record, and find the best design solution to the design goal or human need that underlies the interviewee's suggestion.

In general, considerable agreement about the nature of the new building was found among the different user groups. Disagreements were more often about design solutions than about design goals. The overall theme of most interviews was, "Make the building easily accessible!" Of course, this meant different things in different areas of the building, but accessibility was clearly the key design goal.

To supplement the interviews, we made behavioral observations of the clinic and the offices. Unfortunately, people don't always know what they do, do what they say, or say what they do. Consequently, behavioral observations help to show how people actually use a space. We observed important behavior patterns that no one thought to mention in the interviews, behavior patterns that were different from the impression one would gain from the interviews, and behavior patterns that perfectly confirmed the interview responses.

Interim meetings with board members and the executive director were held to report preliminary findings. Often, a trend in preference or behavior that we spotted was confirmed or further explained by these society officials.

Next, the large task of preparing recommendations was attacked. Literally hundreds of suggestions had been made. We had to decide which would really be beneficial, which were feasible given the financial and design constraints (remember, this was a renovation rather than a new building: the shell of the building could not be altered), and which would be welcomed by different individuals sharing the same part of the building.

In the end, we made 137 recommendations in our report to the

board of directors. Then we met with the board in a marathon meeting to grade each recommendation into one of five categories:

1. *Must* be done now.
2. *Should* be done now.
3. Should be done *someday*.
4. Would be *nice* someday.
5. Should *not* be done.

One of many recommendations for the multiple sclerosis building: place light switches within easy reach of persons in wheelchairs. (Courtesy of the editor, Robert Gifford.)

The report was then given to the architect to incorporate into his plans for the building.

Many of our recommendations were turned into reality; some were not. As I write, the building has been completed and occupied for six months. In another several months, we plan to return to the renovated building to perform a postoccupancy evaluation (POE), a check on how satisfactory the renovated building is to its staff, patients, volunteers, and their supporters.

Preliminary reports are that most building users are very happy with the building. However, environmental psychologists are well aware that occupants of new buildings usually undergo a "honeymoon period" during which their satisfaction is based more on the newness of the building than on its day-to-day performance in the longer run. That is why we wait at least eight months to perform the POE.

Responsible environmental psychologists are not interested in POEs that merely make their work look good; they want to know the truth about how a building is performing. The POE often takes the form of a new set of recommendations, because (a) earlier recommendations were given a low priority but still seem important to the occupants, (b) earlier recommendations were not well incorporated into the design, or (c) unforeseen needs arise, leading to recommendations that were not made in the planning phase. To provide an example of the environmental psychologist's work in a different kind of setting, the next case is a description of the POE of a library. ♦

CASE TWO: EVALUATING A NEW BUILDING

A new branch library was recently constructed in my city. When a large chunk of public money is allocated for a new building, a natural question concerns how well the funds have been spent. Is the new library a good one? What design goals, if any, had been set during the planning phase? To what extent were these design goals met in the completed building?

Not every contract results from the client calling the consultant. Beginning consultants, in particular, but even experienced consultants must be part salesperson, which means approaching potential clients. Or the applied psychologist might spot a project in the community that cries out for expertise; the client is approached even though no one connected with the project had the imagination and foresight to call the consultant. In short, we called the library board and asked for a meeting.

The library studied in the post-occupancy evaluation. (Courtesy of the editor, Robert Gifford.)

My talk concentrated on reminding the board of the size of their investment, the possible effects of poor building design, how these effects can cumulate over the years of the building's life, and how a POE might enable them either to rest easy or to know they should consider remedial renovations now, before the ill effects of the new library drive the public away from the library. Library boards want to see people use their facilities and be happy using them.

The talk was successful and, with my colleague Cheuk Ng, I returned with a specific proposal as to how we would conduct the POE. Apart from the general goals of being a pleasant, cost-effective structure that met basic building codes, the architect had been asked to design a library that provided, in particular:

1. Adequate seating for study and leisure reading.
2. Flexible expansion space for stacks.
3. Easy access for the disabled, elderly, and children in strollers pushed by parents.

4. Open space in the general library area, as free as possible of partitions.

We suggested that three different methods be used to determine how the physical layout of the new library affected its patrons and how well it met these design goals. The three methods included a survey of the patrons and staff, behavior mapping, and behavior tracking. The survey asked patrons a few questions about themselves as well as how often they used the library and their reasons for using the library. It then asked how satisfactory the patron found many features of the library, from noise and lighting to spatial arrangements, amount of space, and aesthetics.

The other two methods were used to check the survey results against actual patterns of library patron behavior. Behavior mapping resembles a snapshot view of overall activity, and behavior tracking resembles a film view of the activity of one patron at a time. In *behavior mapping*, the observer works with a drawing of the library floorplan. At intervals (e.g., every 15 minutes), the observer marks the location of every patron. This information is then compiled across numerous observations of mornings, evenings, weekdays, and weekends to build up an image of where patrons as a whole spend time in the library and which time periods are busy and slow.

In *behavior tracking*, the observer selects an individual patron entering the library and marks on the floorplan the patron's path through the library, noting the total length of time spent at different locations. Once again, by compiling many such trackings, an image of both typical and atypical library use patterns emerges.

The data thus gathered (in this case 126 surveys, 133 behavior maps, and 91 behavior trackings) must then be analyzed. This analysis involves some traditional statistics, such as computing the average satisfaction with items on the survey and the average length of time spent browsing, but it also includes much thought about how these simple facts from different methods fit together. The goal, of course, is to reach some clear conclusions from the data generated by three distinct ways of examining satisfaction and behavior.

In the case of the new library, Cheuk and I found the three methods were indeed necessary to understand some findings that at first appeared contradictory. The patrons were, on the whole, quite pleased with the library: just over 80% gave it an overall evaluation of "very pleasing" or "somewhat pleasing." They especially

liked the windows, natural light, and spaciousness of it. However, some dissatisfaction (over 30%) was expressed with the library's tables and chairs. Numerous patrons felt there were too few tables and chairs and that the tables were too small.

In apparent contrast with this, our behavioral measures clearly showed that, most of the time, there were plenty of tables and chairs. On any given behavior map, many chairs and tables were unoccupied. (Note that had we chosen to use only the survey method or only behavioral mapping, we would have reached opposite conclusions in our report to the library board.) After considering the contradictory findings carefully and talking to patrons, we realized the problem with the spatial layout and the solution to the apparent contradiction. There were indeed plenty of tables and chairs, but they were not placed in the most suitable locations for patrons. When patrons expressed dissatisfaction with the furniture, what they really meant to say was, "I couldn't find a table that was free *where I was working.*"

One might conclude that these dissatisfied patrons should not be so picky or lazy; they should just take a little walk to an open table since the library is not very large. We might agree with such a conclusion if it meant that the library would be faced with a large expenditure for new furniture (which probably would come out of its book-buying budget). However, in this case, the solution is much simpler. We advised the library to move certain tables so their position better fit the pattern of use we had observed. This recommendation was a very inexpensive way to keep patrons happy. After all, as noted earlier, the library board's goal is to have patrons return frequently to use the library.

One other finding in this study reminds us that straight numbers must be viewed with caution. On the face of it, about 85% of the patrons found the library easy to enter. Yet the remaining 15%, who found the library difficult to enter, included a large proportion of the very users the library particularly hoped would find access easy—the elderly, disabled, and parents pushing strollers. The front door conformed to modern fire and building codes, but the heavy-duty closing device made the door quite difficult to push open. We recommended that the library adjust the device or find one that made opening the door less than an Olympic event.

Based on other data and staff interviews, we concluded that the library design had met the other goals (flexible, open space in the general library). ♦

CASE THREE: WHY DO PEOPLE USE WILDERNESS PARKS?

The government was concerned. Use of its parks was steadily declining. Some government managers and researchers decided to investigate. They realized that it is important to understand why people use or do not use parks, that is, park users' motivations. Motivation is a classic area of psychology; parks are an important part of the natural environment; the managers concluded that they needed the expertise of an environmental psychologist.

One manager asked me to discuss the issues with him and his supervisor. In the meeting I outlined some psychological views of motivation that I thought might relate to whether or not a person chooses to visit parks. The manager reminded me that their mission was grounded in the reality of working for taxpayers: Whether their decisions to spend research dollars would be considered good by both political superiors and average citizens; the research they sponsor must have clear practical implications.

A few days later I received a Service Contract outlining the specific tasks I was to undertake. The tasks were based on suggestions that emerged from me and from the managers in the course of our discussion. In contrast to the contract with the MS society, however, the details of the work were much more clearly specified, and were laid out in a written contract. For better or worse, governments must often take a more complete, legalistic, and formal approach to research contracts than private organizations.

This particular contract called for me to complete six tasks. First, I was to review and summarize existing research on why people use or avoid outdoor recreation settings. The managers clearly implied that although I should do a good job of this, I must also be careful not to let this preliminary task dominate the project. Reviewing the literature is an intellectual task that does not, in itself, solve the problem of declining park use.

Second, I was to search for reports describing how park managers in other places had applied research findings to the promotion, development, design, and operation of parks. In short, how are other park officials increasing the use of their parks? Third, I was to assess the strengths and weaknesses of current methods of identifying motives of park users. Psychology has used many ways of discovering an individual's motives: Which of these methods would be best for *this* problem? These first three tasks primarily are reviews of the existing literature, with some added evaluation based on experience. Most research contracts would assume the consult-

ant would do these things, or had already done them, and would only describe the new research to be done. Other contracts consist entirely of review tasks such as these.

My fourth task was one that grew out of the talk with the manager. My preliminary review of motivation research in parks indicated that it is overloaded with questionnaires and surveys. These techniques are the workhorse of applied psychology, but I felt that parks researchers to date had gone too far. One hundred percent of the studies I located had used one variety or another of the good old questionnaire!

Surveys and interviews do have shortcomings. First, motives are not necessarily the same as reasons, stated intentions, or verbal justifications. Motives are what *truly* energize and direct our actions. The reasons, intentions and justifications offered in a survey or interview may not be true motives. People may not wish to reflect on their real motives; they may not be *able* to reflect on them; they may not wish to *express* their real motives even if they are willing and able to accurately reflect on them; or they may not be *able* to express their motives even if all three previous steps are possible.

Consider Mr. Smith, who is being interviewed about why he goes hunting. Assume his true motive is not to bag a four-point deer, but to escape the nagging of Mrs. Smith and to share some quality moonshine with his buddies. However, Mr. Smith is not likely to tell these things to an interviewer he hardly knows or even to write them down on a questionnaire. Possibly, he doesn't even fully realize that escape and drinking are his true motives. The *reasons* Mr. Smith offers in the interview or questionnaire are that he "likes nature" and "wants a nice four-point trophy for his den wall."

But if reasons are not necessarily motives and Mr. Smith isn't even aware of his real motives, how *can* the applied psychologist discover them? One approach, called the *projective method*, attempts to discover motives through various indirect techniques. In one such technique, the respondent is asked to look at a picture (let's say it shows a couple of hunters around a campfire) and asked to create a story about (a) what led up to the present scene, (b) what one person in the picture is thinking and feeling, and (c) what might happen next.

Because Mr. Smith is creating a story, what he says can reflect his own motives more freely than his answers to interview questions might. After all, isn't he merely making up a story about a fictional character? Psychologists have found that many people, except perhaps professional fiction writers, tend to *project* their

own motives into such stories. Mr. Smith has fun making up a story about how one of the hunters doesn't really care a hoot about hunting. He's having a "couple of" drinks with his friends and enjoying his absence from his "old lady" who always "bugs him."

I must point out that projective methods of determining motives also have their drawbacks. They are often difficult and time-consuming to score, judges often disagree on the scoring, and some psychologists assert that the motives "revealed" by projective techniques are still not necessarily the individual's *true* motives.

Nevertheless, I suggested to the park managers that the projective method be tried, mainly because plenty of data based on questionnaires were already available and apparently no researcher had ever tried projective methods of studying leisure motives. Questionnaire studies suggested that a certain set of motives, in a certain order of importance, might govern our recreation behavior. I suggested that it would be useful to know whether motives obtained by a different method confirmed this list or indicated that a different set of motives, in a different order of importance, might organize and direct our recreation behavior. A general principle of science is to confirm the existence or pattern of elusive phenomena (such as motives) by using several methods. This helps to demonstrate that the new knowledge is not merely a product of the method chosen to study the phenomenon.

Thus, my fourth assignment was to develop and test a projective technique for measuring recreation motives. I would create the new method, based on general methods established by projective methods researchers. Then I would try out the new technique with a small sample of individuals.

My fifth task was one that grew out of the managers' more immediate needs. We recognized that even if the projective technique was found to be useful, it would be relatively expensive and time-consuming for both respondents and researchers. Surveys will always be necessary, both to obtain motive information from nonprojective methods and because they are less time-consuming and allow researchers to reach much larger numbers of respondents. So I was asked to design a set of questions for two surveys, one done house-to-house and one done in parks. The main purpose of the house-to-house survey was to investigate the motives of at least some individuals who never visit parks. I was also asked to determine the best way to analyze the data that emerged from these surveys.

Sixth, I was to make a report with recommendations to the management committee based on outcomes of the five previous tasks. Finally, and perhaps the easiest task (given that the first

six were completed successfully), supply three written copies of the report!

Here I will focus on step four, the part of our contract that led to our new method of assessing recreation motives by using a projective test. The other steps also consumed considerable time, but most of them were rather straightforward searches of the research literature followed by a written integration of others' investigations.

Projective tests require some sort of display for the subject's projections. The Rorschach ink blots are the most famous example, but psychologists have also used other displays. One of these is the set of pictures devised by Henry Murray and Christiana Morgan as the Thematic Apperception Test (TAT) (Morgan & Murray, 1935). The scenes show one or two people in ambiguous contexts (e.g., one person in bed and another standing at the door). The subject is asked to create a story; as noted earlier, the themes that emerge in the story are presumed to reflect the storyteller's own motives.

My approach was to create scenes depicting people in recreation scenes, again in poses and contexts that allow for different interpretations. I commissioned a local artist to create six watercolors. We discussed which activities to include and precisely how to arrange the people in the scenes. The six scenes show people (a) canoeing in the wilderness, (b) skiing, (c) visiting an Old West historic town, (d) tanning themselves on a beach, (e) entering a theme park, and (f) sitting around a campfire. With high hopes for its success, we dubbed the new test the Outdoor Recreation Thematic Apperception Test (ORTAT) (see Figure 14-2).

From the telephone book, participants were recruited for *focus groups*, sessions in which small groups of people discuss, under the direction of a psychologist who loosely follows an agenda, the topic of interest to the client. In this case, of course, the agenda was to understand why people do or do not visit parks. To prevent participants from altering the expression of their feelings about parks in either positive or negative ways because they knew our primary concern was park use, the focus group theme was broader. We asked people to tell us about the pros and cons of their recent holidays and vacations to all destinations. We listened especially closely, however, whenever the discussion moved toward parks and outdoor recreation.

The focus group sessions included open-ended discussion (e.g., "What was your favorite vacation, and what made it so good?"), another projective test called the word-association test ("When I say PICNIC what is the first word that comes into your mind?"), a questionnaire that asked about the participant's recent vacations

(where, for how long), and another questionnaire that asked their motives for outdoor recreation in the traditional survey format. Also, of course, each person wrote a story about each of the six scenes in the ORTAT.

Many hypotheses could be tested through analyses of the rich data produced in the focus group sessions which, incidentally, were tape-recorded with the knowledge and consent of the participants.

Figure 14-2 Three scenes from the Outdoor Recreation Thematic Apperception Test (ORTAT). (Courtesy of the editor, Robert Gifford.)

The hypothesis of prime interest to us was whether one's motives for recreation as measured by the new projective test were the same as those produced in response to the traditional survey questions.

If they are the same, we could tentatively conclude that: (a) The motives thus identified are likely to be the person's true motives, because two quite different methods agree on what those motives are; and (b) that future studies could rely primarily on survey methods rather than the much more expensive projective methods, because both methods yield the same answer. However, if the two methods revealed different motives, then one method or the other is probably better at determining one's true motives. (A horrible alternative would be that neither surveys nor projective tests yield a person's true motives!)

To resolve this issue, a relatively complete list of potential recreation motives is necessary so that motives uncovered by different methods can be compared. In our review of past research, we found that many different motives for outdoor recreation had been suggested by researchers and their subjects. As few as four and as many as 40 motives have been described in various studies. No single, agreed-upon list exists.

A useful list must not include too few motives, thereby excluding some that are important, nor should it include too many, introducing redundancy. After considerable effort aimed at integrating previous research, we proposed ten "supermotives" that appear to cover most or all of the forces that energize individuals to undertake outdoor recreation, yet overlap as little as possible. Here is our list:

Ten Supermotives for Outdoor Recreation

1. NATURE: to view beautiful scenery, to be one with nature, to live primitively.
2. ESCAPE: to get away, to be alone, to relax, to find peace and quiet, to avoid routine, cities, and others' expectations.
3. SOCIAL: to be with family, to meet others, to develop relationships.
4. CHALLENGE: to test oneself, to be competitive, to be fit, to hone skills, *not* to seek comfort.
5. DOMINANCE: to make decisions, to lead a group, to be in control.
6. GROWTH: to improve oneself, to learn, to explore, to introspect.

7. RECOGNITION: to make a mark, to be known, to be recognized, to achieve.

8. PLAY: to have fun, to be entertained, to find pleasure.

9. SAFETY: to be secure, to avoid risk, to be safe.

10. ALTRUISM: to help others or the environment.

Now motives could be compared by the two methods. Across the six stories based on the ORTAT scenes, the raters found that the top four motives were (in order): play, escape, social, and nature. Based on the same participants' responses to a questionnaire concerning the same activities depicted in the ORTAT scenes, the top four motives were (in order): nature, challenge, growth, and escape. Thus, the two methods agree that nature and escape are important motives for outdoor recreation, but the projective method (ORTAT) indicates that play and social are important while the questionnaire approach indicates that challenge and growth are important. The biggest difference is for play, the most important projective motive but only the seventh most important survey motive.

The results appear mixed: The two methods agree on some motives but disagree on others. More research is necessary, but one possible conclusion does knit the outcomes together. This conclusion is based on the *social desirability* of motives, that is, how acceptable they would sound to one's friends and family. Projective tests probably can elicit the less socially acceptable motives better than questionnaire methods. To say that you go into the great outdoors for growth and challenge is probably more socially desirable than to say you go out there merely to play.

So what are the main motives for outdoor recreation and which method of discovering them is best? We need both survey and projective methods to discover both the socially acceptable and the socially unacceptable motives. Perhaps nature, escape, play, challenge, and growth are all important motives for outdoor recreation.

The research in this case study is quite theory oriented. I offer it as a counterbalance to the other case studies in this chapter, which were more practical. This project had its more practical side, too. Recall that phase five consisted of designing a questionnaire that could be used for household and park surveys of user satisfaction. So far over 4,000 of these questionnaires have been returned and await my attention! ◆

Becoming an Environmental Psychologist

Education

As with all forms of applied psychology, undergraduate and graduate training is necessary to become an environmental psychologist. At the undergraduate level, a course in environmental psychology is very desirable, but not always necessary. Not every college or university has such a course and graduate programs are aware that students may be unable to take the course. Whether or not your school has one, you should consider taking related courses such as urban geography, environmental sociology, introductory architecture, or human ecology.

For graduate school, of course, you need good to excellent grades and you must meet various other requirements, depending on the school. However, you also need to make some personal decisions. One important decision is what sort of program suits your interests. A few graduate schools offer full programs in environmental psychology—that is, an entire set of prescribed courses, several faculty members who specialize in environmental psychology or closely related disciplines, and classes with at least several other students (although most graduate school classes are much smaller than undergraduate classes).

Many other graduate schools have only one or two faculty members who specialize in environmental psychology. In these schools, the program is an individualized one-on-one set of courses. The few other graduate students with your interests are likely to be at different stages of their degree programs.

The individualized programs are definitely smaller, but they are not necessarily better or worse than the full programs. The advantages of the full program include the opportunity to gain from the expertise of several professors and numerous like-minded students. The individualized program offers more personalized education and it may be the only way to study with that certain professor who was recommended to you or whose work you admire. However, it will lack the breadth of a full program and it may lack the comradeship that occurs when numerous graduate students go through a full program together.

Whether you enter a full program or an individualized set of courses, some features of graduate school remain pretty constant. You will be in class less than before, but you will be expected to do much more reading and research on your own. A supervisor and a committee of two or three other faculty members will officially look

after your progress. A major, original piece of research (or two) under the committee's guidance are required: These are the M.A. thesis and, later, the Ph.D. dissertation.

The oldest established environmental psychology program is at the Graduate Center of the City University of New York; it dates from 1968. Some other full programs in psychology departments and in nonpsychology departments that accept psychology undergraduate degrees include the departments of psychology at Arizona, Arizona State, Claremont, and Utah, the departments of architecture at California (Berkeley and Los Angeles), Georgia Tech, Michigan, Montreal, and Wisconsin (Milwaukee). Two relevant interdisciplinary graduate programs are the Social Ecology Program at the University of California at Irvine and the Design and Environmental Analysis option at Cornell University. For a list of other universities that offer individualized programs see Gifford (1987).

Employment

Graduates of environmental psychology programs work in many different settings. Some jobs might include joining an established environment-behavior consulting firm; starting your own firm; joining a government agency that deals with regional, city, or building planning; managing the facilities of a large organization; or teaching.

Compared to other applied psychology fields, the number of positions is small. However, the number of qualified graduates is also small, relatively speaking. Because environmental psychology has not become as institutionalized as, say, clinical psychology, becoming employed can be more of a challenge. Getting a position as an environmental psychologist depends on your own ability and initiative. Although some positions are labeled "environmental psychologist," most have other titles, such as facility planner, design programmer, or senior researcher (in a design or planning agency) but are open to environmental psychologists.

SUGGESTED READINGS AND REFERENCES

BARKER, R. G. (1968). *Ecological psychology: Concepts and methods for studying the environment of human behavior.* Stanford, CA: Stanford University Press.

BRUNSWIK, E. (1943). Organismic achievement and environmental probability. *Psychological Review, 50,* 255–272.

GIFFORD, R. (1987). *Environmental psychology: Principles and practice.* Boston: Allyn and Bacon.

HERON, W., DOANE, B. K., & SCOTT, T. H. (1956). Visual disturbances after prolonged perceptual isolation. *Canadian Journal of Psychology, 10,* 13–18.

MORGAN, C. D., & MURRAY, H. (1935). A method for investigating fantasies. *Archives of Neurology and Psychiatry, 34,* 289–306.

SOMMER, R. (1983). *Social design: Creating buildings with people in mind.* Englewood Cliffs, NJ: Prentice Hall.

STOKOLS, D., & ALTMAN, I. (1987). *Handbook of environmental psychology.* New York: Wiley.

KATHY MONTGOMERY

Kathy Montgomery was born in Boston, Massachusetts. Her mother worked in nursing homes as she was growing up, and perhaps this familiarity influenced her work focus. Her undergraduate degree in psychology was completed at the University of Massachusetts in Boston, and her M.A. and Ph.D. work at the University of Victoria, British Columbia. She did a brief internship at the Juan de Fuca Hospitals in Victoria, and currently works at the Victoria Mental Health Center. ♦

15

The Geropsychologist

The senior's center meeting came to a close and people filtered out the door or over to the coffee area. As I was about to leave, one of the women I knew well asked if I could stay a bit longer and have a chat with her. We sat in a quiet area of the center and she told me how her grandchildren were progressing, news of ill center members, and such. But that was not why she had asked to talk with me.

"I am afraid I am losing my mind," she said sadly, and then told me how she had occasion to introduce her neighbor of many years to another friend. "To my horror, I couldn't think of Bessie's name to save my life! I know her name as well as my own, but I just couldn't think of it! I went to say it, but nothing come out—my mind was just blank. Bessie and my friend introduced themselves, but I can imagine what they were thinking. This isn't the only time this has happened to me, either. Recently I've been forgetting all sorts of things I know perfectly well. Names are the worst, but how could I forget Bessie! I must be losing my mind, getting senile!"

I told her about *anomia*, the name for her experience, something that happens to people of all ages. We go to say a word we know well and it just won't come, yet it is on the tip of our tongue. Most people pass off this experience and forget about it. But many elderly persons are quite troubled by it and concerned about its significance, as was my friend. Anomia happens to everyone, but becomes more frequent as aging progresses. Yet excessive anomia may also signal the onset of dementing illnesses, as my friend knew. (*Dementia* is the proper term for diseases that are more commonly referred to as senility.) One of the tasks of psychologists in geriatric practice is to quantify anomia and to distinguish between its normal occurrences and excessive ones. This distinction would be made as part of a psychological assessment.

What Is Geropsychology?

There is a distinction between gerontology and geriatrics. Gerontology refers to the study of aging in its broadest aspects. The multidisciplinary nature of gerontology is well demonstrated by the Canadian Association on Gerontology (CAG). Its five divisions, Biological Sciences, Health Sciences, Psychology, Social Sciences, and Social Welfare, include members from at least 35 disciplines. The Gerontological Society, an American organization, is similar. The annual meetings held by these organizations include a very

diverse group of presentations, perhaps ranging from a paper regarding influences of aging on the endocrine system, to one on homesharing, to an exploration of knowledge regarding nutrition, to a discussion entitled, "Is it normal to age?" The CAG's mission is to bring together such diverse specialists for the enrichment of all. Geriatrics refers to clinical problems and pathologies specific to aging populations, again as dealt with by any discipline.

Gerontological psychology is an area of research psychology primarily devoted to discovering psychological changes that occur with aging. Changes may be investigated in sensory functioning and perception, reaction time, cognitive ability, memory, personality, problem solving, or any other topic of interest to psychologists.

Geriatric psychology is an area of applied psychology that focuses on psychological problems and pathologies encountered due to the effects of aging. The aim of geriatric psychology is to promote the psychological well being of elderly people by identifying and managing pathology that occurs as age increases. This rather broad goal encompasses a variety of professional activities. Some psychologists in geriatric practice work directly with elderly people in private practice, hospital, nursing home, or outpatient settings. Others assist families or other caregivers in trying to best maintain an elderly person's well being. This aspect of geriatric practice is conducted at settings such as adult day-care centers, mental health centers, and community senior citizen's organizations.

Geriatric psychologists may also conduct research, much of which focuses on psychological distinctions between normal age-related changes and changes seen in older people due to some form of pathology. Some geriatric psychologists assist governments in policy development and planning for future social and health-care needs of an increasingly aged population.

Obviously there is some overlap between gerontological and geriatric psychology. The term *geropsychology* is often used to indicate the combined areas.

The Background of Geropsychology

Adolphe Quetelet (1835) is considered the founder of the study of aging. In his concern with the concept of the "average man," he studied people of various ages, collecting data on sensory function-

ing, physical properties, hand strength, and productivity. These studies contain elements that modern studies have incorporated.

Sir Francis Galton continued this line of research and used the opportunity of the International Health Exhibition of 1884 to gather data regarding a more extensive set of measures from the fairgoers, whose ages varied widely. Some work was done in exploring variability in psychomotor skills across age during the World War I era, but gerontology and geriatrics as known today did not really gain prominence until after World War II.

In 1946, two centers that emphasize aging research opened. One was the Nuffield Unit for Research into Problems of Aging at Cambridge University in England under the direction of Alan Welford. Although it had a short existence, it provided a training ground for many individuals who spread interest in the study of aging. The other center was at the National Institute of Health in the United States, directed by Nathan Shock. James Birren headed the division for psychological research. A few years later the National Institute of Mental Health opened its section on aging. Since then, an increasing number of federal and private foundations devoted to gerontology have been established. Initially, biological studies of aging were most prominent, but psychological investigations are now moving to the forefront.

The Scope of Geropsychology

Work Settings

There are two main settings for the clinical practice of geropsychologists. One is the community at large. The other includes institutions of various sorts that provide care to disabled elderly.

Clinical Practice in Community Settings

The elderly consume a disproportionately large share of the health-care budget, as one would expect, given that the incidence of disease increases as age increases. Some conditions prevalent among the elderly are preventable, others are treatable, and some are curable. For example, the management of hypertension can help *prevent* strokes and heart attacks. Depression is best *treated* with combined medication and psychotherapy. Many infections are *curable*. Some medical conditions may mimic dementia or senility when in fact the person has a treatable or curable physical illness. A psy-

chologist can differentiate these conditions from dementia and monitor their treatment. Identification of such disorders reduces loss of life enjoyment and unnecessary institutionalization for elderly persons.

The geropsychologist makes the differentiations by conducting a psychological assessment. This service may alternatively be provided by clinical psychologists and neuropsychologists. One of the most frequent referral questions to geropsychologists is the request for assistance in deciding between diagnoses of dementia or depression, a task which is more difficult than most laypeople think. Part of the difficulty is that depressed people, especially elderly depressed people, may show cognitive and memory impairments, which are also characteristics of dementia.

Geropsychologists may also conduct psychotherapy or counseling with appropriate clients. Issues common among the elderly which may lead to consulting a geropsychologist for treatment include: difficulty adjusting to the life changes caused by retirement, loneliness resulting from being some distance from family, the death or relocation of friends, decisions regarding retirement facility entrance, and assistance in the management of grief or bereavement. In addition, family members sometimes consult a geropsychologist. They seek assistance in maintaining a dementing family member at home by devising strategies for coping with problem behaviors, support for themselves in dealing with the institutionalization of an elderly family member, or counseling about relationships with very difficult elderly parents.

Clinical Practice in Institutions

Richards-Wool (1986) outlines the wide range of services a geropsychologist might offer in institutions and techniques for administering such services. They include assessment, psychotherapy, behavior therapy, family counseling, group programs, support groups, and problem behavior management.

Although most services are directed toward elderly residents, another vital role for geropsychologists in institutions is the provision of education for staff members. Programs that train staff in effective communication techniques are a major priority because; for example, some problem behaviors either would not occur or would be milder in nature if staff members had better communication skills. Other areas of staff education include information about normal effects of aging, explorations of geriatric deficits, and the effects of specific neurological and psychiatric diseases prevalent in the elderly.

Research Concerns

Reseach in geropsychology is constantly expanding. Almost every behavior of humans is being studied to discover its response to increasing age. Yet certain basic trends in research exist. The following section is a brief explanation of some of these trends.

An ongoing emphasis in gerontological psychology is the investigation of normal age-related changes in human memory. Memory clearly does change with increasing age, yet the quality and magnitude of change has not been clearly defined or understood. Attempts to compare the memory performances of adults under the age of 65 with those over the age of 65 have highlighted differences between the groups that produce the *appearance* of memory decline, but are not necessarily valid evidence of decline. Older adults approach the memory test situation in a different manner than do younger adults. They are less inclined to give uncertain responses. They tend to be slower but more accurate. They are less willing to work on tasks that appear meaningless or silly to them (e.g., learning nonsense syllables). These differences magnify the amount of apparent decline in memory. When experiments are designed to overcome these effects, the difference between younger and older age groups shrinks. Knowledge about memory functioning also affects memory performance, and educating elderly people about memory functioning serves to improve their performance.

Another broad area of gerontological psychology research is the examination of differences between cross-sectional and longitudinal samples. What does this mean? A *cross-sectional sample* is one in which people of different age groups are selected and studied at one point in time. A *longitudinal sample* is one in which a group of people are selected and then studied at multiple points in time. What difference does this make? The life experiences of people who are now 20 are vastly different than those of people who were 20 in 1930. Because life experiences affect our behavior, perhaps differences between people of various ages (cohorts) are partly due to their biological aging and partly due to the historical times in which they have lived. Current research supports this idea, and tries to ascertain which behaviors and functions are affected and to what degree.

Knowledge accruing from research comparisons of cohort groups does have practical application, and ranges well beyond the field of psychology alone. The attitudes and expectations of an entire generation affect not only the behavior of individuals, but of society as a whole. For example, it is recognized that today's adults

Advanced age is not necessarily any less pleasant than youth. (Courtesy of the editor, Robert Gifford.)

have a greater knowledge of the role of diet and exercise in disease prevention and control. They place great emphasis on a youthful appearance and attitude. They demand that authority figures be accountable and responsive. How will this generation face the challenges of aging? Will they reach age 65 in better physical condition, but with greater distress, and perhaps depression, about each gray hair and wrinkle? Will they maintain a greater involvement in finance and politics?

Much research in geriatric psychology is directed toward identifying effective forms of psychotherapy with elderly clients, particularly those who are depressed. Dolores Gallagher of Palo Alto, California and Peter Lewinsohn in Oregon are prominent researchers in this area (Gallagher & Thompson, 1983; Lewinsohn & Teri, 1983). Studies have examined forms of psychotherapy, depression, grief and bereavement, the combination of psychotherapy with antidepressants or other medication, the use of electro-convulsive therapy (ECT); differences in therapists, long term outcomes; and many other topics.

A new area of research in geriatric psychology is the management of problem behaviors exhibited by elderly residents in long-term care facilities. In the past, physical and chemical restraints were used to control difficult residents. Although these techniques are not desirable, alternative strategies are only now being developed. A geriatric psychologist is particularly suited to this challenge because he or she has expertise in principles of behavior change and is knowledgeable about causes of behavioral dysfunction in the aged. Prominent researchers include Richard Hussian (1985) of Dallas, Marian MacDonald (1983) and Patricia Wisocki (1984), both of Amherst, Massachusetts, among others.

The primary issues in geropsychology research are: What is different about being aged? and What are the effects of increasing age? Given the rapidly increasing percentage of the population over 65 years of age, it is now a social imperative to discover which age-related changes are avoidable, and how to avoid them and, for those changes that are not avoidable, to discover methods that promote effective coping.

CASE STUDIES

The next section presents three case studies from my own work. As such, they reveal more about the scope of my practice than about the scope of geropsychology. Please recognize that geropsychologists do not restrict their activities to institutions, or to the elderly in ill health. I choose these examples because they portray the complexity of geriatric psychology, its clientele, and settings.

CASE ONE: MR. HAWKES

Mr. Hawkes was a businessman who had always enjoyed playing golf in his spare time and had become reasonably proficient. He had even won a number of trophies which he proudly displayed in his home. Once he retired, he devoted much more time to his game. Golf was a great form of exercise for him, especially since his doctor had suggested losing a little weight and avoiding foods high in cholesterol.

Mr. Hawkes's hypertension proved resistant, however, and medication was prescribed to help control his blood pressure. But because he usually felt so well, he was rather sporadic at taking the medication. Mr. Hawkes then started to notice that his vision had deteriorated enough to impair his golf game. Like many elderly, Mr. Hawkes was quite sensitive to glare and found this a handicap. Golf games became less frequent.

Unfortunately, Mr. Hawkes then had a stroke which resulted in his being a little forgetful, sometimes rather irritable, and weak on one side of his body. His wife had died a number of years previously, and his son and daughter-in-law decided to take Mr. Hawkes into their home so that he would have less to manage and they could assist him more readily. However, they found this arrangement less satisfactory than anticipated. Mr. Hawkes's pride in his past business accomplishments made him feel free to advise his son. Being forgetful, he would frequently repeat himself and then become quite irate if asked not to advise so freely and frequently. He found his grandchildren more noisy and confusing than enjoyable. Tension grew in the household.

Then Mr. Hawkes had another, more serious stroke. He was in hospital for a protracted period of time, and spent some time in a rehabilitation unit. He was left with a rather severe difficulty in verbal communication, a severe visual deficit, was unable to get about without a walker, and his irritability was worsened by his anger at his condition. Mr. Hawkes had a dementing condition caused by multiple strokes. Although his family tried having him return to their home, Mr. Hawkes was unable to manage the daytime when everyone was out of the house. The stove would be left on, or he would fall, or he would break things he had not seen well. It was clear that Mr. Hawkes would need to move to a long-term care facility.

The family carefully chose the facility they thought best for Mr. Hawkes. The staff were pleasant and friendly without being overly familiar. The ward was always clean, with well-polished floors and light walls. When he was admitted, they were pleased to see what a nice bright room he had and tried to make it seem more homey for him by decorating it with his golfing trophies and favorite pictures.

But to his family's surprise, Mr. Hawkes had difficulty adjusting to the facility. His nurses complained that they were unable to get him to use his room for any part of the day that he was awake. He would go into other residents' rooms and lie on their beds, which angered the other residents. The aides complained that Mr. Hawkes seemed to need lot of assistance dressing sometimes, although other times he managed easily on his own. Unlike at home, he had a number of falls. Mr. Hawkes seemed restless. Although he could not communicate well, he said "no home, no home" frequently. There were other difficulties as well.

The nurses requested my assistance in helping Mr. Hawkes adjust to facility living. But his ability to use and comprehend spoken or written language was so impaired by the stroke that there was little Mr. Hawkes and I could discuss. Instead, I decided

to observe his behavior on the ward and his interactions with the staff. I also requested that the staff log any falls, note whose beds he lay on, and record a number of other behaviors. I spent much time talking to the staff about difficulties with Mr. Hawkes, and the kinds of approaches they tried to use in their attempts to help him be more comfortable.

Then I started to realize something strange. The aides who helped Mr. Hawkes to dress reported difficulties, but the aides who bathed him were surprised by those reports. The dressing aides further reported that Mr. Hawkes would clutch on to them when they helped him in the morning, but then he would speed down the hall with ease. The falls had occurred in his own room. One observer said Mr. Hawkes had "missed" a chair he was about to sit in. Another complained that Mr. Hawkes had spent the morning gingerly handling fragile items during an activity, but then had carelessly swept a glass to the floor once he returned to his room. It appeared that Mr. Hawkes had difficulties in his room that he did not have elsewhere. How strange!

I went to take another look at his room. Suddenly I thought I knew why he would not stay in the room and had such difficulties when he was there. It had the brightest, sunniest window in the whole facility. The window sill held his shiny gold and silver golf trophies. The walls were pale yellow and covered with large glass-fronted pictures, and the floor was waxed to a high sheen. All these surfaces reflected light around the room and shone into the hall. He probably could not see at all in that room!

The elderly are more impaired by glare than are younger adults. We have probably all had the experience of looking down a hallway toward a window, and seeing the light shine on the floor. The glare from the window will prevent you from seeing something down the hallway as clearly as you would otherwise. The elderly experience this effect more readily and are quite handicapped by it because of normal changes that occur in the visual system as age advances.

Mr. Hawkes was not only elderly, his stroke had further impaired his vision. In his glare-filled room, Mr. Hawkes was unable to see the floor clearly, and he therefore clutched onto the aides in fear of falling. He missed the shiny chair surface because he could not see it properly.

Watching Mr. Hawkes navigate in the halls and in his room seemed to support my hypothesis. I suggested that the nurses request a room-darkening shade and light-filtering curtains, move

the trophies, ask housekeeping not to shine his floor, and either get low-glare glass for his pictures or remove them. These things were done, and a short while later, Mr. Hawkes spent an appropriate amount of time in his room and no longer napped on other residents' beds. ♦

CASE TWO: MRS. ALT

Mr. and Mrs. Alt were a wealthy couple who greatly enjoyed their retirement years. They were able to travel and to participate in activities for which they had never had time previously. Their children thought Mr. Alt was getting rather fussy in his old age because they had observed that he seemed to direct Mrs. Alt in whatever she was doing. He would tell her what dishes to choose in setting the dinner table, when to start cooking, things that he had never bothered with before. They asked their mother how she could stand such constant supervision, but she just smiled and said he was such a great help.

Then Mr. Alt died quite suddenly. Mrs. Alt had trouble coping on her own, but her children thought she was just bereaved and that in time she would manage. But a year and a half passed and finally her children had to admit that Mrs. Alt was demented. The reason for Mr. Alt's diligent supervision became clear to them. It had prevented Mrs. Alt's mental incapacity from being apparent. Thorough medical and psychological investigation concluded that Mrs. Alt was in all probability suffering from Alzheimer's disease.

Eventually, Mrs. Alt was admitted to a long-term care facility. After some initial difficulties, she settled into her new home reasonably well.

But as time passed, Mrs. Alt's dementia became worse. She wandered about the facility in which she resided, once leaving the building and getting lost. The nurses could manage her wandering, with the exception of her intrusion into the room of a bedridden resident, Mr. Thomas, who had a tracheotomy. The equipment to maintain his tracheotomy was by his bedside. Mrs. Alt came into his room and not only fiddled with the equipment, she fiddled with Mr. Thomas's tracheotomy itself! The nurses worried that she would harm the tube and damage the equipment necessary to repair it. How could they keep Mrs. Alt out of the room?

Observation of Mrs. Alt's wandering suggested that she moved toward whatever caught her attention. Mr. Thomas's room was the closest one to the nurse's station, where residents tend to con-

gregate. It was on the right-hand side, which is the direction Mrs. Alt usually turned. His door frame was highlighted against the cream walls by its dark brown paint. This high-contrast coloring made the doorway very conspicuous.

I wondered whether camouflaging Mr. Thomas's door would help. We covered the dark door frame with wide masking tape and papered the door with blank newsprint, making both more similar to the wall. Mrs. Alt did not enter Mr. Thomas's room again. She continued on to the next door on the right—her own!

Such magically simple solutions seldom exist for the kinds of behavioral difficulties experienced in long-term care facilities. Even fewer provide long-lasting benefit. But they do sometimes occur. In Mrs. Alt's case, although she did not enter Mr. Thomas's room, she did continue wandering in other areas of the facility. But at least the nurses could be more assured of Mr. Thomas's safety. ◆

CASE THREE: MRS. BURNS

Mrs. Burns had also moved to a long-term care facility following the death of her husband. He had doted on her, and all their friends said what a loving and caring husband he had been. In a time when most wives catered to their husbands, Mr. Burns had instead catered to his wife. He brought her coffee and toast in bed each morning. He helped her with household tasks. He tried to ensure that her life was as smooth and untroubled as possible.

Mrs. Burns did not make friends easily, and had trouble developing closer relationships with people, but Mr. Burns was quite the opposite. He attracted many people, and with time, they also became close friends of Mrs. Burns. Once Mrs. Burns overcame her initial difficulty, she was a fun-loving and loyal friend. But at the same time she was quite sensitive and her feelings could easily be hurt.

However, the facility staff reported that Mrs. Burns had frequent temper tantrums. The unit director had investigated the situation but was unable to discover what might be causing the difficulties. The director knew the staff well and believed them to be caring people who genuinely tried to help the residents in their care. What could they do to get along with Mrs. Burns better?

Interviewing the staff indicated that they were also quite puzzled by Mrs. Burns' dissatisfactions. They could not identify anything particular that caused the temper tantrums, and in fact thought that things that angered other residents were ignored by Mrs. Burns. At times she was provoked by events that had pre-

viously occurred without comment. But they revealed that her temper tantrums generally occurred in the morning when the nurse's aide was helping her and her roommates get dressed and down to the dining room for breakfast. Temper tantrums were rare at any other time of day.

Mrs. Burns' situation was unusual. I often find it difficult to get an opportunity to actually observe a behavioral problem as it occurs because many such problems occur at unpredictable or infrequent times. In this case, I decided to be on the unit early in the morning in the hope that I might catch a morning when Mrs. Burns had a temper tantrum.

I spent a couple of mornings standing outside the room listening to the aide's interaction with the four residents in that room. She helped Mrs. Burns dress, commenting that here were her pants, her stockings, and so on, and which dress did she want? Their interaction was quite impersonal. She then helped the next resident, Mrs. Yallow, who told her a joke, so the aide told another and they giggled together through morning care. The aide's interaction with Mrs. Yallow was quite warm and companionable. Her interaction with a third inhabitant of the room was very quiet, largely because that resident had very little remaining mental ability. The aide moved on to the final roommate, Mrs. Tate. She assisted the room inhabitants in a different order each morning.

On the second morning, Mrs. Burns had a tantrum, claiming she could not reach her zipper, that no one ever helped her! She burst into Mrs. Yallow's curtained area, and demanded that the aide help her immediately. The aide was angered by Mrs. Burns' intrusion into Mrs. Yallow's privacy, but quietly did her zipper and returned to helping Mrs. Yallow. Mrs. Burns went right down to the nursing station complaining all the way about what little assistance she received and how no one cared for her.

The difference seemed to be that Mrs. Yallow was a much more lively, warm and outgoing person than was Mrs. Burns. She initiated the jokes and fun and giggles that she and the aide shared. Perhaps Mrs. Burns resented the closer relationship between the aide and her roommate and felt left out. Her husband helped Mrs. Burns start closer relationships, but he was not here to do so any longer.

I talked with the aide about her thoughts on my observations of the difference between how she interacted with the two ladies. She agreed that she and Mrs. Yallow had an easier, closer relationship than she and Mrs. Burns did. She liked Mrs. Burns, but she thought that Mrs. Burns' more formal attitude meant she should not joke or laugh when assisting her. I told her about the

Burns' friend's obervations, and how Mr. Burns had assisted Mrs. Burns. I asked whether the aide thought it possible that the temper tantrums were caused by Mrs. Burns' desire for a friendlier interaction, and some jealousy of her relationship with Mrs. Yallow. The aide agreed, but did not know what she might do to change things.

We discussed whether she might tell Mrs. Burns a joke or speak informally as she might with Mrs. Yallow. Perhaps if the aide made the first steps in trying to develop a closer relationship, Mrs. Burns would slowly begin to reciprocate. Perhaps, because the aide did enjoy working with Mrs. Burns, she might say to her, "I like helping you," or some similar comment. I try to be careful about what I suggest staff say to residents about their own feelings because many of them, although caring a great deal about the people they work with, find it hard to specifically *say* that they care. In this instance, the aide was a very competent and caring person who was readily able to communicate her feelings. We also discussed what to do when Mrs. Burns did have temper tantrums.

The aide changed her approach with Mrs. Burns. She provided as much assistance as before, but in a more casual and incidental fashion. She tried telling Mrs. Burns jokes and offering more personal comments. Initially, Mrs. Burns was not particularly responsive, but in time, just as her friends would have predicted, she was better able to take part. The dressing assistance became something that happened as the two talked about other things, rather than the focus of their interaction.

I would like to say that the temper tantrums stopped entirely. But they did not. Instead, the temper tantrums became restricted to periods when Mrs. Burns was assisted by staff members who were either unable or unwilling to engage in a more personal interaction to Mrs. Burns, and then be patient until she was ready to reciprocate. This differential response supported the validity of my ideas about why Mrs. Burns had temper tantrums. As time passed, I could predict whether or not Mrs. Burns was having temper tantrums by knowing which aide was assigned to assist her. ♦

Concluding Comment

The case studies outlined above portray instances where mental decline, sensory impairment, environmental factors, life history, family involvement and interdisciplinary relationships, among other aspects, have to be considered in assisting an elderly individual.

I think that work with impaired individuals who reside in long-term care facilities is one of the most challenging areas of geriatric psychology. But geropsychologists have broad choices among patient populations and settings. Some geropsychologists specialize in assisting elderly clients who are grieving the death of a spouse, adult child, or other close person. Some specialize in consulting with architects regarding the characteristics of environments that aid the elderly in coping with sensory or physical handicaps. In fact, you could probably take most of the applied areas of psychology described in the chapters of this book and find geropsychologists who perform that activity with or for elderly clients!

Becoming a Geropsychologist

Interests and Education

Before deciding on a particular career, it is wise to consider whether the job requirements and job environment suit you. If you are considering geropsychology, you should examine your reaction to spending much of your working day dealing with quite elderly people. Remember that the geropsychologist's clientele is not only elderly, but often ill as well. Even the children of the elderly are middle-aged or elderly. You must like old people if you are to be happy working as a geropsychologist.

Consider, too, whether you could work in a hospital. Although some people feel uncomfortable visiting a hospital, you may find working in one a different experience. Other work sites are possible, but it is wise to be aware of the limitations your personal comfort might place on your choice of employment sites.

A reasonable way to test your response to working with the elderly would be to seek a volunteer or paid position that provides services to the elderly. You might possibly use your paid work with the elderly to finance your education, or to receive course credit, depending on university policy. Positions to investigate include home support worker, adult day-care worker, and nurse aide (although you may be required to pay for a training course first).

In order to conduct an independent practice as a geropsychologist, a Ph.D. is required. With an M.A., you may assist a geropsychologist or you may work under the supervision of someone with a Ph.D. A person with a B.A. may work as a research assistant

or technician, which is a good way to try the area before graduate school. See the article by Lubin, Brady, Thomas, and Whitlock (1986) for further information about graduate programs.

A well-trained geriatric psychologist must know something about many other areas of psychology, including a little medicine. Particularly pertinent psychology areas include neuropsychology, psychopathology, cognition, perception, psychotherapy, and counseling. Some familiarity with psychiatry, neurology, and internal medicine is also very helpful.

At some career point, most geriatric psychologists will also require a knowledge of policy development, administration, and management practices. Those geropsychologists who intend to pass by clinical practice in favor of involvement with government and other agents of social planning and change will require more extensive preparation in these areas.

A very comprehensive example of a curriculum for training in geriatric psychology is given in *Mental Health Care of the Aging: A Multidisciplinary Curriculum for Professional Training* (Eisdorfer & Cohen, 1982).

Research Support

Psychologists engaged in research usually work at a college or university. The institution pays their salary but in order to receive research funds (for equipment, supplies, research assistants, payment to research participants, etc.), they must apply for grants. These applications are reviewed by other researchers familiar with the area and rated according to a predetermined priority system. Then, available research funds are distributed until they are depleted. Grants vary from small amounts granted by local agencies, to larger amounts provided by universities, states or provinces, private philanthropic foundations, and federal governments, which usually manage the largest pool of funds.

In addition to acquiring funds to conduct research, the geropsychologist also must either locate a source of appropriate research subjects and a site at which the research question of interest can be investigated. Sometimes geropsychologists seek their own subjects or sites; at other times, subjects or sites may seek the geropsychologist! My own Ph.D. dissertation is an example of the latter instance, and is described next.

One day I spoke with a woman who was the director of resident care at a local long-term care facility. She told me that one problem

in such facilities is the definition and quantification of problem behavior among the residents. She said that while many rating scales had been published, none seemed to include items regarding the kinds of problem behaviors her nursing staff had to manage on a daily basis.

There are two primary reasons why such information would be desirable. First, knowing which problem behaviors were more frequent would allow a concerted effort at developing better strategies for coping with and managing those particular problems. Second, at times, nurses would request additional help to assist with particularly difficult behaviors. However, staff from various units disagreed about the fair distribution of additional staff, and an objective way of measuring the behavioral burden would be of great benefit. Could a psychologist devise a test that might suit their needs?

This conversation began a long research program for me. First, I needed to understand the ways in which existing scales examined institutional behavior, and why they did not assist the director in her search for a way to measure behavior. Next, behaviors viewed as problematic by the nursing staff had to be identified and defined. Then, a series of attempts to write a behavior rating scale began, followed by investigations of its reliability and validity.

Clinical geropsychology work is obtained in a different fashion. Some clinicians operate a private practice, as do clinicians in other areas of psychology. Their services are sought by parties able to pay their fees directly or by those whose bills will be paid by insurance companies. Other clinicians are employed by agencies with a mandate to supply services to the elderly. These agencies include hospitals and clinics, mental health centers, and long-term care facilities. Patients in need of services are referred by physicians, community agencies, and word of mouth. An option attractive to many clinicians is to divide their time between private practice and other employment.

Employment

Elderly people live in all parts of the country, but relocation after retirement has resulted in an increased concentration of elderly in areas with more pleasant climates, not an unwelcome prospect for future geropsychologists!

Given that the elderly segment of the population is expanding rapidly, the need for services will also increase. At any given time,

only about 5% of the elderly are living in a care facility. But for any one individual, the chance of residing in a long-term care facility even for a brief stay is closer to 50%. Between 20 and 30% of the elderly are residing in care facilities at the time of their death. The young adults of tomorrow will be unable to support their aged parents to the extent that senior citizens of today expect. The burden of caring for increasing numbers of problem behavior residents with diminishing resources will encourage facilities to seek the assistance of psychologists, both in conducting consultations about specific residents and in conducting service education programs for staff.

SUGGESTED READINGS AND REFERENCES

EISDORFER, C., & COHEN, D. (1982). *Mental health care of the aging: A multidisciplinary curriculum for professional training.* New York: Springer.

GALLAGHER, D. E., & THOMPSON, L. W. (1983). Cognitive therapy for depression in the elderly: A promising model for treatment and research. In L. D. Breslau & W. R. Haug (Eds.), *Causes, care and consequences* (pp. 250–274). New York: Springer.

HUSSIAN, R. A. (1985). *Responsive care: Behavioral interventions with elderly persons.* Champaign, IL: Research Press.

LEWINSOHN, P. M., & TERI, L. (1983). *Clinical geropsychology: New directions in assessment and treatment.* New York: Pergamon Press.

LUBIN, B., BRADY, K., THOMAS, E. A., & WHITLOCK, R. V. (1986). Training in geropsychology at the doctoral level. *Journal of Clinical Psychology, 42,* 387–391.

MACDONALD, M. L. (1983). Behavioral consultation in geriatric settings. *The Behavioral Therapist, 6,* 172–174.

QUETELET, A. (1835). *Sur l'homme et le developpement de ses facultés.* Paris: Bachelier.

RICHARDS-WOOL, L. (1986). Growth and healing in extended care: A role for psychology. *The British Columbia Psychologist,* 37–48.

WISOCKI, P. A. (1984). *Behavioral approaches to gerontology.* In M. Hersen, R. M. Eisler, & P. M. Miller (Eds.), *Progress in Behavior Modification* (pp. 239–252). Toronto: Academic Press.

Index

Absenteeism, 275, 283
Accident:
  fatality rates, 255
  litigation, 324
  proneness, 202
Accreditation, 14, 95, 168
Achievement:
  motivation, 154
  test, 50, 115
Acker, L. E., 216–42, 234
Acting-out, 66
Adamson, R., 293, 295
Adjustment errors, 305
Administration, 17
  work, 89
Adult day care:
  centers, 357
  worker, 369
Advertising, 3
Aerospace industry, 303, 324
Affection, 230, 231
Affective behavior, 106
Affiliation, theory of, 186
Ageing, 357, 358
Aggression, 230
  behavior, 63
Air quality, 308, 312
Alcohol, 91
  abuse, 64, 108
  treatment, 188
Alcoholics Anonymous, 66
  Alanon, 66
  Alateen, 66
Allard, F., 155, 169
Allergy, 69
  control, 70
Allison, R. I., 206, 214
Altman, I., 352
Altruism, 349
Alzheimer's disease, 110, 111, 112, 113, 365
American Board of Professional Psychology, 16
American Council on Consumer (ACCI), 200
American Marketing

Association (AMA), 200
American Psychological Association (APA), 8, 14, 18, 44, 50, 53, 56, 61, 70, 71, 81, 95, 96, 126, 142, 200, 212, 249, 268
  accreditation, 72
American Psychologist, 15, 71
Amphetamines, 91
Analgesic medication, 124
Anastasi, A., 46
Andrasik, F., 136
Angell, D., 320, 325
Anomia, 356
Anthropometry, 311, 312, 322
Anti-pollution programs, 224
Antidepressants, 110, 361
Antihypertension medication, 129
Antisocial, 230
  personality, 92
Anxiety, 22, 40, 64, 65, 114, 135, 148, 150, 154, 155, 157, 242
Applied behavior analysis, 218
  background, 221
Aptitude:
  measures, 58
  physiological bases of, 108
  tests, 85
Architecture, 329, 331
  marine, 314
  and psychology, 331
Asbestos, 266
  lawsuits, 266
  litigation, 266
  in textile factory, 266
Assessment, 85, 86
  center, 288, 291
  and diagnosis, 106
  difficulties with, 113
  formal procedures, 60
  strategies of, 109
Association for Consumer Research (ACR), 200

Athletic injuries, 154
Atrophy, cortical, 111, 112
Attention, 158
  deficits, 26, 64, 92, 103, 158
  style, 155
Attention deficit disorder, 36, 37
Attitudes, 154, 308, 312
  case study, 93
  scale, 94
Auditory system dysfunction, 69
Autism, 26
Autogenic training, 140
Automatisms, 64, 65
Autonomy, 79, 94
Aversive events, 234
Axline, V. M., 46

Bahr, H. M., 186, 192
Bandura, A., 32, 46
Barker, R., 330
Barkow, B., 334
Basal metabolic rate, 166
Bathroom design, 336
Baumann, D. J., 172–92
Bayley Scale of Infant Development, 28
Beauvais, C., 192
Becker, M. H., 129
Bed-wetting, 67
Behavior analysis, 218
Behavior analyst, 83
  education of, 237
  employment, 241
Behavior:
  abnormal, 84
  acting out, 63
  change, 165, 362
  map, 342
  mapping, 341
  modification, 53, 62, 218, 220, 225, 227, 233, 237
  observable, 83, 225
  off-task, 61
  patterns, 339

Behavior (*Continued*)
rating scale, 371
records, 220
self cutting, 92
settings, 330
severe problem, 62
therapy, 359
tracking, 341
troublesome, 82
Behavioral, 84
adaptation, 222
change, 177
and cognitive control, 155
control, 228
deficit, 113
dysfunction, 362
engineer, 235
laws, 218
literature, 238
measurement, 231
medicine, 126
models, 32
observations, 57, 336
problems, 52, 367
program, 178
questions, 227
repertoire, 220
results, 310
sciences, 127
self-management, 130
symptoms, 114
techniques, 150
tests, 106
treatment, 131
trends, 83
Behaviorists, 83
Belar, C. D., 123–44, 126, 142,
144
Belongingness, 282
Bender Visual Motor Gestalt
Test, 28
Berliner, C., 320, 325
Bettelheim, B., 46
Binet, A., 46, 80
Binet-Simon intelligence scale,
27
Biofeedback, 127, 159, 242
training, 140, 159
Biological sciences, 222, 239,
356
Biomechanics, 150, 311, 312,
322
and engineering, 312
Biomedical:
researchers, 132
sciences, 126
Biopsychosocial model, 130

Biostatistics, 142
Bird, A. M., 155, 169
Birren, James, 358
Bishop, S., 192
Blackwell, R. D., 197, 214
Blacky Pictures, 29
Blanchard, E. B., 136
Blood pressure, 127, 362
Bohart, A. C., 98
Bornstein, R. A., 116, 120
Boulder conference and model,
55, 81, 95, 96, 97
programs, alternative to, 81
training, 88
Brady, K., 370, 372
Brain:
contusion, 114
damage, 36, 86, 87
diseases, 24
dysfunction, 37
functioning, 85, 86
injuries, 26
left hemisphere, 105
scan, 111
theory, 120
tumors, 106
Brawley, L. R., 155, 169
British Psychological Society
(BPS), 8, 16
Britt, S. H., 199, 214
Broadbent, D. E., 309
Broca, P., 105
Brody, J. G., 192
Brown, C., 180
Brown, D. T., 56, 73
Brown, H., 46
Brunswik, E., 331, 352
Building design process, 328
Business:
entrepreneurs, 246
games, 280
Bus ridership, increasing, 223
Butt, D. S., 169

Califano, J. A., 129, 144
Calorie consumption, 166
Campbell, D. T., 270
Campbell, J. P., 298, 299
Campus administrators, 184
Canadian Association for
Health, Physical Education
and Recreation, 153
Canadian Association of
School Psychologists
(CASP), 56, 61
Canadian Association of Sport
Sciences, 153

Canadian Association on
Gerontology, 356
Canadian Police College, 292,
293, 297
Canadian Psychological
Association (CPA), 8, 15,
119, 298
Canadian Society for
Psychomotor Learning and
Sport Psychology, 153, 162
Cancer, 266
patients, 239
screening, 129
Capital punishment, 255
Cardiovascular disease, 179
Career counseling, 276
Case:
conferences, 61
method, 280
settlement, 261
studies, 4, 6
Cattell Infant Intelligence
Scale, 28
Cattell, J. McK., 27, 80
Central nervous system,
disorders of, 108
Cerebral cortex, 111
palsy, 25
Chad, K. E., 166, 170
Chicago Bureau of Child Study,
55
Child:
abuse, 88
care legislation, 53
disorders, 72
labor laws, 229
management problem, 229
psychiatrist, 39
psychology, 227
rearing, 227, 228
support, 246
Child Behavior Checklist, 30
Childhood:
depression, 26
psychosis, 26
Child-guidance clinics, 28
Child rearing, problems in, 227
Children:
at risk, 68
Children's Apperception Test,
29
Churchill, W., 330
Cholesterol, 362
Chronic pain sufferers, 124,
125, 127, 136, 139
case study, 124, 139
Cigarette smoking, 267

Citizen participation, 179
Civil lawsuits, 261
Classroom:
   environment, 63
   management problems, 236
   situation, 236
Clayman, A., 143
Clinical:
   child psychology, 27
   health psychologist, 125
   neurology, 106
   neuropsychology, 107
   practice, 96
   psychologist, 3
   trials, 142
Clinical neuropsychology, 116
Clinical psychology, 14, 204
   advantages of, 79, 89
   background, 80
   definition of, 79
   disadvantages of, 79, 90
   scope of, 82
Cocaine, 91
Code of ethics, 61, 168
Cognitive:
   ability, 357
   assessment, 43
   behavioral therapies, 136
   deficits, 24, 106
   difficulties, 116
   functioning, 52
   functions, 105
   limitations, 305
   and memory impairments,
      359
   methods, 158
   models, 32
   process, 320
   processes, 310, 370
   rehabilitation therapist, 104
   relaxation techniques, 158
   retraining, 116
   science, 322
   skill development, 154
   strengths, 86
   testing, 65
   weaknesses, 86
Cognitive-behavioral
      therapists, 83
Cohen, D., 372
Cohen, F., 144
Collis, M., 166, 169
Communicaid, 318, 319
   system, 321
Communication, 275, 285, 320
   channels, 285, 294
   model, 295

   network, 286
   patterns, 308
   problems, 286
   process, 292
   skills, 359
   symbolic, 293
   systems, 307
   techniques, 359
Communication-impaired
      travellers, 318, 319
Community:
   center, 227
   consultation, 53
   health center, 233
   mental health center, 11
   programs, 191
   residences, 92
   as social support system,
      176
   systems, 176
Community Mental Health
      Centers Act of 1963, 176
Community psychology, 175
   background of, 176
   scope of, 176
Comparative psychology, 238
Compensation for injuries, 107
Computer:
   ergonomics, 312
   programs, 116
   workstations, 318
Concentration, 115, 154, 158,
      160, 164
   deficits in, 92
   techniques, 157
Concept formation, 103
Conduct:
   disorder, 26
   disordered children, 23
   problem, 23
Confidentiality, 132
Conklin, W. E., 155, 169
Conoley, J. C., 73
Conservatoire National des
      Arts et Metiers, 323
Constructive:
   behaviors, 93
   problem solving, 230
Consumer:
   affairs agencies, 213
   attitudes, 201
   behavior, 196, 197, 201, 213
   complaints, 209
   decision making, 197, 200
   decisions, 199
   education, 196, 212
   research, 201, 202

   researchers, 206
   safety messages to, 199
   satisfaction, 196, 201, 208
   search behavior, 198
   tests, 210
Consumer behavior, 196, 201
Consumer interest:
   issues, 198
   panel, 206, 210
   panel members, 206
   panel method, 206
   perceptions of product
      quality, 208
   protection, 196, 197, 201
   research, 199
Consumer psychology, 3
   background of, 197
   definition of, 196
Consumer Reports, 198, 208
Consumption, 198, 203
   cycle, 198
Contingency, 224, 226
   management, 233
   theory, 284
Contracting, 166
Control:
   fear and anxiety, 149
   of mental conditions, 159
   panels, 307
   weight, 165
Conversion reaction, 130
Cook, T. D., 270
Coping:
   with illness, 128
   with pain, 124, 139
   skills, 129
Corrections, 11, 17
Costa, L., 101–21
Cost-benefit analysis
      techniques, 241
Counselling, 62, 71, 370
   psychology, 14
   service for students, 102
Coutts, L. M., 273–99
Cowen, E. L., 177, 192
Craig, E., 46
Cratty, B. J., 169
Creativity, 275
Crime, 246
   control activities, 178
   prevention, 292
   rate, 251
Criminal:
   cases, 261
   justice, 177, 247, 251
   offenders, 246
   responsibility, 253

Criminally insane, 254
Cripe, L. I., 120, 121
Crisis intervention, 180
  calls, 180
  training, 34
  units, 11
Critical incident technique,
  315
Crowding, 250, 333
  stressors, 189
Cystic fibrosis, 26

Dalton, J., 191, 192
Darrow, C., 259
Davidson, L., 207
Death, 359, 369
  penalty, 255
Decentralized networks, 286
Decision making, 275, 278
  process, 197
Defendants, 249, 254
Degeneration of nervous
  system tissue, 107
Deinstitutionalization, 92
Delusions, 41
Dementia, 356, 358, 359, 365
Demographics, 201
Dependency, 78, 79
Depression, 23, 64, 65, 83, 84,
  86, 91, 94, 111, 113, 135,
  141, 242, 358, 359, 361
  reduction of, 84
  as symptom, 110
Depth interview, 203
Descriptive statistics, 6
Design:
  goal, 337
  programmer, 351
  of work places, 328
Deszca, G., 293
Deutsch, G., 120, 121
Developmental:
  delay, 25, 55, 68
  history, 60, 78
  maturational models, 32
  milestones, 64
  psychology, 44
  tests, 58
Dewey, D., 155, 169
Diabetes, 42, 43, 133
Diagnosis, 58, 61
  of neurological disease, 113
Diagnostic practice, 53
  tests, 58
Dichter, E., 204, 214
Dickson, W. J., 277, 299
Dietary changes, 84

Disabilities, 108
Disabled, 11, 342
  developmentally, 80
  passengers, 305
Disaffiliation, theory of, 186
Disease:
  control, 361
  prevention, 130, 361
  of vascular system, 107
Disobedience, willful, 62
Distress, emotional, 94
Division of Health Psychology
  (APA), 126
Division 40 (APA), 120
Division 16 (APA), 56
Doane, B. K., 330, 352
Doctoral:
  accredited programs, 98
  dissertation, 97
Domestic:
  conflicts, 249
  violence, 246
Dominance, 348
Draw-A-Man Test, 28
Draw-A-Person Test, 29
Droppleman, L., 155, 169
Drug:
  abuse, 26
  and alcohol rehabilitation
    centers, 11
  counselling, 53
  trafficking, 91
  treatment programs, 247
  use, 91
Durkin, J., 146–70

Early childhood education,
  11
Ecological:
  analogy, 176
  psychology, 330, 331
Educably mentally
    handicapped (EMH), 50
Educational:
  assessment, 41
  goal, 236
  psychologists, 106
  records, 60
  treatment strategy, 61
Edwards, R., 73
Edwards preference inventory,
  204
Effect, law of, 221
Eisdorfer, C., 370, 372
Elderly, 11, 342, 358
Electrocardiogram (ECT), 159,
  362

Electromyographic recordings,
  136
Electronic:
  monitoring, 246, 247, 251
  shackle, 251
  transmitters, 246
Elias, M., 191, 192
Emotional:
  adjustment, 88
  difficulties, 161
  disturbance, 45
  problems, 52, 80, 82, 88, 135
  storms, 67
Emotions, 312
Empiricism, 250
Employee:
  assistance programs, 131
  morale, 92, 274
  satisfaction, 284
Employment, 186
  discrimination, 246, 249,
    262, 263
  interviewer, 11
  record, 253
Endocrine system, 357
Endorphins, 128
Energy, conservation, 223
  wasting, 224
Engel, J. F., 197, 214
Engineering psychology, 330
Engineers, 305, 314, 319, 322
Environmental:
  appraisals, 332
  design, 333
  design solutions, 183
  perception, 332
  personality, 332
  psychologist, 312, 350
  restricted stimulation, 330
  sociology, 350
  states, 312
  stress, 265
Environmental psychology,
  322
  background, 329
  what is it, 328
Epidemology, 126, 175
Epilepsy, 26, 66
  and related disorders, 107
Epinephrine, 128
Equal Employment
    Opportunity Commission,
    262
Erectile failure, 133
Ergonomics, 150, 330, 200
  background, 305
  defined, 303

evaluation, 303
macro, 307
model, 307
principles, 308
scope, 307
Ergonomics Society, 307
Ergonomist, 303, 309
becoming an, 321
education of, 321
employment of, 324
Erikson, E. H., 32, 46
Esteem, 282
Ethical:
issues, 161, 162
judgement, 250
Evolutionary history, 222
Exercise, learning, 223
Experimental:
analysis, 223
designs, 226
psychology, 277
Experimentation, 4, 225
Expert systems, 312
Expert witnesses, 248
testimony of, 324
Eyewitness, 261
identification, 248
testimony, 248

Facility planner, 351
Fagan, T. K., 55, 57, 71, 72, 73
Family:
conflicts, 246
counselling, 66, 359
interrelationships, 25
physician, 66
quarrel, 312
therapy, 31
violence, 26, 52
Family and consumer sciences,
213
Family Eduational Rights and
Privacy Act, 60
Fatigue, 308, 312
Feedback, 60, 234
device, 317
Feuerstein, M., 128, 129, 144
Fiedler, F., 284, 299
Field study, 157
Fitness, 152
Fitts, P., 305, 309, 325
Flashing, 218
Fleishman, E. A., 284, 299
Focus group, 203, 346
Follick, M., 126, 144
Ford, D., 311, 325
Franklin, B., 222

French, J. L., 73
Fretz, B. R., 98
Freud, S., 28, 32, 46, 80
theory of, 83
Friendship networks, 183
Frustration tolerance, 103

Gallagher, D., 361, 372
Galton, F., 358
Gardner, H., 120, 121
Gate control theory of pain,
124
Genetic:
disorders, 107
engineering, 108
Gentleness, 230, 231
Geriatric, 356
centers, 107
deficits, 359
practice, 356
psychology, 357, 369
Gerontological psychology, 357
Gerontological Society, 356
Gerontology, 356
Geropsychology, 356, 357
Gesell, A., 46, 55
Gifford, R., 1–19, 326–52
Gifted children, 26
Gilles de la Tourette Syndrome,
24, 25
Glaser, R., 128, 144
Goddard, H. H., 27
Godin, S., 191, 192
Goldman, J., 46
Goldstein, S., 191, 192
Goldwater, B. C., 234, 242
Graduate:
school, 12
training, 240
Graduate Record Exam (GRE),
44, 95
Grandjean, E., 325
Grant, K., 289
Greenberg, J., 46
Greenfield, J., 46
Gregorich, S., 192
Grief, 359
counselling, 53
Griffith, C., 152
Grigsby, C., 187, 192
Group:
cohesion, 154
decisions, 198
dynamics, 278, 283
goal attainment, 284
homes, 11
processes, 283

therapy, 31
think, 283
Guerry, S., 46

Halgin, R. P., 76–98
Hall, G. S., 3, 80
Hallucinations, 41, 91
Halstead-Reitan
Neuropsychological
Battery, 86
Handicapped, physically, 80
Harris, B., 169
Harris, D. V., 169
Harris, E. F., 284, 299
Hawthorne studies, 277, 329
Hayden, T. L., 46
Headache:
characteristics, 138
patients, 136
treatment program, case
study, 135, 136
triggers, 136
Head injury, 87, 104, 105, 106,
109, 115, 116
patients, 104
Health:
behavior, 129
belief model, 129
maintenance organizations,
91
policy, 125
Health care:
budget, 358
culture, 122
economic aspects of, 142
facilities, administrators, 89
political aspects of, 142
providers, 91
Hearing, 59, 60
problems, 59, 69
Heart attacks, 242, 358
Hemispheric specialization, 120
Hepworth, J., 180
Herd, J. A., 144
Heron, R. M., 300–25
Heron, W., 330, 325
High blood pressure, 132
Hildreth, G., 56
Hofer, P., 244–70
Holahan, C. J., 172–92
Holistic systems approach, 307
Holmes, T. H., 128, 144
Home confinement, 246, 247,
251
Homeless, 174, 250
process, 186
and social support, 185

Homelessness, 178, 185
  as a process, 186, 187
  three stages of, 186
Home life, 333
Home support worker, 369
Homosexuality, 249
Hormones and mood states, 130
Horowitz, I. A., 270
Hospitals, 72, 92, 328, 330
House, R., 285, 299
House-Tree-Person Test, 29
Housing, 177, 187
  low-income, 174
Hughes, H., 142
Hughlings-Jackson, J., 105
Human:
  behavior, 331
  conditioning, 238
  development, 80
  ecology, 350
  engineering, 303
  factors, 303, 322, 323, 330
  information-processing, 310
  memory, 360
  motor performance, 150
  operator, 308
  relations movement, 277
  resource planning systems, 287
  systems, 307
  welfare, 176
Human Factors Society, 200
Humanistic-existential psychologists, 84
Humanistic psychology:
  focus of, 84
  psychotherapists, 84
  theorists, 287
Hussian, R., 362, 372
Hutt, R. B. W., 56, 74
Hyperactivity, 37, 61, 63
Hypertension, 129, 358, 362
Hypnosis, 24, 248
Hypochondriasis, 86
Hypothesis:
  generation, 58
  testing, 58

Ilg, F. L., 46
Illinois Test of Psycholinguistic Ability, 28
Illumination, 308
Imagery, 154
  theory, 154
Immune system, 128
In-basket test, 291

Incomplete Sentences Technique, 29
Individualized programs, 350
Industrial:
  design, 312
  designer, 302
  engineering, 277, 322, 323
  psychology, 3
Inferential statistics, 6, 253
Insanity, 248, 254
  defense, 248
Institutional:
  behavior, 371
  change, 183
  environment, 182, 188
Institutionalization, 359
Intellectual:
  abilities, 80
  functioning, 85, 135
  testing, 85
Intelligence, 27, 65, 85, 86
  artificial, 307, 312
  performance, 85
  test, 41, 50, 58, 59, 80, 85, 86, 111, 115
  verbal, 85
Interactional perspective, 305
Interdisciplinary relationships, 368
International Association for Research in Economic Psychology, 200
International Association of Applied Psychology, 18
International Health Exhibition of 1884, 358
International Neuropsychological Society, 116
International Personnel Management Association, 298
International Society of Sports Psychology, 153
Internship, 16, 97
Interpersonal:
  distance, 333
  style, 155
Intervention, 61
  goals, 175
  program, 93
  and rehabilitation, 114
  team member, 67
Interview, 5, 336
  formats, 203
  semi-structured, 4
  structured, 4

techniques, 114
Involuntary nervous system, 159
Ittelson, W., 188

James, W., 80
Job:
  analysis, 278, 289
  dissatisfaction, 283
  involvement, 283, 292
  satisfaction, 275, 283
Job Descriptive Index, 282
Johns, G., 299
Jones, M. C., 29
Jones, R., 305, 325
Joschko, M., 21–47
Journal of Applied Psychology, 3, 201
Judges, 249, 262
Jury, 248
  selection, 257
  shadow, 258, 259
Justice system, 249

Kahneman, D., 309
Kantowitz, B. H., 325
Kanuk, L. L., 197, 214
Keele, S. W., 309
Kelling, G. L., 174, 192
Kiecolt-Glaser, J., 128, 144
Kinaesthetic cues, 317
Kinesiology, 311, 312
Kinetic Family Drawings, 29
Knight, P. A., 299
Koe, Gerald, 49–74
Kollat, D. T., 197, 214
Korchin, S. J., 98
Kuczmierczyk, A. R., 128, 129, 144

Labbe, E. E., 128, 129, 144
Language:
  comprehension, 103
  delays, 70
  disorders, 25
  evaluation, 69
  functioning, 65, 115
  problems, 39
Law:
  enforcement, 178, 179
  firms, 269
  and psychology, 3
  suit, 261
  suits and lawyers, 115
Lawyer-psychologist, 247, 250, 269
  becoming a, 268

Lazarus, A., 128, 144
Leadership, 275, 278
Learning, 197, 333
  as an active process, 234
  assistance teacher, 57, 67, 69
  to concentrate, 160
  disabilities, 24, 25, 37, 39,
    41, 45, 52, 71, 87, 106,
    108, 114, 115, 116
  disabilities class, 67
  disabled students, 50, 107
  disorder, 106
  maladaptive, 83
  mental skills, 149, 153
  rote, 109
  theory, 45
Legal issues, 107
  reasoning, 267
  research, 250
  services, 201
  system, 246
Legislation-oriented research,
  255
Leisure motives, 345
Levin, H., 32
Lewin, K., 8
Lewinsohn, P., 361, 372
Library, 328, 341
Licensing, 15, 119
  examinations, 97
  laws, 97
Lie detector tests, 248, 261
Lighting, 312, 329, 341
Lindstrom, J. P., 73
Litigation consulting
  companies, 248
Littering, 223
Locke, J., 54, 74
Loh, W., 270
Loneliness, 359
Long-term:
  care facilities, 362, 363
  memory, 310
Lorr, M., 155, 169
Lubin, B., 370, 372
Lutzger, J. R., 242

Maccoby, E., 32
MacDonald, M., 362, 372
Machine systems, 307, 308
Make a Picture Story, 29
Management training, 275
  and development, 288
Manufacturing, 201, 307
Marijuana, 91
Marital:
  conflict, 260

problems, 135
Marketing, 197
  program, 199
  research, 199, 201
Martens, R., 155, 169
Martial arts, 163
Martin, G., 242
Martin, J. A., 242
Maslow, A., 277, 282
Matarazzo, J., 116, 120, 125,
  126, 144
May, W. H., 205, 214
McCarthy Scales of Children's
  Abilities, 28
McCormick, E. J., 310, 325
McNair, D., 155, 169
McNeal, J., 201, 214
Measures:
  of central tendency, 6
  of dispersion, 6
Mediation, 53, 261
Medical:
  alert, 66
  care system, 130
  history, 60
  illness, 108
  personnel, 108
  utilization data, 136
Medication, 66, 312, 358
  aids, 106
  usage, 140
Mehrota, S., 202, 214
Meierhoefer, B., 270
Meister, D., 325
Melzack, R., 124, 144
Memory, 102, 103, 357
  deficits, 92, 104, 106
  recent, 103
  short-term auditory, 66
  tests, 113
Mental:
  check-off list, 148
  competence of criminal
    defendants, 261
  decline, 368
  disorders, 62
  film, 148
  hospital, 80, 174
  illness, 85, 254, 265
  incapacity, 365
  retardation, 25, 45, 52, 71
  set, 308
  status, 111, 253
  tests, 80
  trainer, 162
  training, 151, 152, 153, 158,
    160, 161, 162, 163

Mental health, 16, 180, 186,
  283
  agency, 242
  centers, 72, 357
  clinic administrators, 89
  clinicians, 81
  field, 95
  professional, 95
  settings, 89
  system, 92
  worker, 96
Mental Health, National
  Institute of, 81
Mentally handicapped, 107,
  331
Mentally retarded, 50
  children, 55
Merrill-Palmer Scale of Mental
  Tests, 28
Metabolic disorders, 107
  rates, 166
Military, 277, 303, 307, 324
  technology, 305
Miller, G. A., 317, 325
Miller, N. E., 126, 144
Minke, K. M., 56, 73
Minnesota Multiphasic
  Personality Inventory
  (MMPI), 86, 91, 92, 204
Minority groups, 279
Miron, M. S., 205, 214
Modeling, 65, 199
Montgomery, K., 354–72
Mood, 155, 312
Morally retarded children, 55
Morgan, C., 346, 352
Morgan, W. P., 169
Morrow, 143
Motivation, 343
  research, 204, 206, 344
Motor deficits, 103
  impairments, 25
  learning, 150, 152, 153
  limitations, 305
  responses, 311
  skill, 150
Mowen, J. C., 197, 214
Multidisciplinary treatment,
  54
Multiple sclerosis, 108
  patients, 335
  society, 335
  sufferers, 337
Multiple-unit dwellings, 328
Munsterberg, H., 3
Murray, H., 346, 352
Murrell, K. F. H., 307, 325

Musculoskeletal:
  stress, 313
  system, 311

National Association of School
  Psychologists (NASP), 56,
  61, 70, 71
National Board for Certified
  School Psychologists, 71
National Center for State
  Courts, 269
National Conference for
  Training in Community
  Psychology, 176
National health:
  costs, 130
  problems, 127
National Institute for Mental
  Health, 358
National of Teacher Education
  (NCATE), 71
National Research Council
  (Canada), 322
National Science Foundation,
  17
Naturalistic:
  experiment, 180
  observation study, 180
Natural resources, 334
Natural science, 222, 226
Nature, 348
Need theories, 281
Nelms, D., 192
Nervous system, 106
  and behavior, 105
Neuroanatomy, 106, 120
Neurochemical functioning, 84
Neurological:
  activity, 106
  development, 24, 26, 108
  disease, 105, 106, 107, 109,
    113
  disease or trauma, 105
  disorders, 106
  dysfunction, 65
  exam, 103
  impairment, 50
  maturation, 32
  screening test, 65
  tests, 65, 110
  x-ray techniques, 106
Neurologist, 36, 103, 124
Neurology, 102, 107, 120, 370
Neuropsychological:
  assessment, 41, 85, 86, 87,
    112
  diagnosis, 53

disorders, 120
evaluation, 110
tests, 58, 102, 111
therapies, 107
Neuropsychologist, 92, 103,
  104, 106, 116, 359
  becoming one, 116
Neuropsychology, 105, 307
  background of, 105
Neuroscience, 83
  focus of, 84
Ng, C. F., 340
Nideffer, R. M., 155, 169
Nocturnal enuresis, 67, 68
  development of, 67
Noise, 308, 341
  background, 312
Nonverbal abilities, 41
Norman, D. A., 309
North American Society for the
  Psychology of Sport and
  Physical Activity, 153, 162
Nuffield Unit for Research into
  Problems of Ageing, 358
Nurse aide, 84, 369
Nursing, 17

Obsession, 39, 41
Oral examinations, 70, 97
Organizational:
  behavior, 297, 329
  change, 278
  commitment, 283
  design, 275, 287
  processes, 278
  psychologists, 3, 298
  psychology, 16, 322
  punishment, 293
Orlick, T., 169
Orser, B., 163
Orthopedic surgeon, 124
Osgood, C., 205, 214
Oskamp, S., 17, 18
Osmond, H., 331
Outdoor Recreation Thematic
  Apperception Test
  (ORTAT), 346, 347, 349
Outdoor recreation settings,
  343

Paced Auditory Serial Addition
  Test, 103
Pain:
  clinic, 125
  conditioned, 124
  imaginary, 124
  psychophysiological aspects,

125
Paranoia, 86
Paraprofessional, 90
  roles, 96
Parasympathetic nervous
  system, 128
Paredes, R., 180
Parental anxiety, 68
Park, 343
  managers, 345
  users, 343
Parole, 246
  officer, 11
Participant observation, 174,
  206
Partington, J., 169
Path-goal theory, 284
Pear, J., 242
Pediatric:
  clinics, 45
  services, 107
Pediatrician, 24, 36
Peer:
  interactions, 52
  modeling, 31
Perception, 152, 196, 248, 322,
  370
  and learning, 197
  somesthetic, 108
Perceptual:
  capacities, 310
  information, 331
  input, 310
  limitations, 305
  problems, 103, 106
  tests, 58, 111
Performance, 60, 275, 329
  appraisals, 280
  ratings, 280
  school, 60
Personal:
  growth, 84
  safety, 174
  style, 78
Personality, 78, 85, 86, 205,
  308, 312, 357
  factors, 154
  inventories, self report, 86
  measures, 58, 108
  questionnaires, 22
  tests, 79, 85, 86, 113
Personality Inventory for
  Children, 30
Personnel selection, 275
  techniques, 279
Persuasion, 248
Phobias, 242

Physical:
  condition, 361
  defects, 55
  education, 167
  environment, 330
  health, 186
  illness, 358
  sciences, 226
  therapists, 124
Physiology, 322
Physiotherapy clinic, 335
Piaget, J., 26, 32
Pigott, R. E., 169
Pilot errors, 305
Play, 349
  therapy, 26
Plea bargain, 249, 261
Police, 248, 249, 275, 292
  and citizen involvement, 178
  misconduct, 274
Political decision-makers, 257
Positive:
  behavioral repertoires, 230
  self image, 282
  thoughts, 84
Posner, M., 309
Post-occupancy evaluation
  (POE), 339
Post-surgical:
  pain, 139
  sexual functioning, 135
Practicum experience, 96
Prenatal concerns, 64
Presurgical evaluation, 132
Prevention:
  efforts, 189
  primary, 175, 177, 189
  programs, 70
  remodeling, 190
  secondary, 53, 175, 177
Prevention-oriented
  psychologists, 132
Prison, 221, 246, 248, 269
  crowding, 250
Privacy, 182, 333
Problem solving, 230, 357
Process:
  of adaptation, 129
  case study, 78
  theories, 78, 234, 281
  of transferring, 164
Profile of Mood States (POMS),
  155
Program:
  development, 276
  evaluation, 53, 241
  instruction, 280

planning, 70
Projective:
  methods, 344, 345
  techniques, 86, 205, 345
  tests, 86, 205, 346
Prosecutors, 249
Pseudo-shopper, 206
Psychiatric:
  assistant, 11
  hospital, 178, 269
  service and staff, 110
  social work, 95
  ward and support, 188
Psychiatrist, 41, 62, 84, 162
Psychiatry, 107, 370
Psychoanalysis, 28, 204
Psychodynamic, 83, 84
  models, 32, 83;
  psychotherapists, 83
Psychoeducational:
  assessment, 50, 53, 56, 68
  diagnostician, 73
  report, 60
Psychographic, 202
  factors, 201
  profiles, 213
Psycholegal perspective, 249,
  269
Psychological:
  assessments, 84, 91, 359
  assistant, 11
  casualties, 140
  clinics, 80
  components of stress, 128
  disturbances, 83
  help, 94
  limitations, 305
  problems, 83
  stress, 127
  tests, 24, 55, 80, 85
Psychology boards, state, 97
Psychometric:
  assessment, 22
  tradition, 25
Psychometrist, 11
Psychomotor:
  epilepsy, 66
  learning, 152
  skills, 152, 358
Psychoneuroimmunology, 128
Psychopathology, 80, 89, 96,
  134, 370
Psychopathologists, 88
Psychosexual development,
  249
Psychosis, 86, 242, 265
  adjustment to, 26

development of, 22
Psychotherapy, 24, 39, 78, 80,
  81, 82, 84, 87, 89, 93, 94,
  95, 96, 111, 140, 161, 358,
  359, 370
  brief, 43
  clients, 82
  exploratory, 78
  personal issues in, 94
  researcher, 88
Psychotherapeutic:
  interventions, 31
  models, 83
Psychotherapists, 79, 82, 83,
  84
Public:
  accountability, 292
  hearings, 274
  opinion surveys, 203, 204
  prevention, 175
  school, 227
  welfare, 180
Public health, 177
  models of disease, 175
  nurse, 66
  officials, 132
Public Service Commission of
  Canada, 289
Punishment, 220, 230

Questionnaires, 4, 5, 202
Quetelet, A., 357, 372

Rahe, R. H., 128, 144
Rainey, D. W., 155, 169
Rainey, K. W., 155, 169
Rand Corporation, 269
Rating scales, 58, 65
Raynor, R., 29
Reaction time, 152, 157, 357
Reading:
  behavior, 233
  problems, 87
  remedial, 71
Recidivism, 252
Recognition, 309, 349
  system, 296
Recreation:
  behavior, 345
  motive, 345
Recycling, 198, 199, 334
Referral:
  concern, 60
  form, 62
  to a neuropsychologist, 108
Register of Chartered
  Psychologists, 16

Rehabilitation:
  facilities, 107
  program, 104
  treatment, 125
  unit, 363
Reich, J. W., 178
Reinforcement, 223, 225, 226, 228, 230
  contingency, 235
Reis, J., 155, 169
Relaxation, 154, 158, 164, 165
  automation of, 164
  procedures, 159
  technique, 159
  training, 128, 136, 140, 141, 164
  and visualization techniques, 148
Reliability, 5, 58
Relocation, 359, 371
Repetitive:
  muscle stress, 313
Repetitive strain injury (RSI), 311, 314
Research:
  assistant, 369
  assistantships, 241
  contracts, 343
Residencies, 328
Rest cycles, 313
Retirement, 359, 365
Richards-Wools, L., 359, 372
Road safety, 313
Roberts, M. C., 46
Robotics, 307
  system, 314
Rodin, J., 126, 144
Roethlisberger, F. J., 277, 299
Rogers, C., 277
Role playing, 280
Rorschach, H., 41
  test, 29, 86, 346

Saal, F. E., 299
Saegert, S., 189, 190, 192
Safety, 349
  equipment, 223, 224
Salmela, J. H., 154, 170
Sanders, M. S., 310, 325
Schiffman, L. G., 197, 214
Scholastic Aptitude Test (SAT), 85
School, 328
  history, 60
  psychologists, 55
  psychology, 3
  readiness measures, 58

School-based team, 57
Schultz, D. F., 180
Schutz, H. G., 194–214
Scientific litigation:
  research, 259
  techniques, 257
Scientific management, 3
Scott, T. H., 330, 352
Scott, W. D., 3
Screening, 69
  programs, 68, 69
Sears, R., 32
Seizure, 65
  symptoms, 66
Self:
  actualization, 282
  awareness, 84
  concept, 64, 65
  control, 139, 154
  destruction, 225
  destructive pursuits, 92
  esteem, 23, 24, 37, 114, 129
  management of painful situations, 124
  mutilation, 93
  report measures, 86
  stimulation, 221
  understanding, 82
Semantic differential, 205
Senility, 356, 358
Sensory:
  capacities, 310
  deficits, 103
  deprivation, 330
  functioning and perception, 357
  handicaps, 25
  impairment, 368
  limitations, 305
  and motor exam, 111
Sentence completion test, 205
Service:
  agencies, 87
  contract, 343
Settlement:
  conferences, 267
  oriented research, 260
  skills, 261
Sewall, T. J., 73
Sex:
  preoccupation, 41
  stereotyping, 249
Sexual:
  abuse, 26, 52
  activity, 135
  arousal, 219
  behaviors, 218, 219

dysfunction, 132, 242
  functioning, 133
  offenders, 221
Sexuality, 83
Shearer, J. W., 320, 325
Shock, N., 358
Sidman, M., 226, 242
Silva, J. M., 154, 170
Simon, T., 46
Singer, J. E., 126, 144
Skinner, B. F., 223, 242
Sleep:
  cycles, 313
  disorders, 107
Slivinski, L., 289
Smith, D. K., 74
Smith, P., 282
Sociability, 85
Social:
  atmosphere, 184
  behaviors, 218, 278
  desirability, 349
  environment, 330
  interaction, 183, 184, 230
  intervention, 175, 177
  isolation, 182
  learning, 140
  participation, 184
  planning, 370
  problems, 64
  processes, 176
  regulation, 179, 180
  reinforcers, 225
  science, 226, 356
  settings, 175
  skills, 220
  skills group, 66
  support, 187
  support theory, 178
  systems, 175
  welfare, 177, 356
  work, 17
  worker, 84, 91, 115
Socially:
  appropriate behaviors, 93
  isolated, 63
Societal:
  awareness, 177
  need, 178
  processes, 177, 333
Society for Industrial and Organizational Psychology, 297, 298
Society of Behavioral Medicine, 126, 142
Sommer, R., 1, 194–214, 352
Sorkin, R. D., 325

Spatial:
  arrangements, 341
  cognition, 332
  layout, 342
Special:
  children, 22
  education, 55, 72
  masters degree, 266
Speech:
  disorders, 25
  pathology evaluation, 115
  language pathologist, 66, 69
Sport:
  performance enhancement,
    154
  psychologist training, 167
  psychology, 150, 152
  science departments, 167
Sport Competitive Anxiety Test
    (SCAT), 155
Springer, S., 120, 121
Standardized:
  examinations, 97
  psychological tests, 4, 5
  testing conditions, 58
  tests, 64
Stanford Binet-Simon IQ Test,
    27, 28
Stang, D. J., 98
Stein, C. L., 46
Stern, W., 27, 55
Stimulus:
  field, 309
  pattern, 309
Stokols, D., 352
Stone, G. C., 126, 144
Stress, 159, 177, 275, 307
  and illness, 128
  control, 150
  management, theory, 154
  of competition, 149
  reaction, 22
  reduction programs, 87
  response, 128
  treatment for, 67
Stressors, 90, 128
  external, 128
  internal, 128
Stroke, 358, 363
Substance:
  abuse, 52, 92
  use, 92
Suicidal:
  attempts, 85
  depression, 83
  thoughts, 85
Suicide, 42, 162, 264

prevention, 53
Support groups, 359
Surveys, 4, 5, 202
Sympathetic nervous system,
    128
Systems:
  approach, 303
  design, 320
  design, engineering, 323
  interactions, 312, 313
  level intervention, 182
  task analysis, 302

Target:
  population, 203
  shooting, 157
Task:
  analysis, 315, 320
  oriented, 284
Tauber, E. M., 204, 214
Taylor, F. V., 308, 325
Taylor, F. W., 3, 277, 299
Taylor, S. E., 129, 144
Temperature, 308, 312
Temper tantrums, 366, 367,
    368
Teri, L., 361, 372
Terman, L., 27
Territoriality, 333
Test:
  ability, 85
  constructing and scaling,
    105
  employment, 262
  results, 58
  selection, 58
  timed, 50
Testimony-oriented research,
    261
Testing:
  multiple, 61
  rooms, 210
  session, 59, 60, 65
  of significance, 7
Test of Attentional and
    Interpersonal Style (TAIS),
    155
Thayer Conference, 56
Thematic Apperception Test
    (TAT), 29, 30, 41, 86, 92,
    205, 346
Theoretical psychology, 8
Therapeutic:
  direction, 67
  plan, 78
Thomas, E. A., 370, 372
Thompson, L. W., 361, 372

Thorndike, E., 222
Tigert, D. J., 201, 214
Tjosvold, D., 283, 299
Todd, J., 98
Traffic:
  safety, 324
  signs, 313
Training, 116
  programs, 55, 163, 168
  skills, 140
Transfer of learning, 152
Transportation, 307
  ergonomics, 312
  terminals, 318
Treatment:
  behavioral focus plan, 93
  center administrators, 89
  plan, 93
  services for chronic pain,
    124
Trial:
  courts, 248
  strategies, 259

Uhl, K. P., 206, 214
University:
  catalogues, 238
  students, 233
Urban:
  geography, 350
  plaza, 329
  police force, 274
User satisfaction, 349

Vail Conference, 81
Validation process, 60
Validity, 5, 60, 157
  of results, 58
  scales, 86
Values, 203, 293
Vandalism, 174, 181
Verbal:
  abuse, 64
  behavior, 233, 236
  communication, 363
  direction, 63
  praise, 231
  skills, 236
  and visual memory, 114
Video display terminal, 313
Vineland Adaptive Behavior
    Scales, 28
Vineland Social Maturity
    Scale, 28
Vineland Training School, 27
Violence, 250
  in sports, 150

Violent:
    behaviors, 230
    inmates, 248
Vision, 59, 60
Visual:
    defects, 59
    examination, 69
    image, 161
Visualization, 150, 156, 158,
    159, 160, 164
    procedure, 148
    technique, 166
    training, 164
Vocabulary development, 69
Vocational assessments:
    assessments, 64
    interest test, 204
Vroom, V., 282

Walker, C. E., 46

Wall, P. D., 124, 144
Wandersman, A., 175
Watson, J. B., 29
Wechsler, D., 85
Wechsler intelligence tests, 28,
    30, 64, 85, 91, 92
Weight control:
    case study, 165
    difficulties, 150
    programs, 149
Weight loss, 165
Weinberg, R. S., 154, 170
Weiss, S. M., 126, 144
Welford, A. T., 309, 358
Wells, W. D., 201, 202, 214
Wenger, H. A., 166, 170
Western Electric Company,
    277, 329
Whitlock, R. V., 370, 372
Wilcox, B. L., 192

Wilging, T. E., 270
Wilson, E., 142
Wilson, J. Q., 174, 192
Wisocki, P., 362, 372
Witmer, L., 3, 27, 50, 55, 74, 80
Word association, 346
    tests, 205
Work, 275, 281
    behavior, 281
    places, 276
    schedules, problems and
        solutions, 93
    station design, 312
Working, 333
    conditions, 305
    environment, 307
World War I, 27, 305, 358
World War II, 27, 56, 284, 305,
    330, 358
Wrightsman, L. S., 270